The Etruscans

General Editors
James Campbell and Barry Cunliffe

This series is about the European tribes and peoples from their origins in prehistory to the present day. Drawing upon a wide range of archaeological and historical evidence, each volume presents a fresh and absorbing account of a group's culture, society and usually turbulent history.

Already published

The Lombards
Neil Christie

The English
Geoffrey Elton

The Bretons
Patrick Galliou and Michael Jones

The Franks
Edward James

The Russians
Robin Milner-Gulland

The Early Germans
Malcolm Todd

The Etruscans
Graeme Barker and Tom Rasmussen

The Basques
Roger Collins

The Gypsies
Angus Fraser

The Goths
Peter Heather

The Mongols
David Morgan

The Huns
E.A. Thompson

The Illyrians
John Wilkes

In preparation

The Sicilians
David Abulafia

The Irish
Francis John Byrne and Michael Herity

The Normans
Marjorie Chibnall

The Spanish
Roger Collins

The Celts
David Dumville

The Portuguese
Kenneth Maxwell

The Ancient Greeks
Brian Sparkes

The Byzantines
Averil Cameron

The First English
Sonia Chadwick Hawkes

The Serbs
Sima Cirkovic

The Romans
Timothy Cornell

The Scots
Colin Kidd

The Armenians
Elizabeth Redgate

The Picts
Charles Thomas

The Etruscans

Graeme Barker and Tom Rasmussen

BLACKWELL
Publishers

The right of Graeme Barker and Tom Rasmussen to be identified as authors of this work has been asserted in accordance with the Copyright, Designs and Patents Act 1988.

First published 1998

Blackwell Publishers Ltd
108 Cowley Road
Oxford OX4 1JF
UK

Blackwell Publishers Inc.
350 Main Street
Malden, Massachusetts 02148
USA

British Library Cataloguing in Publication Data

A CIP catalogue record for this book is available from the British Library.

Library of Congress Cataloging-in-Publication Data

Barker, Graeme.
    The Etruscans / Graeme Barker and Tom Rasmussen.
       p. cm. — (Peoples of Europe)
    Includes bibliographical references and index.
    ISBN 0-631-17715-9
    1. Etruscans. I. Rasmussen, Tom. II. Title. III. Series.
    DG223.B345 1997
    937'.5—dc21   97–16462
                                      CIP

Typeset in 11 on 12½ pt Sabon
by Graphicraft Typesetters Ltd, Hong Kong
Printed and bound in Great Britain by MPG Books Ltd, Bodmin, Cornwall

This book is printed on acid-free paper.

Contents

List of Figures   vi

Preface and Acknowledgements   x

Introduction   1

1 The Landscape   10

2 Origins   43

3 Sources and Society   85

4 Cultural Transformations   117

5 Settlement and Territory   141

6 Subsistence and Economy   179

7 Life, Cult and Afterlife   216

8 Romanization   262

Appendix: Etruscan Places – a Rough Guide   297

Bibliography   329

Selected Reading   367

Index   369

List of Figures

1   Italy, showing Etruria and the adjacent regions
    affected by the Etruscans   2
2   Central Italy, showing (a) landforms and
    (b) geology   12–13
3   Volcanic crater basins and lakes in southern
    Etruria   14
4   Etruria, showing principal Etruscan settlements   15
5   The Val di Chiana   17
6   The Maremma coastal lowlands   17
7   Typical hill country in northern Etruria near Siena   18
8   Typical *tufo* country in southern Etruria: the plateau   18
9   Typical *tufo* country in southern Etruria: the gorges   19
10 A typical intermontane basin in the pre-Apennines   20
11 The typical karst landscape of the limestone
    Apennine mountains   21
12 Ploughing with an ox team in the recent past   27
13 Modern mechanized ploughing   27
14 The traditional cultivation system of polyculture
    or *coltura promiscua*   28
15 Simplified patterns of recent land use in Etruria   29
16 Transhumant shepherds on the Roman Campagna
    in the nineteenth century   32
17 *Butteri* (herdsmen) on the Maremma in the
    nineteenth century   34
18 Shepherd huts at Ardea in the early twentieth century   35
19 Copper sources and copper age gravegoods in
    central Italy   48
20 'Statue menhirs' from Liguria   50

21 Topographical distributions of bronze age sites
    in Etruria   54
22 The distribution of major late bronze age
    settlements in Etruria   55
23 Sorgenti della Nova: a reconstruction of part of
    the late bronze age settlement   57
24 Changes to the settlement system of southern
    Etruria between the tenth and ninth centuries BC   62
25 Villanovan rural settlement around Narce   64
26 The internal organization of Villanovan centres   66–7
27 Terracotta hut urn of the Early Iron Age   69
28 Plan of the Villanovan cemetery of Quattro
    Fontanili, Veii   71
29 A rich burial at Quattro Fontanili, Veii: tomb
    AA1 (760–730 BC)   78
30 Chronological and regional alphabet chart   88
31 Inscribed stone stele from Lemnos   95
32 Crocefisso del Tufo necropolis, Orvieto,   98
33 Stone sarcophagus of Laris Pulenas at Tarquinia   104
34 Stone sarcophagus of Sethre Vipinans from
    Tuscania   105
35 Engraved bronze mirror showing Dionysus
    and Semele   106
36 Terracotta sarcophagus of Seianti Hanunia Tlesnasa   108
37 Bronze axe-shaped pendant from Bologna, showing
    spinning and work at the loom   110
38 Painting in the François Tomb at Vulci showing
    the killing of Cneve Tarchunies   114
39 Engraved bronze mirror showing Cacu   115
40 Ground-plan of Monte Michele tomb, Veii, with
    finds *in situ*   121
41 Tumulus 2, Banditaccia, Cerveteri   122
42 Geometric-style cups from Quattro Fontanili   126
43 Relief figures from the Tomb of the Statues, Ceri   127
44 Tomb of the Five Chairs, Cerveteri: reconstruction
    of the 'cult room'   129
45 Terracotta cover of canopic urn   130
46 Crocefisso del Tufo necropolis, Orvieto   132
47 *Bucchero* pottery from a tomb at Cerveteri   133
48 *Impasto* bowl on stand, from Ficana   135
49 *Bucchero* distribution in the Mediterranean   138
50 Orvieto: a typical location of an Etruscan city   142

51 The South Etruria survey: the Etruscan settlement
    system   145
52 The Tuscania survey: the Etruscan settlement system   146
53 The Albegna valley survey: the Etruscan
    settlement system   148
54 Polygonal walling at Amelia, probably late
    Etruscan in date   150
55 Typical examples of Etruscan walling   152
56 Tarquinia: detail of street plan   154
57 Doganella: plan established by surface survey   155
58 The fifth century city of Marzabotto   157
59 Marzabotto: footings of a housing block;
    necropolis and town gate   159
60 Plans of structures at San Giovenale and
    Acquarossa   160
61 Murlo: plan of both phases   163
62 Murlo: terracotta relief plaques   164–5
63 Houses at the Etruscan port of Regisvilla   168
64 Podere Tartuchino farm: plans and reconstructions   170
65 An Etruscan road near Tuscania   174
66 Postulated territories of the major Etruscan cities   176
67 Carbonized plant remains from Blera   184
68 Butchery systems practised at Populonia   188
69 Etruscan models of agricultural tools   189
70 The Arezzo ploughman and his team   190
71 The sunken *pithos* at Podere Tartuchino   191
72 Changing patterns of settlement and land use
    near Tuscania   196
73 An Etruscan *cuniculus*   197
74 Domestic wheel-made pottery at Murlo   204
75 The construction of an Etruscan bronze
    incense-burner   208
76 The distribution of vases from the workshop of
    the Micali Painter   213
77 Tomb of the Baron, Tarquinia   217
78 Temple A at Pyrgi: reconstruction model   221
79 Marzabotto: podium of Temple D   221
80 Veii: reconstruction elevation of Portonaccio temple   222
81 Veii: plan of the Portonaccio sanctuary   223
82 Terracotta figure of Menerva from Portonaccio   225
83 Bronze warrior statuette from Monte Falterona   226
84 Bronze Chimaera from Arezzo   227

85	Tomb of the Augurs, Tarquinia: umpire and wrestlers	229
86	Engraved bronze mirror from Tuscania	230
87	Inscribed bronze model of sheep's liver, Piacenza	231
88	The Banditaccia necropolis, Cerveteri	233
89	Etruscan tomb types, compared with Etruscan house plans	235
90	Techniques of corbelling	236
91	Paolozzi urn from Chiusi	237
92	Tomb of Orcus II, Tarquinia: souls in the underworld	240
93	Tomb of the Augurs, Tarquinia: door and mourners	241
94	Querciola II Tomb, Tarquinia: Charun	241
95	Tomb of the Blue Demons, Cerveteri	243
96	Tomb of Orcus II, Tarquinia: Tuchulcha	244
97	Tomb of the Augurs, Tarquinia: Phersu	246
98	Tomb of Hunting and Fishing, Tarquinia: banquet	250
99	Bronze cinerary urn from Bisenzio	252
100	Micali Painter black-figure amphora	253
101	Leg-in-mouth beasts: detail of incised frieze from Capena	256
102	Tomb of Hunting and Fishing, Tarquinia: fishing boat	258
103	Centuriation around Cosa	264
104	The Roman road system in Etruria	268
105	The area of Telamon, Saturnia, Heba and Cosa	270
106	Etruscan and Roman sites around Tuscania	272
107	Roman road at Roselle	276
108	Ara della Regina temple, Tarquinia: plan	278
109	Ara della Regina temple, Tarquinia: terracotta horses	279
110	Terracotta female breasts from Punta della Vipera	280
111	Castel d'Asso: façade tombs	283
112	Norchia: pedimented tombs	284
113	Sovana: Tomb of the Siren	285
114	Volterra urn: journey by wagon	290
115	Mosaic at Musarna	292
116	Falerii Novi: Porta di Giove	295
117	Site location map	300

Preface and Acknowledgements

The Etruscans had its inception one glorious September day ten years ago, as the two of us drove across southern Etruria from Rome to Tuscania during one of the fieldwork seasons of the Tuscania archaeological survey. We were discussing the likely contribution of the Tuscania project to our understanding of the settlement history and archaeology of the region, and in the course of the conversation we found ourselves making the case to each other for a new survey of Etruscan culture as a whole – its origins, development and eventual assimilation by Rome – as a backdrop to the specific results of the Tuscania study of one particular Etruscan centre and its territory. By the time we reached Tuscania the framework of the book had been constructed in the back of one of the project notebooks, from an introduction to the landscape at the beginning to a simple guide to key sites at the end, and in essence it has remained unchanged. GB has had primary responsibility for chapters 1, 2, 5 and 6, TR for chapters 3, 4, 7 and 8, and TR also drafted the Appendix, but the text has gone backwards and forwards between Leicester and Manchester, and we hope that the finished product reads as an integrated study of the Etruscans in terms of marrying both our different perspectives and a very wide set of data sources.

The Etruscans span the twilight zone between prehistory, the study of the past before written records, and history. Before them, Italy was prehistoric, so we can only use archaeology, the study of past human behaviour through material culture, to illuminate the cultures and lifestyles on which their civilization was founded. After them, we use archaeology alongside written sources to study the Romans, who incidentally have left us a number of comments about the Etruscans – though as we discuss, it is often difficult to disentangle the comments which refer to contemporary Etruscans from those on the Etruscans as they had been (or rather as the Romans preferred to think they might have been) before the Romans conquered them. In between prehistory and history, the world of the Etruscans was 'proto-historic': they used an alphabet but wrote no history, though they were in contact with people who did, the Greeks. Hence to study the Etruscans we have to make use of a wide variety of sources: what the Greeks, who knew them, said about them; what the Romans said about them later; and, probably the richest source, the archaeology they have left behind. The relationship between history and archaeology is complex, as we discuss in the Introduction, but we have tried to integrate the widest variety of data at our disposal, be this contemporary and later writings, inscriptions, surviving Etruscan tombs and monuments, excavations, potsherds in the ploughsoil, fossil pollen and river sediments, or human skeletons.

We would like to thank John Davey, formerly of Blackwells, for his unflagging encouragement from the moment of the book's inception and for his professional advice and support. Particular thanks are also due to Deborah Miles (School of Archaeological Studies, University of Leicester) for her skilful redrawing of all line drawings. We would also like to thank Miranda Barker and Andrea Greengrass (Wordwise Edit) for the compilation of the index. TR would like to acknowledge the support of the University of Manchester in providing a grant to visit Italy in the later stages of the preparation of the book. From him, too, goes out a loving thankyou to Ursula for accompanying him to re-check the details of a number of sites listed in the Appendix, and to Naomi who also came, aged seven months – she won't remember it, but her father always will. GB would like to express the same love and gratitude to Annie for living with *The Etruscans* these past years, enjoyably on summer visits to Etruria perhaps, but with forbearance during their overlong genesis in Leicester. We offer *The Etruscans* to Ursula and Annie in small recompense for their love and support.

It is also fitting to dedicate this book to the memory of two scholars. Massimo Pallottino, the father of modern Etruscan studies, sadly died at a great age two years ago. He was always generous to us both with his infectious enthusiasm and wisdom lightly borne. His pupil Mauro Cristofani, whose recent death was tragically premature, contributed to this area of study as much as anyone in the past generation, as our bibliography shows. We wish they might have read *The Etruscans* and hope they would have thought it a useful contribution to their lives' work of bridging what Pallottino once called the 'daft cleavage' between public and academic perceptions of this extraordinary people.

Graeme Barker
Tom Rasmussen
August 1997

Introduction

Most people despise everything B.C. that isn't Greek, for the good reason that it ought to be Greek if it isn't. . . . Myself, the first time I consciously saw Etruscan things, in the museum at Perugia, I was instinctively attracted to them. And it seems to be that way. Either there is instant sympathy, or instant contempt and indifference.

D.H. Lawrence (1932) *Etruscan Places*

This is a book about a remarkable society and the landscape that shaped and sustained it. From the eighth century BC, the Etruscan civilization flourished in Etruria, the region on the western side of central Italy bounded on the north by the Arno and on the south and east by the Tiber (fig. 1). In their heyday in the seventh and sixth centuries BC, the Etruscans were the major power in Italy and disputed the hegemony of the central and western Mediterranean with the Greeks. Greek culture profoundly affected Etruscan culture, and the Etruscans in turn had a profound effect on the early republic of Rome as it grew up on their southern boundary. Between the fourth and first centuries BC, however, the Etruscans gradually yielded their regional hegemony to Rome's aggrandizing power in the face of a combination of military force and cultural assimilation.

The location of the Etruscans in central Italy on Rome's very doorstep, and their contemporaneity with the Greeks and early Romans, are therefore of great significance for the cultural history of the Mediterranean. This history, however, has usually been viewed almost entirely in Greek and Roman terms, and the Etruscan contribution to it is not easy to define, primarily because there are very few Etruscans about whom anything is known other than their name, so the part they played must be, for us today, a somewhat impersonal one. Etruscan archaeology, on the other hand, is very rich and varied and provides an extremely dense and complex body of data for interpretation, one that becomes denser with every year of archaeological research.

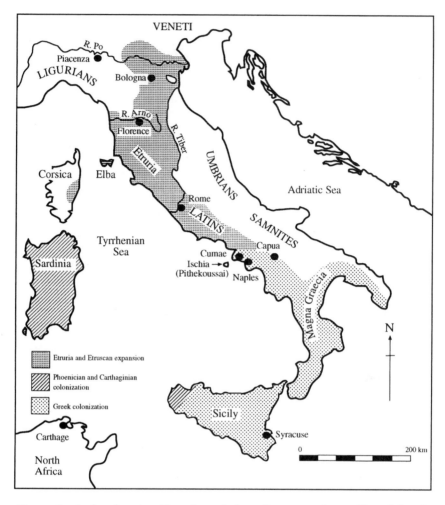

Figure 1   Italy, showing Etruria and the adjacent regions affected by the Etruscans. (After Bonfante, 1990: 7)

Until the early nineteenth century, interpretation of the material remains was blighted by serious misconceptions, such as the view that all painted pots found in Italy were made by Etruscans, an argument accepted by the potter Josiah Wedgwood who founded his own 'Etruria' factory in Staffordshire in 1769 to produce Greek-style vases; or the view promulgated by the draughtsman Giovanni Battista Piranesi that Etruscan buildings were the inspiration behind both Roman and Greek architectural forms. The combination of scientific interest and wild speculation which flavours much thinking of this period originated with a work that focused on the literary references to the Etruscans in the classical authors, the Scotsman Thomas Dempster's *De Etruria Regali*, eventually published in 1723–4. But it was also a period that witnessed the first serious publications of newly formed museum collections, by A.F. Gori in the years around 1750.

It is all too easy to ridicule early theories with the benefit of hindsight, but it is something of a relief to turn to the sober but revolutionary topographical studies of the next century, such as Luigi Canina's *Antica Etruria Marittima* of 1846–51. In the same vein is the book that did most to bring the Etruscans to the English public's attention: George Dennis was an erudite and indefatigable traveller whose official duties in the British consular service in Italy were clearly far from onerous, and his *Cities and Cemeteries of Etruria* came out in 1848, with subsequent editions in 1878 and later. The French, meanwhile, could read *L'Étrurie et les Étrusques* (1862–4) by A. Noël des Vergers, co-discoverer of the François Tomb at Vulci. Knowledge about the Etruscans and their culture was soon widely disseminated beyond Italy itself, though the images of them carried in some minds seem remarkably one-dimensional. In 1871 Friedrich Nietzsche, by profession a classical philologist, could dismiss them in a single phrase as the 'gloomy (*schwermütigen*) Etruscans'.[1]

Ancient literary references to the Etruscans are finite in number; but the history of scientific excavation in Etruria now goes back at least a century, and in that time archaeological research has expanded at an exponential rate. Many earlier books on the Etruscans established a framework from the Greek and Roman sources and fleshed out the skeleton, as it were, with such archaeological evidence as existed. Recently, however, Nigel Spivey and Simon Stoddart demonstrated that the archaeological evidence could be used to write a very different 'archaeological history'.[2] The present book is an attempt to strike a balance by drawing together the disparate evidence of archaeology and history.

The relationship between archaeological and historical data is a critical area of debate for scholars of all periods known to us by material remains and written records, from the first civilizations of Mesopotamia and Egypt to the Industrial Revolution. There was a time, not so long ago, when the relationship between history and archaeology could be characterized – or at least caricatured – as

1   Nietzsche, 1956: 30
2   Spivey and Stoddart, 1990

simple: archaeology was an expensive way of telling historians what they knew already (mostly mundane things like the facts that people lived in houses, used pots, ate food and so on) and if it indicated anything at variance with the written sources, it was obviously wrong! More recently, as the two disciplines have learned to work closer together, historians and archaeologists have tended to describe the relationship as equal: archaeological data and historical data, the argument runs, are neither better nor worse than each other, just different, giving different insights into the past. Today, however, many scholars would say that the 'archaeology versus history' debate is in many respects redundant: history and archaeology are more a single study of the human past than different approaches to it. All our sources, whether written records, inscriptions, monuments or excavated data, are 'archaeology' in the sense that they comprise a single source of material culture that has survived today from the past in complex ways (what archaeologists refer to as 'taphonomic processes') producing numerous biases of survival, preservation and interpretation. At the same time, all these sources are signatures of past human behaviour, and the goal of all those studying them should be the writing of 'history', the holistic study of past human behaviour in all its manifestations – political, demographic, cultural, social, economic, technological, ideological or whatever.

The Etruscans were different from other contemporary societies in their language, attitudes and customs. At least that is what we are told by Roman and especially by Greek writers, and we ourselves may discern other differences as we study the archaeological material – differences, for example, in the materials favoured by artists and craftsmen, in provision for the dead or in the choices of site for settlement. But, as so often when people talk about outsiders and foreigners, the Greeks tended to exaggerate the differences, whereas modern commentators have fluctuated between exaggerating and minimizing them. What is obvious is that many of the outward expressions of Etruscan culture are Greek-inspired – the essential form of temples, the iconography of the major gods, styles of figurative art and the mythological content of many visual narratives. In certain ways the two cultures run so closely parallel that Etruscan and Greek scholars speak in similar terms of stages of development, from 'archaic' to 'classical' and thence to 'Hellenistic' (see below).

Etruscan writing begins some time before 700 BC, which means that in large parts of this book we are dealing with pre-literate society. Even after sections of Etruscan society became literate, however, none of the surviving texts that they produced addresses a wider audience than those few who needed to know the facts being imparted. The texts are either simple statements of fact or instructions about ritual. It is impossible, then, to write a text-based history of the Etruscans. What we are confronted by is a long era of 'proto-history', where the main approach has to be through archaeology and any historical information must be gleaned from other literate societies writing about them. It is an era that stretches back to the first half of the eighth century BC, when the first encounters between Greeks and Etruscans took place. Before then, all is prehistory.

In the strict chronological sense, 'Etruscan' is used by archaeologists to denote the cultural era that began with a distinct set of archaeological phenomena which characterize the 'Orientalizing' period, from about 700 BC. This is, as it happens, at about the time of the earliest Etruscan writing. Not so long ago, the orthodox view held that it was at this time that the Etruscans first appeared on the scene in Italy. However, as chapter 2 describes, most people do not hold this opinion today, but rather the view that Etruscan-speakers must have been in Etruria from long before in prehistory. Exactly when they emerged is an unanswerable question and should worry no-one unduly. (Scholars are similarly uncertain about who the first Greeks were, or the first English for that matter.) Two points are indisputable, however: first, that the origins of the Etruscans must be sought primarily in their prehistoric antecedents in Etruria, not elsewhere; and second, that the Etruscan civilization did not develop in isolation, but was profoundly influenced by contemporary peoples such as the Greeks.

The histories of Etruria and Greece have many parallels (and were frequently intertwined), as the often identical cultural terms used by historians and archaeologists indicate. The Apennine Bronze Age of Etruria which developed during the second millennium BC was roughly contemporary with the Minoan and Mycenaean civilization of Greece and the Aegean, and there is in fact evidence for some kind of trading relationship between Etruria and the Aegean at this time. With the destruction of Mycenae and Troy in about 1100 BC, Greece entered its so-called Dark Age, a period of petty chiefdoms contemporary with the Villanovan iron age chiefdoms of Etruria. In both regions, city states then developed in the eighth and seventh centuries BC. In both regions, too, the seventh century is termed the 'Orientalizing' period, and the city states continued to flourish through the sixth century BC, the 'archaic' period. The

Persian invasion of Greece was first halted with a disastrous defeat at the sea battle of Salamis in 480 BC, and it was also Greek naval expertise that put an end to Etruscan expansion in Italy in 474 BC at the battle of Cumae, both events conveniently marking the end of the archaic period. The fifth century BC was characterized in Greece by the extraordinary intellectual and artistic flowering of classical Athens, but the same period in Etruria witnessed the continued retreat of Etruscan power, now before the infant republic Rome, with the first Etruscan city, Veii, falling in 396 BC. The Hellenistic period in Greece is conventionally dated from the death of Alexander in 323 BC to Augustus' rise to power at Rome in 31 BC, but the term is also used in Etruria to define the last three centuries BC, the period of Roman conquest and acculturation.

It is useful here to name the periods, with their dates, as they are used in this book, because the chronologies vary somewhat in the literature. The dates are only a rough guide, and the onset of various periods will in any case differ slightly in different parts of Etruria. All dates are BC unless otherwise stated (as in the rest of the book):

Early and Middle Bronze Age	2000–1300
Late and Final Bronze Age	1300–900
Early Iron Age (Villanovan)	900–700
Orientalizing	700–570
archaic	570–470
classical	470–300
Hellenistic	300–31

In the case of ancient Greece, labels such as 'archaic', 'classical' and 'Hellenistic' denote defined historical periods as well as visual styles. For Etruscan studies they are also useful for denoting both periods and styles, but the periods are more arbitrarily defined and the Etruscan styles do not display quite the same development.[3] There is no lack of invention in the linear stylizations and decorative patterns of the Etruscan archaic style, and the Etruscans were also attracted by the energy and theatricality of the Greek Hellenistic style. But though they were aware of the Greek classical style, and indeed worked within its formulae for increased naturalism and idealization, it seems to have inspired them rather little: there is little in the way of a Greek High Classical equivalent in Etruria. When it does occur, as in temple decorations at Orvieto and Falerii,

3 Pianu, 1996

it is in isolated instances (at least as far as present finds suggest) rather than as the result of a continuing tradition. Nor could it have been otherwise: only in Greece did the classical style evolve as a process of internal logic.[4]

These art-historical considerations are mentioned here because they have in the past influenced views about the Etruscans, and to a certain extent still do, and always to their detriment. The classical style, with its historically based connotations of excellence and perfection[5] and hence of the imperfection of other and especially pre-classical styles, holds a central place in the public estimation of the Greek achievement but has not at all the same centrality for the Etruscan. 'Why can't a woman be more like a man?', intoned Noel Coward, and there is a common perception – without any of Coward's humour attached to it – that somehow the Etruscans would be more acceptable if only they had been more like the Greeks.

We would do better to think in wider perspectives and reflect that of the many peoples with whom the Greeks came into contact and who learned from them forms and styles of art and architecture, it was the Etruscans who appropriated them most systematically and who, alone of those contemporary with the Greeks, created by these and other means a whole visual culture that lasted many centuries. But Etruria was never a Greek cultural outpost. This is true even though in at least some cases – and leaving Greek exports to Italy aside – it was Greeks who were involved in executing figurative monuments in Etruria; certainly they helped to shape the painted pottery industries, and their presence has been postulated in the tomb-painting workshops, the production of architectural terracottas and work in other media. Although it would be intriguing to know exactly which tomb-paintings and other works Greek craftsmen were responsible for, it would have no bearing on the essential point that these things were made to conform to Etruscan taste in the unique environment of central Italy and are firmly part of the culture of this region.

In many ways art, complex artefacts, and inscribed objects are mere surface froth where the totality of Etruscan society is concerned. They may tell us about the concerns and tastes of an elite section of that society and about its relations with the outside world, they may make for interesting and colourful displays in museums, but they are hardly likely to have been the concern of the bulk of

4 Brendel, 1995: 258
5 Ridgway, 1981: 3

the population. It is generally agreed that one of the ways by which the elites were enabled to prosper was through the control of metal-processing, and so there has in the past been much interest in Etruria's mineral wealth (which no study can ignore – including this one). But it is becoming increasingly clear that in the large spaces between the great cities there were farming communities of villages, hamlets and isolated dwellings of all kinds and that most Etruscans lived agricultural lives far removed from the spin-offs of the extractive industries. Only in recent decades has this population been shown, through painstaking survey and excavation, to have its own archaeological presence.

This book, then, begins with the landscape, explaining how it has changed over great periods of time and how ancient landscapes may be glimpsed through the modern (chapter 1). After an overview of Etruscan prehistory (chapter 2) we move on to consider first the facts and prejudices offered by Greek and Roman writers and then the scope of Etruscan writing, while assessing the evidence they provide for political and social structures (chapter 3). There follow chapters on material culture and its transformations as a consequence of contact with outsiders (chapter 4) and on the various types of settlement and settlement patterns (chapter 5). Much can be said with a fair degree of certainty about the economy, both on the domestic and larger scales (chapter 6), but discussion of cult and belief is inevitably more speculative, and answers have often to be in the form of a series of possibilities (chapter 7). We end with the Romans, but the end is not an abrupt one: archaeologically the period of Romanization is one of the richest (chapter 8).

We hope that the book will provide an up-to-date introduction to the landscape, the artefacts in museums and the sites. Our final section, the Appendix, lists the most important of the latter with descriptions of how best to visit them and brief analyses of their visible (and sometimes invisible) remains. Visiting the sites and museums will make it immediately apparent that the Etruscans were not a homogeneous society but a group of independent-minded states; and noting the varied physical terrain in different parts of Etruria will help to explain their vigorous cultural regionalism. In his introduction to the 1986 edition of D.H. Lawrence's *Etruscan Places*, the great Etruscan scholar Massimo Pallottino wrote:

I don't think there is any other field of human knowledge in which there is such a daft cleavage between what has been scientifically ascertained and the unshakeable beliefs of the public. . . . There is in fact a scholars' Etruria and a writers' Etruria, deriving from two divergent and, in a sense, non-communicating traditions; one, that of objective enquiry; the other, that of poetic intuition.[6]

We are painfully aware that *The Etruscans* cannot match the joyous prose of *Etruscan Places*, but we do hope that we have managed to construct a reasoned account of this extraordinary people in the following pages without losing the wonder at their achievements and love of their landscape that first induced us to embark on this book.

6 Pallottino, in Lawrence, 1932 (1986): 13–14

1

The Landscape

Such a pure, uprising, unsullied country, in the greenness of wheat on an April morning! – and the queer complication of the hills! And in the full, dark, handsome, jovial faces surely you see the lustre still of the life-loving Etruscans!

D.H. Lawrence (1932) Etruscan Places

Introduction

The achievements of the Etruscans cannot be understood divorced from their landscape. Their natural environment offered particular opportunities, such as resources of food, water, space and raw materials, and particular constraints, such as natural hazards, difficult terrain, and biological limiting factors, for them as for all the societies who have lived in Etruria before and afterwards. However, this is not to reduce their civilization to environmental determinism: how the Etruscans responded to their landscape, compared with earlier and later societies, was in terms of their particular social and economic institutions. The relationship between the Etruscans and their landscape was complex: it shaped many aspects of their history, and their activities in turn had a significant impact on it.

We cannot simply take the present-day landscape of Etruria, remove from our mind's eye the more obvious paraphernalia of modern industry and farming, and people it with Etruscans. The landscape of Etruria has been in a state of flux throughout its history, with tectonics and climatic change repeatedly altering it since earliest times and human settlement having an increasingly powerful influence in later prehistory and the historic periods. All these processes can change vegetation, animal populations, soil profiles, soil erosion patterns, river morphology and behaviour.[1] Many of these processes

1 Butzer, 1982

leave well preserved traces in the landscape. To understand the Etruscans' landscape, therefore, we must begin with the geological background that has shaped the major landforms – the robust 'skeleton' of the landscape – that we see today, and then use the findings of pollen analysis, geomorphology and environmental archaeology to try to reconstruct the appearance of the landscape – its 'flesh and blood' – some 2500 years or so ago.

Geological background

Between about 250 and 70 million years ago, the shallow waters of the Tethys Ocean covered much of what is now southern Europe. An immense thickness of limestone was laid down at this time. As the processes of continental drift pushed the continents of Eurasia and Africa towards each other, these limestones were compressed and eventually rose to form the mountain chains of the Mediterranean basin, including the Apennines (fig. 2). (This phase of mountain-building still goes on, reflected in the earthquakes that are a feature of the Mediterranean region.) Further tectonic activity created trenches between the mountains to form what are now the major river valleys and intermontane basins of the Italian peninsula.

During the Pliocene, between about ten and two million years ago, high sea levels submerged much of the landscape except the principal Apennine chain and an archipelago of upland islands to the west, covering many of the flooded areas with sediments such as sands, clays and marls. At the end of the Pliocene, many of these sediments on either side of the Apennines were raised by as much as 800 m as the seabed lifted. Uplift and folding continued to affect the landscape throughout the Pleistocene, the period of the 'Ice Ages' that began about two million years ago and ended with the transition to our present climate about 12,000 years ago.

In Etruria, although Pliocene marine clays are exposed at depth in some river valleys, they have been generally overlain by the volcanic deposits that form one of the most striking characteristics of this landscape.[2] About ten million years ago, a complex sequence of volcanic activity began west of the Apennines which only ended some 50,000 years ago, leading to the formation of the largest expanse of volcanic country in continental Europe. There were

2 Alvarez, 1972

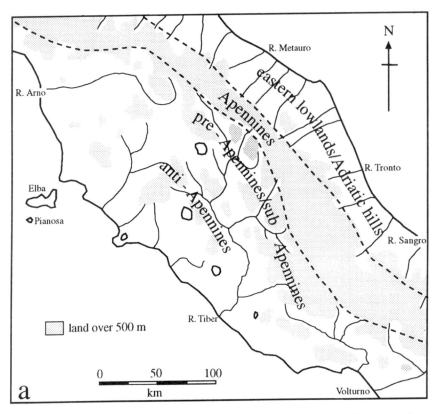

Figure 2a   Central Italy, showing landforms. (Adapted from Barker, 1981: 13)

distinct phases of eruption interspersed with phases of erosion. The first phase of vulcanism led to the creation of the northern volcanic hills in modern-day Tuscany, with Monte Amiata at their centre. About a million years ago, the landscape was convulsed by a second, more profound, sequence of eruptions that formed the dramatic sequence of crater lakes from Bolsena in the north to those of the Alban hills south of Rome and Vesuvius in the Bay of Naples (fig. 3). In south Etruria, the region north of Rome, the scale of the eruptions was such as to force the Tiber eastwards to its present channel.[3] Mud and ash flows of various kinds from the craters cooled

3   Alvarez, 1973

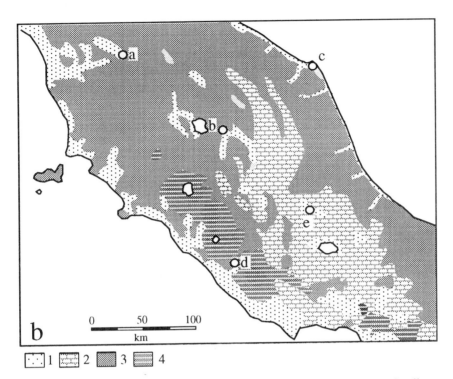

Figure 2b   Central Italy, showing geology. Key: 1 alluvial plains and valleys, and marine terraces; 2 limestone hills; 3 conglomerates, sandstones, clays; 4 volcanic tufo. The regional capitals marked by letters are: a Florence (Tuscany); b Perugia (Umbria); c Ancona (Marche); d Rome (Lazio); e Aquila (Abruzzo). (Adapted from Barker, 1981: 15)

to form tuff or *tufo* rock. Exposed sections often show layers of lava and pumice, a record of the repeated convulsions that fashioned and re-fashioned the landscape at this time.

Over the past 50,000 years, geomorphological processes have added further 'recent' sediments to this geological sequence in the form of colluviation (soil movement downslope caused by erosion) and alluviation (the deposition of alluvium on either side of river channels during flooding). As discussed at the end of this chapter, the extent to which these processes reflect climatic change or human activities is a matter of great debate and of considerable relevance to Etruscan studies.

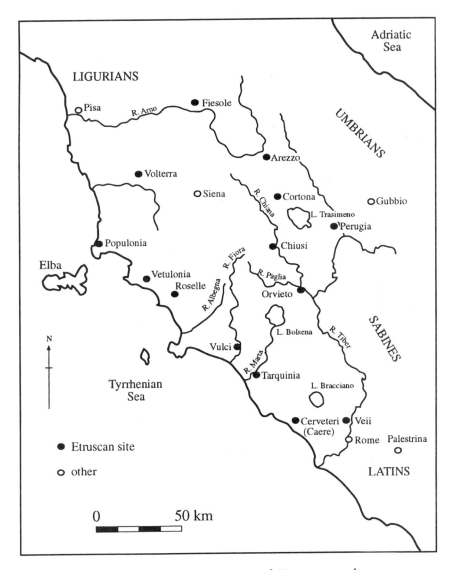

Figure 4 *Etruria, showing principal Etruscan settlements.*

Figure 3 (opposite) Volcanic crater basins and lakes in southern Etruria. Above: air photograph of Baccano crater with, beyond, Lake Martignano and Lake Bracciano. (Photograph by kind permission of the British School at Rome) Below: Lake Bolsena. The hill by the lake edge, in the background to the right, is the site of Bisenzio (Monte Bisenzo). (Photograph: T. Rasmussen)

Landforms and topography

The geological processes described above have fashioned the western side of central Italy into three major structural units: the anti-Apennines, the pre-Apennines and the Apennines (fig. 2). The anti-Apennines were the heartland of the Etruscans (fig. 4). Their eastern boundary is more or less along the line of the modern Autostrada del sole between Rome and Florence, which follows the Tiber valley as far as Orvieto, crosses over into the long trench of the Val di Chiana (fig. 5) and then joins the Arno valley at Arezzo. The main basins and river valleys are floored with alluvial sediments, which are particularly extensive in the lower reaches of the major rivers along the Tyrrhenian littoral, most notably the Cecina and Ombrone as well as the Tiber and Arno. The coastal lowlands here are termed the Maremma – low rolling hills and extensive alluvial plains bordered by littoral sands and shingle, interspersed with lagoons by the major estuaries (fig. 6).

The rugged and broken topography of the island of Elba is paralleled on the mainland opposite, between the Cecina and Ombrone rivers, in the form of the Colline Metallifere (fig. 19, chapter 2), the 'ore mountains', both topographies rising to over 1000 m above sea level. Together they formed the heartland of the mineral wealth of the Etruscans. Northern Tuscany, between the Cecina and Arno rivers eastwards to the hills of Chianti, is also hill country rising several hundred metres above sea level (fig. 7) – a mixture of conglomerates, sandstones and clays interspersed with limestone outcrops, broken principally by the Siena trough, which is mainly floored with Pliocene sediments like the other major basins. Immediately south of the Ombrone, the landscape is dominated by Monte Amiata, its volcanic heights rising to 1738 m above sea level, surrounded by sandstones and clays as to the north.

The Fiora valley on the southern side of this mountain forms the natural boundary with the volcanic *tufo* landscape of southern Etruria. The topography of this region is dominated by a gentle undulating plateau (fig. 8), cut by the narrow valleys of a series of small rivers and streams from the Fiora to the Mignone. These drain predominantly southwestwards from the Monti Volsini, the hills bordering the crater of Lake Bolsena, though only the Marta river flows directly from the lake. In many places the rivers have cut deep trenches through the soft *tufo*, exposing dramatic cliffs that were favourite localities for Etruscan tombs (fig. 9). The Monti

Figure 5   The Val di Chiana. (Photograph: G. Barker)

Figure 6   The Maremma coastal lowlands; in the foreground, the footings of the temple on the hill of Talamonaccio. (Photograph: T. Rasmussen)

Figure 7 Typical hill country in northern Etruria near Siena: the deserted medieval village of Montarrenti. (Photograph: G. Barker)

Figure 8 Typical tufo country in southern Etruria: the plateau. The photograph is looking northwards across the territory of the Tuscania survey shown in fig. 52. (Photograph: G. Barker)

Figure 9   Typical tufo *country in southern Etruria: the gorges. The photograph is of the Marta valley east of Tuscania. (Photograph: T. Rasmussen)*

Volsini rise to just over 600 m above sea level, the lake is at about 300 m and the topography then descends gradually to the sea. South of the Bolsena crater in the bend of the Tiber is the most dramatic crater lake of the region, Vico, the surface of which is about 500 m above sea level, surrounded by a rim of hills rising to almost 1000 m, the Monti Cimini. Some 15 km further south is the last of the big crater lakes, Bracciano, its surface just over 150 m above sea level and its crater rim (the Monti Sabatini) rising to over 500 m. Although the topography southwest of Bracciano consists of a dissected volcanic plateau like that southwest of Bolsena, immediately west of Bracciano are the dramatic hills of Tolfa, which rise steeply to over 500 m.

The pre-Apennines are a rather ill-defined group of predominantly limestone hills cut by wide tectonic basins (fig. 10) and narrow river valleys. On the eastern side of Etruria, the pre-Apennine topography is dominated by the upper Arno and Tiber rivers and their tributaries. The Arno rises in the Casentino, a rather remote basin separated from the rest of Tuscany by the Pratomagno mountain, which projects south from the main Apennine chain forcing the Arno to take a very

Figure 10   A typical intermontane basin in the pre-Apennines: the Gubbio basin. (Photograph: G. Barker)

circuitous route south to Arezzo and then west and north to Florence. To the east of the Val di Chiana, separated by low hills, the Tiber flows down a series of flat intermontane basins in northeastern Tuscany and Umbria from Sansepolcro to Perugia and Todi. Another basin is crossed by the tributary streams which flow from Spoleto past Foligno and Assisi to join the main Tiber near Perugia.

The Apennine mountains form the natural boundary of Etruria on the northern and eastern sides, as the Tiber valley does in the south. They begin on the Tyrrhenian coast north of the Arno as the Alpi Apuane, extraordinarily dramatic mountains which rise almost sheer from sea level to almost 2000 m: for much of the year, the dazzling white of their summits, visible from the coast, is a combination of both snow and the marble of the Carrara quarries. The continuation of the chain on the northern side of the Arno is dominated by clays and shales, forming rounded summits at about 1000 m above sea level separated by wide valleys, an unstable landscape very prone to erosion. From the Pratomagno southwards, however, is the typical landscape of karst uplands: steep ridges rising to some 2000 m enclose basins termed *altopiani* in Italian but more commonly

Figure 11   The typical karst landscape of the limestone Apennine mountains: the Rascino basin in the Cicolano mountains. (Photograph: G. Barker)

poljes by geologists; formed by limestone solution, they have flat floors usually at 1200–1500 m above sea level, made by a combination of sediment accumulation and lateral solution by floodwaters (fig. 11). Like the pre-Apennines, the high mountains bordering Etruria enclose a series of intermontane basins, isolated enclaves of settlement.

The landscape which the Etruscans encountered in their expansion south of the Tiber bears many similarities to the anti-Apennines of Etruria. The volcanic crater country continues past Rome into the Alban hills, and a rolling dissected plateau falls away southwards from these as from Bolsena and Bracciano. The country north and south of the Tiber is termed the Roman Campagna, the middle section of the coastal lowlands that continue southwards as the Pontine plain. Inland of the Pontine plain is a series of limestone ridges such as the Monti Lepini, Monti Ausoni and Monti Aurunci, and then the wide trench of the Liri valley to the east, the principal communication route to the south.

The northern side of the Apennines overlooking the Po plain consists of rolling terrain much damaged by erosion, the clays and shales of the higher ground overlain downslope by Pliocene sands and clays. A series of streams and rivers flows northeastwards through this intermediate terrain onto the alluvial plain itself.

Settlement and communications

We know from archaeological survey that the settlement patterns of Etruria over the past two thousand years have altered drastically, with some periods favouring large nucleated settlements and others more dispersed systems dominated by farmsteads (see chapter 5). The transformations in settlement that have developed since the unification of Italy in 1871 have been particularly profound, and especially so in the past few decades. Nevertheless, the present-day settlement patterns, population distributions and communication networks of Etruria still reflect the constraints and opportunities of the physical environment in many ways. To what extent the present-day settlement patterns reflect those of the Etruscans or were the product of Romanization or later settlement processes such as *incastellamento* (the development of medieval hilltop villages) is one of the themes this book will explore.

In northern Etruria, the principal settlements like Pisa, Florence, Arezzo, Siena and Grosseto are invariably located in major valleys or basins, forming a series of urban enclaves 50–70 km apart along the edge of the hill country, with a few substantial settlements within the hill country, such as Volterra and Massa Marittima (fig. 4). In the diverse geology and broken topography of the hill country, the population is relatively low and is concentrated for the most part in small hamlets and villages, mostly on hilltops such as San Gimignano. In 1927 D.H. Lawrence described the country between Volterra and Sam Gimignano as 'queer and empty – very hilly in sharp little hills, and rather bare, and no villages'.[4] There is a similar pattern of small hilltop settlements around Monte Amiata. Despite the increase of dispersed settlement in recent centuries in response to improved communications, industrialization (the construction of factories on drained valley floors that were formerly too wet for settlement) and social trends (the flight to the countryside of the industrial middle class), the hill settlements of Tuscany still largely retain their traditional functions as 'agro-towns' or 'agro-villages', providing homes for people who farm their land on a daily basis,

4 Kezich, 1986: 159

returning to the settlements in the evening. In the volcanic lowlands of southern Etruria, by contrast, where the topography is gentler and the soils more fertile, there are fewer very large settlements but many more small towns and substantial villages, with a relatively high dispersed population in the countryside as well.

In the pre-Apennines and Apennines, population levels are lower and the major basins form the foci of settlement, supporting local centres 20–30 km apart such as Sansepolcro, Todi, Assisi and Spoleto, with outliers in the Apennine basins such as Gubbio and Norcia. The main urban enclaves in the interior are always at key communication nodes such as Perugia in the middle Tiber valley and Terni and Rieti on the middle Velino. The mountain villages vary from thriving and substantial settlements, where the traditional employment in farming can be augmented by an easy commute to major centres nearby, to remote and dying hamlets that are the home for a few elderly people, visited in the summer by relatives now settled in northern Italy, northern Europe, America or Australia. The main centres are generally 400–600 m above sea level, and most of the hill villages above the basin floors are at 600–1000 m, but there are a few villages right up in the Apennine *altopiani*, such as Castelluccio above Norcia at 1452 m above sea level.

The main roads constructed by the Romans (see fig. 104 chapter 8), the basis for the modern state highway system (but not the Autostrade), are a good guide to some of the best natural communication routes according to the topography.[5] The Aurelia followed the Tyrrhenian littoral, generally several kilometres inland where it crossed the plains to avoid the marshiest terrain. East of the Aurelia was the Via Clodia, which cut across the *tufo* plateau of southern Etruria south of Lake Bracciano to Tuscania and thence took a more circuitous route across central Tuscany past Volterra to the Arno valley. Further east was the main overland route through Etruria, the Via Cassia: this crossed the *tufo* east of Bracciano and Bolsena, skirting round the Monti Cimini between the two, and then used a series of river valleys (the Paglia, Orcia, Ombrone and Arbia) to cross the difficult country of the *crete senese*, the grey rolling claylands south of Siena. From Siena the natural route north is to follow the line of the Elsa valley northwest to the Arno, rather than to cut north through the Chianti hills to Florence like the modern *superstrada*. The next major route is the Flaminia, which skirts the edge of the *tufo* avoiding the Tiber valley, crosses the

5 Gualandi, 1990

Tiber and then uses a series of river valleys and intermontane basins to cut through the Apennines to the Adriatic at Fano. The other major trans-Apennine route, the Salaria, likewise skirts the Tiber valley, though on its eastern side, then crosses the Sabine hills to the Rieti basin and goes up the Velino and down the Tronto valleys to the Adriatic beyond Ascoli Piceno. South of Rome one main route (the Via Latina) followed the Liri valley, and the other (the Via Appia) crossed the Alban hills and the Pontine plain to the coast at Terracina.

These roads have acted as the main arteries of transport in the region since their construction, and the railways built in the last century generally follow them. The routes followed by most English lords on their Grand Tours in the eighteenth and early nineteenth centuries were invariably the same as those taken by Italy's many invading armies in the medieval and post-medieval periods. As the accounts of the former relate, even these major routes were very liable to destruction from landslips in the rainy season, and away from them the communication system linking many hill villages with the outside world consisted of little more than mule tracks. Only in recent decades has the traditional road and rail system been overlain by new systems as a result of the application of modern engineering technologies in draining wetlands, bridge and tunnel building, and the like. The Autostrada del Sole and the new electrified rail line from Rome to Florence have both been constructed straight across the alluvium of the lower and middle Tiber, much of it a malarial marshland till the present century; the same is true of the autostrada from Florence to Pisa down the Arno valley. Similarly, whereas the old route east across the peninsula, the Via Claudia and Via Valeria, followed a tortuous line from one valley or basin to another, the modern autostrada is an unending succession of dramatic bridges, viaducts and tunnels, culminating in a tunnel more than ten kilometres long that goes straight under the Gran Sasso, the highest peak of the Apennines.

Natural communication routes also include the sea, rivers and mountains. A recent advertisement to attract British tourists described Italy as the 'longest pier in Europe', and obviously both the Tyrrhenian and Adriatic coastal waters are ideally suited for moving people and goods up and down the peninsula. Although well protected deep harbours are relatively few, there are many small sheltered bays well suited to the kind of shipping used in the ancient world, and maritime trade was certainly a critical feature of the Etruscan economy (see chapter 6). Within the peninsula, the lower and middle stretches of the major rivers could be navigated by quite substantial barges: Rome in the imperial period received much of its food supply not only from other parts of the Mediterranean basin through its port of Ostia but also from upriver, and both Rome and Florence depended heavily on river supply in the medieval period also.

The smaller rivers and streams are too small and too capricious for boat transport on any scale, though many of their valleys provided the easiest all-weather communication routes through the mountains. It must also be remembered that the mountains themselves could act as a means of communication as much as a barrier, at least on a seasonal basis: for centuries the Apennines have provided their inhabitants with abundant wood for charcoal production and summer pasture for grazing animals, and the exploitation of such resources inevitably brings together peoples from adjacent valleys and basins.

Environment and land use

The Italian peninsula, like most regions of the Mediterranean, is characterized by dramatic differences in topography. The rises in altitude over short distances are such that on a clear day you can see the sea from some of the Apennine ski resorts, and both the Tyrrhenian and Adriatic seas from some of the highest peaks. Such variability is inevitably reflected in climate, environment and land use.

The climate of Etruria is Mediterranean, with hot summers and humid winters, but average summer temperatures on the lowlands and uplands vary between 25 and 20°C respectively, and average winter temperatures between about 7 and 2°C. Rainfall also varies greatly with altitude: under 700 mm on the coastal lowlands, 700–1000 mm further inland, 1000–1500 mm in the Apennine basins, and over 1500 mm at high altitudes. Most rain falls in autumn and winter, but there are less than seventy days of rainfall on the lowlands compared with well over a hundred in the interior. In bad summers the coastal lowlands can be almost entirely rainless. The high Apennines like the Pratomagno are sub-alpine in their winter conditions, with prolonged frosts and snow, and in bad winters snow may cover the mountains for months, with high villages regularly cut off for days at a time. Winter conditions on Monte Amiata are sufficiently severe to support a small ski resort.

Patterns of land use in Etruria have undergone immense transformations since the last war. Mechanized agriculture began to be a feature of the Etrurian landscape during the fascist era but has only become widespread in recent decades. Traditional iron ploughs pulled by horses, donkeys or oxen cultivated down to about 20 cm depth (fig. 12), but most farmers now use caterpillar tractors to pull steel ploughs which cut huge furrows down to almost a metre's depth (fig. 13). The technology also allows them to plough steeply sloping ground which was formerly left to woodland or pasture. Modern market pressures, supported by government and EU subsidies, have encouraged the development of monoculture rather than mixed cropping. The combination of heavy tractors and monoculture has promoted the destruction of field boundaries to create larger, more efficient units. The effect of the changes on the landscape in terms of accelerated erosion rates in regions such as Tuscany has been simply horrific[6] and, very belatedly, less destructive systems of cultivation are being re-introduced.

Separate fields of cereals, vines or olives have now almost entirely replaced the traditional mixed system of polyculture or *coltura promiscua* (fig. 14). In the latter system, the roots of the vines, olives and cereals grow at different depths, so they do not compete with each other and also help to prevent erosion by binding the soil. Above ground the system raises the surface temperature by several degrees, so prolonging the growing season. *Coltura promiscua* has been common in Italy since the Roman period, when it was described by Columella, Pliny, Varro and Virgil.[7] Olives certainly and vines probably were not grown by prehistoric farmers in Etruria.[8] Whether or not olive and vine cultivation, and polyculture, characterized Etruscan as well as Roman farming will be discussed in chapter 6.

Useful guides to land use in Etruria before these changes are the *Carte della Utilizzazione del Suolo* published by the Touring Club Italiano in the 1950s and early 1960s, produced at 1:200,000 scale from air photographs (fig. 15). They show pine groves along the coast and extensive areas of deciduous (predominantly oak) forest on the lowlands inland, but the dominant form of land use shown on the maps is cereal farming. Rice was being grown on the wettest reclaimed lands of the Maremma and Pontine plain, Mussolini's *bonifica*. Interspersed within the cultivated land and forest of the coastal lowlands are extensive areas of pasture. Further inland, in the hillier areas, many villages have the classic radial pattern of

6   Coles et al., 1984; Gilbertson et al., 1983, 1992
7   White, 1970: 47–9
8   Barker, 1981

Figure 12   Ploughing with an ox team in the Biferno valley (Molise) in the 1970s. (Photograph: G. Barker)

Figure 13   Modern mechanized ploughing in Tuscany in the 1980s. (Photograph: G. Barker)

Figure 14 The traditional cultivation system of polyculture or coltura promiscua: *olive trees, vines between them and grass crops grown below. (Photograph: G. Barker)*

Mediterranean land use: vegetable plots on the edge of the village, olive and vine plantations (frequently mixed) on the slopes immediately below, cereal fields further away, and pasture and woodland at a distance.[9] Olives are not grown much above about 600 m, and vines above about 800 m, and they are only grown at these heights if the aspect is favourable. The Apennine basins have mixed cereal and tree farming, the slopes of the mountains are covered in forest, the *altopiani* are generally under pasture and there is sub-alpine pasture above the tree line on the peaks. Not shown on the land use maps is the scale of cultivation: as altitude increases, field and farm sizes get smaller, yields diminish and land use is more marginal.

For English readers, some of the most evocative insights into the rural life that lay behind these systems of land use in Etruria before mechanization are the descriptions by escaped prisoners of war of the peasant families (*contadini*) who sheltered them in the second world war during the German occupation after the Italian armistice. With most of the able-bodied men still in the armed forces in Russia,

9 Chisholm, 1968

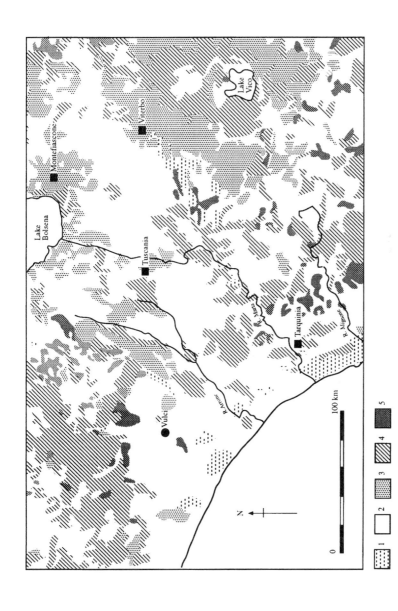

Figure 15 *Simplified patterns of recent land use in Etruria: 1. drained land; 2. arable; 3. polyculture (cereals, olives, vines); 4. woodland; 5. pasture; ■ modern town; ● ancient site. (Adapted from the* Carta del Utilizzazione del Suolo d'Italia, *1959, sheet 12)*

or in hiding in the woods as fugitives or partisans, farms were being cultivated by women, children and the elderly, and many allied soldiers in hiding ended up learning to farm the land in return for food and shelter. In the best known account, *Love and War in the Apennines*,[10] Eric Newby entered into the dawn-to-dusk grind of one peasant family high up in the northern Apennines above Parma: clearing fields of stones, ploughing with a pair of oxen, hoeing with the *zappa*, milking, cheese-making, tending the animals, repairing equipment, and so on.

I had always thought of the Italian *contadini* as a race of people who sat basking in the sun before the doors of their houses while the seed which they had inserted in the earth in the course of a couple of mornings' work burgeoned without their having to do anything but watch this process taking place. I now knew differently. These people were fighting to survive.[11]

Stuart Hood encountered a similar world in the Chianti hills and John Verney in Abruzzo.[12] When Newby returned twelve years later, he found many of the mountain farms abandoned and the traditional way of life of the *carbonari*, charcoal-burners from the Maremma who came into the Apennines each winter, already consigned to history by the advent of methane gas for cooking.

Before mechanization, farmers needed oxen, horses or donkeys not only to cultivate their land but also for transporting goods, the donkey or mule being particularly critical as an all-purpose pack animal for the *contadino*. Modern feeds mean that cow's milk can now be produced at little more cost than in northern Europe, and refrigeration allows it to be transported from producer to consumer, however hot the climate. Herds of Friesian dairy cattle are quite a common sight around the major cities of Italy today, as well as (on the coastal lowlands) the buffalo which produce the highly prized *mozzarella di bufalo*. However, the Italian climate and environment do not naturally favour dairy cattle, and before the introduction of modern fodder crops it was a major investment for most farmers to keep a team of plough oxen, let alone a large herd of cattle. The Roman agronomists Cato and Columella simply advised farmers to collect whatever leaves they could find between March and September to keep their ploughing team alive, and if necessary to keep their own family short of grain in the autumn to feed up the oxen

10 Newby, 1971
11 Newby, 1971: 114–15
12 Hood, 1963; Verney, 1955

ready for ploughing.[13] Subsistence farmers in the Apennines still collect branches and leaves from the forest for animal fodder.

The pig is a very useful animal for the Italian *contadino*, given that if necessary it can more or less fend for itself on rubbish around the settlement, as well as rooting in fields and woods. It also breeds prolifically. The Roman and medieval authors describe a range of pig-keeping systems in Italy, with sties at one end of the spectrum and, at the other, half-wild herds left in the woods for months on end, gathered from time to time rather like British hill sheep. Whilst almost every part of the pig can be eaten, and the Roman writers were rapturous in their descriptions of the 1001 ways in which you could cook it,[14] the drawback is that the pig is only useful dead. It cannot provide useful 'secondary products' when alive as cattle, sheep, goats and horses do (such as milk, wool, pulling power or transport) and will only manure a field at the price of rooting the soil up. Hence, for many peasant families in Italy, keeping a pig has been something of a luxury, its slaughter still the occasion for family get-togethers when city workers return to their home village to help their relatives deal with the carcass.

Sheep and goats are well adapted to the Mediterranean climate and vegetation. They were the principal stock for many prehistoric farmers in Italy[15] and since Roman times have been kept in large numbers in both small- and large-scale systems of husbandry. In the former, a small flock of between about twenty-five and a hundred animals is grazed during the day around the settlement on pasture, stubble fields, fallow land and wasteland, and penned overnight. In the worst weather, they are normally penned and fed on hay (and, nowadays, concentrates). This system is therefore termed *stanziale*, denoting the use of stalls or pens. Keeping sheep on a large scale in Italy, as elsewhere in the Mediterranean, invariably relies on transhumance, *transumanza*, moving the animals from lowland grazing in the winter to summer grazing in the mountains.

Today the transhumant flocks are transported by truck, whereas earlier this century and in the second half of the last century they were moved by rail to railheads and then walked to pasture. Before this, they were moved on the hoof, on droveroads or *tratturi*.[16] This kind of movement requires organization at the regional scale and has invariably been a capitalist enterprise, the flocks being owned

13   White, 1970: 219
14   White, 1970: 321
15   Barker, 1981
16   Sprengel, 1975

Figure 16 The Roman Campagna in the nineteenth century: Henry Coleman's painting of the winter camp of transhumant shepherds near Rome. (Reproduced by kind permission of Pier Andrea de Rosa, from de Rosa and Trastulli, 1988)

by wealthy families, the Church or the state. In the sixteenth century, millions of sheep were involved in such long-distance transhumance in the Italian peninsula each year. The largest droves were on the eastern side of the peninsula between the Abruzzo mountains and the Tavoliere plain in southeast Italy, controlled by the Dogana delle Pecore for the Kingdom of Naples.[17] At the same time, however, hundreds of thousands of animals were also driven between the high Apennines and the western lowlands, particularly to winter pastures on the Maremma and the Pontine plains.

There were no true *tratturi* here as on the eastern side of the peninsula, and the flocks were driven along normal mule and cart tracks. (In the early 1950s, transhumant flocks were still driven through Rome down the Corso – the equivalent of London's Oxford Street – *en route* to the winter pastures!) Most of these flocks belonged to shepherds from villages in the Apennines, who camped out on the lowlands in thatch huts (fig. 16). In the last century, Augustus Hare travelled across the Pontine plain where, he wrote, 'the most frequent landmarks are the conical shepherds' huts . . . inhabited during about half the year by a race of men so cut off from all social and civilizing influences that one might expect to find the lowest brutality, and all the fiercest passions in a moral soil thus neglected'.[18] A less judgemental description comes from Stuart Hood, writing of Chianti in the spring of 1944:

one evening the shepherds from the Maremma passed on their way to the high Apennine to spend the summer on the short-grassed pastures. Through the winter and the lambing they had kept their flocks among the Etruscan tombs. They slept in the hay. In the morning they paid their lodging in milk and curds and moved slowly on, tall men in long black cloaks, taciturn and close. Their dogs were always at heel lolling their tongues – gaunt, shaggy, with a spiked collar on their lean necks.[19]

It is difficult for the modern visitor, driving down the Aurelia or the Autostrada del Sole, to appreciate the extraordinary changes to the landscape of western Etruria that have taken place since the 1920s and 1930s. Before the land reclamation programmes of the fascist era, the Maremma, Campagna and Pontine plains were not unlike the prairies of the Wild West, inhabited not only by the transhumant shepherds who so offended Augustus Hare but also by herdsmen, *butteri*, who lived there all year round herding the

17 Braudel, 1972
18 Hare, 1875: 21
19 Hood, 1963: 114–15

Figure 17   Butteri *(herdsmen) on the Maremma in the nineteenth century: Charles Coleman's painting of herds being driven to Rome. (Reproduced by kind permission of Pier Andrea de Rosa, from de Rosa and Trastulli, 1988)*

long-horned white Maremmano cattle (fig. 17). They had the same skills and wild reputation of the American cowboys: when Buffalo Bill brought his circus to Rome, the *butteri* of the Maremma took on his cowboys and indians in horsemanship trials and, the story goes, won. Many of the paintings of rural life on the Roman Campagna, the plains around Rome, made in the nineteenth century by the Coleman family,[20] or the photographs taken here in the early twentieth century by Thomas Ashby,[21] could be of Montana or Wyoming save for a Roman viaduct or the dome of St Peter's in the backgrand. Earl Brewster, the friend and travelling companion of D.H. Lawrence on his journey through Etruria in 1927, described their drive from Tarquinia to Vulci as crossing 'the wildest country I have seen in Italy'.[22] For Edward Hutton, the Campagna was 'this immense and universal thing which lies unregarded at the gates of the Eternal City . . . too vast and too silent for intimacy'.[23] Figure 18

20   de Rosa and Trastulli, 1988
21   Martinelli and Scott, 1986
22   Kezich, 1986: 161
23   Hutton, 1909: 334

Figure 18   The huts of transhumant shepherds at Ardea near Rome in the early twentieth century. (A Thomas Ashby photograph, by kind permission of the British School at Rome and the Istituto Centrale per il Catalogo e la Documentazione)

shows the huts of transhumant shepherds outside Ardea in Lazio photographed by Thomas Ashby at the turn of the century. One of the communities he photographed was on the site of what is now Rome's international airport at Fiumicino.

Inscriptions and references in the classical writers make it clear that long-distance transhumance was practised in Italy in the Roman republican and imperial periods, the most important product probably being wool.[24] Whether or not long-distance transhumance was also a feature of the Etruscan rural economy will be discussed in chapter 6. The practice continued on a smaller scale in early medieval times,[25] though the market for wool did not expand again until bulk cargoes could be shipped to the burgeoning cities of northern Italy after the twelfth century.[26] Today the main market is

24   Gabba, 1985, 1988; Pasquinucci, 1979
25   Clementi, 1984
26   Wickham, 1982: 50–8

for very young lamb, the *abbacchio* that is one of Rome's specialities in the spring, though the milk produced by the flocks (both the hard *pecorino* and the soft *ricotta*) also brings in useful income.[27]

Abbacchio, pecorino – they conjure up the wonderful regional cuisines of Etruria that, washed down with a bottle of Chianti or Frascati, are one of the main reasons most of us have for holidaying in the region (forget all those Etruscan tombs!).

Tuscan cuisine is inextricably bound to the culture and personality of Tuscany and its people. I do not mean by Tuscan cuisine the elaborate food that one might eat in one of the region's many grand and elegant restaurants; I mean the sort of food that the waiter will eat when he goes home, the recipes that the grandmother of the chef might cook every day. . . . Those who dwell here live in medieval houses, pray before altarpieces painted by Renaissance masters and prepare their food with the grace and balance instilled into them by hundreds of years of measured civilization.[28]

However, it has to be emphasized how recent this cuisine in fact is and how, for all the 'peasant cooking' that is its greatest charm, most Italian peasants in the past saw little of it. At the end of the last century, for example, in most rural Italian households, 'meat was a rare luxury, eaten only on feast days or family celebrations. Foods which we think of today as typically Italian – tomato purée, for example – were virtually unknown, or far too expensive for most people. Even wine was beyond the means of most peasants, who had to content themselves with *vinello*, mostly water, but passed through the must.'[29] The staple food for most peasants was a wheat gruel, with bread, pasta, polenta and vegetables being reserved for festival days and even fruit a real luxury. The same was almost certainly true for most Roman and medieval peasants, too, with religious festivals probably the main occasions on which they tasted meat.

It is tempting to look at the model of the Etruscan ploughman behind his ox team (see fig. 70, chapter 6), compare it with images of recent ploughing using similar technologies and assume that we can people the Etruscan landscape with the peasant farmers of yesterday. Watching a Tuscan peasant ploughing between rows of olives and vines with his ox team at the turn of the century, Bernard Berenson wrote in his diary how 'it gave me a moment of happiness.

27 Barker and Grant, 1991
28 Romer, 1984: 1, 3
29 Clark, 1984: 19

Why? The spectacle in itself was beautiful. At the same time it gave me a feeling that I was looking at what has been going on ever since civilization began.'[30] In the same way, the intellectual Carlo Levi, banished from Rome by Mussolini before the last war to a remote village in Basilicata in the south, felt that he must be witnessing a way of life that went back more or less unchanged for thousands of years: 'the seasons pass today over the toil of the peasants, just as they did three thousand years before Christ. . . . Of the two Italys that share the land between them, the peasant Italy is by far the older. . . . Every outside influence has broken over it like a wave without leaving a trace.'[31]

In fact the backwardness and poverty Levi witnessed in the Italian Mezzogiorno were largely a product of feudalism in the post-medieval period, and rural societies here three thousand years before Christ were totally different from those of 2000 BC, 1000 BC, the beginning of the Christian era, or even AD 1000.[32] Quite apart from the social, economic and political institutions that separate modern and ancient farming, we know that crop systems have changed fundamentally since farming was first introduced. The first Mediterranean farmers sowed different kinds of cereals from today, preferred wet soils that were generally avoided in later periods, sowed their crops in spring (whereas autumn sowing is ubiquitous today), did not cultivate olives and vines, and probably kept animals only on a very small scale, mainly for meat.[33] Whilst of course we can learn much from pre-modern systems of land use in Etruria, we cannot simply transpose them back to the first millennium BC. We have to understand Etruscan farming in its particular social and economic context.

The landscape of the Etruscans

The modern vegetation of Etruria, as elsewhere in Italy, is the product of more than a million years of natural processes, substantially modified by several millennia of human activity. Without human disturbance, most of the landscape would be forested. The natural or climax vegetation of the coastal belt would be dominated by pine

30 Raison, 1983: 187–8
31 Levi, 1947: 12–13
32 Barker, 1995
33 Halstead, 1987

trees with shrubs such as rosemary and lentisk below. There would be evergreen oak and juniper forest further inland at low altitudes. Higher than 200–300 m above sea level this would give way to deciduous forest, with willows and alders in the valley bottoms near water and trees like oak, ash, elm, lime, sycamore, sweet chestnut and hornbeam on the slopes up to about 1000 m. Between here and about 1500 m there would be beech with ash, elm and sycamore on drier soils, and silver fir and pine on wetter soils. Above this would be dwarf juniper and sub-alpine pasture where the soil cover was sufficient to sustain vegetation growth.

In fact, of course, much of the landscape bears little relation to this description. The coastal pinetum is protected and in places is being enlarged to attract tourists to the beaches. The inland lowland forests survive only in patches, though abandoned arable and pasture is now being colonized by a scrubby *macchia* of rosemary, cistus, broom, lentisk, juniper, evergreen oak and acacia, which if left ungrazed would regenerate to evergreen oak forest. Drainage and forest clearance have created huge areas under the plough. Soils have been eroded and exhausted by millennia of farming, in places creating bleak badlands like the *balze* moonscape around Volterra. Forest-cutting for firewood and charcoal-burning, especially in the post-medieval period, has in places greatly reduced the upland forests, though regeneration is now so well advanced that wolves are returning to the mountains of Tuscany.

Etruria is fortunate in the number of pollen analyses that have been carried out, at least in the southern part, which allow us to reconstruct vegetation cover during the Etruscan period. Most of the pollen diagrams have been constructed from cores taken in the sediments of the volcanic crater lakes or basins (from north to south): Lagaccione di Mezzano, a small lake 8 km west of Bolsena; Vico; Monterosi, a small lake between Vico and Bracciano; Martignano, a small lake just over 1 km east of Bracciano; and Baccano, a crater drained by the Romans and crossed by the Via Cassia a few kilometres further south.[34] There is also a diagram from the drained crater lake of Valle di Castiglione 20 km east of Rome,[35] and another from Mezzaluna on the eastern edge of the Pontine plain.[36] For northern

---

34 Lagaccione di Mezzano: Hunt, 1988; Vico: Frank, 1969; Monterosi: Bonatti, 1961, 1966, 1970; Martignano: Kelly and Huntley, 1991; Baccano: Bonatti, 1963
35 Alessio et al., 1986; Follieri et al., 1988
36 Eisner et al., 1986; Hunt and Eisner, 1991

Etruria, there is only one diagram, from lacustrine sediments in the Farma valley.[37]

In the closing stages of the Pleistocene, according to all these diagrams, the landscape of Etruria consisted predominantly of an arid steppe vegetation with grasses and artemisia. The shift towards present-day climatic conditions began with the Holocene some 12,000 years ago, and as rainfall and temperature increased so did the amount of forest cover. The early deciduous woodland formed an open canopy, with steppe vegetation persisting into the early Holocene, but by about 6000 BC there was dense forest. The uplands of the peninsula were also densely forested by this time.[38]

According to the pollen diagrams from the crater lakes there was a decline in woodland between c.2000 and 1000 BC. Frank attributed this to human actions, but Bonatti, Hunt, Kelly and Huntley suggested that it is more likely that a change in climate towards drier conditions was responsible.[39] In the Valle di Castiglione, too, there was an increase in dry-loving vegetation from the latter part of the second millennium BC, indicating the development of warmer and drier conditions, and there is parallel evidence from molluscan remains at the site for climatic warming, so the investigators here also see the opening up of the forest at this time as primarily reflecting climatic change rather than human activities.[40] There is also widespread evidence for the shrinkage of lake levels during this same period.[41]

The development of more open vegetation may have started earlier on the coastal lowlands: *macchia*-type vegetation is recorded in the Mezzaluna diagram in a phase dated between about 4500 and 3000 BC. What happened in the uplands is not at all clear. A change to warm, dry conditions was not noted in the pollen diagram from the Farma valley.[42] The only published study from the central Apennines is that of Chiarugi, long before radiocarbon dating:[43] pollen from lake and peat sediments indicate a shift from oak and beech forest to fir and ash in the middle Holocene, but precisely when is not clear. On the other side of the Apennines, however, a diagram taken from the floor of the Adriatic ocean 30 km off the coast recorded a decline in oak and beech forest and a rise in fir and ash

37 Ferrarini and Marraccini, 1978
38 Grüger, 1977; Watts, 1985
39 Bonatti, 1970; Frank, 1969; Hunt, 1988; Kelly and Huntley, 1991
40 Alessio et al., 1986; Follieri et al., 1988
41 Carancini et al., 1986; Fugazzola Delpino, 1982
42 Ferrarini and Marraccini, 1978
43 Chiarugi, 1939

from about 1000 BC, thought to reflect vegetational changes in the Apennines.[44]

Despite the limitations of the palaeoenvironmental evidence, we can conclude that the landscape of the Etruscans was somewhere between the closed woodland of earlier periods (akin to the climax vegetation described earlier) and the predominantly open landscape of the classical period. Coastal lowlands like the Pontine plain were a mosaic of marsh, fen and forest depending on groundwater levels.[45] The lowlands, intermontane valleys and basins, and the main Apennines themselves, must have been predominantly forested, but the composition and thickness of the forest would have varied considerably, from densely wooded valley bottoms and steep hillsides to more open country on some of the interfluves that would have been more conducive to settlement. The tree cover over the high Apennines was also beginning to open up by this time.

Although the pollen studies indicate that climatic warming had played the major role in opening up the landscape by the time of Etruscan settlement, the palynologists also recognize the influence of early farmers in contributing to the process. Cereals were in fact being cultivated by neolithic farmers in Etruria from about 5000 BC, and there is consistent evidence for a substantial increase in settlement during the Bronze Age, the second millennium BC, especially in the latter part (see chapter 2). This was also the period when the settlement record suggests that the high Apennines were being exploited systematically for the first time, probably by shepherds and herders from communities in the adjacent valleys and basins – hitherto they were almost certainly too densely forested.[46] In the first millennium BC, the vegetation on the Pontine plain around Mezzaluna consisted of alder carr and some willow, with oak, elm and hornbeam forest on the hills beyond, but there are also indicators in the pollen diagrams of arable and pasture land nearby. Although the radiocarbon dating at Baccano and Monterosi is not very satisfactory, the indications are that cereals were occasionally being grown in the vicinity before 1000 BC and were present consistently after 1000 BC, but the quantities of cereal and grass pollen in these diagrams then increased dramatically after Romanization.

In 1969, the geomorphologist Claudio Vita-Finzi published an important study of Mediterranean river systems in which he argued

44   Bottema, 1974
45   Hunt and Eisner, 1991
46   Barker and Grant, 1991

that, at some time in the Holocene, the regimes of rivers throughout the Mediterranean changed, the result being the dumping of huge quantities of sediment in their middle and lower channels.[47] He termed these sediments the Younger Fill, to distinguish them from Older Fill sediments deposited in the late Pleistocene. Dating evidence in the form of radiocarbon samples and potsherds collected from the river sections suggested that the Younger Fill sediments were probably deposited in the main during the first millennium AD, and Vita-Finzi concluded that the likeliest cause of such a widespread and broadly contemporaneous phenomenon must be a change to a wetter climate.

Since his study, however, it has been found that the history of Holocene alluviation in the Mediterranean is more complex than he supposed. Geomorphologists have found evidence for alluvial episodes in prehistoric, classical, medieval and post-medieval times rather than the more or less single phase of alluviation predicted by the Younger Fill model.[48] Archaeologists have also noted that alluviation episodes often correlate with phases of population increase and/or agricultural intensification,[49] suggesting that human activities such as forest clearance for farming and grazing were the likeliest culprit, though it remains likely that climatic change made things much worse in Roman times.[50]

The sedimentary record in central Italy correlates with the evidence of the pollen diagrams in the indications of the accelerating impact of human settlement on the landscape: small scale and spasmodic before about 1000 BC; consistent but limited during the Iron Age and Etruscan periods; and only large scale in classical and later times.[51] The record of settlement trends according to regional archaeological surveys conforms with this picture.[52] Certainly in southern Etruria, Romanization marked a profound shift in the relationship between the Etruscans and their landscape, for it led to an increase in settlement densities in the countryside to levels probably not reached again until the modern period (see chapter 5).

47 Vita-Finzi, 1969
48 Bruckner, 1986; Davidson, 1980; Gilbertson et al., 1983, 1992; Hunt, 1995; Neboit, 1984; Pope and van Andel, 1984; van Andel et al., 1985; Wagstaff, 1981
49 Barker, 1995; van Andel and Runnels, 1987
50 Greene, 1986; Randsborg, 1991
51 Barker, 1995; Cherkauer, 1976; Hunt, 1988; Hunt et al., 1990; Jones, 1985; Judson, 1963; Mazzanti et al., 1986
52 Barker and Lloyd, 1991: Potter, 1979

Whilst we are beginning to be able to reconstruct the landscape of the Etruscans, it is important to recognize that this is far from being able to measure the perception of that landscape by the Etruscans themselves. This may seem an impossible task, but in recent years archaeologists have begun to make some headway in understanding the 'mental maps' of ancient peoples by using techniques developed by the geographical sciences for visualizing human perceptions of geographical space. Such an approach has been used with some success in the case of the peoples contemporary with the Etruscans living south of Rome in the Pontine region[53] but has not yet been applied in Etruria proper. However, as discussed in the ensuing chapters, we can draw a number of inferences from other evidence, such as Etruscan funerary architecture and material culture, regarding how Etruscans perceived their landscape, and their place within it.

53 Attema, 1992

2

Origins

The Etruscans sailed the seas. They are even said to have come by sea, from Lydia in Asia Minor, at some date far back in the dim mists before the eighth century B.C. But that a whole people, even a whole host, sailed in the tiny ships of those days, all at once, to people a sparsely inhabited central Italy, seems hard to imagine.

D.H. Lawrence (1932) *Etruscan Places*

Introduction

Before the development of systematic archaeological research, scholars interested in the origins of the Etruscans could only scrutinize the writings of the Greek and Roman authors, given the absence of Etruscan literature. The impossibility of treating such sources as 'factual history' will be discussed at length in the next chapter. Suffice to say here that the ancient writers were conspicuously inconsistent in what they said regarding the question of Etruscan origins.

At one end of the spectrum is the comment made by Herodotus in the fifth century BC (*Histories* 1.94) that the Lydians of Asia Minor (modern western Turkey), forced by famine to leave their homeland, sailed westwards under their leader Tyrrhenus and established themselves in Etruria, founding the Etruscan cities. A diametrically opposite view, however, was put forward by Dionysius of Halicarnassus (1.30.2) in the first century BC, who pronounced that the Etruscans were indigenous to Italy: they called themselves Rasenna and were an ancient nation 'which does not resemble any other people in their language or in their way of life, or customs'. A third (modern) theory, which springs in part from the Roman historian Livy, is that the Etruscans came down into Italy overland from the north across the Alps: he pointed to similarities between the Etruscans and the inhabitants of Rhaetia in the region of the river Danube.

As the Etruscan scholar David Randall-MacIver emphasized, to reconstruct the cultural background that preceded the emergence of a recognizably Etruscan culture in the eighth century BC, we have to put aside the writings of the Greek and Roman authors and turn instead to archaeology 'on which alone any valid arguments can be based'.[1] It has to be said, however, that archaeological data can be just as ambigious and amenable to alternative interpretations as documentary data. Since systematic archaeological research began in the mid nineteenth century, for example, some archaeologists have detected evidence in the material culture in support of the original 'oriental' theory of Etruscan origins, some have favoured the 'indigenous' theory and others have favoured an origin going back to the preceding Iron Age but have seen the origin of that culture north of the Alps!

Virtually all archaeologists now agree that the evidence is overwhelmingly in favour of the 'indigenous' theory of Etruscan origins: the development of Etruscan culture has to be understood within an evolutionary sequence of social elaboration in Etruria. Explaining this process, however, is still far more difficult than describing it. For example, contact with the outside world, particularly with the Greeks and Phoenicians, was certainly an important factor within the final stages of this process, but scholars disagree about the extent to which such contact was a cause of increasing cultural complexity in Etruria, or a result, or both.

The most important developments in social complexity presaging the emergence of Etruscan culture took place in the preceding 500 years or so, the Late Bronze Age and Iron Age, when the settlement system changed from one based on hamlets and farms to one that included, on top of this, substantial villages and proto-urban centres. The Late Bronze Age certainly marked significant cultural changes in Etruria compared with before, which have sometimes been intepreted in terms of the arrival of new peoples (the colonization movement from the north referred to above). However, while the period 1300–800 BC remains the principal focus of interest, to answer the question 'Who were the Etruscans?' we also have to sketch in briefly the earlier settlement history of Etruria in order to establish the amount of continuity or change in the population of the region before the Late Bronze Age, and to understand the social foundations of the stratified societies which we can discern in the archaeological record in the centuries immediately preceding the Etruscan civilization.

1   MacIver, 1928

The first settlers

To begin at the very beginning, people have probably been living in Etruria from about three quarters of a million years ago, though the evidence is exceptionally sparse before about 100,000 years ago.[2] Before then, the archaeological record consists of a number of locations in which primitive flint implements and animal bones have been found together, meagre testimony to the activities of nomadic bands of foragers and scavengers over this immense period of time.[3] Between about 100,000 and 40,000 years ago there were bands of Neanderthals subsisting on the lowlands of Etruria by a mixture of ambush-hunting and scavenging to obtain meat, and probably plant-collecting as well, though evidence for the latter has not survived.[4] Anatomically modern humans had replaced (or evolved from? – the evidence is not clear) Neanderthals by about 40,000–35,000 years ago.[5] Their appearance coincides in the archaeological record with evidence for profound transformations in technology, subsistence, systems of communication and ideologies, all of which were effective adaptations to the hostile glacial climate of the time.[6] The hunting bands probably spent the winter months on the lowlands but followed animals like red deer into the hills in the summer.[7]

With the onset of modern climatic conditions after about 12,000 years ago, people in Etruria had to adapt to the rapid growth of forest that ensued. Mixed systems of hunting, fishing and gathering were developed by these 'mesolithic' or 'epipalaeolithic' communities, the resources of the sea, lakes and rivers becoming especially important over time.[8] Although European prehistorians have traditionally regarded such societies as egalitarian, there are signs that a few localities with exceptionally rich food resources may have sustained relatively large communities living in more or less permanent settlements who – like farmers later – built houses, stored food, built ceremonial monuments and organized themselves within distinct households.[9] The most striking evidence for complex social relationships amongst such communities has come from cemeteries,

---

2 Peretto et al., 1983
3 Piperno, 1992
4 Peretto, 1992
5 Guerreschi, 1992
6 Gamble, 1982; Mithen, 1990
7 Barker, 1981; Donahue, 1988
8 Lewthwaite, 1986
9 Bender, 1978; Rowley-Conwy, 1981

where the gravegoods imply that different age and sex groups were clearly differentiated from each other by their dress, ornaments and equipment. Although the large cemeteries are mostly in northern Europe, there are a number of burial sites in Italy, including several caves in Liguria immediately northwest of Tuscany, near the modern border with France.[10] Such burials suggest that already in these early societies there were particular individuals of high status singled out as leaders of some kind.

The first agricultural communities

The beginnings of farming in Etruria *c.*5000 BC have traditionally been explained in terms of the arrival of a new people, neolithic colonists from the eastern Mediterranean. However, here, as in many other parts of Europe, the 'colonist hypothesis' has looked increasingly less attractive in recent years as we have learned more about the previous mesolithic societies and about the chronology and nature of the transition from hunting to farming.[11] The discovery of neolithic pottery reliably associated with mesolithic flint tools at Petriolo in Tuscany in a hearth dated by radiocarbon to *c.*5000 BC is typical of the evidence now widespread in the Mediterranean for the gradual incorporation of new resources into existing subsistence systems at this time.[12]

Although isolated neolithic sherds have been found at many locations in Etruria by recent archaeological surveys,[13] excavated settlement sites of the initial phase of farming are still very few.[14] Most communities were very small, perhaps one or two families, living in huts made variously of branches, reeds, straw and daub, probably not dissimilar to those still constructed by Italian farmers, shepherds and charcoal-burners as temporary shelters and stores. Their diet was probably dominated by cereals and pulses,[15] the heavily forested landscape making it impracticable to keep large numbers of stock, though sheep (especially), goats, cattle and pigs were all kept.[16]

10 Cardini, 1980
11 Barker, 1985; Lewthwaite, 1982, 1985, 1986, 1987; Zvelebil and Rowley-Conwy, 1984
12 Donahue et al., 1993
13 Anzidei, 1987; Fugazzola Delpino, 1987; Negroni Catacchio, 1987
14 Calvi Rezia, 1972, 1973; Malone and Stoddart, 1992
15 Castelletti, 1974–5
16 Wilkens, 1987

The crops were grown in small fields – gardens, really – around the settlement, the ground cultivated with hoes, mattocks and digging sticks and fertilized with household rubbish.

Early neolithic societies were acephalous (that is, without elaborate ranking of individuals), but they seem to have developed elaborate initiation rites for particular age and sex groups as a way of maintaining group unity and the traditional social boundaries within it.[17] Many caves were used as burial and/or ritual sites, their underground springs and rock formations often forming a critical part of the ceremonies.[18] There are several examples of these in Etruria, the best known being the Grotta Patrizi, a cave on the edge of the Tolfa mountains northwest of Rome, where an adult male was buried with ceramic vessels, flint blades and a variety of pendants and other ornaments; in another part of the cave there was an adult woman with a young child, and nearby was a teenager.[19]

During the fourth millennium BC, the emphasis of ritual changed from the group to the individual, and there were well developed exchange networks involving high-quality pottery, obsidian (a volcanic glass with flint-like properties found in the Tyrrhenian islands of Lipari, Palmarola, Pantelleria and Sardinia), flint and greenstone axes.[20] There is the first clear evidence for the management of animals for their secondary products as well as for their meat: changes in the mortality structures of the faunal samples[21] coincide with the appearance of spindle whorls and perforated strainer sherds, the latter presumed to be for cheese-making.[22] Settlement sites became larger, with evidence for rectangular houses and grain silos.[23] The evidence suggests that particular individuals were increasingly able to control aspects of the production, distribution and consumption of resources, achieving higher rank than their fellows in the process.

The social transformations of the Copper Age

These trends in social change accelerated during the third millennium BC, the chalcolithic or Copper Age, when for the first time

---

17 Skeates, 1991; Whitehouse, 1990
18 Whitehouse, 1992
19 Radmilli, 1951–2, 1953
20 Malone, 1985
21 Wilkens, 1991
22 Grifoni Cremonesi, 1987
23 Bietti Sestieri, 1984a; Pitti and Tozzi, 1976; Tozzi, 1982

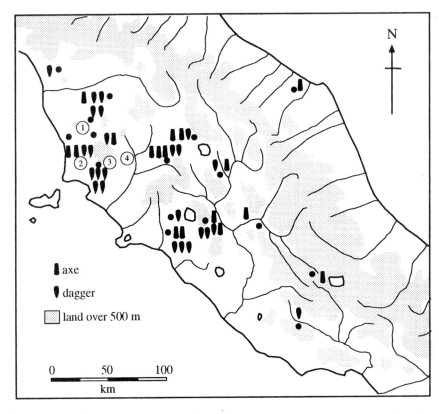

Figure 19   Copper sources and copper age gravegoods in central Italy. Principal copper ores in the Colline Metallifere: 1 Montecatini; 2 Campiglia Marittima; 3 Massa Marittima; 4 Pari. (After Barker, 1981: 77)

elites can be distinguished clearly in the archaeological record. Although the whole of Italy was involved in this process, the changes were particularly profound in Etruria. The indications are that the period marked the beginnings of the process of cultural separation between this region and the rest of Italy that was to crystallize eventually in the Etruscan city states. Certainly the exploitation of the Tuscan metal ores that was to be a cornerstone of the Etruscan economy began in this period.

The Italian Copper Age is best known for its rich burials,[24] the main concentrations in Etruria occurring in the Colline Metallifere and the Fiora valley (fig. 19). The bodies were normally buried on

24   Cardarelli, 1992; Guidi, 1992; Negroni Catacchio, 1988; Pellegrini, 1992

their side in the foetal position, the knees drawn up towards the chest. Most of the rock-cut tombs consist of a short entrance tunnel leading into a small burial chamber sealed by a stone slab. The gravegoods placed with the bodies include special pottery, superb pressure-flaked daggers and arrowheads made of high-quality imported flint, perforated stone weapons and, occasionally, primitive copper artefacts. The pottery is mainly of a particular regional type, but occasionally includes elaborately decorated beakers of the kind used as status-markers across much of western Europe at this time.[25] Most of the metalwork consists of thin triangular daggers and blades, axes and awls. Despite their warlike appearance, the metal artefacts were ineffective weapons: analysis shows that they are of almost pure copper rather than the tin-bronze developed in the Bronze Age.[26] Such a composition, compounded by the thin structure, means that the daggers would have buckled if used in earnest. In the same way, the pressure-flaked daggers and arrowheads are exquisite, but would have easily snapped in combat.

There is a remarkable series of stone 'statue menhirs' from Liguria in this period, perhaps originally grave-markers of some kind, showing individuals bearing exactly these kinds of artefacts (fig. 20).[27] The assumption is, therefore, that many gravegoods were important status-indicators and that their owners were distinguished from the rest of their communities (we presume in life as well as in death) by their clothing, personal ornaments and weaponry. Although most of our information about these societies is derived from graves excavated many years ago, recent careful excavation of the cemetery of Poggialti Vallelunga[28] has found indications in the architectural arrangements of the tombs of hierarchically organized clans. In one of the best studied skeletal groups, too, kinship and family groups could be discerned within the community.[29]

As figure 19 shows, most of the metalwork found in the copper age burials of central Italy is restricted to within about 100 km of the Colline Metallifere. The similarities between the composition of the copper ores and that of the metalwork make it clear that the Etrurian coppersmiths must have begun to mine the Colline Metallifere; they may also have begun to exploit the copper ores of Elba

25 Barfield, 1977
26 Barker and Slater, 1971
27 Anati, 1981
28 Negroni Catacchio, pers. comm.
29 Corrain and Capitanio, 1975

Figure 20   'Statue menhirs' from Liguria. (After Anati, 1981: 31)

at this time.[30] Miniature ceramic vessels in the Poggialti Vallelunga cemetery have been interpreted as symbolic representations of the primitive crucibles that would have been used in this initial phase of metallurgy.[31]

The third millennium BC was also characterized in Etruria by significant changes in settlement and subsistence. There are the first indications of the selection of defensible locations for settlements and there was a major expansion of settlement into the interior Apennine regions that had been only lightly settled hitherto, a process accompanied by evidence in the pollen diagrams for the increasing deforestation of the landscape.[32] The mortality data in copper age faunal samples indicate the increasing importance of animal secondary products,[33] a trend supported by the frequency of spindle whorls and strainer sherds. Perhaps animals were becoming significant items of wealth and exchange for these early Etrurian elites, alongside the artefacts they seem to have used as trappings of their authority.

---

30   Zecchini, 1968
31   Negroni Catacchio, pers. comm.
32   Defensive settlements: di Gennaro and Pennacchioni, 1988; Östenberg, 1967; pollen: Cruise, 1991
33   Wilkens, 1991

Early and middle bronze age societies, 2000–1300 BC

The Early Bronze Age, the period between *c*.2000 and 1700 BC, is still poorly defined archaeologically in Etruria, as elsewhere in central Italy.[34] However, it is possible that it was a period of significant social change characterized by a decline in the prestige systems of the Copper Age and the authority of the elites who controlled them. The widespread distribution of fine flint daggers suggests that high-status items were still being exchanged, though metal was still extremely rare and as restricted in its distribution.[35] Our best information concerning social organization is from the settlement of Torre Spaccata near Rome, where the internal arrangements of occupation debris and burials have been interpreted in terms of a series of family households, with few, if any, indications of social differentiation.[36]

The Middle Bronze Age (*c*.1700–1300 BC), also termed the Apennine Bronze Age, witnessed a gradual filling out of the landscape.[37] On the lowlands of Etruria, numbers of sites increased dramatically at this time:[38] in the Fiora and Albegna valleys, for example, most parts of the topography were used for settlement, but for the first time these included naturally defensible locations.[39] Further inland, the intermontane valleys and basins were now permanently occupied, some of them densely;[40] lakeside locations were increasingly preferred.[41] The extension of settlement and land use is documented by increased evidence for clearance activities, both on the lowlands[42] and in the mountains.[43]

Despite the numbers of sites found, we still know remarkably little about the internal organization of settlements at this time. The best known settlement is the *tufo* acropolis of Luni on the Mignone river in southern Etruria, continuously occupied from the Bronze Age to Etruscan times.[44] The excavators discovered three trenches cut into the *tufo* filled with occupation debris of this period and

34 Cremonesi, 1978; Holloway, 1975; Peroni, 1971
35 Carancini, 1991–2
36 Anzidei et al., 1985
37 Barker and Stoddart, 1994
38 Bietti Sestieri et al., 1991–2; di Gennaro, 1991–2
39 Miari, 1987; Negroni Catacchio and Miari, 1991–2
40 Barker et al., 1986; Malone and Stoddart, 1994
41 Balista et al., 1991–2; Carancini et al., 1986
42 Alessio et al., 1986; Hunt and Eisner, 1991
43 Cruise, 1991
44 Östenberg, 1967

interpreted them as the foundations of longhouses with drystone upper walling and thatched roofs; charcoal clusters within the trench fills were interpreted as the separate hearths of groups within extended families. However, doubts have since been raised about the relationship between the trenches and the domestic rubbish filling them: it is possible that the trenches were cut later, and that soil with middle bronze age material from a settlement zone elsewhere on the site was used as backfill. Certainly the settlement at Luni is unique in its scale: at Narce, for example, a contemporary settlement in the Treia valley in southern Etruria, the few pits and stakeholes found suggest an encampment of one or two simple huts.[45]

Both on the lowlands and in the intermontane valleys and basins, these communities grew a range of cereals and legumes, and managed their stock for both meat and secondary products.[46] However, the evidence of high-altitude sites (a few have been found in places now used as winter ski resorts) and pollen diagrams showing high-altitude clearances indicate that this period also marked the first systematic use of the Apennine pastures, probably for short-distance transhumant grazing from communities living in the immediately adjacent valleys and basins.[47]

Metal remained in restricted circulation: most hoards have been found within 100 km of the Tuscan ores[48] and none of the excavated settlements has produced more than a few scraps of bronze. Lithic technologies remained important. Although people decorated their pottery with designs selected from a common repertoire used throughout the peninsula, thin section and X-ray analysis indicate that almost all production was local, probably still at the household level.[49] There are no signs of significant status differentiation amongst the (very few) burials known. The dominant rituals known consist of food offerings by springs in caves, very different from the elaborate and apparently competitive public ceremonies practised by many bronze age societies elsewhere in Europe.[50] In short, at the threshold of the period that was to witness the most dramatic process of social change in Etruria, the indications are of an agricultural society

45 Potter, 1976
46 Agostini et al., 1991–2; Barker, 1976; Barker and Stallibrass, 1987; de Grossi Mazzorin, 1985a, 1995; Jarman, 1976; Wilkens, 1991, 1991–2
47 Barker, 1989
48 Carancini, 1991–2
49 Loney, 1996; Nash, 1979
50 Whitehouse, 1992

with few social divisions within individual communities or within regional groups.

The Late Bronze Age, *c.*1300–900 BC: the first chiefdoms?

The Late Bronze Age, the period between *c.*1300 and 900 BC, marked the first crucial phase in the transition between village and state societies in Etruria. It seems likely that before the Late Bronze Age the high-status individuals we can discern in the archaeological record had generally achieved their status by their actions, rather than by birthright. In contrast, the Late Bronze Age – particularly by its later stages (the Final Bronze Age in the Italian chronological system, dated *c.*1100–900 BC) – provides consistent and repeated indications of a limited but nonetheless concrete hierarchy. There are also clear signs of significant demographic increase and economic intensification. Put together, they imply the development of the chiefdom societies from which Etruscan state societies swiftly developed.

Settlement trends have been closely studied in the Albegna and Fiora valleys:[51] whereas middle bronze age settlement spanned all parts of the topography from valley floor to hilltop with few preferences for particular situations, more than two thirds of the late bronze age settlements are on bluffs and hilltops overlooking the rivers, often narrow *tufo* promontories with steep ground on three sides making them easily defensible (fig. 21). In the Sabine hills, there was much the same trend.[52] Despite the shift, however, there are few signs of defence works being constructed. Caves were almost entirely abandoned as occupation sites, except perhaps as seasonal pastoral camps.

As di Gennaro[53] has pointed out, the distribution of the main late bronze age settlements in much of southern Etruria is remarkably regular: if all the land is divided between them, most sites have a territory of about 10 km^2 (fig. 22). He estimated populations between 100 and 1000, given the average size of outcrop of 4–5 ha. However, virtually none of these sites has been investigated in detail, and where one has been (the Luni acropolis), the area of settlement shown by surface remains and excavation was far smaller than the total area available.[54] Presumably average populations were nearer

51 Miari, 1987
52 Angle et al., 1982
53 di Gennaro, 1982, 1986, 1988
54 Östenberg, 1967

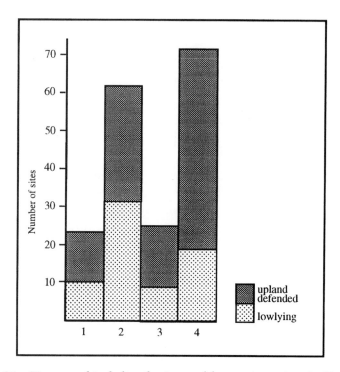

Figure 21 Topographical distributions of bronze age sites in Etruria: 1 early bronze age; 2 middle bronze age; 3 late bronze age; 4 final bronze age. (Adapted from Barker and Stoddart, 1994 and Miari, 1987).

100 than 1000. Moreover, we should probably not exaggerate the process of nucleation indicated by the crude distribution maps of known settlements. When intensive field-walking on a systematic basis was applied to the postulated territory of one of the 'major' late bronze age settlements in figure 22, the San Pietro acropolis of Tuscania, we found more than a dozen small sites contemporary with the San Pietro settlement, some on low hills, some in streamside positions on valley bottoms and some on the intervening slopes.[55] Field survey indicates similar distributions around the late bronze age settlement of Narce.[56] Undoubtedly the process of nucleation that was to develop into full Etruscan urbanization had begun in this period, but the countryside was certainly not denuded of its population.

55 Barker and Rasmussen, 1988; Barker et al., 1993
56 Potter, 1979: 59

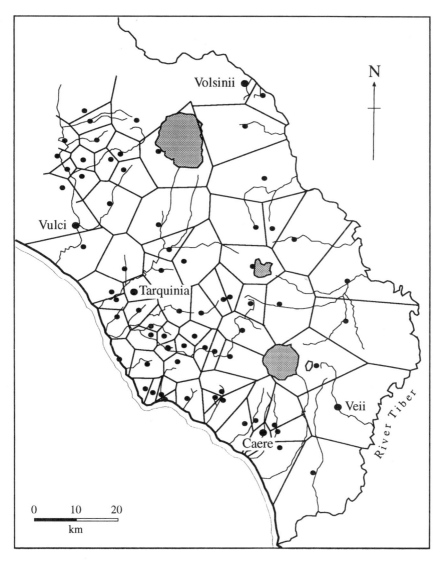

Figure 22 The distribution of major late bronze age settlements in Etruria, with hypothetical territories ('Thiessen polygons'). (Adapted from di Gennaro, 1982)

In northern Etruria, by contrast, surveys indicate far lower settlement densities and no evidence for settlement hierarchies in the Late Bronze Age,[57] except perhaps around Monte Cetona.[58] Much the same is true of the intermontane basins such as Gubbio.[59] In the Gubbio basin the shift to hilltop locations began in the Middle Bronze Age, and there was then an expansion of settlement during the Late Bronze Age, both along the hills overlooking the basin and down to the lower slopes.

Although there are few signs of elaborate political hierarchization at this time, it is tempting to suggest that central sites in southern Etruria like San Pietro, Luni and Narce acted as foci of some kind for the small sites in their hinterland, as Pacciarelli has argued in the case of Luni.[60] Certainly it must be significant that all of these, like so many of the other acropolis settlements in figure 22, continued as local centres into the Etruscan period. We also have to bear in mind that we know little about the extent of settlement at this time on the sites of the major Etruscan cities: late bronze age material has been found in recent years at most of the major Etruscan sites in southern Etruria such as Bisenzio, Cerveteri, Orvieto, Tarquinia and Veii,[61] and it is conceivable that Etruscan urban sites had quite substantial late bronze age occupations.

By far the best evidence for internal organization in the major late bronze age settlements is from Sorgenti della Nova, a 15-ha *tufo* outcrop in the Fiora valley (fig. 23).[62] On the top of the hill there were rock-cut pits interpreted as hut foundations, and along an artificial terrace cut into the hillside was a series of small oval huts, each measuring some 10 × 5 m, surviving as rock-cut depressions and post-holes. Artificial caves near the huts were also used for domestic activities on the evidence of midden deposits and hearths. The excavators argue that the community was stratified socially, the elite living in the huts on the hilltop and the commoners on the hillside.[63] They may be right, though there seem to be few if any differences in the structural evidence and cultural residues. On the other hand, the high frequency of pig at the site may be significant:

57   Barker and Symonds, 1984; Barker et al., 1986; Tracchi, 1978
58   Cipolloni, 1971
59   Malone and Stoddart, 1984, 1986, 1994
60   Pacciarelli, 1982
61   Bonghi Jovino, 1986b; Cardarelli et al., 1980; di Gennaro, 1986; Fugazzola Delpino and Delpino, 1979
62   Negroni Catacchio, 1981, 1986, 1989
63   Negroni Catacchio, 1989; Negroni Catacchio and Domanico, 1986

Figure 23   Sorgenti della Nova: a reconstruction of part of the late bronze age settlement. (Reproduced with kind permission of N. Negroni Catacchio)

as we described in chapter 1, it is something of a luxury to keep an animal that only provides meat: in Britain, for example, prehistoric, Roman and medieval sites identified on other grounds as being of high status very often have high frequencies of pig.[64] Monte Rovello, another major settlement, had a large central building measuring some 12 × 8 m, cut into the rock to a depth of up to 3 m.[65]

It does at least seem clear that a 'central place' settlement such as Sorgenti della Nova was significantly different in its scale from the small sites in the countryside. Torrionaccio, for example, which is in the vicinity of Sorgenti della Nova, probably consisted of a cluster of small huts.[66] At Narce, the hut settlement of the Middle Bronze Age was succeeded in the Late Bronze Age by rectangular huts on stone footings, probably enclosed within a timber stockade.[67]

The development of some kind of settlement hierarchy coincided with significant changes in economy. There is evidence for intensification in the agricultural system in the form of new crops.[68]

64   Grant, 1988, 1989
65   Biancofiore and Toti, 1973
66   Cassano and Manfredini, 1978
67   Potter, 1976
68   Follieri, 1981; Jarman, 1976

Locational studies indicate that many lowland sites were positioned to have easy access to increased areas of arable soils.[69] An expansion in arable cultivation is registered in the pollen diagrams.[70] Animal secondary products were increasingly important,[71] and there may have been diversification and specialization: sheep are the most frequent stock at Narce and Torrionaccio, cattle at Luni and Monte Rovello, pig at Sorgenti della Nova.[72] The amount of metal in circulation increased dramatically, as did the range of types, produced now consistently in tin bronze.[73] New settlement clusters developed around the metal ores, suggesting that control of mineral resources was increasingly critical.[74] Many of the objects produced were items of dress and display such as dress and cloak pins, but there were also effective tools and weapons such as axes, knives and sickles. Flint became more or less redundant as the manufacture of small tools like chisels, blades and needles resulted in dramatic advancements in the technologies for working other materials such as wood, bone and textiles.

Although Mycenaean trading posts and perhaps colonies were established on the southern coasts of the Italian peninsula from the fourteenth century BC, Etruria was at the very end of the exchange network and there is no evidence that it was in direct contact with Mycenaeans.[75] Similarly, the bronze age communities of the Po valley were in trading contact with the communities on the other side of the Alps, but there is little evidence that Etruria was involved in such long-distance commerce. Rather, the artefact distributions emphasize the importance of regional exchange networks in Etruria.[76]

Another significant change in the archaeological record of the Late Bronze Age is the appearance of cremation cemeteries, the beginning of a new way of burial that was to be particularly common in the ensuing centuries. In Etruria, most of the tomb groups are small, in the order of five to fifteen cremations, though there are occasional examples of large cemeteries with up to fifty burials.[77] It

69   Pacciarelli, 1982
70   Alessio et al., 1986; Frank, 1969; Hunt and Eisner, 1991
71   Barker, 1976; de Grossi Mazzorin, 1995
72   Narce and Torrionaccio: Placidi, 1978; Luni: Gejvall, 1967; Monte Rovello: Caloi et al., 1988; Sorgenti della Nova: Caloi and Palombo, 1981
73   Barker and Slater, 1971; Bietti Sestieri, 1973
74   Giardino, 1984
75   Marazzi and Tusa 1976
76   Bietti Sestieri, 1976, 1984b; Stoddart, 1987
77   Bietti Sestieri, 1984b

used to be thought that the appearance of the burial rite marked the arrival of new people from central Europe, where the rite appears first,[78] but the theory is now discounted. Differences in the burial arrangements (most are in simple pits, others are in stone cists, a few are under mounds) and in the associated gravegoods (most people were buried with one or two pots and metal items, a few were buried with more, some were buried with nothing) make it clear that everybody now was definitely not of the same status. In this respect the funerary archaeology correlates with the settlement archaeology and the evidence of the hoards for unequal access to resources.

In recent and contemporary ethnography, 'chiefdom societies' have been classically defined as 'ranked', with a chief acting as the focus for the economic, social, political and religious activity of the group, a principal role being to act as the permanent central agency of coordination for systems of redistribution of goods and services within the chiefdom territory.[79] The archaeological correlates for the development of chiefdoms have been taken to include larger populations, higher settlement densities, larger residence units, evidence of ranking (most visibly in burials), increased subsistence production, and improved craft specialization and exchange.[80] As we have seen, the archaeological record for the Late Bronze Age in Etruria contains evidence for all of these changes. We should probably not exaggerate the degree of competitiveness in Etrurian society at this time, but whilst some of the characteristics of recent chiefdoms cannot be discerned, the evidence suggests that Etrurian societies were by now organized within comparable systems of ranking.

The reasons for the emergence of bronze age elites is one of the great debating issues of European prehistory, and where we have the best information of all, the Greek Bronze Age, we are furthest away from consensus. To simplify the theories at the risk of unfairness to their proponents, one extreme view has been that the elites of the Greek Bronze Age developed because they were fundamentally advantageous for their communities in their control of the economy, so people easily acquiesced to their authority.[81] At the other end of the spectrum is the view that these elites were more like the worst feudal barons of medieval times, seizing power (particularly the critical means of production such as ox teams) for their own

78 Hencken, 1968a, 1968b
79 Service, 1962
80 Renfrew, 1972, 1973
81 Renfrew, 1972

ends and exploiting the peasantry for all their worth.[82] A related theory holds that control over people would have been more important than over any other resources.[83] Between such views is the 'social storage' theory that much of the economy stayed at a subsistence level but that a limited public sector developed whereby the commoners were required to pay the elites gifts of agricultural surplus in return for elite assurance of assistance in times of bad harvests.[84] The role of the elites of late bronze age Etruria could have had any or none of these characteristics. With so little precise data for the organization of the production, distribution and consumption of resources, we can do little more than speculate. But of the existence of comparable elites in Etruria there seems little doubt.

The 'Villanovan' Iron Age, 900–700 BC

The Iron Age of Etruria is usually named 'Villanovan' after a cemetery which Giovanni Gozzadini excavated in 1853 on his land at Caselle near Villanova on the outskirts of Bologna.[85] From then until very recently, Villanovan cemeteries and their associated rite of cremation have often been taken as evidence for the arrival of a new people in Italy from north of the Alps, archaeological proof of the 'continental' theory of Etruscan origins.[86] However, as explained above, the consensus now is that the rite of cremation was adopted in late bronze age and iron age Italy, as elsewhere in Europe, in much the same way as it was in Britain or the United States in the twentieth century: the spread of a cultural phenomenon that certainly reflected important developments in ideology and social relations, but not a new people.[87] In the following discussion, therefore, it is important to remember that Villanovan is simply a descriptive term for the Etrurian Iron Age, not a reference to incoming Villanovans.

Settlement trends

The ninth century BC witnessed profound developments in settlement structure in Etruria, where – at least in the southern part –

---

82 Bintliff, 1982; Gilman, 1981
83 Webster, 1990
84 Halstead and O'Shea, 1982
85 Bartoloni, 1989a
86 Hencken, 1968a, 1968b
87 Champion et al., 1984

there are signs of a dramatic process of nucleation. Here, the number of major sites (the kind of settlements shown in figure 22, not the very small sites found, for example, in our Tuscania Survey) shrank from about fifty to just over ten. Whereas in the tenth century most sites measured between 1 and 5 ha, with a few measuring 5–15 ha, in the ninth century in southern Etruria five huge centres developed measuring between 100 and 200 ha, followed by a succession of far smaller sites (fig. 24).[88] South of the Tiber, by contrast, the size-ranking of settlements throughout the tenth and ninth centuries was fundamentally the same as the tenth century pattern in southern Etruria. To the east of southern Etruria, in the Sabine hills, there is no evidence for the dramatic polarization in settlement size suggested for southern Etruria in the ninth century, though the fact that settlement declines at this time have been noted by surveys in the pre-Apennine hills and intermontane basins [89] has been taken by some as further proof of a 'flight from the countryside' to large population centres.

The five centres at the top of the Villanovan settlement hierarchy in southern Etruria all developed into the major Etruscan and Roman cities of this region: Caere (Cerveteri), Tarquinia, Veii, Volsinii (Orvieto) and Vulci (fig. 22). Accordingly, several scholars have been tempted to draw a political map for ninth century Etruria with the Villanovan centres controlling large territories like those which the later cities may have controlled: if all the land is divided between them by standard geographical techniques such as Thiessen polygons, each Villanovan centre ends up with a theoretical territory of between 1000 and 2000 km².[90] The location of smaller centres within these territories has also led di Gennaro to argue that the earlier part of the ninth century was characterized by competing pairs of local centres controlling smaller territories, the successful centres then expanding rapidly both in their own size and in the size of the territories they controlled.

A problem with this model is that all of the finer dating for the ninth century has been developed from the study of cemetery material, little or none of which is likely to be found on small domestic sites in the countryside. In the case of the Tuscania Survey, for example, the paucity of domestic sites precisely dated to the ninth century could be taken as evidence for a process of sudden nucleation

88   Guidi, 1985
89   Angle et al., 1982; Bonomi Ponzi, 1985; Carancini et al., 1986
90   Bartoloni, 1991; di Gennaro, 1982, 1986, 1988

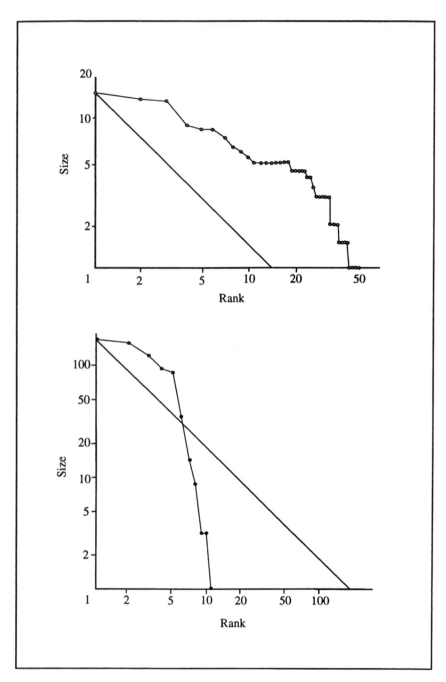

Figure 24 Changes to the settlement system of southern Etruria between the tenth and ninth centuries BC (above and below, respectively). The points mark individual settlements of the kind shown in figure 22, with their size shown in hectares. The five Villanovan sites over 100 ha in size in the lower figure are Caere (Cerveteri), Tarquinia, Veii, Volsinii (Orvieto) and Vulci. (Adapted from Guidi, 1985)

at Tuscania, where evidence of ninth century settlement has been adduced from burial material. Yet the survey record shows a number of small rural sites around Tuscania with pottery that can only be dated loosely between the tenth and eighth centuries BC, which could therefore indicate the continued existence of dispersed settlement around Tuscania in the ninth century. In the territory of Veii, too, Potter[91] has argued that the occurrence on survey sites of red *impasto* pottery, a domestic ware which he suggests on the basis of his excavations of the Narce settlement can be reliably dated to the ninth and eighth centuries, indicates a pattern of dense rural settlement in the countryside around Veii rather than large-scale desertions (fig. 25). At Narce itself, the period was marked by an extension of the settlement zone from the river terrace occupied in the Bronze Age to include the rock summits to the north and south. Survey has also shown that the Iron Age was marked by a significant increase in the number of small rural settlements around Cerveteri[92] and within the territory of the modern city of Rome.[93]

The debate about the scale of aggregation in southern Etruria is only likely to advance if we can establish reliable chronologies for the domestic coarse wares that make up the bulk of the surface assemblages of settlements, and extend systematic survey of the kind practised around Tuscania, Veii and the Albegna valley[94] to the rest of the region. The argument about whether or not the major centres controlled large territories will also run and run without significant progress until we can map settlement sufficiently to judge whether or not there were boundary zones empty of settlement. In the meantime, it is at least clear that, whatever the nature of settlement in the countryside, the ninth century in southern Etruria was certainly characterized by the development of nucleated population centres, a few of them very large indeed.

Much less is understood of contemporary settlement trends in northern Etruria. On the western lowlands, most late bronze age settlements found by surveys are concentrated on the coast,[95] but during the ninth century – on the evidence of cemeteries, it has to be said, rather than settlement sites – there seems to have been a process of settlement clustering around the sites of the later Etruscan

---

91   Potter, 1979: 59
92   Enei, 1995
93   Bietti Sestieri, 1984a
94   Attolini et al., 1991
95   Cucini, 1985; Fedeli, 1984

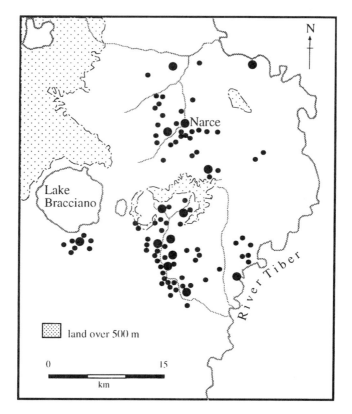

Figure 25   Villanovan rural settlement around Narce: the Villanovan Iron Age marked a massive change in the scale and density of settlement. Large circles: bronze age sites; small circles: iron age sites. The distribution of small sites approximately denotes the size of the British School at Rome's South Etruria survey. (After Potter, 1979: 59)

cities, a less extreme version of the process of nucleation further south.[96] In the Etruscan period, the two main settlements here were Populonia and Vetulonia, assumed to be mining centres given their geographical position. On the promontory of Piombino opposite the island of Elba, the distribution of Villanovan cemeteries suggests that there was a cluster of distinct but grouped settlements in the ninth century, preceding the development of the single settlement of Populonia in the middle of the eighth century.[97] Further inland,

96   Bartolini, 1991
97   Fedeli, 1983

there seems to have been a pattern of small more or less undifferentiated settlements at this time, some of which (such as Chiusi) were to develop into substantial Etruscan centres, whereas others (such as Montepulciano, Chanciano and Sarteano) were not. In the Siena region, systematic survey at Montarrenti has indicated a landscape of small farms at this time.[98] In many parts of northern Etruria, the lack of systematic survey is such that we know almost nothing about iron age settlement, apart from a few negative hints such as the lack of evidence for settlement of this period under the Etruscan city of Arezzo. Despite the unevenness of research, however, it seems clear that there were dramatic shifts in settlement in the ninth century in southern Etruria and comparable, if less extreme, trends on the lowlands further north, with little significant change in the interior.

Settlement structure

The major Villanovan centres are frequently described as 'proto-urban', but in fact their internal organization is not clear (fig. 26). The fact that most of them were used for later occupation has made systematic research difficult. Many of the theories about their possible size and character have been based on inferences made from their surrounding cemeteries rather than from direct evidence from the settlements. Opinions have varied from one extreme, that they were no more than collections of hamlets or villages separated by open ground, to the other, that they were proto-towns with large continuous zones of occupation and large numbers of inhabitants.

Veii has been proposed as an example of both settlement models! Limited field-walking within the 2000 ha enclosed by the Etruscan walls suggested to Ward-Perkins[99] that the Villanovan settlement was simply a collection of perhaps five hamlets, each placed at the margin of the settlement zone with a related cemetery nearby outside the acropolis area. However, more extensive field-walking across the middle of the acropolis area indicated to Guaitoli[100] that it was more likely to have been a large and continuous settlement. In fact this detailed survey still found large areas of empty ground, and some of the surface material mapped may be the result of the inhabitants using household rubbish to manure their garden plots rather than occupation debris. Hence the likelihood is that the Villanovan

98   Barker et al., 1986
99   Ward-Perkins, 1961
100   Guaitoli, 1982

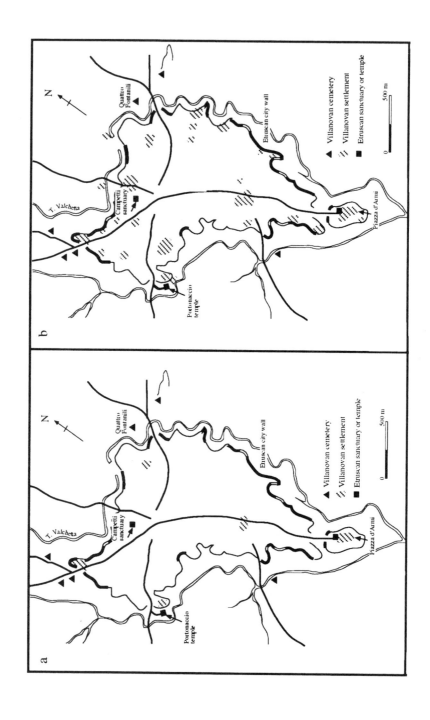

N

a

T. Valchetta

Campetti
sanctuary

Quattro
Fontanili

Portonaccio
temple

Piazza d'Armi

Etruscan city wall

▲ Villanovan cemetery

⫽ Villanovan settlement

■ Etruscan sanctuary or temple

0   500 m

N

b

T. Valchetta

Campetti
sanctuary

Quattro
Fontanili

Portonaccio
temple

Piazza d'Armi

Etruscan city wall

▲ Villanovan cemetery

⫽ Villanovan settlement

■ Etruscan sanctuary or temple

0   500 m

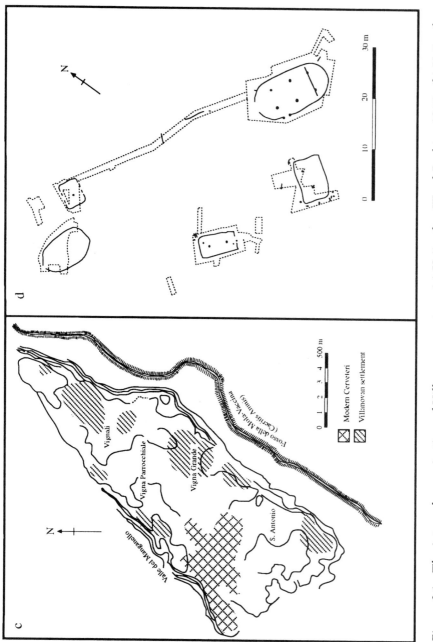

Figure 26 The internal organization of Villanovan centres: (a) Veii, after Ward-Perkins 1961; (b) Veii, after Guaitoli, 1982; (c) Cerveteri, after Merlino and Mirenda, 1990; (d) Tarquinia after Linington, 1982.

settlement of Veii was somewhere between the two extreme models: a very substantial settlement of a scale that was entirely new to Etruria, but in its structure and density not yet a town or city of the kind that was to develop later on the same site.

The evidence from the other major settlements supports this interpretation. At Tarquinia, the iron age settlement seems to have consisted of a series of habitation zones forming clusters across two adjacent spurs of high ground. At Cerveteri, eight zones of settlement have been defined along the plateau behind the later town, and whilst these partly reflect different levels of archaeological visibility, their similarities with the settlement zones of Veii and Tarquinia are striking.[101] The evidence of cemetery distribution suggests that Vulci was probably settled along similar lines, and at Orvieto there were probably at least two distinct occupation areas at either end of the acropolis.[102]

At Tarquinia, moreover, geophysical survey of one of the settlement zones by the Lerici Foundation followed up by excavation showed that it consisted of a series of huts which varied considerably in shape and size: there were a few oval structures, generally rather large (up to 15×7 m), and several smaller rectangular structures (generally $6–8 \times 4$ m), though the arrangements of the postholes inside suggest they probably all had pitched roofs of thatch.[103] Fragments of daub found in the excavations presumably come from the walls. There are indications of the same range of structures at Veii.[104] The similarities with the two kinds of huts at Sorgenti della Nova are striking, as Negroni Catacchio and Domanico have pointed out.[105] One possible interpretation is that Villanovan settlements consisted of several distinct social groups or clans. Bartoloni[106] argues that the smaller huts would have housed nuclear families and the larger dwellings extended families, though it is possible that the latter had administrative functions like the large 'public' buildings on Aegean early bronze age centres that were used for administrative control of the agricultural and other products involved in redistribution and exchange.[107]

101 Tarquinia: Spivey and Stoddart, 1990: 51; Cerveteri: Merlino and Mirenda, 1990
102 Vulci: Pacciarelli, 1989–90; Orvieto: Bartoloni, 1989a: 110
103 Linington, 1982
104 Stefani, 1944, 1953
105 Negroni Catacchio and Domanico, 1986
106 Bartoloni, 1989a: 116
107 Renfrew, 1972

Figure 27   Terracotta hut urn of the Early Iron Age, from near Castel Gandolfo (Latium), in the British Museum, London. (Photograph: copyright British Museum)

Structural evidence from 'lower order' sites is extremely rare. A small Villanovan village has been preserved in lake muds on the eastern shore of Lake Bolsena at Gran Carro. The site consisted of rectangular wooden and thatch huts, the settlement zone being about a ha.[108] We know nothing of the appearance of the very small rural sites found by the systematic surveys around Tuscania and Veii.

Both the oval and rectangular structures of Tarquinia are represented in the ceramic 'hut urns' that are found in Villanovan cemeteries, the details of which suggest that they were, to some extent at least, modelled on domestic structures (fig. 27). There are indications on a few of them of the subterranean foundations that have

108 Tamburini, 1986

been found at some sites: one from a cemetery at Vulci, for example, has a clearly demarcated plinth below the floor of the house indicated by the door threshold.[109] The walls shown on the urns seem sometimes to be wattle and daub laid directly on the ground surface, in other cases laid on drystone foundation walling, with external timber posts supporting the roofs. The single door is usually on one of the shorter walls, frequently under a protective porch. In the interior there is often a circular hearth outlined on the floor at the centre of the dwelling. The walls and roofs of the huts are frequently decorated with incised patterns, the central roof ridge and the front roof lines with elaborate moulded decoration. Whilst much of this decoration echoes that of other funerary pottery vessels and no doubt served to emphasize the role of the hut urns within Villanovan funerary ideology, it does seem likely that Villanovan houses were decorated with clearly visible symbols, perhaps of the particular social group to which the inhabitants belonged, like the lodge or wigwam decorations and totem poles of Native American settlements.

Burial ritual

The settlement changes were paralleled by as dramatic changes in the size and formality of cemeteries. We have already noted how the major centres were surrounded by several cemeteries: each of these might now contain burials in many hundreds. By far the best studied in Etruria is that of Quattro Fontanili, one of Veii's cemeteries, excavated by the British School at Rome between 1961 and 1972.[110] It was used as a burial ground from the ninth to the seventh centuries BC (fig. 28), and the analysis of its 650 excavated burials (first by Joanna Close-Brooks, one of the excavators, and latterly by Judith Toms) has provided the cornerstone of Villanovan funerary chronology.[111] It is probably typical of most cemeteries in that the earliest burials were on the summit of the hill and ensuing burials spread outwards downslope.

Pits were cut into the bedrock and sometimes lined with stones, and the ashes were placed in the burial urn covered by an upturned bowl. Some burials were marked above ground by gravestones. The burial urn is generally of a standard type also found on settlement sites, thought to have been used in domestic contexts as a water

109   Bartoloni, 1989a: 113
110   Ward-Perkins et al., 1968b
111   Close-Brooks, 1965; Toms, 1986

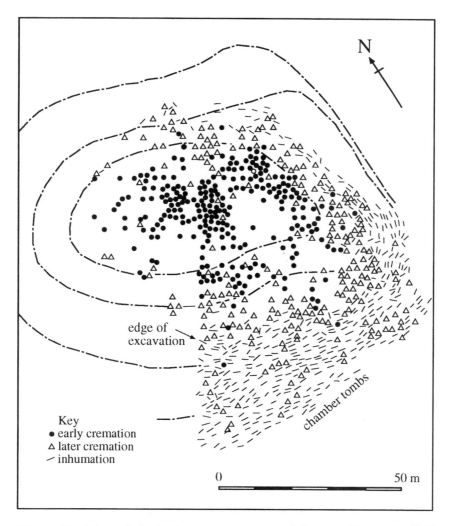

Figure 28 Plan of the Villanovan cemetery of Quattro Fontanili, Veii. (After Potter, 1979: 64, following Close-Brooks, 1965)

carrier,[112] though occasionally other types of vessel were used such as a hut urn. There were a few unusually rich graves at one end of the spectrum and, at the other, some with no gravegoods, but most people were buried with a small number of artefacts. The commonest gravegoods divide into two groups: fibulas (large safety pins for cloaks) and spindle whorls; or fibulas, knives and razors. The shapes

112 Bartoloni, 1989a: 124

of the fibulas in the two groups are different. The assumption is that the former set of artefacts was buried with women and the latter with men, but the cremated bones with them are so fragmentary that the hypothesis cannot be proved by skeletal analysis.

The details of the burial rite varied somewhat from region to region: in the cemeteries around Populonia and Vetulonia, for example, inhumation graves are mixed in with cremations from an early date, and there are also a few chambered tombs.[113] What does seem clear is that the distinctions are not simply to do with different levels of status and wealth: as well as the common group identity indicated by membership of the cemetery population, there were important allegiances to particular social sub-sets such as kin-groups or clans.[114] The parallels with the social groupings discernible within the settlement archaeology are obvious.

The most important iron age cemetery excavated in recent years is that of Osteria dell'Osa on the eastern outskirts of Rome.[115] Though just outside Etruria, the quality of information from its exemplary investigation has provided invaluable insights into social structure at this time. Like Quattro Fontanili, it was used from the ninth to the seventh centuries for a similar number of burials, and the layout shows clear evidence of a formal structure. The burials cluster into distinct groups according to burial type, location and gravegoods. The main groups identified include: cremated males buried in central positions accompanied by miniature versions of pottery vessels and weapons that indicate particular status; cremated males in peripheral locations buried with miniature or normal-sized gravegoods; inhumation burials of juvenile males without high-status gravegoods; children buried with or without gravegoods (and, if present, not sexually differentiated); adult and old women, mainly buried around the central males, with personal ornaments as their gravegoods; young women and girls with rich sets of personal ornaments; and children buried with personal ornaments indicating their sex. The differences are interpreted as evidence for the division of this community into extended families or clans, which were in turn stratified vertically into different social levels mostly according to age and sex but including adult males of particular high status, assumed to be the clan chiefs. A similar structure has been identified in the ninth century cemeteries around Bologna: the burials were 'concentrated in groups internally distinguished both according to sex and

113   Bartoloni, 1991
114   Teegen, 1995
115   Bietti Sestieri, 1979, 1992a, 1992b; Bietti Sestieri and de Santis, 1985

according to the role of individuals' which were interpreted as 'family units (extended families or aristocratic groups) linked to one or two privileged male burials'.[116]

Subsistence and exchange

Given the tremendous changes to the landscape implied by the settlement archaeology, and the equivalent implications of the cemetery archaeology for social change, it is very frustrating how little evidence exists for the Villanovan way of life. It is assumed that the basis of the economy was agriculture, but in fact almost no direct evidence has been collected in the form of botanical and faunal remains. One exception is the settlement of Narce. The ninth century plant residues here included emmer wheat, barley, millet and a range of legumes,[117] which were associated with weed and parasite infestations suggesting increasingly intensive agricultural systems. Another important indicator of change comes from the lakeside settlement of Gran Carro, where the plant remains show, in addition to the cultivation of cereals and legumes and the collection of fruits and nuts, the systematic exploitation of vines at this time.[118] As later chapters describe, wine production was an important component of Etruscan agriculture, and wine-drinking was of great social importance for Etruscan elites, so although there is as yet no direct evidence for wine production in the Iron Age, it would certainly not be surprising to find that the systematic cultivation of the vine began at this time in Etruria to provide wine for the emergent elites. The kind of fine tableware that would have been associated with wine-drinking would almost certainly have been urns and bowls of the kind buried in the cemeteries.

The animals whose remains have been most frequently identified in tombs (presumably food offerings placed with the dead) are pigs, but pigs were identified far less frequently in the food refuse of the Villanovan levels at the settlement of Narce.[119] The stock of the Villanovan community here consisted mostly of sheep and goats, and the mortality data indicate that they were being kept increasingly for milk and (in the case of sheep) wool, a trend that correlates with the large numbers of loom weights and spindle whorls found in Villanovan cemeteries. Cattle were also important at Narce,

116 Giardino et al., 1991: 17
117 Jarman, 1976
118 Costantini and Costantini Biasini, 1987
119 Barker, 1976

their age suggesting they were mainly plough cattle killed at the end of their working lives. The small faunal sample from Gran Carro is somewhat similar in the proportions of the species and the (admittedly restricted) mortality data.[120] It seems likely that pigs were becoming something of a luxury food (like wine?), with most of the meat eaten on the ordinary settlements coming from adult sheep and cattle raised primarily for their secondary products. The increased emphasis on secondary products makes sense in terms of the food requirements of the rapidly expanding population, which was presumably dependent on an increasingly cereal-dominated diet. Producing the cereals to feed them must have entailed increasing amounts of arable land, and therefore more cattle to work and manure the fields. In the same way, it would have been more efficient to use flocks to produce cheese as the main fat and protein supplement to the diet, rather than kill off most surplus animals for meat.

Studies of the fabrics of Villanovan pottery, both domestic and funerary, suggest that production was still mainly at the household level, even though the regional similarities in shape and design show well defined traditions of craftsmanship. In the case of metalwork, the period witnessed a rapid expansion in the amount of metal in circulation, sufficient to meet the needs of people in both life and death. There was a sudden expansion, too, in the repertoire of forms produced. Numbers of hoards, consisting mainly of everyday objects such as axes, many of them broken, indicate that bronze-smiths may have been moving from community to community, selling new pieces, repairing others and acquiring broken pieces for re-casting. Bartoloni[121] argued from the typologies of these hoards that the raw materials for most of the metalwork in central Italy were being mined now in the Colline Metallifere, with Populonia and Vetulonia developing as centres of metalworking.

Metal objects moved freely over considerable distances: a burial at Populonia, for example, has two vases with applied metal decoration from Tarquinia, two fibulas from the Bologna region, and a bronze button and a sheet bronze container from Sardinia.[122] The repertoire also includes a few bronze pieces recognized as being from regions outside peninsular Italy such as Sardinia, Sicily, Spain and Cyprus. The metalwork at Populonia demonstrates links with Sardinia on the one hand and Bologna on the other, and Bologna's

120   Scali, 1987
121   Bartoloni, 1991
122   Bartoloni, 1991: 109–11

metalwork has as many links with continental Europe as with Etruria. What mechanism or mechanisms caused these movements? It is unlikely that we can talk of formalized trade at this time: most of the movement of valuable metal objects probably took place within a system of competitive exchange or 'ritualized friendship', as the emergent elites of Etruria endeavoured to cement alliances with their neighbours or with more distant contacts.[123] A similar system of prestige gift exchange was to characterize the Etruscan aristocracy.[124] Interestingly, most of the exotic objects at Populonia are in female burials, leading Bartoloni[125] to conclude that 'we must assign to the institution of marriage an important role in the exchanges that took place in the Villanovan world. Marriage appears to have been the main instrument of trade between communities (or families).'

Greeks and Phoenicians

In the late ninth century, and more particularly during the course of the eighth century, the Villanovan chieftains of Etruria came into contact with Phoenicians and Greeks as the latter expanded westwards across the Mediterranean.[126] The Phoenicians (from the Levant, around modern Lebanon) established colonies on the north coast of Africa, western Sicily, Sardinia and southern Spain, and the Greeks settled in southern Italy, eastern Sicily, Corsica, southern France and eastern Spain (see fig. 1 in the Introduction).[127] In Italy, the first Greek colony was established by people from the island of Euboea at Pithekoussai (or Pithecusae) on the island of Ischia in the Bay of Naples. Whilst the exact date of the foundation is disputed, excavations have revealed a substantial population on the site by 750 BC.[128] Cumae on the mainland opposite was founded in about 745 BC, and another colony was established overlooking the site of the modern city of Naples at the beginning of the seventh century. Other colonies were founded at the instep of the Italian peninsula towards the end of the eighth century or early in the seventh century BC.[129] The colonies were established to provide new land for the expanding population of the Greek mainland and to develop

123 Bartoloni, 1989b
124 Cristofani, 1975a
125 Bartoloni, 1991: 111
126 Ridgway, 1992
127 Boardman, 1980; Sherratt and Sherratt, 1993
128 Buchner, 1979; Frederiksen, 1979; Ridgway, 1973
129 de la Genière, 1979

trade networks to supply the homeland with raw materials. Once established, they could trade directly with the indigenous populations and act as 'ports of trade' or intermediaries for trade with the homeland. An indication of the remarkably polyglot nature of these early trading ports is an Aramaic and a Phoenician inscription at Pithekoussai.[130]

Greek and Phoenician trade with the Italian peninsula certainly preceded the foundation of the Greek colonies, and it is commonly assumed that the search for metal ore was the principal stimulus.[131] Etruria was especially attractive in having copper, tin and lead near the coast in the Colline Metallifere, and rich sources of iron on the island of Elba. However, the distribution of Greek objects indicates that contacts were not just with this region: for example, there are Greek objects in rich eighth-century graves at Bologna, Bisenzio (on Lake Bolsena in inland central Etruria), Tarquinia, Vulci, Veii and Osteria dell'Osa,[132] as well as in cemeteries nearer the colonies in Campania. Villanovan objects have also been found at Pithekoussai and in Greece.[133]

By the mid eighth century there must have been direct exchanges between the elites of the Greek colonies and of Etruria. Although a piece of iron ore from Elba has been found at Pithekoussai, most Greek imports have been found in the cemeteries of the major Villanovan centres of southern Etruria: one of the most celebrated early pieces from Cerveteri is a Greek mixing bowl for wine and water (*krater*) signed in Euboean Greek by one Aristonothos, who probably lived in Cumae.[134] There is no evidence for such contact with Populonia and Vetulonia, the centres nearest the metal ores. It has therefore been suggested that the elites of Veii, Tarquinia, Cerveteri and Vulci may have acted as intermediaries in some way, providing safe conduct through their territories and perhaps armed escort into the hinterland.[135] Any maritime trade from the Greek colonies up the Tyrrhenian coast had to pass through waters that could be easily controlled by Cerveteri, Tarquinia and Vulci, and Veii had a similarly strategic location for controlling access up the Tiber. The elites of Populonia and Vetulonia seem to have had more

130 Frederiksen, 1979: 283
131 de la Genière, 1979; Frederiksen, 1979
132 Bartoloni, 1987; Bietti Sestieri 1992a, 1992b; Boitani et al., 1985b; Delpino, 1982, 1984; Descoeudres and Kearsley, 1983
133 Ridgway, 1973
134 Martelli, 1987
135 Bartoloni, 1987; Cristofani, 1983b; Delpino, 1984, 1987; Torelli, 1982

effective alliances westwards across the sea to Sardinia, both with indigenous peoples there and with Phoenicians: in addition to the Sardinian metal pieces noted earlier, Phoenician pottery occurs in graves outside the two centres dated to the second half of the eighth century.[136]

As far as we can tell from well dated tomb groups, no sooner had fine Greek drinking services started to appear in Etruria than local copies were being produced (certainly by the mid eighth century). Analysis of the clay fabrics of the two types of vessel has shown such similarities in potting technology that it is thought that the local copies must have been made by Greek craftsmen who had come to work in the major Villanovan settlements like Veii, Tarquinia and (a few decades later) Vulci.[137] Local craftsmen were then able to copy and develop the technology. From the mid eighth century the workshops of southern Etruria concentrated on producing fine vessels to accompany wining and dining, either closely imitating Greek style or faithful to Villanovan traditions.[138] Both kinds of pottery entered the internal exchange system linking the Villanovan elites and have been found, for example, at Bologna.[139]

Villanovan society and economy

Villanovan society has frequently been described as 'proto-urban', though what precisely such a term might mean has not been properly defined. Certainly the cemetery archaeology indicates a social structure divided both horizontally (into clearly demarcated social groups such as clans) and vertically (into well defined degrees of status) – in anthropological terms, respectively, segmented and stratified. It also seems clear that vertical ranking had increased substantially by the middle of the eighth century, when the first really rich burials appear in the cemeteries. At Quattro Fontanili, for example, the cremated remains of one individual were interred in a pit grave inside a decorated bronze casket, accompanied by more than fifty gravegoods: the casket was covered by the warrior's bronze and iron armour including a shield, sword, spear, axe and helmet, together with his horse's bridle bit (fig. 29), and there were sixteen

136 Bartoloni, 1991
137 Boitani et al., 1985b
138 Bartoloni, 1987; Delpino, 1984
139 Giardino et al., 1991

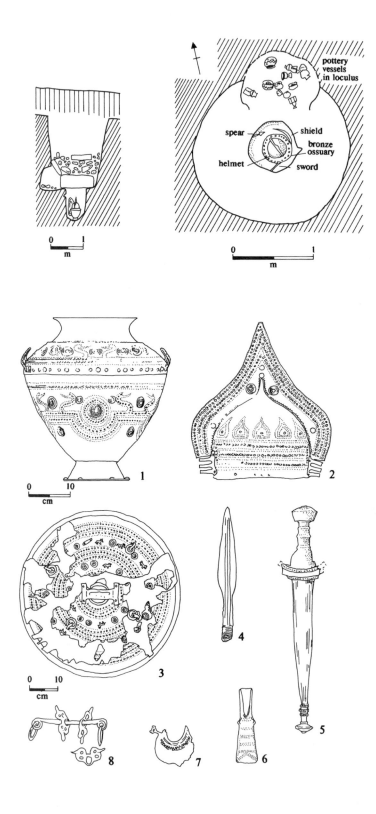

pottery
vessels
in loculus

spear   shield
               bronze
               ossuary
helmet   sword

0   1
    m

0   1
    m

0   10
    cm

1

2

0   10
    cm

3

4

5

8   7   6

pottery vessels and a set of personal possessions including metal bracelets, rings, brooches, ear-rings, a razor, glass beads and a 'scarab' or seal of faience (a glass paste) almost certainly from Egypt.[140] There are female graves with equally notable wealth. At Osteria dell'Osa, too, there are male and female burials of equivalent status at this time, one of the richest 'warrior' burials including the metal fittings of a wooden chariot. Four chariot burials have also been found at Castel di Decima immediately south of Rome. The presence in the richest graves of exotic imported materials such as gold, silver, lead and amber, and of metal objects manufactured to the highest standards of craftsmanship, shows that access to valuables and the control of production were increasingly in the hands of a few powerful individuals in each community.

As we have seen, the settlement archaeology indicates similar complexity. In southern Etruria in particular, there was a hierarchy of domestic sites, with numerous small farms or hamlets forming the base of the triangle, villages or local centres the middle layer, and the few huge centres at the apex. The centres in turn seem to have been divided into distinct communities, interpreted as specific kin-groups, each perhaps occupying (on the evidence of Tarquinia) a settlement unit consisting of a set of smaller structures grouped around a larger one.

Given the evidence for horizontal and vertical divisions, and the dominance of particular locations and individuals in the control of the production and distribution of resources, the likelihood is that Villanovan society was characterized by a well developed system of clientship, with local chiefs controlling dependent groups, and these chiefs in turn acting as vassals to more powerful 'paramount' chiefs. By the later eighth century there may even have been a few all-powerful individuals controlling large regions, though the different chronologies of Greek imports at the major centres suggest that, if so, such power was short-lived and no centre had a particular monopoly.

140   QF, 1970

Figure 29   (opposite) A rich burial at Quattro Fontanili, Veii: tomb AA1 (760–730 BC). Top: section and plan. Bottom: some of the objects: 1 bronze ossuary; 2 bronze helmet; 3 bronze shield with an iron rim; 4 bronze spearhead; 5 iron sword with an ivory and bone hilt and a bronze scabbard; 6 bronze axe; 7 bronze razor; 8 bronze and iron horse bit. 1 and 2 are drawn at the same scale. (After Potter, 1979: 65 and 66, following Close-Brooks, 1965)

Local leaders would have been linked to their clients in a set of mutual obligations, such as receiving gifts, tribute, labour and so on in return for providing protection, communal services and food-stuffs. In turn, they would have been beholden to more powerful leaders in parallel systems of clientship. The economic systems associated with social structures of this kind typically involve the use of the labour of the paramount's dependent group to produce foodstuffs and domestic prestige items for redistribution, as well as commodities for external trade.[141] Given the biases of the data, we can best discern the latter part of the system, but it is highly likely that the production and distribution of foodstuffs such as cereals and legumes, meat, cheese and wine (together with important side-products such as wool), and the technology of agricultural produc-tion such as cattle or ox teams and ploughs, were also increasingly within the control of the Villanovan elites. Presumably the control of raw materials such as metal ores, or at least access to them, was also critical.

The problem of the Etruscan language

The social context of Etruscan literacy is discussed in the next chapter, but a few comments are needed here on the vexed problem of the origins of the Etruscan language. Although, as described in the preceding sections of this chapter, the archaeological evidence overwhelmingly suggests that Etruscan society developed out of the preceding societies of Etruria, the linguistic evidence has frequently been cited as conclusively pointing to exotic origins. Virtually all the languages of Europe share a number of common word stems that indicate they belong to a 'family' of related languages, termed Indo-European; Etruscan, however, along with Basque, Hungarian and Finnish, is not part of this family. Thus in Indo-European lan-guages, both ancient and modern, numerals typically have common roots which we can recognize even if we don't know the language: one, two, three; un, deux, trois; ein, zwei, drei; uno, duo, tre, etc. The same numbers in Etruscan are the completely unfamiliar *thu*, *zal* and *ci*. The Etruscan language is unrelated to any of the other (Indo-European) ancient languages spoken in Italy such as Umbrian, Oscan and Latin.[142] The only known similarity is with a dialect that

---

141 Frankenstein and Rowlands, 1978; Webster, 1990
142 Bonfante, 1990; Bonfante and Bonfante, 1983

was being spoken on the island of Lemnos in the northern Aegean, according to inscriptions found there dating to the second half of the sixth century BC (see chapter 3, p. 94 and fig. 31), which in turn was different from all the other languages being spoken in Greece at that time. (Nobody knows how and when it was first spoken there.) 'The problem of Etruscan origins is encapsulated in the peculiarity of their language.'[143]

The first texts written in the Etruscan language date to around 700 BC. The language was written in a version of the Greek alphabet, which in turn was developed and adapted from the Phoenician and was probably adopted in Etruria from Euboean Greek, not much later than its adoption in Greece;[144] it was presumably acquired from contact with the Greek colonies in the Bay of Naples.[145] Of course the Lemnos inscription has provided invaluable grist to the mill for those looking for Etruscan origins in the eastern Mediterranean, but given that it dates over a century later than the first Etruscan inscriptions in Etruria, it could logically be used to argue that Etruscans did the colonizing, not the other way round! The Etruscan language must have been spoken in Etruria long before it was first written down, though how early we cannot tell, but certainly we must assume that people were speaking a version of the language at least during the Villanovan period.

Why Etruscan was so different from the other ancient languages we know were spoken in the Mediterranean region remains a mystery. Ever since the Indo-European language group was recognized in the nineteenth century, archaeologists have tried to identify evidence for folk movements from the east that might have introduced a core Indo-European language. Some have favoured the second millennium BC,[146] others the third millennium BC,[147] though the evidence cited is no longer accepted. More recently, Renfrew[148] has argued that the only satisfactory context for such a folk movement would have been the spread of agriculture in the fifth and fourth millennia BC, though explaining the transition to farming in Europe in terms of a folk movement no longer seems as convincing as a decade or so ago.

143   Bonfante, 1990
144   McCarter, 1975
145   Colonna, 1976
146   Gimbutas, 1965
147   Piggott, 1965
148   Renfrew, 1987

As Renfrew has recently argued, the most important advances in the study of the origins of ancient languages may well come from the biomolecular studies of DNA in modern populations.[149]

The evidence of physical type

The bones of Etruscans have also been studied for evidence of their origins. Physical anthropologists a hundred years ago confidently divided Etruscan skulls into two types, interpreted respectively as 'indigenous' and 'eastern Mediterranean', in support of the prevailing theories of colonization, and as late as the 1950s Etruscan skulls were still being classified by de Beer as having a 'typically Near Eastern cranial form'.[150] He also interpreted blood group variation in present-day Etrurian populations as evidence for an ancient migration of Etruscans from the eastern Mediterranean. By the 1960s, however, the variability in skull shape was being regarded simply as 'typically Mediterranean' and de Beer's blood group theory completely abandoned. Today most of the anthropological studies of Etruscan burials are concentrating on information regarding diet, nutrition and health (see chapter 6), but where population characteristics have been investigated, at one end of the spectrum there is evidence of strong homogeneity in local Etruscan burial populations suggestive of kin groups,[151] and at the other, of broad similarities between Etruscans and contemporary iron age societies south of the Tiber and east of the Apennines.[152] In exactly the same way, whereas nineteenth-century studies of neolithic, copper age and bronze age skeletons from central Italy invariably divided them into 'local' and 'eastern' types on the basis of skull measurements, the physical anthropologists now emphasize the broad homogeneity of central Mediterranean prehistoric populations.[153] A preliminary study of the mitochondrial DNA of modern Tuscans in the region of Siena has also indicated a long history of similarity with other Causasian populations rather than unusual genetic patterning.[154] (It is intended to develop this study by comparing the DNA of these modern Tuscan populations with that of human remains from Etruscan tombs.) At

149   Renfrew, 1992
150   de Beer, 1955
151   Pardini and Mannucci, 1981
152   Saloi, 1981
153   Corrain and Capitanio, 1975; Robb, 1994
154   Cinelli, 1993

present there is no evidence in the skeletal material for significant 'different-ness' between Etruscans and the people living in Etruria before them, or between Etruscans and their neighbours, or even between Etruscans and their successors in this part of Italy.

The origins of the Etruscans

The Etruscans – at least as recorded by the Greek and Roman writers – certainly had a strong sense of their own ethnicity, of the fact that they were Etruscans, or *Rasenna*. As their culture was absorbed into the Roman world, the folk memory of Etruscan 'different-ness' understandably must have taken on an ever greater importance in their psyche. However, although a few people today still prefer the romantic myth of Etruscan exotic origins, it must be viewed as just that – a myth. As we have seen, there is no evidence for the kind of cultural break at the Villanovan/Etruscan transition envisaged by either of the 'plantation' models (an entire 'exotic people', or just an 'exotic elite') from the eastern Mediterranean, or for a folk movement of either kind from continental Europe in the Late Bronze Age or Iron Age. The overwhelming evidence of the archaeological record is that the origins of Etruscan society lie fundamentally in the later prehistoric communities of Etruria. By the close of the Villanovan Iron Age the framework of the Etruscan economic, social and political system (and presumably their language) had already been established, and the roots go back certainly to the late second millennium BC.

Many scholars who have accepted the general thrust of the 'indigenous' argument still prefer to use the evidence for external contact to explain the critical transition from Villanovan to Etruscan society in the eighth century BC. Cristofani's view is typical: 'within iron age villages . . . class differences came into being at an early stage, as a result of contacts with the Phoenicians and Greeks'.[155] Undoubtedly the appearance of Greek imports and the evidence for Greek craftsmen resident in Villanovan centres coincide with the evidence for much more drastic social stratification than hitherto. But did the arrival of Greek traders stimulate the emergence of powerful chiefs, or was the existence of powerful chiefs in southern Etruria the reason why the Greeks chose to trade with them? The obvious problem in trying to separate the chicken from the egg is

155 Cristofani, 1979b: 30

that the rich burials and the Greek imports are contemporary – in fact, of course, the latter date the former given the precision of Greek ceramic chronologies. However, it does seem unwise to use Greek and Phoenician trade as a simple *deus ex machina c.*750 BC, given the clear evidence from both the settlements and the cemeteries for an accelerating process of social intensification during the ninth century, that in turn can be understood in the context of the important cultural transformations of the Late Bronze Age. Greek contact must be regarded as fundamentally a symptom of Villanovan social intensification rather than its cause, just as initial European contact accelerated social intensification amongst indigenous North American societies rather than caused it.

That being so, can we explain, rather than simply describe, the process of social intensification in Etruria? In addition to the development of centralized spatial organization, the intensification in production and the emergence of more rigid personal ranking between 1000 and 700 BC, interactions *between* local centres may have been particularly critical. Renfrew and Cherry[156] have argued that such competitive interaction between neighbouring chiefdoms is likely to have been the critical stimulus of early state formation. The examples which they cite of the processes that might have been involved in such 'peer polity interaction' range from the expansion of one polity's ideological system at the expense of others, competition in the construction of public works and increasing levels of exchange, to outright warfare. The Greek city states developed at about the same time as the Etruscan city states, and several scholars have argued that there is much evidence for such competitive interaction amongst the preceding iron age societies in Greece.[157] A similar variety of expressions of increasing 'ritualized friendship' can be discerned amongst late bronze age Villanovan and early Etruscan societies. Whilst we are still a long way from understanding why the Etruscans developed as they did, it is at least clear that the patterns of cultural change in Etruria between 1000 and 700 BC have many parallels with those of Greece over the same period. The formation of the Etruscan city states needs to be understood most of all as a parallel trajectory of state formation to that of Greece, not as one that only took place in the aftermath of the Greek experience.

156 Renfrew and Cherry, 1986
157 Morris, 1987, 1991; Snodgrass, 1986; Whitley, 1991

3

Sources and Society

Besides, the Etruscans were vicious. We know it because their enemies and exterminators said so.

D.H. Lawrence (1932) *Etruscan Places*

Greek and Roman sources: early and late

The Etruscans possess little by way of voice, and for the most part their monuments and artefacts have to speak for them. But while keeping the archaeological data in mind, this chapter will be concerned primarily with building up a picture of the Etruscans from the written sources. These fall into two categories: inscriptions, which can provide important but haphazard snippets of information; and the writings of the Greek and Roman authors, which offer more connected historical accounts but which can hardly ever be taken at face value.

We begin with the latter, and with a passage from an early Greek poet that is not without difficulties: 'And Circe, daughter of Helios, Hyperion's son, bore in love to steadfast Odysseus, Agrios and Latinus, noble and strong, who far away in the remote holy islands ruled over the famous Tyrsenians.' So Hesiod wrote, in *Theogony* 1011–6. The Etruscans called themselves Rasna or Rasenna; to the Greeks they were the Tyrsenoi/Tyrrhenoi, to the Romans Tusci or Etrusci. The Hesiod passage, which includes one of the earliest references to Tyrrhenians, was probably added in the sixth century BC to the main body of the poem, which was composed around 700 BC.[1] One could argue, from the mention of Latinus, that the passage refers to the Latins alone. However, 'Tyrrhenian' is the usual Greek appellation for the Etruscans; possibly here it embraces both the Etruscans and their southern neighbours as undifferentiated inhabitants of central Italy – which might explain why two rulers are

1 Gras, 1985: 632

mentioned.[2] Equally ill-defined is the geographical setting: although the Tyrrhenians are well known ('famous'), their homeland is localized in only the vaguest terms. As for the mythological genealogy, it was a Greek convention (and presumption) to attribute to most 'barbarian' ethnic groups origins stemming from Greek heroes.

Neither Greeks nor Romans had particular cause to like the Etruscans. When the former were beginning to colonize the western Mediterranean, the Etruscans were already firmly in place to bar their way up the Italian coast, clearly masters of the sea which the Greeks knew as the Tyrrhenian, a mastery that would in later centuries be under constant threat from the Greeks of Sicily and southern Italy. At Rome there were Etruscan rulers for the duration of the Tarquin dynasty and again briefly under Lars Porsenna of Clusium (Tacitus, *Hist.* 3.72.1). Thereafter the Etruscans presented a formidable barrier to Roman expansion northwards, which was penetrated only in the fourth century BC.

Hesiod's Agrios translates as 'savage' or 'wild man', tallying with the early Greeks' perception of the Etruscans as pirates to be feared. It is the image of them that is presented in the seventh Homeric Hymn, probably also of the sixth century BC, which tells of the Tyrrhenian pirates' capture of Dionysos. Although – as we shall see – there were populations known as Tyrrhenoi in other parts of the Mediterranean far from Italy, later Roman versions of this story assume that it is the Etruscans who were involved. The earliest unambiguous illustration of the god's punishment of his tormenters, whom he turned into dolphins, is on an Etruscan black-figure pot of the late sixth century BC.[3]

Literary references to Etruria which are contemporary with the early Etruscans are very few indeed. Rather more numerous are those that refer to early times but which were written very much later. Most plentiful of all are those that were written late, often in the late Roman Empire or later, and refer to the latest periods of Etruscan history. The value of the second and third categories depends almost entirely on the quality of any earlier sources consulted by the authors.

A small clutch of references of the second kind takes us back to early Tarquinia and concerns the arrival of the Corinthian exile Demaratus.[4] Clearly the accounts are only in part reliable at best, but a combination of the passages in Polybius, Livy, Pliny and Tacitus

2   West, 1966: 433–6
3   Spivey and Rasmussen, 1986
4   Blakeway, 1935

(written between the second century BC and the second century AD), gives a narrative of a man who had made his wealth through trade with the Etruscans, was then forced out of Corinth for political reasons in the mid seventh century, and settled in Etruria bringing with him craftsmen who introduced to the Etruscans the art of modelling in clay. His son married a Tarquinian lady and moved to Rome, where he succeeded in becoming the first of the Tarquin kings.

This is certainly a long train of events, but there is nothing inherently improbable about any of it. So, for example, modelling in clay would include the skills involved in making roof tiles and architectural terracottas: the earliest tiled roofs known are at Corinth, of the first half of the seventh century BC, and it looks very much as if the idea was introduced into Etruria in the middle of the century.[5] However, Tacitus introduced one other element into the story, that it was Demaratus who taught the Etruscans alphabetic writing, and archaeology can at least disprove that. Corinthian influence may explain the use of the crescent gamma (Ɔ) and the sibilant *san* (M) in Etruria (fig. 30), but there is general agreement that the primary source of the Etruscan alphabet is colonial Euboean from Pithekoussai (Ischia). The earliest inscriptions are in any case earlier than Demaratus by some generations. Demaratus himself seems a plausible enough figure, one of many Greeks who did well out of the trading with Etruria.

To the following century belongs an illuminating inscription written on a stone anchor by another Greek who may have made good in this way. Found at the port of Graviscae and now in the Tarquinia Museum, it reads: 'I belong to Aeginetan Apollo. Sostratos, son of (...), had me made.' The author of this dedication is probably the same Sostratos from Aegina mentioned by Herodotus as one of the most successful of all sea-traders. But that he should also be the same man who scratched the undersides of many Athenian pots from Etruria with the trademark SO is too great a coincidence for most to swallow.[6]

Kingship and nationhood

Mentions of kings of individual cities are numerous. Although many float in a chronological vacuum, there is some evidence to suggest

5 Wikander, 1993: 160; but see also p. 165
6 Sostratos in Herodotus: Johnston, 1972; scepticism concerning link with SO marks: Gill, 1994: 101

Transcription/ phonetic value	Seventh century south Etruscan (Caere)	Seventh century north Etruscan	Hellenistic south Etruscan	Hellenistic north Etruscan
a	A	A	A	A
c (k)	Ɔ		Ɔ	Ɔ
e	Ⅎ	Ⅎ	Ⅎ	Ⅎ
v	⅃	⅃	⅃	⅃
z	I	I	I	ⱦ
h	⊟	⊟	⊟	⊟ ⊘
θ (th)	⊗ ⊕	⊕ o	O	O
i	I	I	I	I
k	Ϟ	Ϟ		Ϟ
l	Ⅎ	Ⅎ	Ⅎ	Ⅎ
m	⋔	⋔	m	m Λ
n	⌐	⌐	n	n
p	1	1	1	1
q	φ			
ś		M		M
r	ꟼ ◁	ꟼ	ꟼ	◁ ꟼ
s	ξ	ξ	ξ	ξ
ś	ξ		3	
t	T	T	T	✝
u	Y V Y	V	V	V
φ (ph)	φ	φ	φ	φ
χ (kh)	Y	Y	↓	↓
ṡ	+			
f			8	8

Figure 30 Chronological and regional alphabet chart. (Not all variant letter-forms are shown)

that kingship persisted for a long time in some Etruscan city states, long after it had been abolished in Rome and most parts of the Greek world. Several kings from Veii are known by name, and one, Lars Tolumnius, was defeated and killed by the Romans, according to Livy, in the 430s or 420s BC.[7] Livy also recorded (5.1.3) that in appointing their last king a generation later, the people of Veii succeeded in alienating the other Etruscans for whom kingship was by now an anathema and who allowed Veii to be destroyed by Rome without coming to its aid; though he may here simply have been reflecting contemporary Roman distaste for monarchy in general.

The nature of royal power is a matter for speculation, but presumably it included high priestly office and leadership in war. More is known about kingly regalia, thanks especially to a passage in Dionysius of Halicarnassus (3.61). The king was distinguished, among other trappings, by a purple robe, an eagle-topped sceptre and an ivory throne which visual representations suggest was in the form of a folding stool (though the setting for it is by no means always regal). In processions he was preceded by a magistrate carrying the *fasces*, a bundle of rods with an axe in the centre, symbolizing the power to punish and execute and showing that the king was also supreme arbiter in matters of justice. Much of this paraphernalia, along with its inherent symbolism, was passed on to the consuls of the Roman Republic via the Etruscan kings of Rome.

Not all the 'kings' we hear about seem to have held their authority constitutionally. The picture that Virgil (*Aeneid* 8) paints of Mezentius of Agylla (an originally Greek name for the city of Caere, modern Cerveteri in southern Etruria) is of a leader with little support from among his people, a monster who tortures and kills his enemies by attaching their living bodies to rotting corpses (an accusation made against the Etruscans in general, and Etruscan pirates in particular, that goes back as far as Aristotle). The common view has been that he is an entirely fictitious creation, though more recently Gras[8] has made a concerted attempt to show that behind the image lies a sixth century historical character.

Thefarie Velianas, another leader of Caere, certainly existed, though his constitutional position is again problematical. Nothing was known about him until 1964, when three inscribed gold tablets dating to about 500 BC were excavated at Pyrgi. One of them provides the only Phoenician/Punic inscription so far found in Etruria

7 Ogilvie, 1965: 558
8 Gras, 1985: 454ff

and offers considerable help in construing the longer of the Etruscan texts.[9] Together they record a dedication made by Thefarie, a
gift possibly of a statue and probably also of the earlier of the two
temples on the site (Temple B) which dates to this period. The
Phoenician text styles him king of Kysry (Caere, the Etruscan name
for which was Cisra) and mentions the beneficiary of his gift as the
Phoenician goddess Astarte. She is given her Etruscan name Uni in
the other text, which also refers to him not as king but *zilac/zilath*,
the title of the highest annual magistracy, but which he seems to
have held for three years in succession. Both inscriptions talk of the
gift in terms of a thanks-offering for services rendered by the goddess, which many commentators have interpreted as enabling Thefarie
Velianas to seize power, possibly through the agency of Carthaginian
backers.[10] Clearly relations between Carthage and Etruria (especially Caere) were close in the sixth century: the two peoples co-
operated closely in driving the Phocaean Greeks out of Corsica
(chapter 4, p. 137); a close trading treaty between the two mentioned by Aristotle (*Politics* 3.5.10–11) may well belong in this
period; while Carthage itself has produced a 'visitor's card' in Etruscan, consisting of a short introductory inscription on ivory for use
in Etruria by a Carthaginian merchant.[11]

We rarely hear of kings with wider jurisdiction than over a single
city, though Lars Porsenna took on something approaching national
importance in trying to restore the Tarquin dynasty at Rome at
the end of the sixth century. Arimnestos, who has gone down in
the records as the first non-Greek to make a dedication to Zeus
at Olympia, is styled simply 'king of the Tyrrhenians', presumably
because Pausanias (5.12.5) did not know any further details of his
city or did not bother to record them. However, Livy and others are
insistent that there was a mechanism whereby the Etruscans could
come together to elect a national leader: at the meetings of the
concilium Etruriae (which seem to have been annual) at the Sanctuary of Voltumna (Fanum Voltumnae), delegates of the League of
Twelve Cities could elect one of their leaders to the supreme position. This office, which in Etruscan and Roman inscriptions is probably what is meant by *zilath mechl rasnal* and *praetor Etruriae*
respectively, may normally have been simply titulary, or it may have
been concerned primarily with the religious aspects and organization

9   Bonfante and Bonfante, 1983: 53ff
10 Pallottino, 1975: 90
11 Cristofani, 1991b: 72

of the annual meetings. Dionysius (3.61), however, speaks of the command of joint military forces being entrusted to a supremo, to whom were handed the twelve *fasces* of the individual cities, though there is little evidence that this happened on any regular basis.

There has been endless discussion about which cities may have belonged to the League; possible candidates are more than twelve in number and its composition may have been a shifting one over the generations. Much effort, too, has been expended on attempting to locate the site of Fanum Voltumnae, where the meetings seem to have been part of an important festival with games and a fair. They continued to be held in the late Roman Empire in the territory of Volsinii (Bolsena), but the major fixtures on the site may have been very few, the crowds of participants having camped in tents. The Panionion in Ionia, with which comparisons are sometimes made, preserves only an altar and a few rows of rock-cut benches.

In this area, as in many others, the correlations between written sources and archaeology are poor. So far the burial place of no known king has been discovered, though the area around Chiusi has been combed for the fabled tomb of Porsenna described by Varro. There are many 'princely burials' from the seventh century BC, when kingship was probably the norm, but without inscriptional or very obvious iconographic evidence, there is no means of proving that any of these are burials of rulers. However, it must be from the families to which such tombs belong that the early rulers of the Etruscan communities were drawn.

Religion

As I have already said, the Athenians are far more devoted to religion than any other people. (Pausanias, 1.24.3)

So the nation [the Etruscans] whose devotion to religious matters exceeded that of any other people and was matched by their skill in the conduct of them, ... (Livy, 5.1.6)

The first statement has received scant comment, the second is often quoted as a great truth. Pausanias' remark, made in the course of a description of the innumerable cult places of Athens, has not altered the common perception of the Athenians as a people concerned with rationality and logical argument, with humanistic ideals rather than with intercourse with the supernatural. Livy's words, on the other hand, are felt by many to go to the heart of Etruscan preoccupations, reinforced as they were by other ancient writers, including Arnobius, who wrote of Etruria as 'the mother and creator of superstitious practices'.

In point of fact there is much truth in the assertions of both Pausanias and Livy, but at the same time there was nowhere in the ancient world where cult and 'superstition' (Arnobius was writing from a Christian standpoint) were not of great importance. Athens, as well as being host to great numbers of cults connected with the Greek pantheon, was rife with soothsayers and oracle-mongers, and Aristophanes made fun of a good many in his plays. Rome, too, was replete not only with its many official cults and an increasing number of imported ones, but also with astrologers and occultists of all kinds from all over the Mediterranean; so much so that three centuries before Arnobius, the emperor Augustus (Dio Cassius 56.25.5) and his successor Tiberius (Suetonius, *Tiberius* 63) made attempts to restrict their practices. It is clear that many Romans such as Cato and Cicero regarded Etruscan diviners or haruspices, who also operated in the city, as practitioners of the same kind of quackery as the emperors later tried to suppress.

One of the main differences between Etruscan religion and most others of its time is that behind it lay a set body of doctrine which was thought in origin to be the word of the gods. Roman writers refer to it as the *etrusca disciplina*. According to them it was composed of several separate treatises, among the most important of which were the *libri haruspicini* on divining through the examination of entrails, the *libri fulgurales* on interpreting lightning, and the *libri rituales*. An attempt to sketch some of the principles of the first two is made in chapter 7. The last seems to have contained a wide range of material, from rites to be carried out in the laying out of towns and field systems to specific rituals of worship. It has often been suggested that an actual fragment of it is preserved in the longest of the surviving Etruscan texts, written – to everyone's astonishment – on an Egyptian linen mummy wrapping of second century BC date, now in Zagreb,[12] which appears to give in calendar form a list of what offerings are to be made to which gods on which days of the year. In their prescriptive nature and in their attention to the minutiae of observances, the *libri rituales* may be compared very loosely with the statutes of the Law of Moses in the second to fifth books of the Old Testament.

It should be stressed that references to the *etrusca disciplina* are very scattered and of late date, and it may well be that it was only

12 Roncalli, 1985

in the very latest period of Etruscan literary activity – around the first century BC – that most of it was composed in the form in which Roman and Greek writers knew it in translation. This may partly explain the fatalistic tone of some of its contents, in particular the doctrine of Great Generations (*saecula*) of variable duration lasting up to well over a hundred years each, and of which the Etruscan nation had only ten allotted to it.[13] Plutarch (*Sulla* 7) seems to imply that the eighth ended in 88 BC, while other sources say that the ninth lasted only until 44 BC; but the earliest source for the *saecula* is Varro (quoted by Censorinus in the third century AD), who stated that the eighth was still in progress when the records were written down. It is therefore conceivable that the whole system was thought up retrospectively to explain in cosmic terms what was already very apparent by the second and first centuries BC: that the Etruscans as an ethnic entity were at their last gasp.

One does not have to look far to see why the Etruscans have gone down in history as being so obsessed with matters religious. The *saecula* doctrine apart (and even that has some correspondences with Hesiod's Ages of Man), there is little in the area of religion that cannot be matched in some way with Greek practice. In the Greek world, too, appropriate rituals were necessary to accompany most actions of any consequence, public or private, whether founding and laying out a colony, opening a meeting of the town council or even commencing a drinking and dining 'symposium'. Early Rome, however, seems to have borrowed many of its procedures from the Etruscans, especially in the sphere of divination, and in this field alone the Romans regarded them as their superiors, employing their priests and haruspices on a regular basis to assist them in seeking out and interpreting signs from the gods.

The position of the haruspices was given a considerable boost by the emperor Claudius when he revived their ancient colleges by decree (Tacitus, *Annals* 11.15), and they continued to be consulted at Rome for centuries afterwards. If a Livy or a Seneca of the early Empire had been asked to summon up a picture of *contemporary* Etruscans, it is the learned haruspices, steeped in their arcane specialism, who would have sprung quickest to mind, for there simply were no others around who were visibly keeping Etruscan traditions alive. Such writers, writing about the Etruscans in their heyday centuries earlier, would have found it very difficult, almost impossible, not to project backwards the image of a society dominated by haruspication and the *etrusca disciplina*.

13   Pfiffig, 1975: 159ff

Etruscan sources and writing

In addition to the snippets by Greek and Roman writers, there is information to be gleaned from the surviving Etruscan texts. About 13,000 inscriptions are known to date, most of them published in the *Corpus Inscriptionum Etruscarum* (*CIE*), with new additions reported annually in the journal *Studi Etruschi*. The great bulk of them are funerary in nature, a few of the longer ones liturgical. Truly historical documents such as the Pyrgi plaques are conspicuous by their scarcity.

The Etruscan language is only imperfectly known, but given the limited scope of the material for study, it is remarkable how much headway has been made in understanding it – the result of much hard work by numerous, mainly Italian, researchers. What are hoped for now are longer and more varied texts, plus a sprinkling of Etrusco-Roman bilingual texts, hopes that may well be fulfilled in the future as excavators continue to concentrate more on urban and sanctuary sites. The crucial period is the third to first centuries BC when Etruria was under Roman rule and when there is likely to have been a need for commemorative, dedicatory and even proclamatory inscriptions in both languages. Such a scenario may seem unlikely to some,[14] but the prospect of new finds is an exciting one.

Etruscan is the only non-Indo-European language of ancient Italy (see chapter 2, p. 80), and its uniqueness was noted by ancient writers. The only language so far known that is remotely similar, apparently spoken on the Aegean island of Lemnos in the archaic period, survives only on an inscribed tombstone (fig. 31) and on incised pottery sherds. The script is very close to archaic Etruscan; the language is not itself Etruscan but is clearly a not-too-distant relation of it and even shares the same formula for expressing a person's age.[15] Consequently, one school of thought views Lemnos as an Etruscan outpost for trade and piracy,[16] even though no other Etruscan material has as yet been found there. Interestingly, Thucydides (4.109) said that the island was inhabited by Tyrrhenians; but in this context these were a branch of the Pelasgian race who inhabited the Aegean area in pre-Hellenic times.

Herodotus (1.57) recorded that the Pelasgians spoke their own language and that they were in possession of Lemnos until it was

14   Wilkins, 1990: 68
15   Script: de Simone, 1994; language: Heurgon, 1989
16   Grant, 1980: 57; Gras, 1976

Figure 31 Inscribed stone stele from Lemnos, sixth century BC, *in the National Museum, Athens. (After Bonfante and Bonfante, 1983: fig. 4)*

overrun by the Athenians in the early fifth century BC. Further, he appears to add that there were Tyrrhenian communities living in northern Greece in his own day. In the fourth century BC and later, Greek references to Tyrrhenians in the Aegean proliferate, especially in the context of piracy,[17] and it seems probable that they are remnants of these same populations. To the Greeks, then, *Tyrrhenoi*

17 Giuffrida Ientile, 1983; Musti, 1989

had several meanings: the Etruscans of central Italy; a related ethnic group spread thinly in the Aegean area; and (possibly, by extension) any non-Greek-speaking community of the Aegean or Italy with a penchant for piracy. Putting this evidence together, it is possible to come up with a picture of the Etruscans as part of a wider group of non-Indo-European speakers who once occupied large areas of the Mediterranean, the only part to survive later population incursions substantially intact into the historical period.

Most books on the Etruscan language begin with a discussion of the script,[18] which presents few problems in reading; as most shorter inscriptions consist in the main of personal names, they can be understood without a great depth of linguistic knowledge. The letter-forms are of western Greek type, and their likeliest source is the island of Ischia (p. 87). The earliest Etruscan inscriptions are from around 700 BC, and until recently these were the earliest of any kind from central Italy, but an inscription in Greek letters is now known from the early iron age cemetery at Osteria dell'Osa in Latium, too short to make certain sense, but which pushes knowledge of the Greek alphabet back to within the first half of the eighth century BC.[19] For the history of the alphabet, the Phoenician/Euboean community on Ischia now begins to look doubly important, both as the likeliest base of those Greeks who transmitted it to central Italy and the Etruscans, and also as the place where the Greeks may have learned it from the Phoenicians in the first place.[20] The Osa pot was found in the grave of a woman, and perhaps either she or whoever scratched the letters was a Greek from further south. It will be interesting to see for how long it remains an isolated find from the region including not only Latium, where early inscriptions are very few, but also southern Etruria, where it is far more likely that other early written material will turn up.

There are about 120 Etruscan inscriptions from the seventh century BC. Some of them are in the form of learning aids such as alphabets and syllabaries, which include Phoenician/Greek letters that were never needed to reproduce Etruscan sounds. It is remarkable that these 'model' alphabets continue to the end of the century. Otherwise such letters – including the signs for *b*, *d*, *g* and *o* – were dropped immediately, and even within the century certain of the remaining letters began to undergo small changes.[21] In later centuries

18 For example: Bonfante and Bonfante, 1983; Cristofani, 1991a; Pallottino, 1975
19 Bietti Sestieri, 1992: 185; Ridgway, 1994
20 Holloway and Holloway, 1993
21 Colonna, 1970

there were more modifications and even the appearance of one or two new signs. This development, combined with some regional variation of the alphabet (which concerns in particular the use of *k* and *c* and the signs for the various sibilants), makes it possible to separate out, at least roughly, northern from southern inscriptions, and late from early (fig. 30).

Most early Etruscan writing, like the earliest Greek, runs from right to left. But whereas Greek finally settled for the opposite direction in the sixth century, Etruscan persisted with its retrograde script to the end. This might reflect – or might have produced – some difference in the psychology of vision, for it has been suggested that the visual narratives in the art of both cultures do tend to run in opposite directions from each other. Only one area, that of black-figure vase-painting, has been tested, but with statistically interesting results.[22] Another feature that archaic Etruscan and Greek inscriptions have in common is the lack of word separation, though in Etruscan there is a tendency to mark the ends of words with one or more dots or puncts; a similar system marking the ends of syllables disappeared when word division came into use.

It is clear that few people in the seventh century had writing skills, and that those who did were restricted mainly to the ruling class. Inscriptions on objects from 'princely tombs' suggest a symbolic, perhaps even magical, importance by which those who had access to this new power were separated out from those who did not. Some of the earliest texts, from Tarquinia,[23] are scratched on pottery as dedications to gods (here to Uni), a use of writing that never wanes. In the sixth and fifth centuries, the number of inscriptions increases dramatically, a phenomenon that is usually explained in terms of the rise of a new wealthy 'middle class' with writing ability.[24] It is very possible that those making dedications at sanctuaries had their gifts inscribed by priests, who may also have been responsible for inscriptions over tomb doorways, as at Orvieto (fig. 32), and even for those on sarcophagi and ash-urns, though there has yet to be any palaeographic study of hands. However, the wide range of texts on objects for personal use, the many inscribed mythological scenes, the labels on items that were primarily for female delectation such as mirrors (fig. 35), all argue strongly against the view that writing was chiefly in the hands of a priestly caste.

22   Small, 1987
23   Bonghi Jovino, 1986a: 172
24   Stoddart and Whitley, 1988

Figure 32   Crocefisso del Tufo necropolis, Orvieto: chamber tomb with inscription on lintel. (Photograph: G. Barker)

The limitations imposed by the nature of the written evidence can be compared with an attempt, by somone with only rudimentary knowledge of English, to reconstruct the language and society of seven centuries of English history from the survival of inscribed tombstones, numerous fragments of illuminated manuscripts and far fewer of the Book of Common Prayer, inscribed church plate and records of church donations, along with Christmas presents of the upper classes with their gift tags attached. What working vocabulary would he or she be able to build up, and what picture of English life? For Etruscan, the known core vocabulary is therefore small, but it is slowly growing with new finds. Heading the list are proper names of private people, gods, mythological heroes (mainly Greek), cities[25] and some months of the year. Many of the numerals are now known, along with some numerical signs.[26] So, too, are several terms denoting familial relations such as 'father', 'daughter'. The list also includes a number of common verbs, names of vase

25   Pallottino, 1937a
26   Bonfante, 1990: 22, 48

shapes[27] and some rather enigmatic titles of magistracies. Work on the language continues all the time: it has only recently been confirmed, for example, that that most characteristic of vase shapes, the cup with two vertical handles we refer to by the Greek name *kantharos* (see fig. 47, chapter 4, lower right), was actually called a *zavena*.[28]

Social structure

Putting the written evidence together, literary and epigraphic, and combining it with the archaeological, it is extremely difficult to come to definite and uncontroversial conclusions as to how power was exercised within the city states. Even terminology presents major problems. When we published a preliminary report on our field survey around Tuscania, we entitled it, perhaps somewhat rashly, 'The archaeology of an Etruscan *polis*'.[29] It is in fact very questionable whether any Etruscan town and its surrounding territory, even the large ones like Tarquinia, should be given a Greek label that presupposes a social framework embracing political, cult and legal institutions, all of them the result of long development on Greek soil. An additional problem is that the term *polis* conjures up some of the more politically progressive cities like Athens, with their open government, law courts, assemblies and voting rights, whereas it is worth bearing in mind that many Greek *poleis* were controlled by a narrow clique of families or even a single ruler, or were in matters of external policy subject to more powerful neighbours. Many, too, were very small.

In Etruria it is likely that at any one time there would also have been a wide range of political regimes – only not quite so wide, for one hears from no quarter of any move towards democratization. Kingship and tyranny have already been discussed; otherwise the norm was some form of oligarchy. Under the latter, the main offices of state, held probably annually, were those of *zilath*, *purth* and *maru*, which are mentioned in many inscriptions, but most of them admittedly of late date.[30] It is very unclear what responsibilities each had and therefore how we should translate them, but the function

27 Colonna, 1973–4
28 Cristofani, 1989–90: 357–8
29 Barker and Rasmussen, 1988
30 Lambrechts, 1959

of the *maru* seems to have been in part priestly, and the *zilath* (of which there seem to have been several kinds) appears to have been the most important. The fact that men could attain this office in their twenties and hold it several times in one lifetime (up to seven times is recorded) suggests that it was open to only a small aristocratic circle.

One feature, among many, that Etruscan cities had in common with Greek *poleis* is that they controlled large territories around them, which might also include smaller towns. This is nowhere stated explicitly in any ancient source, but it is clear enough from the distribution of major cities on the map of Etruria, clear enough, too, from such factors as the regionalism of architectural and craft production – though artistic influence does not stop at state boundaries. It is also the probable reason why, during the course of the sixth century BC, a number of smaller and medium-sized centres such as Murlo and Acquarossa were destroyed or abandoned at a time when the major cities were increasing in size and power. It is of course impossible to trace political territories with precision, and in any case their borders must have been subject to constant re-alignment as the states jostled with each other for superiority. Two sources, one Latin, one Etruscan, may illustrate the last point. One of the Tarquinian *elogia* (p. 112), written in Latin but perhaps distilled from some earlier Etruscan version, commemorates a local man who is said to have beaten a king of Caere in battle and defeated Arretium (Arezzo), while another concerns a leader who also led an army against Caere.[31] The second source is the painting in the François Tomb at Vulci which shows murderous encounters between named Etruscans from different towns, including Volsinii (Orvieto) and Sovana.[32]

That the territories were under the effective control of the leading family groups (or the Roman equivalent: *gentes*) of the cities is suggested by (late) epigraphic evidence. At Musarna, for example, two of the leading families were the Alethna and the Hulchnie, who around 100 BC built a sumptuous bath-building with a mosaic floor inscribed with their names; the former are found on sarcophagi from the cemetery, but both names are known from funerary inscriptions from Tarquinia.[33] Furthermore, seventy years ago an epigraphic study of the Chiusi region concluded that a wide area around the city was in the possession of no more than around

31   Torelli, 1975
32   Buranelli, 1987: 97
33   de Casanove and Jolivet, 1983

twenty families.[34] Quite how control was exerted by the cities on the smaller centres is, however, another matter. To go back to the Alethna of Musarna, several members of this family held magistracies, including that of *zilath*, while two other small towns in Tarquinian territory, Norchia and Tuscania, also produced magistrates of all three kinds,[35] but it is unclear whether their jurisdiction was purely local or was based at Tarquinia and covered the whole territory.

The discussion so far has concerned only the aristocracy. In addition it is probable that there were families who were free but not so privileged, perhaps roughly equivalent to the Roman *plebs*, and beneath these in status the many slaves and ex-slaves. Greek and Roman sources have much to say about the tensions between the ruling classes and those without access to political power, and for a number of cities insurrections are recorded, of which there is no need to mention more than a couple. Again we are dealing with a late period of Etruscan history, though conditions may well have been similar centuries before. In 302 BC, the ruling family of the Cilnii at Arretium (Arezzo) was threatened with an uprising and called in the Romans to help them; according to Livy (10.3–5), those stirring up trouble were what he called the *plebs*. Then, a generation later, there was a revolution at Volsinii (Orvieto), the result of a slow process, according to the Byzantine writer Zonaras, as the ruling classes out of laziness had allowed their freed slaves to run more and more of the machinery of government, until they found their position usurped altogether. In none of these cases was it working slaves who were attempting to overthrow their masters: they were freedmen at Orvieto, and probably of higher status at Arezzo.

The freed or manumitted slave has an archaeological presence in Etruria. He or she is a *lautni* or *lautnitha* in funerary inscriptions, as is proved by the Latin equivalent *libertus* that is found in bilingual texts[36] – though precise equivalence in rights and status is unlikely. For his family name the *lautni* took one of his master's names and no doubt continued to owe allegiance to him; he might also be buried in some style in an inscribed cinerary urn. Slaves, however, received no such distinction; their burial places are unknown, their lives undocumented. Considerable numbers were no doubt employed in the unpleasant manual tasks in the mining, smelting and quarrying industries, and probably in agricultural work

34 Bianchi Bandinelli, 1925: 500
35 Scullard, 1967: 230
36 Heurgon, 1964: 62

too (see chapter 6). We can see them sometimes in domestic situations in tomb-paintings, occasionally identified by first name alone, for they were without a family name. Slave uprisings were rare: there was one in Etruria in 196 BC (Livy 33.36.1–2) which was quickly suppressed by Roman legionary force.

Another class of dependant is signalled by the term *etera*, but modern opinion is divided as to whether its status is between slave and *lautni*, or *lautni* and free man. But whether *lautni* itself possessed the same meaning after the Roman takeover (and after the imposition of Roman law) as before is very questionable.[37] Once again it needs to be stressed that all this evidence is of the latest period: there is almost nothing that carries us back beyond the fourth century BC.

The family

In some areas, Etruscan epigraphy is very informative. The age of death is given in many funerary inscriptions (see fig. 94, chapter 7), according to which a life of seventy or eighty years was not uncommon. One old soldier called Felsnas was involved in the Hannibalic wars and died at Tarquinia aged 106,[38] and there is other evidence of extreme longevity too – or of the capacity of descendants to exaggerate age or lose track of time.

Even when texts include little more than names, they may give considerable information about how families were structured. How people are named can vary with time and for a variety of reasons. At the beginning of the twentieth century most inhabitants of Turkey had only a single name, but by the end of the 1930s there was no-one who did not also have a family name or surname, the result of a decree passed by Atatürk out of a wish that his country should modernize and follow western conventions. In Etruria, too, in the inscriptions of the early and mid seventh century BC, one personal name suffices: 'I am Larth's', written on a silver vessel,[39] was all that was required for those who needed to know to whom the object belonged. If any greater precision was needed, one could give one's father's name, or patronymic, in addition.

During the course of the seventh century, however, two names became standard. So the text scratched on an amphora from Cerveteri made in *bucchero*, the fine black pottery of the Etruscans, informs

37   Harris, 1971: 126–7
38   *TLE* 890
39   *TLE* 54

us that Arnth gave it to a lady called Ramtha, who is also given her family name Vestirikina.[40] The Etruscans, unlike the Turks, were not suddenly inventing second names for themselves out of thin air; such names, many of them derived originally from a patronymic, are likely to have existed already, but were now employed more prominently because new social conditions made it desirable. Two interconnected factors spring to mind: the dramatic rise in population that there undoubtedly was during the period (see chapter 5); and the growing scale and increasing urbanization of the main centres of habitation. The single name with patronymic works well enough in a small village, less so in a sophisticated urban environment (as the Icelanders of Rekyavik would probably agree).

Possibly many different but interrelated family units, of father, mother and offspring, would have had the same family name, so in order to differentiate oneself further it was often necessary, as in the period of single names, to state one's father's name and perhaps those of other progenitors. Such formulations in funerary texts could be very elaborate, as on the stone sarcophagus of Laris Pulenas at Tarquinia (fig. 33), who names not only his father and grandfather but also his great-grandfather and uncle.[41] Inscriptions like this go beyond mere expediency in identification and are more concerned with glorying in familial connections and illustrious lineage, offering eloquent, if pompous, testimony to the importance of the family in society.

A final development is the appearance of a third name to designate a particular branch of a family, as in the example Laris Tarnas Herma.[42] This is similar to the *cognomen* of a Roman tripartite name, and indeed the Roman usage may have preceded the Etruscan.

Women and society

Etruscan society was patriarchal, where, as inscriptions make clear, the family name was carried through the male line. However, the fact that women were given individual first names, unlike their counterparts at Rome who had to make do with the merely familial 'Clodia', 'Flavia Minor' and the like, is one of many factors that suggest they possessed considerable social standing. One may also point to the use of matronymics in inscriptions, of which there are a considerable number, though admittedly they are not as common

40   *TLE* 868
41   *TLE* 131
42   *TLE* 5904

Figure 33   Stone sarcophagus of Laris Pulenas, early second century BC,
in the Museo Nazionale, Tarquinia. (Photograph: Alinari)

as patronymics. Moreover a woman, even when she married, might
carry her own patronymic, or her family name, through to the
grave. This usage has a rather modern ring to it considering that
even now in some traditional English circles a woman may be completely subsumed under her husband's name, at any rate in corres-
pondence ('Mrs John Smith'). A sarcophagus from Tuscania in the
British Museum (fig. 34) bears an inscription that illustrates these
points well:[43] the name of the deceased, Sethre Vipinans, is followed
by that of his father Velthur, together with his mother Thanchvilu
and her family name Meclasia (or patronymic: 'daughter of Meclas').
   A number of inscriptions record gifts to, or objects possessed by,
women. There would be little point in adding the donor inscription
to the *bucchero* amphora mentioned above unless Ramtha could
read it herself, which suggests that some women were literate already by the later seventh century. Two female owners' names,
Culni and Ati, were also found scratched on pottery from the sixth/

43   *TLE* 180

Figure 34 Stone sarcophagus of Sethre Vipinans from Tuscania, third century BC, in the British Museum, London. (Photograph: copyright British Museum)

fifth century Tomb of the Greek Vases at Cerveteri, so these women may have helped put together one of the largest and finest collections of Greek painted pottery ever recovered in a single find.[44] They, too, were not only literate but also seemed to have possessed a remarkable taste for objects that displayed complex imagery with which they were probably familiar, at least in part.

Decorated bronze mirrors point in this same direction. Although they need not all have been used exclusively by women, mirrors were essentially part of a woman's personal equipment and are common in female burials. On their engraved (and occasionally relief) reverses there is as wide a repertory of mythological scenes as can be found anywhere in Etruscan art (fig. 35), and in fact a number of episodes concerning Greek heroes and gods are seen here and nowhere else, not even in Greece.[45] On many mirrors and other

44 Heurgon, 1964: 91
45 Carpino, 1996; de Grummond, 1982; van der Meer, 1995

Figure 35   Engraved bronze mirror: Dionysus (Etruscan: Fufluns) reunited with his mother Semele (Semla) in the company of Apollo (Apulu) and a young satyr. Fourth century BC, *formerly in the Staatliche Museen, Berlin (now lost). (After Herbig, 1965: fig. 2)*

objects the key figures are labelled, and where the names are Greek they are no mere transliterations but are adapted to the developing patterns of Etruscan speech. Hence Agamemnon is Achmemrun in Etruscan, while his wife Klytaemestra is at first Clutumustha, then

– by a process of syncopation – Clutumsta and finally Clutmsta.
Greek mythology was alive in Etruria: it was not simply something
to be admired uncomprehendingly on works of art, but was discussed and retold in the language of everyday speech – by women
as well as men.

At least this is likely to have been the case in aristocratic circles,
and one obvious venue for the recounting of such tales is the banquet/
symposium (chapter 7, p. 249), to which women were freely admitted,
a custom that prompted much disapproval among the Greeks and
elicited such outbursts of moral indignation as that of Theopompos
(chapter 6, p. 179). The difference between Etruscan women of the
Tarquin family reclining at banquet (with an implication of accompanying licentiousness) and Roman women who preferred to sit and
spin wool is also a central point in Livy's dramatic story (1.57) of
court life at the time of the fall of the Roman monarchy.[46] On the
left wall of the painted Cardarelli Tomb at Tarquinia, in a scene of
symposiastic dancing in which both men and women participate, a
young girl carries a cup in one hand and a mirror in the other.[47]
In such settings, mythological narrative could be enjoyed on two
levels, both aural and visual.

Within the spheres of family and social life, women enjoyed considerable freedom, but it seems unlikely that they exercised in the
nude, as Theopompos feverishly imagined (Athenaeus 12.517d), or
played an active part in sports, though they might spectate at them,
as tomb-paintings such as those in the Tomb of the Chariots at
Tarquinia make clear.[48] There is no hint, either, of their exercising
any real political power; even the most strong-willed of Livy's Etruscan women exert their influence only through the men around them.
To what extent they could own property (as opposed to Greek
pots) is unclear. At Orvieto, out of 124 façades of chamber tombs
inscribed with the names of the occupants, half a dozen display
female names.[49] To some these are proof of a significant female
property-owning sector; to others they are merely the exception to
the general patriarchal rule.[50]

The costly, even extravagant, dress and accessories that are so
conspicuous on female figures featured on funerary monuments (compared with which, women on Athenian grave reliefs look remark-

---

46 Bonfante, 1973; Heurgon, 1964: 79
47 Steingräber, 1986: plate 55
48 Steingräber, 1986: 289
49 Cristofani, 1974: 309
50 Respectively: Bonfante, 1986b: 236; Cristofani, 1979a: 28

Figure 36   Terracotta sarcophagus of Seianti Hanunia Tlesnasa, second century BC, *from near Chiusi, in the British Museum, London. (Photograph: copyright British Museum)*

ably restrained) should be no surprise if we are to believe Posidonius' remark that lavish attention in costume was given even to Etruscan slaves (Diodorus 5.40). The main garments were the long tunic and, draped over it, a mantle. These were also the essential male draperies, except that for men the tunic was often of a special cut with a curved hem – the forerunner of the Roman toga. Other notable fashions include shoes with pointed curved-up toes, for both sexes, and similarly in the archaic period, but for women only, the headgear to which the Romans gave the Etruscan-sounding term *tutulus*. The latter was as much a hair-style as anything, for the hair had to be carefully piled up beneath the linen cloth or cap that covered it (fig. 77). All these modes were Greek-inspired, many of them coming originally from Ionia.[51]

51   Bonfante, 1975

What contributed most to the opulence of appearance was the gold jewellery,[52] which is of outstanding workmanship but receives no mention from the ancient writers. Unlike most modern brooches, ancient brooches or fibulas had a job of work to do, pinning together the hems of tunics and mantles. They reach a peak of elaboration and craftsmanship early, in the seventh century BC, when the granulation technique of applying decorative motifs by means of tiny gold spherules is unsurpassed anywhere in the ancient world (see chapter 6). Like fibulas, the lentoid pendants or (Latin) *bullae* were worn by both sexes, but especially by women who from the fifth century onwards displayed them suspended from necklaces, as seen on the stone sarcophagus lid from Tarquinia in the British Museum.[53] The terracotta sarcophagus of Seianti Hanunia Tlesnasa, also in the British Museum, shows well the range of accessories sported by a member of the aristocracy of the Chiusi region in the second century BC (fig. 36): bracelet, armlet, necklace, tiara and earrings (the last were worn by women only).

To turn from physical appearance to daily activity, it seems clear that women were heavily involved in spinning and weaving, notwithstanding Livy's innuendoes to the contrary (see above). The proof is finds of spindles, spindle whorls and loom weights from female graves of all kinds, from the richest to the poorer.[54] Although it is possible to question the orthodox view about textile manufacture being in female hands,[55] it is in fact a pattern that is very visible in central Italy already in the Early Iron Age.[56] In later periods some of this work may have been given to female slaves, but the most detailed representation of spinning and work at the loom, on a large axe-shaped pendant in Bologna,[57] shows the women seated on curving high-backed chairs (fig. 37), which in northern Etruria seem to denote high rank, as at Murlo (fig. 62b).

Other women seen in action seem to be mainly of lower status. In tomb-paintings, females shown in simple tunics are likely to be domestics,[58] though some may conceivably be children of the family. They are shown performing simple tasks like carrying household objects or preparing garlands (fig. 98, chapter 7). Interestingly, the

52 Cristofani and Martelli, 1983
53 Haynes, 1971: plate 11
54 Bartoloni, 1989a; Rallo, 1989
55 Spivey, 1991b: 59
56 Bietti Sestieri, 1992b: 108
57 Bonfante, 1981: 16
58 Rallo, 1989

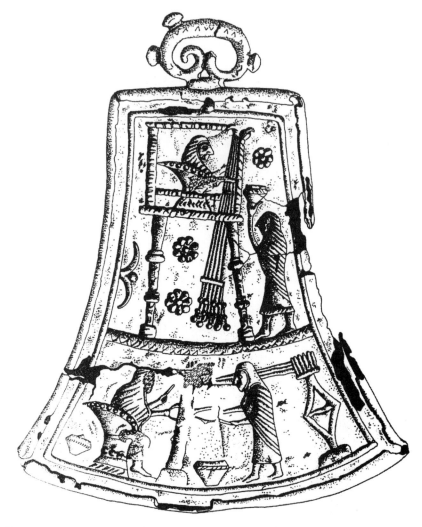

Figure 37   Bronze axe-shaped pendant showing spinning and work at the loom, from the Tomba degli Ori, Bologna, c.600 BC, in the Museo Civico, Bologna. (After Morigi Govi, 1971: plate 52)

most complete scene of food preparation in the kitchen, in the painted Golini I tomb at Orvieto, depicts most of the work being done by men. Then there are the many performers in musical and display contexts. The tumblers, seen in the Tomb of the Jugglers (Tarquinia) and the Tomb of the Monkey (Chiusi), the musicians with castanets or (Greek) *krotala*, and perhaps some of the dancers too, are likely to be professionals, hired for the occasion and again of low or servile status.

Of colleges of priestesses there is scant evidence. At Pyrgi it has been suggested that there were temple courtesans in the service of the love goddess Astarte.[59] There may also have been a line of priestesses of a rather more exalted kind at Vulci. At least, this is the likeliest explanation for the predominantly female burials of the Tomb of the Inscriptions in the Ponte Rotto necropolis.[60]

One of the more illuminating pieces of recent research has been a simple statistical study of male and female burials, focusing on the sarcophagi and ash-urns of the Hellenistic period, where sex can be determined by the inscription and/or by the figure of the deceased carved on the lid.[61] One immediate conclusion is that, in Etruria generally, more men are commemorated in death than women, the ratio being about 60:40. Only at Tuscania is the ratio even, and then only in the category of stone sarcophagi. However, around Asciano in the north it was noted that 'female' objects such as mirrors and ear-rings were sometimes deposited in urns for men, so here (and no doubt elsewhere) it looks as if women could be buried in their husbands' urns without this being made clear by inscription or other means. Almost certainly in these cases the husband would have died first. Almost certainly, too, a wife was more likely to be given her own burial container if she died before her husband. But to be given a container in one's own right, with inscription and/or sculptural representation of oneself, must have been an obvious criterion of esteem in the context of family and society, and so the ratio of 60:40 in favour of men is a telling one.

Etruscan legend and historical traditions

That there existed Etruscan writings on matters of cult and religion we can be certain, but was there at any time a body of secular literature which consequently suffered the severe misfortune to have been entirely lost? An allusion in Varro (quoted by Pliny 36.93) to Etruscan *fabulae* does not take us far, for the word can mean any kind of narrative and from the context is hardly likely to mean 'plays'. Only one literary figure, Volnius, gets a mention in the

59   Colonna, 1985: 128
60   Nielsen, 1989: 88
61   Nielsen, 1989

ancient sources, again by Varro, who said that he wrote 'Etruscan tragedies'. The name certainly appears to have an Etruscan stem, and there is reason for placing him in the second or first century BC. For Heurgon[62] he is the last in a line of forgotten creative writers, whose influence is to be seen in the subject-matter of the countless funerary urns from northern Etruria. Most of the urns with narrative content, especially those from Volterra and Chiusi, show Greek mythological themes;[63] an attempt to re-interpret some of the scenes as Etruscan/Roman/Italic works with very few.[64] If the urns have any connection at all with the likes of Volnius, then he must have written adaptations of Greek plays, like a number of Roman contemporaries such as Ennius and Accius. What seems very unlikely is that his work, had it survived, would have given us any insight into Etruscan life and thought.

Varro also knew of certain 'Etruscan histories' (*historiae*), and from the chronological indications he gives, they should have been written down no earlier than the second century BC (Censorinus 17.6). No authors are mentioned, and scant information is given about content, which may have included little other than material relating to the *saecula* (see p. 93) and to other religious doctrine.[65] However, it is very possible that they did contain records of events based on earlier chronicles, and indeed we may catch a glimpse of such archival material from the fragments of public inscriptions (*elogia*) in Latin from Tarquinia, originally set up in the first century AD but extolling the exploits of members of the Spurinna family of many centuries earlier (see above, p. 100).

If chronicles were kept in any kind of systematic way, it is probable that each city, or – more likely still – each great family, was responsible for its own.[66] From such documentary material, Claudius, the emperor and author of a lost Etruscan history (and spouse of an Etruscan lady), may have derived the information, which he gave out in a speech to the Senate, about Servius Tullius who reigned after the first Tarquin at Rome, that according to certain 'Etruscan authors' he was called Mastarna in Etruscan. We see this Mastarna (Macstrna) depicted in the François Tomb at Vulci, in the one Etruscan painting that has any truly historical content.[67] In a complex

62 Heurgon, 1964: 247
63 van der Meer, 1977–8
64 Small, 1981
65 Harris, 1971: 12
66 Spivey and Stoddart, 1990: 108
67 Buranelli, 1987: 96

series of bloody scenes, he is shown freeing Caile Vipinas from his chains. The setting may well be Rome, for one of the Tarquins is present (by name Cneve, otherwise unknown), in the process of being murdered (fig. 38). Putting the evidence of various Roman writers together with the painting and its inscriptions, it is fairly clear that the brothers Avle and Caile Vipinas (Aulus and Caelus Vibenna in Latin) and other men of Vulci, along with Mastarna himself, are on one side, ranged against a coalition of leaders from various towns including Volsinii, Sovana and Rome.[68]

Although the events depicted are of the sixth century BC, a date for the painting in the later fourth century is generally accepted,[69] at a time when glorying in past victories against the Romans may have provided some comfort to the Vulcentines who were now threatened by them. Probably the story became well known and was passed down (and embroidered) in an oral tradition; eventually it may have become part of a local chronicle compiled at Vulci, of the kind to which Claudius may have had access. The additional piece of information emanating from the emperor, that Servius and Mastarna were, in the Etruscan tradition, one and the same person, is crucial, though one modern view is that Claudius was slightly misled by his sources.[70] Even without that evidence, the painting shows that there were murderous encounters during the period of the Tarquin dynasty that were not chronicled in the Roman accounts. If Claudius got it right, however, then the Roman historians were simply wrong about the accession of Servius: he was a king with (royal) blood on his hands.

The Vibenna brothers of Vulci were historical figures, of that there can be little doubt. Archaeological evidence provides further proof with the find of a stemmed foot of a large *bucchero* vessel from the Portonaccio sanctuary at Veii with a dedicatory inscription bearing Aulus' name (Avile Vipiiennas), dating to the first half of the sixth century BC.[71] Later, other stories seem to have sprung up around the pair, including one concerning a hostile encounter with a seer whose sacred texts or oracles they attempted to steal. On a fine engraved mirror in the British Museum (fig. 39), the Apollo-like seer in the centre is labelled Cacu, otherwise known in Roman sources as a legendary figure of early Rome, which may be the

68   Bonfante, 1978; Heurgon, 1964: 47; Sordi, 1989: 43
69   Cristofani, 1967
70   Cornell, 1995: 140
71   Cristofani, 1990: 19

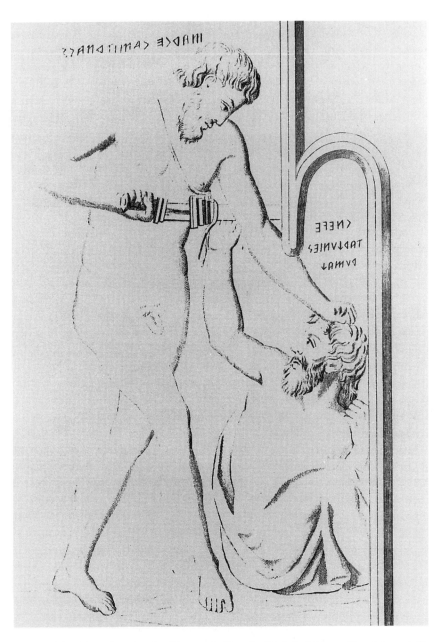

Figure 38 Painting in the François Tomb, Vulci: Marce Camitlnas kills Cneve Tarchunies. Fourth century BC. *(After Noël des Vergers, 1862–4: plate 30)*

Figure 39 Engraved bronze mirror showing Cacu, his acolyte(?) Artile, and the Vibenna brothers, from Bolsena, third century BC, in the British Museum, London. (Drawing: copyright British Museum)

setting for the scene. The story seems to have been widely known, and is illustrated on four relief cinerary urns, two of them from Chiusi.[72]

The cycle of stories surrounding the Vibenna brothers is so far unique in the Etruscan record. There are very few other narratives illustrated that involve named or recognizable figures from Etruscan history or legend, but they include the Tarchon episode on the mirror from Tuscania (see fig. 86, chapter 7), and it is possible that some of the unexplained and unlabelled scenes on other mirrors may concern local traditions now lost. If there was any tradition of historical writing in Etruria, or if there was any circulation of local epic, it is surprising how little impact they made on the visual arts.

Sifting carefully through the various kinds of written sources does provide some useful information, but in itself it is not enough. The following chapter also utilizes literary accounts, but its emphasis is more on the material remains.

72   Buranelli, 1987: 243; Small, 1986

4

Cultural Transformations

Now, we know nothing about the Etruscans except what we find in their tombs. . . . So to the tombs we must go: or the museums containing the things that have been rifled from the tombs. The garden of Florence museum is vastly instructive, if you want object-lessons about the Etruscans. But who wants object-lessons about vanished races? What one wants is contact. The Etruscans are not a theory or a thesis. If they are anything, they are an experience.

D.H. Lawrence (1932) *Etruscan Places*

Introduction

The archaeology of bronze age and early iron age Etruria does not prepare us for the levels of wealth and conspicuous consumption that were to follow. Conspicuous consumption was not so much in living accommodation – this has for the most part eluded excavators so far – but in funerary provision, in tombs and their contents. From the later eighth century BC there is a transformation in the material record, and the lavishness with which the dead were now equipped has helped to fill many museums in Italy and worldwide. Many of the objects concerned are imports from further east, from various parts of the eastern Mediterranean and the Near East[1] and especially from Greece. These in turn inspired local craftsmen to produce work in similar styles. Hence the term 'Orientalizing' is used both for the new style and the period, which extends from the late eighth to the early sixth centuries BC. Exposed to new ideas and to visitors and immigrants from abroad, Etruscan society was bound to undergo profound social and cultural changes.

Pre-Orientalizing Etruria has been the province of archaeological specialists; Etruria after the Early Iron Age is the object of large-scale tourism, with visitors flocking to all corners of the region to admire the exotic gravegoods and the monumental cemeteries that

1 Rathje, 1979

have yielded them. To the museum visitor, the developments of this period are obvious in the new materials that can be seen: objects not just of pottery and bronze, but also ivory, gold, silver and iron. Equally apparent are changes in style, in particular a new interest in animal and human forms revealing a marked indebtedness to the art of Greece and the eastern Mediterranean. Whereas the earlier archaeology of Etruria can in large part be explained without recourse to moving beyond the confines of central Italy, Etruscan culture emerges now, after 700 BC, as one of the leading lights on the Mediterranean stage and, with its international contacts, can only be properly discussed in the context of the wider Mediterranean setting.

It is now that the monumental Etruscan cemeteries began to be laid out, at first with great tombs and tumuli arranged haphazardly. These appear to have been the burials of a privileged class or members of the ruling aristocracy, for even the average Orientalizing tomb contained a fair range of expensive gravegoods. But every so often enormous stacks of precious goods are found in very large tomb assemblages, in what Italian archaeologists call *tombe principesche* – 'princely tombs'. Until fairly recently, they were thought to be a peculiarly Etruscan phenomenon, even though some of the tombs concerned lie outside Etruria proper in Latium (such as at Praeneste/Palestrina and Castel di Decima) and Campania (such as Cumae and Pontecagnano). In fact it is unlikely that all these Latian and Campanian tombs were the resting-places of Etruscan princelings, given that the bulk of the literary and archaeological evidence for Etruscan occupation south of Rome refers us to a later period – to the later seventh and sixth centuries. It is true, though, that had the contents of the Bernardini Tomb at Palestrina been found at Cerveteri, say, or Tarquinia, no-one would ever have doubted that they were the possessions of an Etruscan.

In connection with the Bernardini Tomb, it is interesting to note the controversy that surrounds the silver cup found in it, on which opinion is divided as to whether its incription *vetusia* is a Latin feminine name[2] or whether it is Etruscan – 'I belong to Vetus'.[3] Actually the answer would have little bearing on the ethnic origins of the person buried, who was almost certainly Latin. The inscription may well be Etruscan, but such objects could travel far by gift or trade.

Literacy, figurative art, monumental tombs: all are obvious signs of a sophisticated level of culture, and none of them would have

2 Cornell, 1991: 18
3 Cristofani, 1985a: 128

developed in the way they did (and might not have developed at all) without major outside influence. Clearly the Etruscans were in possession of sufficient wealth to acquire materials that were unobtainable locally such as ivory and gold, and also to support foreign craftsmen. That there should have been a ready supply of the latter is easily explained by momentous events in the eastern Mediterranean: in the eighth century BC, Assyria was aggressively expanding its territory at the expense of the inhabitants of Syria and Phoenicia, from where communities of displaced artisans may have found emigration westwards the only viable course of action. The Phoenicians were also important as traders and are often mentioned as such in Homer, and no doubt at least some of the Near Eastern goods found in Etruria were carried there on Phoenician ships. Their interest in the western Mediterranean began early, and the traditional foundation date of their colony of Carthage is 814 BC. Rather later, the Greeks were also settling in the south of the Italian peninsula, partly for reasons of land hunger but also for trade with the Etruscans further north. Their earliest settlement on the island of Ischia seems to have consisted at least in part of a mixed community of Greek and Phoenician traders. Near Eastern and Greek goods and craftsmen now have an important role to play in Etruria, and, not surprisingly, the indigenous craftsmen were deeply responsive to both.

The resulting transformation of Etruscan art and material culture was very rapid. However, art is not life; it may not even mirror life, and an artist may copy images from a model that are quite alien to his own surroundings. So, for example, the lion is an important subject of Etruscan art,[4] but there were no lions to be seen in Italy (nor, for that matter, would there have been many opportunities to see them in Greece). Further, however much good sense we may make of the conventions and cultural references displayed in visual representations, it is very difficult to gauge how far down the social scale they penetrated. To varying degrees, this is true of the ancient world generally. An extreme case is that of Assyria, where, apart from cylinder seals, the material remains (and written texts) are centred almost wholly on palaces and temples, where the viewpoint is restricted to the king, his courtiers and priests.

Much Etruscan art, however, is private rather than official. We are, therefore, able to glimpse the tastes and predilections of individuals, even if these are still from a rather narrow sector of society. This sector seems to have become more than superficially acquainted with Oriental and Greek lifestyles and art forms, and

4 Brown, 1960

much of the complex imagery decorating the artefacts produced for it would have made little sense without considerable knowledge of the stories of Greek mythology. There is little doubt, too, that many Etruscans were versed in the Greek language.

The world of the *principes*

Personal possessions laid in tombs may tell us a considerable amount about the lives and status of their owners, though they are no substitute for the houses of the living, of which we lack evidence for this period. The goods from a single grave complex at Cerveteri, the Regolini-Galassi Tomb, found intact and badly excavated in 1836, fill several rooms of the Museo Gregoriano Etrusco at the Vatican, while the contents of the Barberini and Bernardini tombs at Palestrina form one of the principal display features of the Villa Giulia museum in Rome. A more recently discovered tomb of the mid seventh century at the Monte Michele necropolis at Veii,[5] also found intact but scientifically excavated, is of this same order of opulence. It was a chamber tomb, and in the single chamber were burials of a man and a woman (fig. 40). The bulkiest item of furniture was a four-wheeled funerary cart decorated with intricate strips of repoussé bronzework, but there were also many personal ornaments of bronze, silver and silver-gilt, and a great array of locally made fine pottery as well as iron utensils and a decorated ivory ornament of Near Eastern workmanship. A long passage or *dromos* led to the chamber, and to either side of it were niches with subsidiary burials, one of a youth, one of an infant, and with the youth was found a Greek perfume pot (*aryballos*) imported from Corinth.

Tombs like the Regolini-Galassi are works of architecture, the first monumental architecture in stone found in mainland Italy. Early iron age practice had been to bury in simple trench graves, a tradition that was never to die out entirely, but now the fashion among the most wealthy changed in favour of tombs with chambers hewn out of the solid *tufo* and covered by a tumulus resting on a circular drum that was itself either rock-cut or built up in blocks (or a combination of the two). Some of the tumuli are of very large dimensions, such as the Montetosto tumulus outside Cerveteri with a diameter of 60 m.[6] Many, too, contain tombs of varying dates,

5 Boitani, 1982, 1983
6 Rizzo, 1989

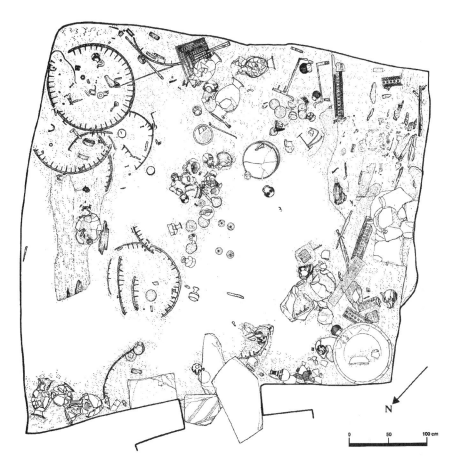

Figure 40   Ground-plan of tomb-chamber with finds in situ, *Monte Michele necropolis, Veii, seventh century* BC. *(After Boitani, 1982: fig. 5)*

and the tumulus may not be contemporary with the earliest of them, as in the case of one of the grandest of the mounds at Cerveteri, Tumulus 2 (fig. 41). Here it has been suggested that the great drum was built along with the construction of the latest of the four tombs (the late sixth century Tomb of the Greek Vases) – the only one of them that is on a radial axis; so that in effect the tumulus served to unite several tombs belonging to a single family group.[7]

The new monumental tombs of southern Etruria usually have rock-cut couches for the dead to be laid out. However, inhumation

7   Gran Aymerich, 1979

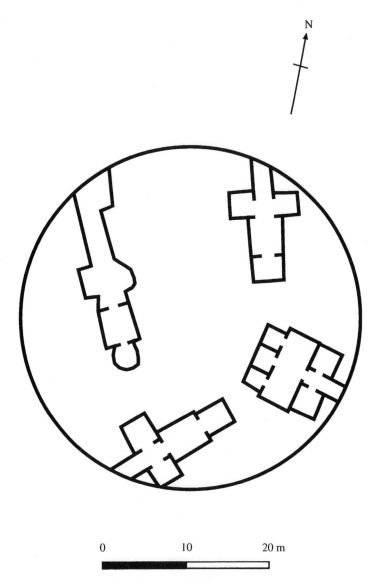

N

0   10   20 m

Figure 41   Plan of Tumulus 2, Banditaccia necropolis, Cerveteri, with its four chamber tombs (the Tomb of the Greek Vases is bottom right).

was not adopted uniformly across Etruria, and in the north, especially around Chiusi, cremation burials continued uninterrupted. More- over, in the great 'princely tombs', the occupants were often cre- mated, seemingly as a mark of special status, perhaps partly because the rite allowed greater pomp and spectacle. In the Monte Michele tomb at Veii, the deceased were all cremated with the exception of the infant. As for the tombs themselves, there are certainly remarkable parallels to be drawn with the great tumulus fields at Sardis in Lydia,[8] but the idea of the chamber tomb itself is one that can be shown to have evolved gradually from the earlier trench graves.[9]

In surveying the diversity of Etruscan burial practices, it is worth bearing in mind that 'in the vast majority of cases known ethnographically, a culture or society is not characterized by one type of burial only, but . . . on the contrary, one society will undertake several different forms of burial, and . . . these forms will often be correlated with the status of the deceased',[10] together with Binford's principle of effort-expenditure: the higher the social rank of the deceased, the greater the corporate involvement in the funeral, and the greater the amount of energy expended in the interment ritual.[11] In a sense, funerals are theatre and display: apart from the elaborate rituals acted out and the expensive gravegoods carried in procession, they provide an unequalled opportunity for the ruling class to reinforce its superior position in society and to maintain it by means of a permanent architectural monument for posterity to wonder at. Among the various components that made up Orientalizing Etruscan society, it is clear that the occupants of the Montetosto and Regolini-Galassi tumuli and their many counterparts throughout the country were at the top of the hierarchy.

In the central part of the Regolini-Galassi tomb there were two occupants, a man and a woman. To the woman belonged a gold fibula ornamented with animals in repoussé and granulation, in all some 15 cm long.[12] Many items such as this, which is far too large for normal wear, must have been made specially for the tomb. Others were simply possessions amassed during life. It would be nice to think we knew the name of the woman, but the name incised on three silver vessels buried with her can be read either as 'Larthi' (feminine) or 'Larth' (masculine). However, the general message of the tomb is clear: that on death one took one's personal treasury with one.

We read about these kinds of treasury in Homer, and we might compare *Odyssey* Book 2 where Odysseus' son Telemachus goes

---

8   Boëthius, 1978: 228
9   Linington, 1980; Prayon, 1975a: fig. 3, 1986: 174
10 Ucko, 1969: 270
11 Quoted in Chapman et al., 1981: 9
12 Sprenger and Bartoloni, 1983: plate 18

down into his father's store-room 'where gold and copper lay piled up, along with clothing in chests'. In Homer, the metal is usually shaped into goblets, tripods or cauldrons. In another passage, Telemachus is in Sparta at the palace of Menelaos to enquire after news of his father, and when he leaves the king offers him 'three horses, a chariot-board of polished metal and a fine goblet'. In Homer's world no-one leaves his host empty-handed, and so it may have been in Etruria, too. This is how in a pre-coinage society portable wealth could be used to form friendships and to seal alliances and treaties.[13]

We can never reconstruct the lives of those buried in the Regolini-Galassi and other great tombs, but we could do worse than imagine them living in the surroundings of Homer's aristocrats, that is in 'palace' complexes (not necessarily of grand dimensions), surrounded by many retainers, and in not a few cases with skilled craftsmen attached to the household. A gold fibula of the late seventh century in the Louvre[14] certainly points in this direction, with its inscription carried out in granulation along the catchplate: 'I am the fibula of Arath Velavesna, given by Mamurke Tursikana'. It is a piece that can only have been made to order and suggests a very close relationship between craftsman and patron.

In the *Iliad*, heroes such as Patroklos are given grand burials that also have many echoes in Etruscan practice. Patroklos was cremated along with his favourite chariot team, funeral games were held in his honour and a great mound was thrown up over his tomb. In central Italy, chariot burials are known from several sites, including San Giuliano, Castelnuovo Berardenga,[15] and Castel di Decima in Latium;[16] whether games were also held in these cases is not known, though they are common enough in later funerary iconography (see chapter 7, p. 245). When alive and not fighting, Homer's heroes spend a lot of their time feasting and drinking from exquisitely wrought vessels, and it is just these kinds of metalware and pottery that form the bulk of grave gifts in Etruria, so drinking in this style may be a concept the inhabitants of central Italy (such banqueting sets are also found in Latium and Campania) learned from contact with the Greeks.[17] It is the *style* of drinking we are talking about

13   Cristofani, 1975b, and see chapter 6
14   Cristofani and Martelli, 1983: plate 103
15   Mangani, 1985: 159
16   Zevi et al., 1975
17   Rathje, 1990

here, which concerns in particular the kinds of vessels employed. Communal drinking itself had probably been a part of the life of the well-to-do in Italy and Sicily long before the Orientalizing period.[18]

Stimuli for change: arrival of the Greeks

However carefully one examines the material from an Orientalizing tomb, there is never any sure means of knowing how an individual amassed his riches, which in any case is likely to have varied from locality to locality. What is generally agreed to have raised the overall level of wealth is the exploitation of metal deposits on a truly massive scale, especially in northern Etruria (see chapter 6, p. 205). Harder to understand is how and where the trade and interaction between Greeks and Etruscans took place. There is little trace of an early Greek presence in northern Etruria; the nearest to the mineral-bearing areas that the Greeks settled is a long way south, at Ischia and Cumae. Presumably it was from these bases that traders and prospectors proceeded up-country to conduct their negotiations, and we can perhaps follow their progress by noting the distribution of the Greek geometric cups, including the 'chevron skyphoi', that they must have taken with them among other trade goods. In southern Etruria there are notable clutches of these vessels at Veii (fig. 42), and their style points to the island of Euboea, the original home of the Ischian settlers.[19] Perhaps, too, some Etruscans of entrepreneurial spirit were more than glad to travel to do business with the foreigners where they had settled. One such may have ended up around 700 BC in the Artiaco Tomb at Cumae surrounded by splendid and entirely Etruscan-looking gravegoods.[20]

One recent suggestion is that the Euboean settlers arrived as single males and in the course of their excursions into central Italy took Etruscan wives and brought them back to their base.[21] The idea is not mere speculation, for the female dress ornaments found in the Ischian graves are of the identical kinds to be seen in early iron age Etruria, notably in the Quattro Fontanili cemetery at Veii. A phase of intermarriage might best explain how Greek cultural concepts became important to the indigenous population, and it is surely significant that the Greeks on Ischia not only cremated their

18   Holloway, 1994: 191
19   Ridgway, 1988b
20   Strøm, 1971: 147; 1990: 90
21   Coldstream, 1993

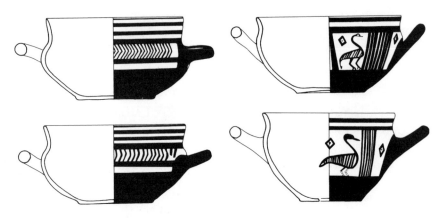

Figure 42   Greek cups (skyphoi) of geometric style from the Quattro Fontanili cemetery, Veii. Scientific analysis proves the clay of the two on the left to be local; these were probably made by a Euboean craftsman at Veii, while the other two are imported. First half of the eighth century BC, in the Villa Giulia Museum, Rome. (After Ridgway, 1988b: fig. 1)

dead and built tumuli for them in Homeric fashion but also made allusion to Homeric epic on painted as well as inscribed pots.[22] It would also solve the problem of how the Etruscans began to use Greek alphabetic writing so suddenly, specifically the alphabet of Cumae/Ischia, for the intricacies of a writing system are unlikely to be learned simply through casual trading encounters. But inter-marriage entails a second generation at least partly bilingual, and its members would have been in the best position to promote the new script. Able to mix freely among both ethnic groups, they may also have been among the first to prosper from the international trading opportunities opened out by the arrival of the Greeks in the first place. The Artiaco Tomb at Cumae, mentioned above, may then be the resting place not of an Etruscan, but of a half-Greek half-Etruscan of the second generation.[23]

Honouring the dead with sculptural form

Some seventh century tombs provide the earliest monumental sculpture from Etruria. A recent find is from a necropolis at Ceri, near

22 Ridgway, 1992: 56, 58
23 Coldstream, 1993

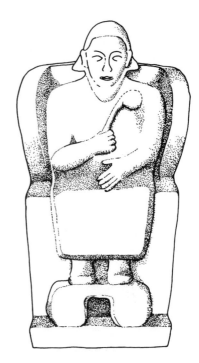

Figure 43   Relief figures from the Tomb of the Statues, Ceri, seventh century BC. *(After Colonna and von Hase, 1984: fig. 11)*

Cerveteri: the remarkable Tomb of the Statues.[24] The figures concerned are in fact not statues but carved in high relief out of the solid *tufo*, two seated males, under life-size, facing each other across the interior of the tomb (fig. 43). This part of the tomb is a kind of vestibule leading to a burial chamber with two rock-cut couches. Also from the mid century are some comparable figures (statues) in stone from the Pietrera Tumulus at Vetulonia,[25] but the way they were set up within the tomb is far from clear. A little later in date are some terracotta seated statuettes which had originally been placed on a row of rock-cut chairs in the Tomb of the Five Chairs at Caere (Cerveteri).[26] Three survive, including two in the British Museum.[27]

These are striking pieces, impressive for their early date, and the expenditure of effort involved in their execution is proof of the high

24   Colonna and von Hase, 1984
25   Cristofani, 1978: figs. 33–5
26   Prayon, 1975b: fig. 1
27   Andersen, 1993: fig. 57c–d; Macnamara, 1990: fig. 30

status of those buried in their vicinity. But in no case is it clear-cut that it is the tomb occupants who are represented. The Ceri duo are both male, but, as Colonna points out, the two buried in the inner chamber are likely to have been a man and woman, for most Orientalizing tombs were made for the nuclear family of husband and wife plus any children who died before child-rearing age.[28] One of them holds what is perhaps a curved stick or *lituus*, the other a fan or sceptre terminating in a palmette. They might be ancestors or even gods. The Pietrera female figures have their hands crossed between their breasts, as does a rather later series of funerary female figures in stone from Chiusi.[29] It is a familiar pose of supplication, and it is likely that in both cases these are figures of mourners. In the case of the Caere tomb, there were carved stone tables in front of the seated terracotta figures (fig. 44), who were clearly shown as if at banquet, a setting that would again suit not only the immediate dead but also ancestors of the family, as well as survivors shown as if at a perpetual funeral feast.

There is, however, one early class of sculpture that is unambiguous in its intention of representing the deceased, commonly found in inland northern Etruria, especially in the area around Chiusi. The so-called canopic urns (fig. 45) are containers for the ashes of the dead;[30] they may be of terracotta or bronze, but their lids are in the form of terracotta heads of either sex, and sometimes they were placed (in the tomb) on elaborate curved thrones which are known from other contexts to denote high rank. The series begins in the seventh century BC and continues through the sixth.

Who were the sculptors of the stone figures? Colonna argues that Syrian sculptors were responsible for the Ceri reliefs, a view that has found general favour.[31] As for the others, they were almost certainly more used to working in other materials and on a smaller scale, and the nudity of the Pietrera females suggests the carvers had seen figures of Near Eastern fertility goddesses; but there is no need to suppose they were other than local craftsmen. This is certainly the case with the canopic heads, which can be seen to emerge from an indigenous tradition. The earliest examples of them are engagingly crude,[32] but later they come increasingly under the influence of Greek styles.

28 Colonna and von Hase, 1984
29 Brendel, 1995: fig. 65
30 Gempeler, 1974
31 Andersen, 1993; Tuck, 1994
32 Sprenger and Bartoloni, 1983: plates 13–15

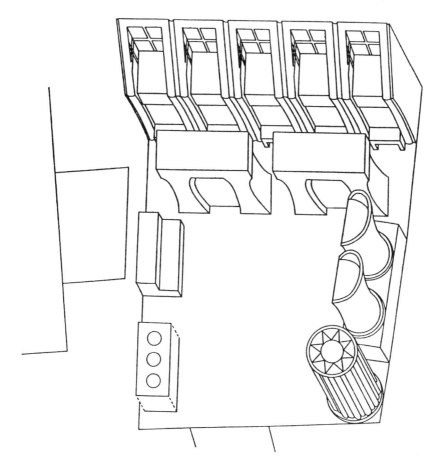

Figure 44 Reconstruction of the 'cult room' of the Tomb of the Five Chairs, Caere (Cerveteri), seventh century BC. *(After Prayon, 1975b: fig. 1)*

Tombs and levels of wealth

Early Etruscan settlements are discussed in the next chapter, but there is as yet no evidence from any settlement that allows us to relate individual tombs to occupants of specific houses. As it is, it is difficult to be sure how the typical resident of an Etruscan town was buried, for the chamber tombs we see may not be the burial places of 'average' folk. Almost certainly, access to formal burial in the larger cemeteries was restricted in some way to the families of power and influence,[33] so in walking through the necropolis areas

33 Spivey and Stoddart, 1990: 143

Figure 45   Terracotta cover of canopic urn, sixth century BC, *in the Ashmolean Museum, Oxford. (Photograph: Ashmolean Museum)*

of Cerveteri or Populonia, one does not see the whole social picture. This may also be true of some of the smaller cemeteries. There is a further limitation, too, in the evidence provided by tombs, which is that the quantity and quality of gravegoods deposited in them seem never to be constant through the generations. The staggering riches of the Orientalizing era are never quite repeated in later periods: the sixth century archaic tombs are often rich but hardly spectacularly so (even taking into account the depredations of tomb-robbing), and later the deposits become poorer with some notable Hellenistic exceptions.

The point to be made is that funerary provision does not necessarily reflect the wealth of the individual or the community. There may be many reasons why some generations chose not to put valuables in the tombs of their kin, and they need not be economic: they may have to do with a wish to channel energies and wealth elsewhere, or with changes in religious belief, or even with simple fashion. The issues are well discussed by Morris[34] in relation to Corinth, where there is a sudden decrease in gravegoods around 750 BC but no evidence for general economic decline and, closer to Etruria, by Cornell,[35] in relation to Latium in the first half of the sixth century. But the poverty of such material in fifth century Etruria, along with the temporary demise in tomb-painting, has often been explained in simple terms of economic collapse.[36] There may be some truth in this, and there are naval defeats at the hands of the Greeks that could help to explain it (see below), but it may also be an over-simplification. Whereas rich tombs are certainly an indicator of economic status, poor tombs (whether in terms of contents, decoration or architecture) need not be.

All the evidence goes to show that, with time, access in the necropolises was gradually opened up to wider and wider circles of families, but this did not happen evenly over the country. In the Banditaccia cemetery at Cerveteri, for example, the grand seventh century tombs, comparatively few in number and not planned in any coherent pattern, soon give way to the smaller, more standardized and regimented chamber tombs of the second half of the sixth century and later.[37] The most striking example of this latter kind of regular planning is the Crocefisso del Tufo necropolis at Orvieto, where tombs of identical size are laid out in streets in a true grid pattern (fig. 46), each with the name of the (principal) occupant incised over the door (see figure 32, chapter 3). Further north, however, the dominance of a very small number of families in each centre seems to persist longer, so that at Cortona, for example, visible sixth century burials are confined to a small handful of giant tumuli.[38]

34   Morris, 1992: 25
35   Cornell, 1991: 15
36   For example, Torelli, 1986a: 56, 1986b: 62
37   Prayon, 1975a: fig. 2, 1986: fig. V.9a
38   Zamarchi Grassi, 1992

Figure 46   Crocefisso del Tufo necropolis, Orvieto, where the tombs are laid out in 'streets' in a regular grid pattern: chambered tombs surmounted by mounds and by stone markers. (Photograph: G. Barker)

Pottery in tombs

Pots were placed in tombs often in great quantities. This may have been done for a multiplicity of reasons, but no doubt principally, as in Greece, for the use and comfort of the deceased in the afterlife. So now, wherever we turn in Etruscan museums, we are confronted by shelves of pots mainly from cemeteries. Among the wares made locally is the fine *impasto* of varying shades of brown and grey, and the shiny greyish-black *bucchero* (fig. 47). The earliest *bucchero* is from Cerveteri, but over the generations it becomes, in its various manifestations, the primary fine tableware throughout Etruscan Italy.[39] Various painted wares were imported from Greece: from Corinth, Laconia, the Aegean islands, but in greatest numbers from Athens. It is a remarkable fact that most black- and red-figured Athenian pottery has survived to the present day because it was

39   Bonghi Jovino, 1993; Rasmussen, 1979

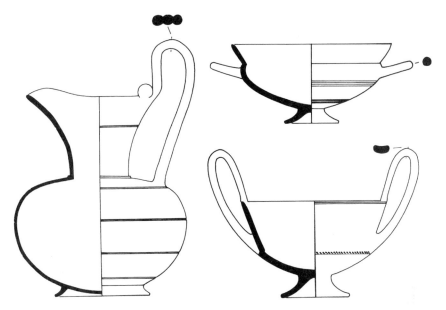

Figure 47   Bucchero *pottery from a tomb in the Monte Abatone necropolis, Cerveteri, c.600* BC, *in the Museo Nazionale Cerite, Cerveteri. (After Rasmussen, 1979: figs. 53, 168, 229)*

acquired by the Etruscans and placed in their secure tombs, and that without this phenomenon we would know hardly anything about some of its greatest exponents such as Exekias and Euphronios.

It has been recently suggested that fine pottery, including Athenian figured ware, was of very low value and was deposited in tombs as the cheapest available substitute for the metal vases used in real life.[40] The argument runs that, after the Orientalizing period, the Etruscans realized that it was foolish to put precious metal out of circulation, and that it was better to keep the metal vases for use above-ground and to place in the tombs specially made or bought ceramic vessels as mere tokens. There are many difficulties with this theory. To start with, there were almost certainly many more metal vessels among post-Orientalizing gravegoods than is apparent today, for the simple reason that most tombs have been plundered and the metalware removed. Some pots may have been special purchases for the grave, but others were definitely not, such as those –

40   Vickers, 1985–6: 165. For Greece: Hoffmann, 1988: 153

including some 'cheap' *bucchero* and black-gloss vessels – repaired with metal rivets. Even some items, which from their over-blown ostentation look like prime candidates for special funerary purchase, need not be. So the vase-carrier supporting a wine bowl, known from tombs in both *impasto* and metal versions often several feet high, has been found in a purely domestic context in Latium – in *impasto* (fig. 48).

As for Athenian painted pots, it has been shown that they were relatively inexpensive but not cheap: a large red-figured water jar might set a skilled workman back three days' wages in fifth century Athens,[41] and no doubt the price in Etruria would have been similar if not more, given the additional costs of transport. If the value of painted pottery was minimal, it is odd that Athenian potters took the trouble to copy some of the Etruscan shapes for their export drives to Etruria,[42] odd too that painted vases were sometimes so faithfully represented on the frescoed walls of Etruscan tombs.[43] And if the function of Greek pottery in Etruria was primarily to fill chamber tombs and for dedication at sanctuaries, which in both cases would remove it from the public domain altogether, it is difficult to envisage how it could have had such a profound effect on the Etruscan pottery industry, inspiring imitations produced on a very large scale:[44] Etrusco-Corinthian (main production centres: Vulci and Caere), Etruscan black-figure (primarily Vulci) and Etruscan red-figure (various centres, including Falerii, Caere and Volterra). The truth is that fine pottery, both decorated and undecorated, was very much in use among the living, the well-to-do living at that, as the site at Murlo (see chapter 5, p. 166) makes very clear, where amidst the debris of the earlier building there were painted cups from various parts of Greece, great quantities of *bucchero*, and Etrusco-Corinthian plates[45] – all for real banquets rather than for the feasts of the dead. Fine pottery recently excavated from a domestic dump at Cerveteri[46] points firmly in the same direction, as does the finding of Athenian painted cups and Etruscan *bucchero* in an archaic house at Roselle outside a room that was almost certainly used for dining.[47]

41   Johnston, 1991: 224, 227
42   Rasmussen, 1985
43   Spivey, 1991a: 135
44   Martelli, 1987
45   Nielsen and Phillips, 1985: 74ff
46   Cristofani, 1992/3
47   Donati, 1994: 100

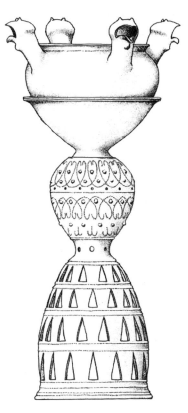

Figure 48 Impasto *griffin-bowl on stand, from Ficana (Latium), second half of the seventh century* BC. *(After Rathje, 1983: fig. 5)*

Further encounters with Greeks and others

Greek trade with Etruria in the sixth century was obviously intense, and pottery must have been just a small part of it. Most ships, whether Greek or Etruscan, will have carried mixed cargoes, as the one that foundered off the island of Giglio soon after 600 BC illustrates (see chapter 6, p. 214). There never were any Greek colonies in Italy further north than Cumae, a fact that speaks volumes for early Etruscan military muscle and naval power, but one that also, until quite recently, made it difficult to picture how the trade operated. As it turns out, there were indeed communities of Greeks in southern Etruria, not organized in independent colonies but in trading enclaves on the coast.[48] The first to be identified was adjacent

48 Cristofani, 1983a

to the present-day lido of Tarquinia, a site that was later to be chosen for the Roman *colonia* of Graviscae, where rescue excavation revealed a series of shrines to Greek divinities such as Hera and Demeter, along with a large body of votive material with dedications scratched in Greek. Further up the coast, an archaic harbour settlement at Regisvilla looks very much like a second emporium serving the city of Vulci, whilst a third is currently under excavation at Pyrgi, the port of Caere. Caere was called Agylla by the Greeks, and Pyrgi is also a Greek name ('towers'). At about the time that the Giglio ship was plying its trade around this coastline, the Greek emporia were just beginning to be established.

The Greeks came to trade, but some eventually to settle, as they had done earlier when we find the names of Etruscanized Greeks such as Larth Telicles and Rutile Hipucrates scratched on seventh century pots.[49] According to the inscriptions from Graviscae and other evidence, many of them seem to have come from eastern Greece, perhaps displaced by the Persian assaults on the cities of the Ionian seaboard. Among them were craftsmen, including – not surprisingly – potters, like those responsible for the elegant Caeretan *hydriai* made for an exclusively Caeretan clientele.[50] They may also have included painters on a more monumental scale, for it is at this time that the large series of figurative painted tombs begins at Tarquinia, and the style of them is markedly Greek. There have even been attempts to analyze them in terms of the regional styles of eastern Greece,[51] with the implication that the various painting workshops at Tarquinia were supervised by Greeks from different areas of Ionia. There is a similar and contemporary phenomenon at the other end of the Mediterranean, at Elmali in Lycia, where there are painted interiors of (built) tombs in comparable style. When it was first discovered, its general resemblance to Etruscan painting was noted,[52] a resemblance that is simply due to their common source. In both cases, we are witnessing the adoption and adaptation of Greek styles of painting by indigenous peoples.

Enterprises in the western Mediterranean

Most Etruscan goods for export, unlike the Greek goods coming in, are not detectable by archaeology, consisting as they must have

49   *TLE* 761, 155
50   Hemelrijk, 1984
51   Cristofani, 1976a
52   Mellink, 1970: 253

done of unworked metal ores. But again pottery was included, which at least helps to pinpoint the areas to which trade products were directed (fig. 49). Most Etruscan pottery found beyond Etruria is of *bucchero*, and its distribution in the seventh and sixth centuries has been analyzed a number of times, most recently by von Hase.[53] From this it is clear that Caere was heavily involved and, judging by the Etrusco-Corinthian pottery, Tarquinia and Vulci were also included. It is unfortunately impossible to know which ships were the carriers, but in some cases the exports are so numerous as to leave one wondering whether there were not Etruscans living abroad channelling the goods into the area, possibly at Carthage, Tharros on the west coast of Sardinia, Megara Hyblaea in Sicily and St Blaise in southern France – several hundred *bucchero* fragments have been found at the last two of these town sites. A lot of the transport may have been in Greek and Phoenician hands, but very likely it was Etruscan ships that dealt with southern France, and here one of the more important commodities traded can be identified as wine. Etruscan transport amphorae, used for wine as well as other bulk produce, are found in Provence and Languedoc in especially great numbers, along with *bucchero* jugs and cups – the complete drinking equipment in fact. A trading vessel that foundered off Cap d'Antibes was carrying a couple of hundred such amphorae, as well as a considerable quantity of the accompanying *bucchero* tableware.[54]

By no means all relations with the Greeks were friendly, however, and on both sides trade was liable to lapse into piracy. The situation was exacerbated when the Greek inhabitants of Phocaea in Ionia, fleeing the Persian threat to their city, moved to Alalia on the east coast of Corsica, from where, according to Herodotus (1.166), they marauded widely. An attempt to put a stop to this was made by a combined Etruscan and Carthaginian fleet (the former contributing half of the 120 ships), and after the ensuing battle (*c.*540 BC) off Sardinia, the Phocaeans, though apparently the victors, retreated in a body to southern Italy. From the material excavated at Alalia, the modern Aléria,[55] it seems that the site was a mixed one open to Etruscan, Greek and Carthaginian traders and settlers, and that here at least there was a sizeable Etruscan community living beyond the confines of the Italian mainland, an element in the population

53   von Hase, 1989
54   Bouloumié, 1982
55   Jehasse and Jehasse, 1979

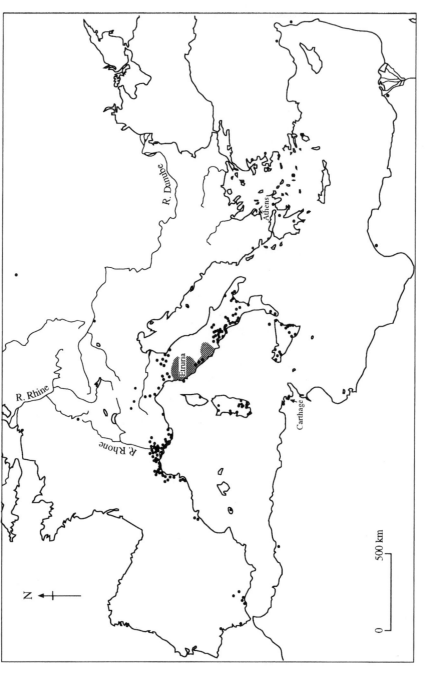

Figure 49 Bucchero distribution in Etruria, the Mediterranean and beyond. (After von Hase, 1989: 329)

that can only have become more dominant after the events of 540. It is possible that an Etruscan with a first name of Venel, who was active in southern France in the fifth century and involved in a transaction recorded on a fragmentary lead tablet found at Pech-Maho, was an entrepreneur from here; at any rate it has been argued that the script tallies with Alérian inscriptions.[56]

Expansion in Italy

Servius, in his commentary on Virgil's *Aeneid* (11.567) wrote that 'nearly all Italy was under the domination of the Etruscans'. That was never literally true, though Etruscan influence must have been felt far and wide. It was certainly felt at Rome, where there were generations of Etruscan kings, though Rome was never an Etruscan city and the bulk of the population remained Roman and Latin-speaking. According to the Roman annalists, the Tarquin dynasty lasted from 616 to 509 BC, but some modern authorities would place its beginning later: Cornell, for example, argues for a date towards the middle of the sixth century.[57] What is at stake here is whether or not the Etruscans were a major influence on Rome's early urbanization, for it is during the period traditionally assigned to the Tarquins that Rome for the first time took on the trappings and amenities of a major urban centre, with big temples and planned public spaces; by the end of the period, its outward appearance was in the same league as the larger cities of Etruria and Greece. Rome's power and prestige in the sixth century were very considerable, as comes across in the catalogue to the vast exhibition held in Rome in 1990 documenting early Roman material culture as uncovered by excavation.[58] The organizers of the show followed the traditional chronology, as is clear from their title – *La grande Roma dei Tarquini*.

It may have been before the period of the Etruscan dynasty at Rome that bands of Etruscans began to push further south to colonize the rich lands of Campania, the culture of which in the Early Iron Age and Orientalizing phase had been closely related to that of Etruria itself – indeed, from indications given by Velleius Paterculus, they may even have founded Capua around 800 BC. The scripts of the graffiti on pottery suggest that the coastal southern cities such as Pontecagnano and Fratte were reached by sea from coastal southern

56 Cristofani, 1995
57 Cornell, 1995: 126. For a contrary view: Rasmussen, 1997
58 Cristofani, 1990

Etruria, but the push towards the inland northern centres such as Capua and Nola seems to have been made overland from the area around Veii.[59] The ancient sources speak of an Etruscan league of Campanian cities, but major centralized control seems unlikely,[60] and although the Etruscans may have provided the leaders, the populations of the individual settlements are likely to have been of mixed stock: Etruscan, Greek, Italic. Such seems to have been the make-up of early Pompeii, where an Etruscan presence is proved by graffiti on *bucchero*. The Etruscan influx into Campania included craftsmen, notably potters who set up *bucchero* workshops at Capua and elsewhere[61] and Etrusco-Corinthian workshops at Pontecagnano.

A similarly loose political system may have existed in the Po valley, where the major settlements were at Bologna and Mantua. To this area Etruscans from northern Etruria brought the initial impulse towards urbanization, which is best seen at Marzabotto (see chapter 5, p. 156), and which around Bologna replaced the essentially village culture of the Villanovan Iron Age. Here already at the end of the seventh century there were Etruscan-speakers,[62] but most inscriptions from around the Po are of the following two centuries; few have been found in context, with the notable exception of those excavated at Bagnolo San Vito.[63] The east coast towns of Adria and Spina were Etruscan-controlled trading emporia where Etruscans and Greeks seem to have lived and worked in close co-operation, and through which enormous numbers of Greek goods, especially painted pots, were channelled into the interior of northern Italy (see chapter 6).

The Etruscans suffered reversals of fortune in these new areas of settlement already at the end of the sixth century, first at Rome, from where the Tarquins were expelled in 509 BC, and then in Latium, where a major Etruscan force was defeated a few years later at Aricia by a combined army of Latins and Cumaean Greeks. In Campania, relations with the Greeks worsened, culminating in the defeat of an Etruscan fleet off Cumae in 474 BC at the hands of the Greeks of Cumae and Syracuse. So the Campanian Etruscans became further isolated; but in the north, the urban settlements of the Po valley suffered a series of incursions from the Gauls, and many of them, including Marzabotto, were abandoned in the fourth century.

59 Cristofani, 1979b: 384
60 Frederiksen, 1984: 126
61 Rasmussen, 1986
62 C. Morigi Govi in Cristofani, 1985a: 87
63 Pandolfini, 1988

5

Settlement and Territory

Probably in Etruscan days it was much the same, but there must have been far more people on the land, and probably there were many little straw huts, little temporary houses, among the green corn: and fine roads, such as the Etruscans taught the Romans to build, went between the hills: and the high black walls, with towers, wound along the hill-crest.

D.H. Lawrence (1932) *Etruscan Places*

Introduction

Our understanding of Etruscan settlement is still far less comprehensive than we would wish. Until a generation ago, most discussions of Etruscan settlement largely had to have recourse to two sets of indirect evidence: the comments made by later Greek and Roman writers (the biases of which will be all too clear from the discussion in chapter 3); and the inferences that could be drawn from the location, architecture and contents of Etruscan tombs. The astonishing riches of the Etruscan cemeteries inevitably created a research tradition which focused on the aristocracy, rather than on Etruscan society as a whole. The development of Roman, medieval and modern cities on top of several of the major Etruscan sites – Orvieto (fig. 50) is a good example of this phenomenon – made the investigation of their layout and organization a daunting proposition. Such urban excavation as had taken place was limited largely to clearance operations in the monumental centres, rather than stratigraphic excavation of domestic or industrial areas. Knowledge of settlement in the countryside was even more rudimentary. In retrospect, much of the oft-quoted 'mystery of the Etruscans' was largely a product of the bias in the history of archaeological research in the nineteenth and early twentieth centuries: most Etruscans were more invisible than mysterious!

Figure 50 Orvieto: a typical location of an Etruscan city, occupied from Etruscan times to the present day. (Photograph: G. Barker)

As this chapter describes, however, the picture has been transformed by archaeological research since the 1970s, many of the most significant results coming from field projects that have either been completed very recently or are still in progress. Whilst we still know all too little about the internal appearance of the major centres, the domestic landscape of the Etruscans can be described with increasing confidence both in terms of the structure and appearance of the major classes of settlement type, and in terms of their regional diversity.

The Etruscan settlement hierarchy

The Etruscan settlement system was of course dominated by the major centres of population, the cities. There seem to have been about fifteen major centres between the Arno and the Tiber (see figure 4, chapter 1): (from north to south) Faesulae (Fiesole) above Florence in the middle Arno valley; Volaterrae (Volterra) in the north Tuscan hills; Arretium (Arezzo), Cortona and Clusium (Chiusi) in the Val di Chiana; in Umbria, Perusia (Perugia) in the upper Tiber valley and Orvieto in the basin of the Paglia valley near its junction with the middle Tiber; Populonia, Vetulonia and Rusellae (Roselle) on the Tuscan Maremma; and on the volcanic lowlands of southern Etruria, Vulci in the lower Fiora valley, Tarquinii (Tarquinia) in the lower Marta valley, Caere (Cerveteri) and Veii south of Lake Bracciano.

The major Etruscan cities of southern Etruria, which, as chapter 2 described, had all been significant population centres from Villanovan times, were – in terms of their size at least – at the top of a distinct settlement hierarchy, each measuring some 200–300 ha.[1] The next level of settlement consisted of minor centres, a few of which, such as Falerii Veteres, Acquarossa, Nepi, Castel d'Asso and Narce, were between 100 and 10 ha in size, but most of which (more than forty) were between 10 and 2 ha. There was also a clear settlement hierarchy in northern Etruria, but without such dramatic differences between the larger and smaller centres. Further north in the Po valley, there are similar indications of settlement hierarchy, with major sites such as Felsina (modern Bologna) and the Adriatic port of Spina in the upper level and sites such as Bagnolo San Vito, Casalecchio di Reno, San Polo d'Enza and Voghiera in the

1 Judson and Hemphill, 1981

intermediate level. Some scholars argue that Felsina was a regional capital at the top of the hierarchy.

Throughout the Etruscan world, on the evidence of a number of intensive programmes of field-walking, there was a variety of still smaller settlements below the minor centres. Some of these measured about a hectare, but most measured less than 50 × 50 m in their surface remains. These can probably be interpreted as hamlets and farms. The discovery of these sites – where the majority of Etruscans probably lived – has been one of the most important results of modern archaeological research in Etruria.

The first indications of the density of Etruscan rural settlement were provided by the British School at Rome's survey of part of the Ager Veientanus, the territory of the city of Veii, in the 1950s and 1960s. Teams of students traversed the fields every autumn after ploughing, picking up the archaeological artefacts they could see on the surface, mainly pieces of tile and pottery. In this way they were able to map the distribution of ancient sites preserved as discrete concentrations of artefacts, normally in dense scatters some 50–100 m in diameter. The distribution of sites with *bucchero* pottery was astonishingly dense: 137, compared with sixteen sites with Villanovan pottery in the same area. The evidence suggested that the development of the Etruscan city coincided with an extraordinary population explosion in the countryside as well.[2] Comparable regional studies were undertaken by the British School around Sutri, Narce and Capena.[3] Whilst there were regional variations in the data (in part probably due to different search and collection methods), the total number of sites rose from seventy-nine Villanovan to 314 early Etruscan (fig. 51).[4]

Further confirmation that this density of rural settlement was the rule rather than the exception has been provided by regional field-walking surveys conducted in recent years. Our own survey of the countryside around Tuscania, for example, has provided significant new information about the remarkable density and complexity of rural settlement around this minor Etruscan centre, which was probably within the political sphere of the city of Tarquinia.[5] We investigated a circular territory with a radius of 10 km centred on the San Pietro acropolis, an area which we regarded as large enough to have encompassed the likely territory of the town in antiquity, given

2 Potter, 1979; Ward-Perkins et al., 1968a
3 Sutri: Duncan, 1958; Narce: Potter, 1979; Capena: Jones, 1962, 1963
4 Potter, 1979: 74
5 Barker and Rasmussen, 1988; Barker et al., 1993; Rasmussen, 1991

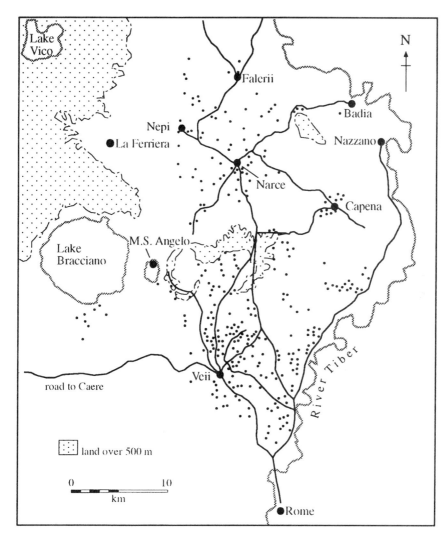

*Figure 51   The South Etruria survey: the Etruscan settlement system in
the seventh and sixth centuries* BC. *(After Potter, 1979: 73)*

that the neighbouring Etruscan centres of Bisenzio, Musarna, Castel
d'Asso, Norchia, Tarquinia and Vulci are between 10 and 20 km
away.[6]

Because the area was too large to search systematically in its
entirety, we decided to investigate a representative zone intensively.
There is a lively debate amongst survey archaeologists today about

6   Barker, 1988; Barker and Rasmussen, 1988; Rasmussen, 1991

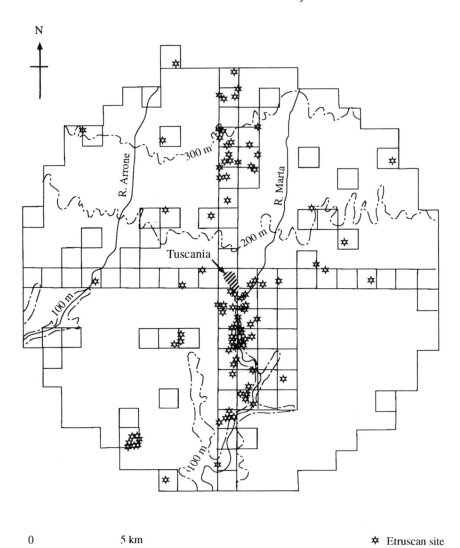

0   5 km   ✿ Etruscan site

Figure 52   The Tuscania survey: the Etruscan settlement system located by field-walking within the composite sample investigated of transects, random squares and judgement squares.

the pros and cons of different sampling strategies, so we deliberately decided to use three systems, to allow comparison of the results of different methods (fig. 52): a 'transect' sample of 40 km², comprising four transects each 1 km wide and 10 km long running north, east, south and west from the town; a 'random' sample of 40 km² selected on a statistically random basis throughout the survey area; and a 'judgemental' sample of 20 km², selected deliberately to study areas not covered by the first two systems – the whole amounting to about a third of the total 'territory' we had defined.

As in the case of Veii, the survey has shown that, with the development of the Etruscan cities, there was a transformation of the landscape around Tuscania. We recovered Etruscan pottery from 43 per cent of all the units walked, more than double the number that produced prehistoric pottery. There was a gradual 'filling up' of the landscape compared with the preceding centuries: many more settlement sites appeared, and these in turn were – unlike the prehistoric sites – surrounded by dispersed scatters of sporadic material, a phenomenon taken to indicate the practice of manuring the land, with household rubbish being thrown onto farmyard manure heaps and thence finding its way onto the land.[7] The greatest densities of Etruscan sites were found in the first 3 km from the town, with numerous others up to 7 km away, averaging four sites per square kilometre. Fewer were found in the eighth to tenth squares of the transects, suggesting that there was a discrete agricultural enclave of farms and cottages around the town – a remarkable density of agrarian settlement. When we came to compare the results of the random squares, however, we found evidence for isolated sites and for several distinct clusters of sites elsewhere in the territory, suggesting a rather complex hierarchy of rural settlement, with major and minor farms around local centres (we think hamlets or villages) as well as around Tuscania itself. The 'judgemental' sample confirmed the model of Etruscan rural settlement around Tuscania established on the basis of the first two sampling strategies.

Further evidence for the density of Etruscan rural settlement comes from the Albegna valley, intensively surveyed by teams from Pisa and Siena Universities during the 1980s.[8] This valley, at least its southern part, was probably within the sphere of Vulci in the Etruscan period. Field-walking was conducted in a series of L-shaped transects laid out with the river at their axis (fig. 53). The lower valley and the coastal plain were characterized by small nucleated settlements or villages, often as little as 1 km apart, with what are presumed to be their cemeteries nearby; only a few isolated farms were found in between. In the middle valley, by contrast, although a number of substantial Etruscan cemeteries were known, the domestic

7   Bintliff and Snodgrass, 1988
8   Attolini et al., 1991

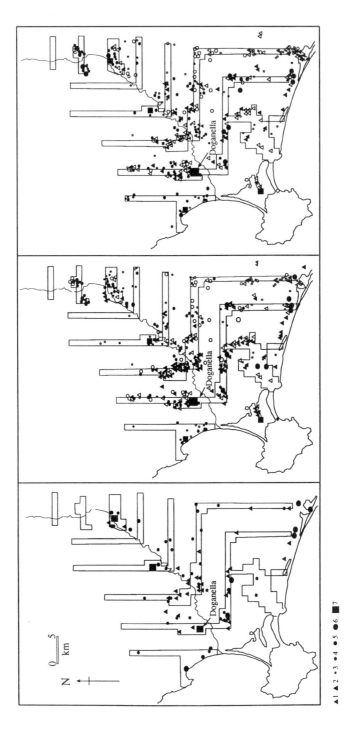

Figure 53 The Albegna valley survey: the Etruscan settlement system of the seventh (left), sixth (centre) and fifth (right) centuries BC. Interpretation: 1 tomb; 2 necropolis; 3 house or tomb; 4 small house; 5 large house; 6 village; 7 centre. Lines indicate sampled areas. (After Perkins, 1991)

▲1 ▲2 •3 •4 ●5 ●6 ■6 ■7

settlements found were predominantly small and dispersed. In the upper valley, in a further contrast, the survey found a hierarchy of rural settlement, from small farms to villages. (We shall return to the possible social interpretations of these variations in rural settlement at the end of this chapter.) Calculations based on the different sizes of the various categories of site indicate a fourfold increase in the population of the valley from the seventh to the sixth centuries BC.[9] Such a dramatic increase (mirrored in the other surveys of southern Etruria) implies an annual growth rate of about 3 per cent, not dissimilar to that suggested for the Athenian city state at the comparable stage of its development in the late eighth century BC.[10]

Very little is known of rural settlement in northern Etruria because of the limited extent of systematic archaeological survey, but where it has been practised, for example around the coastal centres of Populonia, Vetulonia and Roselle,[11] in the central Tuscan hills at Montarrenti near Siena[12] and in the Gubbio basin in Umbria,[13] it has uncovered evidence for networks of small hamlets and farms similar to those further south. Further north in the Po valley, even less is known of small-scale settlement, but survey in the Reno valley found surface remains of a small domestic site outside the town of Marzabotto, as well as numerous traces of small cemeteries every kilometre or so down the valley as far as the minor centre of Casalecchio di Reno, evidence which is taken together to indicate that the agrarian population lived in numerous small farms as well as in the centres.[14]

The major centres

The Etruscan cities and smaller centres of Etruria were invariably located in positions of great natural strength (fig. 50) and further strengthened by impressive walls.[15] Masonry below later Roman and medieval walling or incorporated into entrance gates has been identified at several cities as Etruscan, though much probably dates to the later centuries of Etruscan settlement around the time of Romanization (see chapter 8); typical examples include Amelia (fig. 54),

9 Perkins, in press
10 Snodgrass, 1977
11 Cucini, 1985; Fedeli, 1983, 1984
12 Barker and Symonds, 1984; Barker et al., 1986
13 Malone and Stoddart, 1994
14 de Maria, 1991
15 Boitani et al., 1975

Figure 54   Etruscan-period polygonal walling at Amelia (Umbria), probably late Etruscan in date. (Photograph: G. Barker)

Perugia and Volterra. Etruscan stone walling was either 'polygonal', cut as irregularly shaped blocks and laid as a kind of vertical crazy paving, or 'ashlar', cut into roughly rectangular blocks and laid like modern bricks as headers and stretchers in courses. One of the best known – and most photographed – examples is the sixth century BC defences of Roselle, where almost 4 km of walling surrounded the city area. Traces of similarly substantial walls have been found in Rome dating to about the same period.[16] Figure 55 presents some examples of Etruscan walling as shown in the charming drawings used by George Dennis to illustrate his *Cities and Cemeteries of Etruria*. At Roselle (Rusellae), excavations on the northern boundary of the town have also found evidence for a seventh century wall constructed of sun-dried mud-brick on stone foundations;[17] no doubt the same technique was used elsewhere in Etruria. It is probably no coincidence that Rusellae replaced its mud-brick defences in the sixth century with a massive stone wall at just about the time that its great neighbour Vetulonia underwent a sudden decline.

One of the best studied defence systems is that of Veii (see figure 26, chapter 2). The acropolis or natural citadel of the town immediately south of the main city site, Piazza d'Armi, was enclosed by a well constructed wall of ashlar masonry with a rubble core, with a gateway through it protected by a large guardhouse.[18] The city itself was encircled by a defence system more than 6 km long, consisting of a massive earthen rampart more than 20 m thick fronted by an ashlar stone wall some 2 m thick, which survives in places to a height of 6 m.[19] The lower part of the wall-facing was much rougher than the upper section, suggesting that there may have been a sloping 'glacis' or earthen ramp between the edge of the cliff and the wall, to make an even more difficult angle of approach for an attacker. The system was probably constructed shortly before the Roman attack of 396 BC.

For the reasons mentioned in the introduction to this chapter, few of the major Etruscan cities have been adequately investigated by archaeologists and little is understood of town planning. The indications are that most Etruscan cities were laid out rather haphazardly, more like medieval hill towns than planned Roman towns. As yet no overall pattern emerges, though it seems likely that, as in

16   Cristofani, 1990
17   Canocchi, 1980
18   Stefani, 1922
19   Ward-Perkins, 1959, 1961

Figure 55 Typical examples of Etruscan walling, redrawn from illustrations in Dennis (1883): Volterra (above), Populonia (centre) and Roselle (below). Volterra and Populonia as drawn by Dennis, Roselle as drawn by S.J. Ainsley.

Greece, the growth of the old established centres was organic and rather haphazard, but that more formal planning was applied to new foundations. At Veii, there seems to have been a single main road running down the spine of the hill with streets branching off, an informal layout with curving streets has been revealed in a quarter of Vetulonia, and geophysical survey at Tarquinia has shown that the axes of the streets vary in different parts of the site (fig. 56).[20] A more formal approach is probable (but only small areas have been tested) at Regisvilla[21] and Doganella, both founded in the sixth century, and has long been known at Marzabotto south of Bologna (see below).

There were probably public spaces at the centre of the towns, with other areas reserved for the monumental buildings. Such buildings differed radically from developed Greek architecture because the soft *tufo* rock of the region was ill-suited to sculpture in the round with intricate carved detail. Stone was often employed only for the footings of walls, the rest of the structures making extensive use of less durable materials of which the country has an abundant supply: mud-brick for walls; wood for columns, architraves and the framework of the roof; and fired clay (terracotta) for the tiles, the sheathing of exposed beams and all sculptural and architectural ornament.

Etruscan temples are discussed in detail in chapter 7, but a few comments on their physical appearance are apposite here. The temple stood on a stone platform, with a central flight of steps leading up to the entrance. The superstructure was mounted on a wooden frame of columns and cross beams, the walls being built mainly of unfired brick covered with plaster. The principal form consisted of an open colonnaded front and a closed rear space commonly divided into three rooms or *cellae*, the whole structure covered with a ridged roof decorated at the ridge, gable ends and edges with terracotta 'antefixes' and statues. The pediment, the triangular gap at the front of the temple formed by the roof pitch, was left open in the early temples but sometimes later decorated with sculpture. The terracotta decorations and probably exposed wood as well were painted in bright colours like red, white and green, so Etruscan temples must have been very striking, not to say gaudy.

Doganella, in the Albegna valley, has provided us with some of the best evidence for urban layout from the study of its surface artefacts, as the city is under the plough today (fig. 57).[22] The city walls enclosed an area of 140 ha; as at Veii there seems to have been a central cobbled street, with access to it via side streets from the different parts of the town. The distribution of surface debris indicates that the northern and western zones were used for food-processing,

20   Cavagnaro Vanoni, 1989
21   Tortorici, 1981
22   Perkins and Walker, 1990; L. Walker, 1985

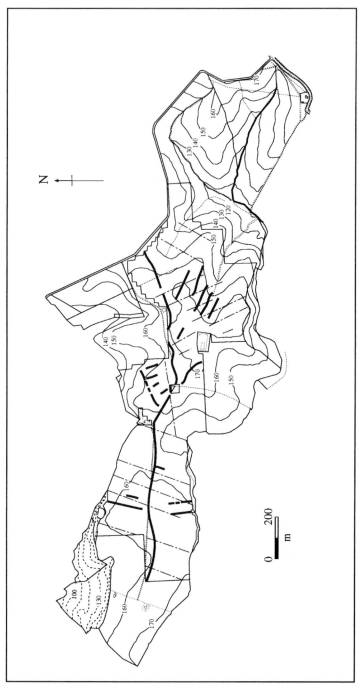

Figure 56 Tarquinia: detail of street plan. (After Rasmussen, 1986a, courtesy of L. Cavagnaro Vanoni)

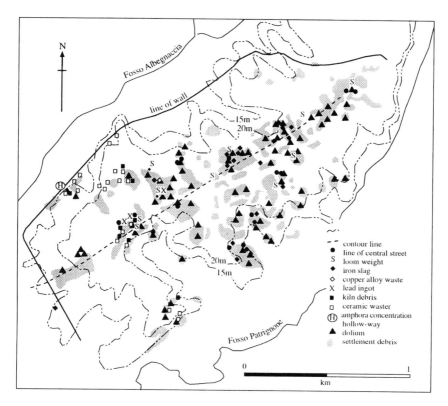

Figure 57 Doganella: plan established by surface survey. (After L. Walker, 1985)

food storage, metalworking and weaving; probably most of the population lived here, with many agricultural and craft activities operating at the household level. The western part of the site was used for amphorae production, suggesting that this activity was on a more organized, industrial basis – indications of the complexity of the Etruscan agricultural economy, to which we shall return in the next chapter. Some parts of Etruscan cities may well have remained open areas used for cultivation or grazing, like parts of some medieval cities in Italy. Perkins and Walker[23] calculated a population of between 8000 and 15,000 people at Doganella, whilst on the basis of population estimates for smaller settlements excavated comprehensively (see below), Spivey and Stoddart[24] suggested maximum

23   Perkins and Walker, 1990
24   Spivey and Stoddart, 1990: 61

populations for each of the main Etruscan cities of about 35,000 people.

There are no standing structures at Doganella, but we can begin to picture the appearance of the living quarters of the urban population from excavations elsewhere. In the area of the northwest gate at Veii, a Villanovan round hut with wattle and daub walls, timber posts and thatch roofs was replaced in the sixth century BC by a rectangular wooden house measuring about 12 × 5 m, divided by wooden partitions into three rooms and fronted by a wooden portico.[25] This was replaced after a few decades by a rectangular building of stone, with a tiled roof. On the northern side of the town, Stefani found evidence of terraced houses with their ground floor rooms cut back into the bedrock, first floor rooms fashioned (at least in part) of drystone walling – timber was probably also used – and roofs of terracotta tiles.[26] Similar houses have been excavated by the northern perimeter wall at Roselle.[27] The traditional terraced housing of many Italian hill towns and villages today is comparable in its design and – before the days of the ubiquitous cement rendering – probably not dissimilar in appearance. In such housing, the lower floors have traditionally been used for storage and stabling, the upper floors for living and domestic work.

In the late sixth and fifth centuries BC, when Etruscan power expanded north of the Apennines into the Po valley, the city of Marzabotto was established as a new centre to a carefully planned design (fig. 58). Streets of regular widths were laid out at right-angles to form housing blocks of *c*.165 m in length, with a sanctuary area on rising ground to the northwest.[28] The religious complex included a series of square temples and altars (see figure 79, chapter 7). Each housing block contained seven or eight houses built as separate units within them (fig. 59 (above)). The houses were rectangular, with a series of small rooms laid out round a central courtyard. Rainfall from the roofs was collected in drainage channels between the houses and then guided by secondary channels through a perforated slab into stone-lined cisterns at the centre of each courtyard. Other drainage channels along the sides of the houses connected with street drains laid out at a careful gradient to take rainwater and effluent from the settlement to the river Reno below.

25   Ward-Perkins, 1959
26   Stefani, 1922
27   Canocchi, 1980
28   Mansuelli, 1972; Sassatelli, 1989

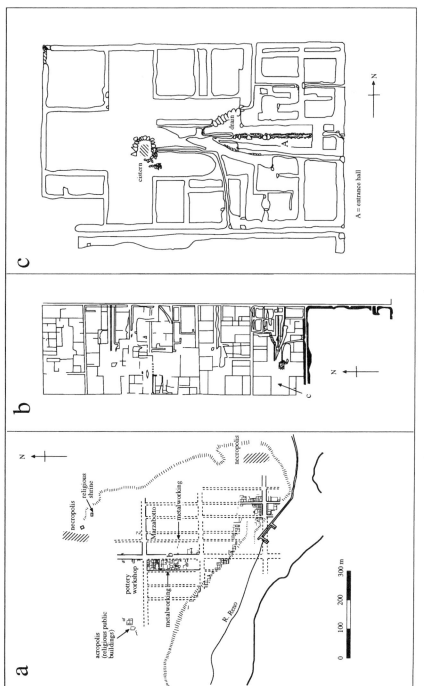

Figure 58 The fifth century BC city of Marzabotto, showing (a) its overall structure, (b) the ground-plan of one of the insulae, and (c) one of the houses within this insula. (After Sassatelli, 1989)

The city plan shows well the urban Mediterranean penchant both for grouping together workshop areas of similar trades (metalworking, for example) and for placing cemetery areas outside the walls and gates of the settlement (fig. 59 (below)). This type of regular street plan, which probably originated through contact with the Greeks of Sicily and southern Italy, is also very noticeable in some of the larger necropolises further south, especially at Orvieto (Crocefisso del Tufo) and Caere (Banditaccia).

The other well known Etruscan planned settlement in the Po valley was the Adriatic port of Spina.[29] Founded in the later sixth century BC, the port was laid out on an orthagonal grid plan still visible in air photographs today. Much of the communication system consisted of navigable canals connected to the sea as well as normal streets. Organic remains are well preserved because of the waterlogged conditions of the site: the houses were built on the drier higher ground, on platforms of timber and brushwood, with timber frames, wattle and daub walls and thatch roofs.

The smaller centres

Like the cities, most Etruscan minor centres were situated in positions of great natural strength, defended by stout walls. In the case of some promontory locations, the protection of the site from attack was further strengthened by a ditch across the promontory neck. The cemeteries were located outside the walls, cut into the flanks of the main hill or on neighbouring hills. Information about the internal organization of the medium-sized and minor centres is derived mostly from the Swedish excavations of San Giovenale and Acquarossa in southern Etruria.[30] The site at Murlo to the south of Siena, which began to be investigated in 1966 and is still under excavation, is particularly important as an early example of non-funerary architecture and planning on a monumental scale. The Etruscan names of the three sites are unknown.

San Giovenale and Acquarossa

Both sites (fig. 60) lie in the interior of southern Etruria, and so may not necessarily be typical of the minor centres that were within the

29 Alfieri, 1979
30 Wikander and Roos, 1986

Figure 59   Marzabotto. Above: footings of a housing block. Below: eastern necropolis, with town gate in the background. (Photographs: T. Rasmussen)

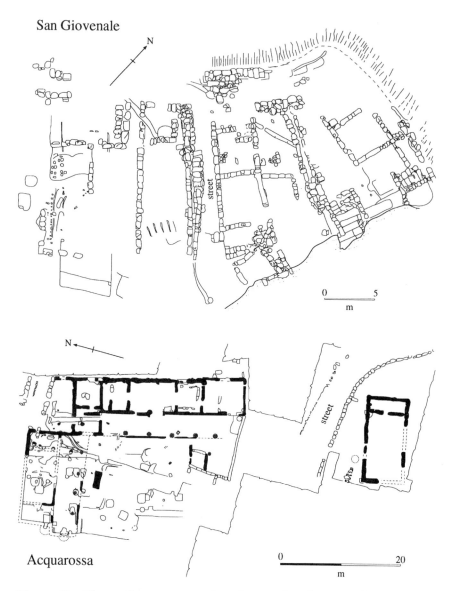

Figure 60   Plans of structures at San Giovenale (above) and Acquarossa
(below). (After Colonna, 1986)

political spheres of influence of the major cities. San Giovenale is situated on the eastern side of the Tolfa mountains and was the site of a Villanovan village of oval huts. The Etruscan settlement that succeeded this measured about 3.5 ha and consisted of a cluster of dwellings rather like those of Veii, with their foundations cut into the bedrock and their superstructures built of large ashlar *tufo* blocks which were found preserved to a metre or more.[31] The houses were two-roomed with pitched roofs of terracotta tiles, separated from one another by alleys. One of the houses had a low bench made of river cobbles running along three walls of the main room like the *triclinium* of a Roman dining room; others were identified as storage facilities from the presence of *dolia*, large clay jars. Rainwater was drained from the habitation area by channels and collected in cisterns as at Marzabotto. During the course of the fourth century BC, the eastern end of the acropolis area was enclosed by a substantial defensive wall of ashlar blocks.

Acquarossa, 6 km north of Viterbo, flourished during the seventh and sixth centuries BC. The site covered a maximum area of 23 ha, with a population estimated at about 5000.[32] The settlement seems to have developed in an irregular fashion without a preconceived plan. It was built on a plateau of about 1 km² with steep sides. In the northwestern part of the hill, a road some 7 m wide brought the visitor up from the valley into a public space demarcated by two monumental buildings at right-angles to each other, each consisting of a series of rooms fronted by a portico. These structures were elaborately decorated with terracotta antefixes and facing slabs showing images borrowed from Greek mythology, such as the labours of Herakles, as well as scenes of feasting and banqueting.[33] This part of the site is assumed to have been its politico-religious centre.

About twenty houses have been uncovered elsewhere on the acropolis, laid out in irregular groups, built of *pisé* (mud) or wattle and daub on stone footings. The more common version measures about 10 × 5 m, with two or three rooms usually entered from the side. Some of these plans are strikingly reminiscent of contemporary chamber tombs, especially the type that features three inner chambers facing onto a transverse hall, as exemplified by the Tomb of the Greek Vases at Caere. Fragments of domestic pottery, cooking stands, clay spindle whorls and loom weights indicate that the

31 Boëthius, 1978; Hanell, 1962
32 Östenberg, 1975; Wikander and Roos, 1986
33 Wikander, 1981, 1988

houses were used for a variety of craft activities as well as living and sleeping. Other buildings were used for storing food and equipment and stabling animals, the intervening courtyards no doubt being the focal area for much of the life of each household. In the central part of the settlement, presumably reserved for the richer people, were a few larger houses distinguished from the others by the addition of an extra room and a portico. Both types of houses had foundations cut into bedrock, walls of sun-dried mud-brick or wattle and daub on stone block foundations, and tile roofs. The wealthiest houses had revetments decorated with griffins or rosettes and similarly elaborate terracotta cornices.[34] Many of the houses, like the temples, were modified during use, confirming the impression of piecemeal development.

Murlo

The principal building excavated at Murlo was at its grandest in the first half of the sixth century, when its hub was a complex of rooms with *pisé* and mud-brick walls arranged around a courtyard in a 60 m square and with an interior wooden colonnade on three sides (fig. 61). But this was only a replacement for a similar, though smaller, construction that had burned down at the end of the previous century, the remains of which were found under the west and south flanks (seen in the solid lines of fig. 61). Especially arresting are the terracotta revetments and roofing systems of both phases. To the later phase belong life-size *akroteria* (roof sculptures) of standing and seated human figures, of which two wear 'cowboy' hats; these were placed along the ridge-pole of the northern flank, which was probably two storeys high, and were flanked by figures of animals and monsters.[35] Also of this phase are the four series of moulded plaques that possibly adorned the wooden architraves above the colonnades (fig. 62a–d). But the earlier (Orientalizing) building can boast architectural terracottas of almost equal sophistication, including elaborate figurative openwork or 'cut-out' *akroteria*.

Despite the widely held and persuasive view that the standard tiling system for a ridge roof, along with its optional decorations, was a concept imported from Greece, the early date of the installation at Murlo (the second half of the seventh century) has given

---

34   Wikander, 1993
35   For the building complex: Phillips, 1993; Nielsen and Phillips, 1985. For the
      statue *akroteria*: Edlund-Berry, 1992

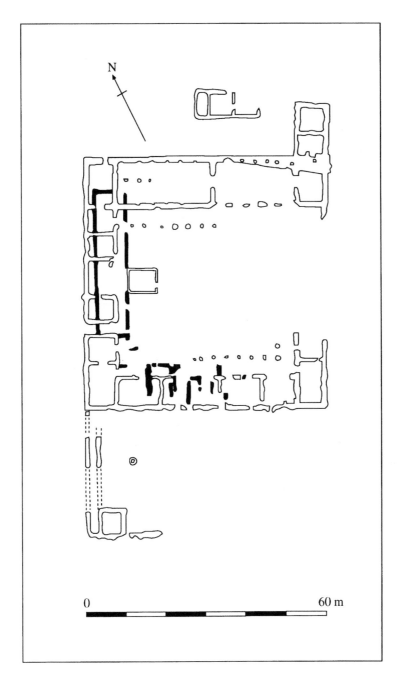

N

0   60 m

Figure 61 Plan of Murlo, Poggio Civitate: the building of the Orientaliz-ing period is shown in black, under the archaic-period structure. (After Stopponi, 1985a)

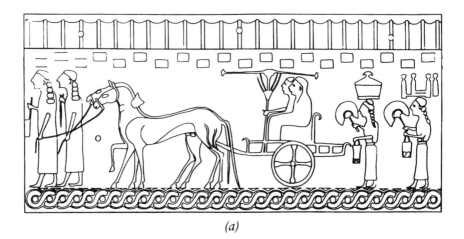

(a)

(c)

rise to the argument[36] that the system may have been developed
from native traditions such as are visible in the 'hut urns' of
the Early Iron Age (see figure 27, chapter 2). However, although the
treatment of the ridge-beam – supporting cut-out *akroteria* in the
seventh century[37] and full-scale statues in the sixth – clearly does
follow local inspiration and traditions, the basic elements of the
tiled roof are still very likely to be a principle learned from the

36 Ridgway and Ridgway, 1994
37 Rystedt, 1983

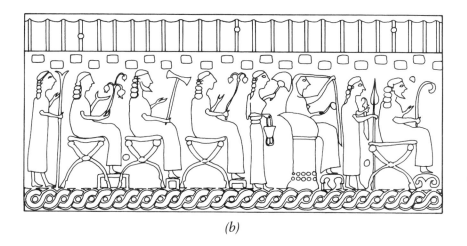

(b)

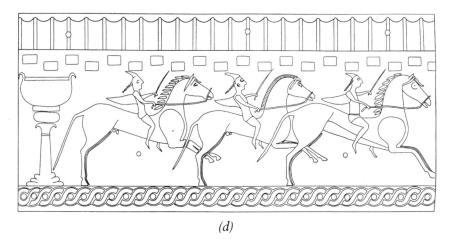

(d)

Figure 62   Murlo: terracotta relief plaques from the sixth-century building. ((a) After Gantz, 1974: fig. 1 (b) After Gantz, 1971: fig. 1 (c) After Small, 1971: fig. 1 (d) After Root, 1973: fig. 1)

Greeks. At Murlo, the terracotta work was done on the spot, for in the immediate vicinity was a building nearly 50 m in length that was in part used as a tilery: stacks of unfired tiles were found here *in situ*, along with decorative terracotta elements.[38]

The conflagration that consumed the Orientalizing complex is thought to have been accidental (the workshop building also burned

38   Nielsen, 1987, 1991

down at about the same time). It was so sudden that many of the portable objects within it were left there, including vast quantities of pottery for use in eating and drinking: more than 400 plates, sets of elaborate *bucchero* cups, imported Greek vessels, as well as large storage jars set into the floor. There is much luxury evident, which must have considerable bearing on the function of the site. Italian archaeologists have tended to see it in terms of a residence for a local ruler, and one can 'read' the terracotta plaques to conform with such a view without too much difficulty (fig. 62): his family arrives at the palace on wheeled transport (fig. 62a: note the status symbol of the sunshade), they sit in state on elaborate thrones (fig. 62b), they recline at banquet (fig. 62c). In the early years of excavation, the site was interpreted as a sanctuary pure and simple, in which case the big human statues can be viewed as gods rather than members and ancestors of a ruling family. Kyle Phillips, who excavated the site, came to the opinion that it was a meeting place for an alliance or league of local settlements, a political and religious centre of a kind known in Latium and in Greece. It seems to have posed a threat to neighbouring states, for in the second half of the sixth century it was deliberately destroyed and levelled (by Chiusi flexing its muscles?) and the terracotta statues carefully hidden away, along with whatever power they were thought to possess.

All this is basically informed speculation. Murlo is the one site so far known that is on a par with the opulence of the Orientalizing tombs, but so much background, so much detail, is at present lost to us. One of the small finds was a fragmentary ivory lion with the name Avil incised on it. Who was this: a local leader, a worshipper from a village in the hills, the resident caretaker of the centre . . . ?

Montetosto, a sanctuary site outside Caere built in about 525 BC, seems to have been a version of the Murlo building.[39] The site selected was 4 km from the city on the road to Pyrgi near an enormous burial mound of the Orientalizing period. The structure measured about 55 m on each side, with two major wings of rooms on the northern and southern sides built of massive squared blocks of *tufo*. The principal entrance seems to have been through a vestibule on the western side. Like the other Etruscan religious buildings, its roof and façade were lavishly decorated with terracottas.

---

39   Colonna, 1985: 192–6

Ports

Ports also seem to have been laid out carefully. One example is Regisvilla, the port of Vulci founded about 525 BC.[40] A settlement was laid out with a grid plan within a rectangular area of about 20 ha enclosed within a defensive wall. The principal street of the settlement running down to the sea was some 2.5 m wide, well surfaced with stone blocks and carefully drained. The houses seem to have been much like those of Marzabotto. The main one that has been excavated measured some 20 × 16 m, the long axis laid out at right-angles to the street to which there was access from two of the front rooms (fig. 63). There was a central empty space which, if (as was probably the case) it was open to the sky, would have provided the house with an atrium-like focus exactly like the classic Pompeian house.

Gravisca, modern Porto Clementino, the port of Tarquinia founded in the early sixth century BC, seems to have been laid out much like Regisvilla, with a grid plan of streets, private houses backing onto these, and a separate sanctuary area.[41] Pyrgi, the principal port of Caere, was another planned settlement, probably founded in the seventh century BC. It was connected to Caere by a monumental road 13 km long, flanked by tumuli. The port was enclosed by a defensive wall, with access to it from the Caere road through an impressive gateway that brought the visitor before two splendidly adorned temples. It was between these temples that the sensational discovery was made in 1964 of three gold plaques inscribed with Etruscan and Phoenician texts (see p. 89).

Rural settlements

Very few small rural Etruscan sites have been excavated, but a consistent picture of their construction and layout is emerging from those that have. The best example is that of Podere Tartuchino, one of the surface sites discovered by the Albegna survey.[42] The surface remains in the ploughsoil consisted of a dense scatter of roof tiles and building stone over an area of some 300 m². Excavation discovered the stone footings of a suite of rooms on one side of a court-

40   Colonna, 1986: 462
41   Torelli and Boitani, 1971
42   Perkins and Attolini, 1992

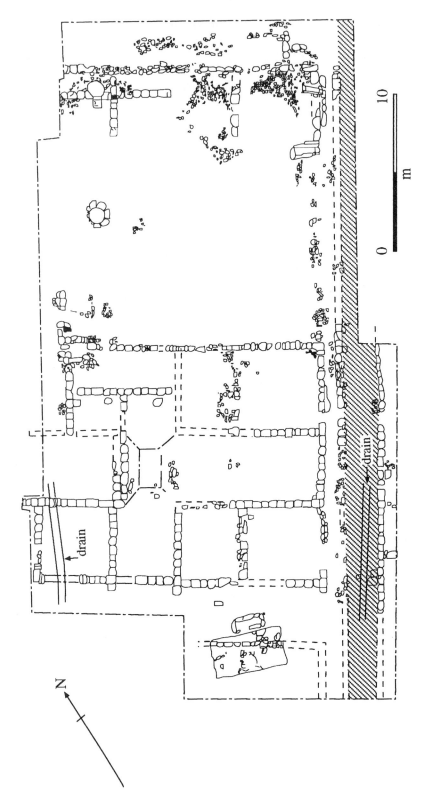

N

drain

drain

0   m   10

Figure 63   Houses at the Etruscan port of Regisvilla. (After Colonna, 1986)

yard, the enclosure wall attached to it standing almost a metre high; there was probably another range of buildings on the other side, downslope, but this part of the site had been destroyed by deep ploughing and erosion (fig. 64). The internal floors were made of gravel and clay, the lower walls of the building were constructed of unshaped stone blocks bound with clean clay, the upper walls were probably built at least in part of mud-brick or *pisé* (on the evidence of lumps of burnt clay found in the rubble) and the roofs were of fired clay tiles. Partition walls were probably of timber and/or *pisé*.

During the occupation of the site, from the late sixth to the early fourth centuries BC, the building underwent two distinct phases of design. On the evidence of changing arrangements of post-holes indicating where timbers supported the superstructure, it was enlarged and strengthened, the latter probably because of the instability of the location. In the first phase, there was an asymmetrical roof and a wooden portico overlooking the courtyard. In the second phase, the floor area was doubled, the building was strengthened with thicker stone walls, three rooms were added, two narrow corridors were created on either side of the central room and the structure was capped with a symmetrical ridged roof. Rainwater was drained off the courtyard by a system of channels. Artefactual and biological remains (discussed in the next chapter) make it clear that the site was a working farm, the size of the rooms indicating that it was occupied by a single family in the first phase and by an extended family of perhaps three generations in the second phase.

Recent studies have shown how the elaborate town houses of rich Roman families were divided rather formally into public and private, major and minor spaces, with a person's place in society (different age and sex groups, slaves, guests and so on) controlling their access to one space or another.[43] There was none of this at Podere Tartuchino. Heating, cooking and eating took place in the central room, industrial tasks and sleeping probably in the adjacent rooms. The rooms all opened onto the courtyard, which must also have been a focal point of the family's life. The general impression is that the life of an Etruscan farming family was lived without much personal privacy.

Podere Tartuchino is the first Etruscan farm to have been excavated on a scale and to a standard that allow its design and function to be reconstructed in some detail. Parts of similar structures have now been found at a number of other rural sites. A rescue excavation at Montereggi, north of Fiesole, for example, found traces of a small

43 Wallace-Hadrill, 1988

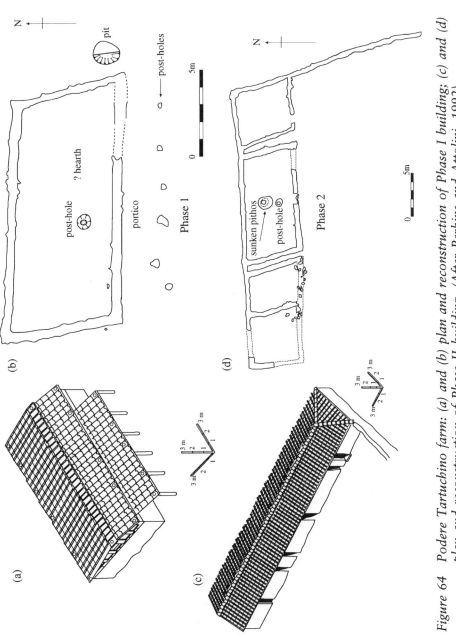

Figure 64 *Podere Tartuchino farm: (a) and (b) plan and reconstruction of Phase I building; (c) and (d) plan and reconstruction of Phase II building. (After Perkins and Attolini, 1992)*

rectangular building with drystone walls of roughly shaped sandstone blocks, the rooms being grouped round a courtyard of beaten earth, channels across it guiding water to a central cistern.[44] The material culture – fragments of coarse pottery, storage amphorae, loom weights, grindstones and the like – indicates a small agricultural building, though decorated terracottas are evidence that ritual activities intermeshed with the domestic life of the community, much as a future excavation of a modern Tuscan farm would find crucifixes amidst the secular agricultural debris. The farm was probably established in the sixth century, though occupation continued for many centuries.

Evidence for an even more modest structure was found when we excavated one of the small Etruscan sites found in our Tuscania survey.[45] We chose one of the few Etruscan sites we thought had not been destroyed by deep ploughing, on a terrace overlooking the Marta valley, 2 km south of the Etruscan town, midway between two important cemeteries. The excavations revealed a simple cottage-like structure with stone footings, walls of *tufo* blocks and *pisé* and a tiled roof, used from the sixth to the second centuries BC. Artefacts and structural details show that a variety of agricultural processes were going on in and around the building (see chapter 6), yet, as at Montereggi, there are also indications that the secular life of the household took place within religious bounds.

Podere Tartuchino was a medium-sized surface scatter, whereas the Tuscania farm was found below a surface scatter measuring about 50 × 50 m. The occurrence of very small surface sites in the Tuscania and Montarrenti surveys, with surface remains only a few metres across, suggests that the bottom of the Etruscan settlement hierarchy probably consisted of very small structures such as cottages, hovels and huts, none of which has yet been investigated by excavation. Whether or not all the larger surface sites represent substantial farms like Podere Tartuchino, or small villages or hamlets formed of clusters of houses, must also remain an unanswerable question until a representative collection has been excavated. Unfortunately this task gets harder each year with the continuing damage to the archaeological record caused by modern mechanized ploughing, particularly that part of it consisting of small unprepossessing collections of domestic pottery and tile fragments in the ploughsoil.

In addition to the farms at lower elevations that have been mapped by the surveys of the plough zone, it is difficult to believe that

44 Berti et al., 1985
45 Grant et al., 1992

the hills and mountains of Etruria were not also dotted with small settlements, cottages and temporary camps of the kind built by farmers, shepherds and charcoal-burners in the Apennines in recent times.[46] Again, we know almost nothing of these, though Monte Bibele, a small hilltop 30 km southeast of Bologna, may well be fairly typical: excavations found a terrace of small one-roomed cottages cut back into the bedrock, with post-hole settings indicating a second floor.[47] Each house had a small hearth at one end of the main room. As in the major and minor sites described earlier, water was carefully drained away from the house by surface channels and some of it was collected in storage cisterns.

Communications

Our knowledge of the Etruscan road system is based partly on extrapolation from the quite sophisticated technology of road construction and drainage demonstrated on Etruscan urban sites, described in preceding sections, and partly on traces that survive in the countryside.[48] The deep gorges common throughout the dissected volcanic landscape of southern Etruria present formidable problems of communication: tracks have to be angled down across the cliff faces and the streams below have to be bridged or forded. There are many traces of ancient road cuttings through the *tufo* in this part of Etruria. Some, like the Valle la Fata track near Veii, preserve the routes of what must have been trackways for pedestrians or mules; Villanovan tombs along its route are a clear indication of its antiquity.[49] Presumably there was a system of such trackways connecting settlements like Sorgenti della Nova with its neighbours in Villanovan times.[50]

With the development of the Etruscan city states and the economic system that accompanied this process, these trackways were augmented by routeways capable of taking the two- and four-wheeled vehicles that the Etruscans used. One of the most photographed examples is a road leading off from the Banditaccia cemetery, where the parallel grooves of wheeled carts are still well preserved; figure 65 shows a similarly impressive example near Tuscania. Most

46   Barker and Grant, 1991
47   Vitali, 1988
48   Boitani et al., 1985b; Quilici, 1985
49   Ward-Perkins, 1961
50   Potter, 1979\

such cuttings are extremely difficult to date – a celebrated exception is a cutting near Corchiano with the Etruscan name of its maker carved into the wall: Larth Vel Arnies.[51] The rest can only be dated by association with adjacent archaeological monuments. However, on the evidence of such associations, it seems clear that a system of substantial roads was engineered across southern Etruria connecting the cities and minor settlements during the seventh and sixth centuries BC, parallel with the appearance of imported goods and the remains of wheeled vehicles (or models of such) in the richest Etruscan tombs.[52] Detailed fieldwork suggests that a city like Caere was at the centre of a comprehensive network of roads radiating out into the surrounding countryside.[53]

Etruscan road engineering is extremely impressive. One of the cuttings made for the road that linked Nepi with Falerii Veteres was 200 m long and 15 m deep.[54] As figure 65 shows, the fact that *tufo* is easy to cut means that it is also very liable to wear and tear from traffic. Instead of undertaking the huge labour of importing slabs of harder stone to surface these roads, the Etruscans seem to have re-cut and levelled stretches as they deteriorated – there are examples of side ledges and steps from earlier surfaces that show this. Many streams must simply have been forded, others crossed using primitive plank bridges. More elaborate bridges must have been built, but very few of them survive: one example is near San Giovanale, where two massive bridge supports of *tufo* blocks were constructed on either side of the Pietrisco stream; the span between the two is 20 m, and piles of blocks in the river bed suggest that the bridge must have been a substantial construction of wooden beams on stone pillars.[55] Water was also canalized by aqueduct – yet another feature of Roman civil engineering that had its origins in Etruscan times.

As the description of well planned ports earlier in this chapter has implied, Etruscan boat technology was also extremely well developed. The Tyrrhenian coast allowed easy communication along the length of Etruria, and the navigable lower stretches of the major rivers like the Tiber and Arno also facilitated the movement of people and goods into the interior. The Etruscans' skills as sailors were fundamental to the development and maintenance of their economic systems.[56]

51 *CIE* 8379
52 Hemphill, 1975; Potter, 1979: 82
53 Nardi, 1985: 165
54 Frederiksen and Ward-Perkins, 1957
55 Hanell, 1962: 304–6
56 *Commercio Etrusco Arcaico*, 1983; Cristofani, 1983a

Figure 65   An Etruscan road near Tuscania. (Photograph: G. Barker)

Landscapes of power

It is one thing thing to describe the cultural landscape of the Etruscans in terms of the physical appearance of their settlements and
cemeteries, roads and bridges, but quite another to reconstruct how
these components articulated with one another as a political landscape. Boundaries are rarely neat and absolute between adjacent
communities – even the people living on either side of Hadrian's

Wall in Roman Britain were linked by many social and economic ties. Etruscan communities must have been variously linked or divided by ties of ethnicity, ideology and clientship. Political control must have operated in terms of the control of land, of the population living in it and of the resources they produced, as well as in terms of military coercion. The territories of Etruscan cities cannot have been the one-dimensional constructs they sometimes appear from archaeologists' maps.

However, archaeologists have tried several approaches in trying to measure the territories that may have been controlled by the major cities. One of these has been to 'read back' the boundaries that can be reconstructed from comments made by Roman authors,[57] but the dangers of applying boundaries that may have operated in one period to another several centuries earlier are obvious. Another has been to model the maximum size of potential territories in a theoretical way by drawing 'Thiessen polygons' round the cities:[58] the technique simply involves placing boundaries on the map midway between one centre and its neighbour, at right-angles to a line drawn between them. As figure 66 shows, there is quite considerable regularity in the territories that are created in this way.

One weakness of Thiessen polygons is that they only model the maximum spaces that would have 'belonged' to each city if all the land was controlled or owned. Another is that they have to assume that all the centres were of equal importance and the land divided up equally between them, but we know that the power of different centres waxed and waned. Stoddart[59] has attempted to overcome these problems in weighting the calculations mathematically to take account of the projected size and influence of centres. The application of the technique indicated that there were probably highly competitive boundaries between the major centres of coastal Etruria, natural boundaries like rivers and watersheds being particularly important. Such boundaries were often 'reinforced' in a ritual sense (as in the case of the Greek city states) by the placing of sanctuaries beside them.[60] The political control of the major cities probably extended directly to the minor centres – Tuscania, for example, is assumed to have been within the greater political territory of Tarquinia for much of its history.

57 Pallottino, 1937a
58 di Gennaro, 1988; Potter, 1991b
59 Stoddart, 1988, 1990
60 Zifferero, 1993

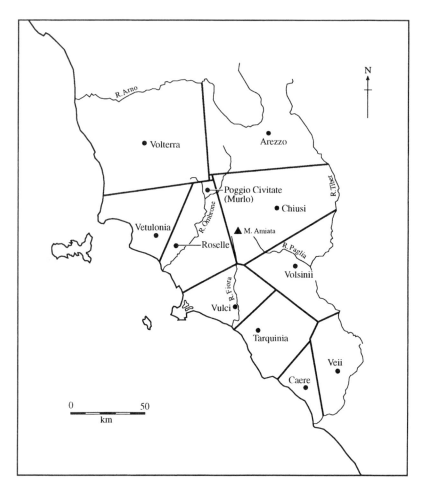

Figure 66 Postulated territories of the major Etruscan cities. (After di Gennaro, 1988; Edlund-Berry, 1991; Potter, 1991b)

Inland, however, it seems likely that the political authority of these centres faded away to leave buffer areas in which minor centres were able to develop more or less independently. Acquarossa was probably such a settlement, together with Bisenzio on Lake Bolsena, Marsiliana in the Albegna valley, and Murlo. In the sixth century, however, the major centres extended their territorial authority, and all these sites declined or were destroyed. Given Murlo's location central to the territories of the major centres of Volterra, Arezzo, Chiusi, Roselle and Vetulonia (fig. 66), and the evidence for its ritual status, Edlund-Berry argued that the site might have operated as a neutral meeting place for the confederation of these cities, under divine protection, until the confederation was abolished when Chiusi changed its political affiliation to the Tarquin dynasty at the end of the sixth century BC.[61] The development of the monumental complex at Acquarossa suggests that its importance for ritual activities may have been important in the survival of this site, too, in terms of its relations with its more powerful neighbours, though ultimately it met the same fate as Murlo.

Territorial relationships have mostly been studied at the level of the cities and minor centres, and there are many suggestions that the relationships of relative power detected in settlement networks were paralleled in clientship systems linking the aristocracies that dwelt in them. In the same way, it is likely that similar relationships linked local aristocracies not just with the lower-order populations that lived in the same settlements but also with the rural population. Certainly the parallels between the domestic and burial hierarchies around Tuscania described earlier suggest strongly that the rural population here was socially stratified in defined levels of lower status relative to the town's aristocracy. The potential complexity of these relationships has best been studied in the Albegna valley by Perkins, arguing from the different distributions of different sizes and kinds of surface site found by the survey in the different parts of the valley (fig. 53).[62]

The area around Cosa on the coast contained several large villages as well as farms. This area was within the territorial control of Vulci, and Perkins suggested that there were clientship links between Vulci's aristocracy and leading families in the villages, the *principes* of the urban *gens* protecting a *familia* which was in part made up of the rural population, with further client links downwards to the scattered population outside the villages. In the lower Albegna valley, marked social stratification in the cemeteries is not paralleled in the settlement record, which is dominated by small scattered settlements, suggesting that power resided with local individuals or families. In the middle valley, a well defined settlement hierarchy contrasts with large communal cemeteries: the region's social networking is interpreted as transitional between the coastal system dominated by urban families and the lower valley system of rural territorial groups. The upper valley has much less evidence for marked stratification in either the settlement or burial archaeology,

61   Edlund-Berry, 1991
62   Perkins, 1991

suggesting fairly autonomous communities probably living fairly close to subsistence.

This is a pioneering study and extremely speculative, but it provides a powerful argument for the potential information to be gleaned from modern systematic surveys of Etruscan regional settlement systems. The study of the total settlement record mapped by this kind of approach, from Doganella to the most remote farm, particularly when (as currently in the case of the Tuscania and Albegna data) enhanced by computerized analysis using Geographical Information Systems and combined with the excavation of representative rural sites like Podere Tartuchino, surely holds the key to an entirely new understanding of the Etruscan political landscape.

6

Subsistence and Economy

The Etruscans, though they grew rich as traders and metal-workers, seem to have lived chiefly by the land.

D.H. Lawrence (1932) *Etruscan Places*

Introduction

The word 'economy' derives from a Greek word denoting the management or stewardship of a household, but has been expanded to cover the management of resources at any scale from the household to the state. At the most basic level, economy may be much the same as subsistence, the provision of food, whereas at the other end of the social and political scale, Adam Smith defined economy for the nation state as the art of managing the resources of a people and its government.[1] This chapter, likewise, is concerned with how resources were managed by Etruscans at these different scales.

Whilst some of the ancient writers have a lot to say about how the Etruscans lived, much of it reads like a British tabloid Sunday newspaper reporting on New Age travellers or an acid house party, and probably bears as much relation to reality.[2] Certainly there is the same feeling of prurient titillation in one of the most oft-quoted passages by Athenaeus, a Greek writer of around AD 200, citing an account by the fourth century BC historian Theopompos:

Among the Etruscans, who were extraordinarily pleasure-loving, Timaeus says . . . that the slave girls wait on the men naked. Theopompos . . . also says that it is normal for the Etruscans to share their women in common. These women take great care of their bodies, and exercise bare, exposing their bodies even before men, and among themselves: for it is not shameful for them to appear almost naked. He also says they dine not with their husbands, but with any man who happens to be present; and they toast anyone they want to. The Etruscans raise all the children that are born,

1   Onions, 1973: 628
2   Ampolo, 1987

not knowing who the father is of each one. The children also eventually live like those who brought them up, and have many drinking parties, and they make love with all the women. It is no shame for Etruscans to be seen having sexual experiences. . . . When they come together in parties with their relations, this is what they do: first, when they stop drinking and are ready to go to bed, the servants bring in to them – with the lights left on! – either party girls or very beautful boys, or even their wives. When they have enjoyed these, they then bring in young boys in bloom. . . . They make love sometimes within sight of each other, but mostly with screens set up around the bed. . . . They live luxuriously and smooth their bodies . . . they have many barber shops.

The other ancient writers provide similar, if less lurid, accounts of dedicated partying. Diadorus Siculus (5.40) recounts how 'twice a day sumptuous tables are laid and everything brought that goes with exaggerated luxury – flowers, robes, and numerous silver goblets of various shapes; nor is the number of slaves who are in attendance small. Among them some are distinguished by their beauty, some by the price of their clothes.' In Roman times, terms like *pinguis Tyrrhenus* (Virgil, *Georgics* 2.193) or *Etruscus obesus* (Catullus 39.11) were the equivalent of the modern couch potato. No wonder that many modern writers have followed suit: 'the life of the Etruscan aristocrats must . . . have been . . . a round of luxury and pleasure'.[3]

Although the wilder descriptions of debauchery tell us more about Greek or Roman xenophobia than about the Etruscans, it is certainly true that the fifth century BC paintings adorning the walls of the aristocratic tombs of Tarquinia depict many scenes of people enjoying themselves feasting at the banquet table (the *symposion*) or indulging in what we would now term leisure pursuits such as hunting, rather than in honest toil. In fact, as chapter 7 discusses, the *symposion* was an important device in structuring the social relations of the Etruscan elite, not just a simple binge, and the range of motifs selected to accompany the dead cannot be taken as a straightforward mirror of everyday life. Exaggerated or not, however, the feasting depicted in the tomb-paintings did not come free of charge: the food, drink and fine utensils had to be produced, the supporting cast of servants and craftsmen had to be maintained.

We get some impression of the potential scale of economic production in the heyday of the Etruscan economy from Livy's description of the products supplied by the Etruscan cities to the general Scipio Africanus in 205 BC in preparation for the attack on Carthage:

3   Bloch, 1958: 126

Populonia – iron; Volterra – corn and rigging for the ships; Arezzo – 3000 bucklers, a like number of helmets, of Roman and Gaulish javelins and long pikes, to a total of 50,000 arms, axes, picks, scythes, buckets and oars to equip forty long ships, a hundred bushels of wheat and supplies for the decurions and rowers; Perugia, Chiusi and Rusellae gave pine wood for the construction of the ships and large quantities of wheat. (27.45)

Livy also tells us that in the fifth century BC, a famine at Rome was relieved by corn supplies from Etruria (2.34.5, 4.52.5).

Given the biases of the ancient writers, however, any discussion of the Etruscan economy has to depend above all on archaeology. Unfortunately, the techniques of modern archaeological science that have been used since the 1960s so effectively to study the economic systems of many other ancient societies have only recently been applied to Etruscan material, and still very partially. Many past accounts of the Etruscans have, as a result, offered little on this critical aspect of their culture beyond quoting the written sources and adding a few comments on 'everyday life' (in fact of course of the elite) gleaned from the tomb-paintings and their contents.[4] Similarly, those archaeologists who have addressed the nature of the Etruscan economy more directly have had to rely principally on indirect evidence, drawing inferences from the quantities of metalwork in tombs about Etruscan metallurgy, from imported Greek pottery about the nature of exchange and trade, and from artefact and tomb decoration (pictures of ploughing, hunting and the like) about the exploitation of the countryside.[5]

Of course this information is useful, as the present discussion will make clear. At the same time, however, recent archaeological studies have begun to contribute important new data that inform directly on Etruscan agriculture, technology, production and trade. We have already described in the previous chapter how the recent archaeological surveys have transformed our understanding of the appearance of the Etruscan countryside, demonstrating a complex settlement hierarchy that implies as complex systems of resource production and distribution to sustain it. As this chapter will attempt to demonstrate, we can begin to discern – at least in outline – the workings of the economic system that was functioning behind the wining and dining of the *symposion*.

4   For example, Bloch, 1958; Bonfante, 1986b; Heurgon, 1961; Hus, 1961; Pallottino, 1975
5   For example, Ampolo, 1980; Cristofani, 1979b, 1985a, 1985d; Macnamara, 1990

Food and farming

Until recently, descriptions of Etruscan farming relied principally on the comments made by classical authors such as Livy, Columella, Pliny and Varro.[6] In addition to Livy's description of the contributions to Scipio, we learn from Pliny and Columella that Pisa produced grain of excellent quality and a wine as good as that of Paros in Greece and that other areas producing good wine included Caere and Gravisca, whereas both Horace and Martial are very scathing about the wine from Veii. Livy and Pliny tell us that the upper Arno valley was very fertile, with an abundance of wheat and livestock, and that the Val di Chiana by Chiusi was another region of prime wheat; they also describe the varieties of vines that were grown in these regions. Varro and Diodorus both comment on the fertility of the soils of Etruria. Livy refers to flocks around Roselle and Pliny to flocks near Orvieto. Columella tells us that Etruria produced good strong plough cattle and, according to Polybius, the Etruscan pig was a phenomenal breeder.

Apart from the fact that most of these comments are very general, the principal difficulty is the extent to which they can be taken as a useful guide to what was happening in the Etruscan countryside several centuries earlier. (English historians would never use comments by the landed gentry of the English countryside at the time of the Agricultural Revolution as a useful guide to the structure of the medieval landscape.) Ampolo argues from the Livy passage that cereals were probably both a staple food and a key commodity for export in archaic Etruria as well as in the period to which the text refers.[7] However, we have to remember that the fertility of areas such as the Val di Chiana was extracted from their heavy soils because the Romans had the technologies and manpower to drain and cultivate them effectively. Such soils were often cultivated much less intensively in the very different economic, social and demographic context of the medieval period. We cannot assume *a priori* that Etruscan farming was on the Roman scale, and indeed the Tuscania and Albegna valley surveys suggest strongly that this was not the case.[8]

Archaeological evidence for Etruscan agriculture in the form of plant remains and animal bones from excavations is still extremely exiguous. Such material can inform not just on what cereals and animals were kept, but also on the systems of husbandry practised

6   Ampolo, 1987; Moscati, 1987
7   Ampolo, 1987
8   Attolini et al., 1991; Barker et al., 1993

and their relation to the wider economic, social and ideological frameworks of the communities under investigation.[9] To get the maximum information from such data demands time-consuming and expensive programmes of systematic sampling of excavated deposits: screening soil through fine meshes to collect all the animal bones including small fragments, and washing and sieving bulk samples of soil to collect both the seeds (which may survive in carbonized, mineralized or waterlogged form) and other parts of the plant such as the cereal husks and ear spikelets discarded during threshing. However, even today many Etruscan archaeologists do not appreciate the potential importance of this material, and collection remains haphazard.

The archaeobotanical evidence

Until the late 1980s, the main body of botanical data was that collected from the Swedish excavations in the 1950s of archaic deposits in Rome.[10] Important new material of the same antiquity has been collected by John Giorgi using systematic sampling procedures on a number of Italian and foreign excavations, for example on the Palatine and in the region of the Via Sacra, and is in course of study.[11] The new samples are dominated by carbonized cereal seeds and chaff fragments, invariably of emmer and barley. The combined material from archaic Rome, however, also includes einkorn, bread wheat, millet, oats, horsebeans and peas, fruits such as elderberry, raspberry, sloe and blackberry, olive stones, fig seeds and grape pips. Giorgi's study of the composition of the samples he collected (in terms of the relative frequencies of the different species, the proportion of seeds to chaff, the size of grains, the associated weed seeds and so on) provides invaluable insights into how the crops were processed after harvesting: some of the residues can be identified as threshing debris, others as the material discarded when the threshed crops were sieved to separate them from weed seeds, grit and so on, and others as cleaned crops discarded after being burned accidentally in cooking.

In Etruria proper, data are few and far between but are consistent with the evidence from Rome. A bronze vessel containing olives was found in the Tomb of the Olives at Cerveteri dated to 575–550 BC. The excavations at San Giovenale yielded a few carbonized grains

9   Barker and Gamble, 1985
10   Helbaek, 1953, 1956, 1960
11   Giorgi, pers. comm.

*Figure 67   Carbonized grains of barley from the Etruscan settlement of
Blera. (Photograph: Lorenzo Costantini)*

of emmer and barley,[12] and at Acquarossa emmer, barley, oats and
fragments of pea were identified,[13] whilst in burnt daub from one
of the Acquarossa houses were found impressions of barley, emmer,
einkorn, bread wheat, oats, rye, spelt, pea and weeds such as darnel.[14]
The material from the Hellenistic period settlement of La Piana near
Siena included a few seeds of barley, millet and cereals, together
with a storage jar containing sediments which yielded a number of
grape pips, probably of a cultivated variety.[15] Podere Tartuchino
(where systematic sampling for plant remains was a feature of the
excavation) yielded carbonized grains of emmer and spelt, cereal
chaff, over a thousand grape pips, a single olive stone and many
seeds of weeds associated with cereal cultivation.[16] The residues
from a fourth century pit at Blera (fig. 67) were dominated by grape
pips but also included barley seeds, olive and wild cherry stones, fig
seeds, hazelnuts, acorns and a pear pip;[17] morphological and metric
criteria confirm that the grapes were cultivated rather than wild.

   In short, whilst the archaeobotanical evidence is still limited, it is
clear that Etruscan crop husbandry was characterized by an expansion in the number of cereals and legumes cultivated and by the
cultivation of tree crops such as olives, vines and figs. A variety of
cereals and legumes had been cultivated in Etruria since neolithic
times, and grapes were being cultivated by the Villanovan period on
the evidence of Gran Carro,[18] but Etruscan farming offers the first

12   Pohl, 1987
13   Scheffer, 1987a
14   Hjelmqvist, 1989
15   Giorgi, pers. comm.
16   Perkins and Attolini, 1992: 108–10
17   Costantini and Giorgi, 1987
18   Costantini and Costantini Biasini, 1987

reliable evidence in Italy of the integration of all the key elements of traditional Mediterranean crop husbandry. There is no clear evidence for the classic system of *coltura promiscua* (see figure 14, chapter 1), which certainly was practised in Roman times,[19] though a frieze in the Tomb of the Bulls at Tarquinia could be interpreted as representing mixed crops in rows.[20]

The archaeozoological evidence

Substantial well collected faunal samples from Etruscan sites are still extremely rare. Quite apart from the low priority given to this material on most previous excavations and the general dearth of settlement excavation, the volcanic soils of Etruria are not very favourable to bone survival – no bone was preserved at Podere Tartuchino, for example, or at the farm near Tuscania. Like the plant remains, however, the faunal evidence indicates significant developments in husbandry compared with Villanovan times. There was a wider range of domestic resources, now including horses, donkeys and chickens as well as cattle, sheep, goats, pigs and dogs; systems of production were intensified to supply the domestic sector with meat and secondary products and the religious sector with foodstuffs and sacrifices; and more specialized butchery systems were developed for the more efficient production of food and bone tools.

A small but important sample of early Etruscan animal bones has been published from excavations of domestic deposits in Cerveteri.[21] The material, dating to the late sixth century BC, was identified as a mixture of food refuse and industrial waste discarded from bone-working activities. The sample was dominated by cattle, sheep/goat (the skeletons of these animals are almost identical, so most small fragments of the kind found on archaeological sites cannot be distinguished reliably as belonging to one or other of the two species) and pig, with horse, red deer, dog, bird and fish also represented. Minimum numbers of twelve cattle, eight sheep or goats and seven pigs were identified. The presence of all parts of the skeletons of these species shows that the animals were slaughtered on site.

Of the cattle, one had died between fifteen and eighteen months old (using ageing criteria for modern stock), some were mature, and some were old on the evidence of their very worn teeth. The measurements of the metapodials of the mature and old animals also

19 White, 1970
20 Roncalli, 1986: 624
21 Clark, 1994

indicated two distinct groups, one of medium size and one very large. Similar patterning in the mortality and metric data has been found in the cattle samples from other Etruscan sites. At Acquarossa and San Giovenale, for example, a few cattle were killed young, most cattle were killed in middle age and others at a great age.[22] The same trends can be discerned in the cattle samples from later settlements such as Montecatino[23] and Populonia.[24] All these sites, except Montecatino, were significant centres of population rather than farms, and the faunal material presumably represents consumption much more than production. However, the evidence implies that Etruscan farmers at sites like Podere Tartuchino were probably supplying their local centres with surplus young male cattle, infertile cows and worked-out plough cattle.

Lots of very young sheep in an archaeological faunal sample are generally taken as an indicator of the importance of meat, lots of old animals as an indicator of the importance of wool, and a predominance of middle-aged animals as the evidence for an unspecialized flock in which ewes are kept for breeding, milk and wool – in the latter system, a few surplus males could be killed young for meat, and any milk over the requirements of the lambs would be available for human consumption. The sheep mortality data from Etruscan sites are surprisingly variable. Cerveteri seems to be an example of the 'wool' model: a few animals had died in the first year but most were surprisingly old, four or five years old or more. On the other hand, the faunal samples of San Giovenale, Montecatini and Narce[25] indicate less specialized flocks kept for meat, milk and wool. Populonia contrasts again: most sheep were killed at one, two or three years old, implying that by the third century BC local sheep husbandry was supplying the town with good-quality meat animals.

As pigs do not provide any useful secondary products, it is normal to kill most of them when they reach a reasonable meat-weight, apart from the breeding boars and sows. Today we can fatten pigs so quickly that, whether raised for pork or bacon, most are killed when they are only a few months old. Etruscan pigs, like other pigs in antiquity, took much longer to mature: most were killed in their second or third years, sometimes even older. Pigs fattened quickly in confined spaces in modern systems of intensive management are very prone to diseases like osteoporosis and osteomyelitis; the absence of signs of such disease in the Etruscan faunal material indicates

22   Gejvall, 1982; Sorrentino, 1981a, 1981b
23   Ciampoltrini et al., 1989–90
24   de Grossi Mazzorin, 1985b, 1987
25   Barker, 1976

that Etruscan pigs were raised in extensive systems in the woods and wasteground around the settlements.[26]

The second group of faunal material from Etruscan contexts has been collected from excavations of cemeteries or ritual areas and consists of either foodstuffs deposited with the dead or the remains of meals associated with funerary rituals. In the archaic period in Rome, for example, the animals sacrificed and consumed in funerary rituals consisted mainly of the major domestic stock, but other species represented include game such as red deer, birds and fish. A similar range of species has been reported from the cemeteries and sanctuaries of Etruria: at Pyrgi, for example, the food refuse by the temples included domestic and wild animals, birds, fish and shellfish.[27] As faunal samples begin to be collected more systematically from these sites, there is an impression (as in the domestic samples) of considerable variability – over half the faunal sample by the Spring Building at San Giovenale consisted of red deer, for example.[28] It is also clear that the rituals at these sites included the slaughter and deposition of complete animals: one pit at Pyrgi contained a piglet and a badger, another had three foxes, another a sheep and another a dog.[29]

Where butchery marks have been recorded, at Populonia and Cerveteri, there are indications of much more standardized systems of carcass-processing than previously. At Populonia, for example (fig. 68), in the case of cattle, sheep and goats, the head was first removed from the trunk by a cut near the top of the cervical vertebrae and the tongue was removed by cracking open the lower jaw. The fore-limb was removed at the base of the shoulder-blade, the hind-limb at the top of the femur, and the main sections of the limb were then separated at the articulations. Pig butchery was rather similar except that the trotters were used as food whereas the cattle, sheep and goat metapodials were set aside for tool manufacture.

Equid bones are relatively common on Etruscan sites. Donkeys were probably increasingly important as beasts of burden in the countryside, whereas horses were important indicators of wealth and prestige. There are many motifs of horses being used in ceremonial and sporting contexts by the elite (as illustrated, for example, in figures 62a and 62d), horse trappings are relatively common amongst gravegoods, and there are several examples of *tombe principesche* containing horses and chariots or waggons.

26 de Grossi Mazzorin, 1985b: 146
27 Colonna, 1987a
28 Sorrentino, 1981b
29 Colonna, 1987a

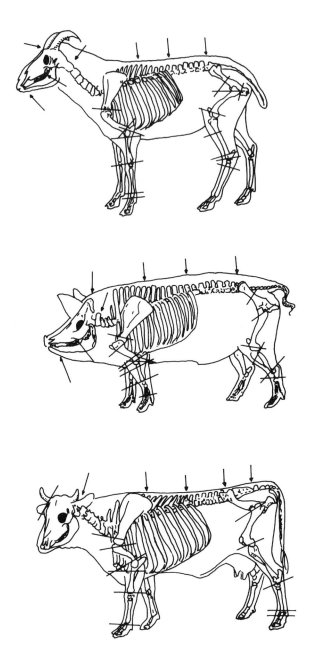

Figure 68 Butchery systems practised at Populonia in the third century BC; *arrows and lines indicate chop- and cut-marks. (After de Grossi Mazzorin, 1985b)*

Figure 69   Etruscan models of agricultural tools (from a votive deposit at Talamonaccio). Above: hoes and mattocks. Below: a yoke and a sickle. Different scales. (Photograph: Museo Archeologico, Florence, Soprintendenza Archeologica per la Toscana)

Agricultural technologies

A wide range of agricultural artefacts in durable materials such as fired clay, bronze and iron, or models in the same materials, allows us to discern something of the technology that was used by Etruscan farmers,[30] though presumably everyday technology must have relied heavily on organic materials such as wood, leather and basketry which have not survived on most settlements.

The land was tilled by hand using a variety of iron picks and mattocks that have a striking resemblance to those of recent Italian peasant farmers, such as the horseshoe-shaped *zappa* (fig. 69), or by ploughs pulled by teams of oxen or cattle, as in the charming model from Arezzo (fig. 70). The main plough frame would have been wooden, tipped with an iron share – the Etruscan plough was of the simple 'ard' type that scratches a furrow in the soil rather than

30   Barbieri, 1987a: 143–7; Cristofani, 1985a, 1986

Figure 70　The Arezzo ploughman and his team: a fourth century BC
*model in bronze. (Photograph: Villa Giulia Museum, Rome, Soprintendenza
Archeologica per l'Etruria Meridionale)*

turning it over. The crops were harvested with metal sickles and
could then be brought back to the farm in wooden carts: a bronze
model from Bolsena suggests that they had a wooden frame and
wicker walls, with wooden wheels made of three pieces pinned
together.[31] The cereals could have been threshed with a simple flail,
though none has survived, nor have threshing floors been found –
presumably the courtyard of a farm like that of Podere Tartuchino
(see fig. 64, chapter 5) was the location for many such activities.
Almost nothing is known of the technology of olive and vine cultivation, though a bronze sickle-like implement from the Lago dell'Accesa
settlement has been identified as a tool for pruning vines[32] and deep
trenches, almost certainly for vines, have been found at Blera dating
to late Etruscan times.[33]

　　Farms like Podere Tartuchino were clearly equipped with barns
and store-rooms, in which most cereals and legumes were probably
stored in clay amphorae to protect them from vermin – over half of

31　Barbieri, 1987a: 144
32　Camporeale, 1985: 135
33　Ricciardi, 1987

Figure 71   The sunken pithos *at Podere Tartuchino: an Etruscan wine
still? Scales measure two metres. (Photograph: Phil Perkins)*

the potsherds collected in the excavation were from storage amphorae. Spikelets of spelt in the main workroom at Podere Tartuchino
indicate that food was prepared there, since spelt is stored in the
husk and only roasted and stripped prior to cooking. The Etruscans
used simple saddle querns to grind their grain.[34]

Podere Tartuchino has also provided the clearest evidence for
wine-processing. At the centre of the main workroom was a large
sunken *pithos* or *dolium* (fig. 71), with its external surface covered
in a slip to make it more waterproof. Lipid analysis of the clay also
indicated that the interior had been sealed with a softwood resin.
Scenes on Attic black-figure vases show that the Greeks used sunken
storage jars of this kind in wine-making, and a *pithos* sherd from
Gravisca with the word *vinun* scratched on it indicates similar use
in Etruscan times.[35] The Roman agronomists tell us that sunken
storage jars of this kind were used for the second fermentation of
wine and for the storage of wine, oil and dregs.[36] Two stone footings

34   Barbieri, 1987a: 143
35   Cristofani, 1985c: 143
36   White, 1970: 145–6

and a post close to the Podere Tartuchino *pithos* may be traces of the supporting structure for a beam press. A small hearth beside it may also have been associated with wine-making if the Etruscans made reduced wine of the kind described by Columella (2.21).

We must assume that the technology for olive oil production was somewhat similar, though the Podere Tartuchino *pithos* cannot have been used for storing oil as the resin would have reacted with it to produce acidic oil.[37] On the other hand, it could have been used for other agricultural processes including cheese-making, washing wool, or storing grain or water. A sunken *dolium* was also found in the small farm we excavated near Tuscania,[38] and pressing equipment for oil or wine has been identified at Blera.[39] Rooms containing hearths and *pithoi* have also been found at Veii[40] and at Lavinium south of Rome.[41]

Many activities of traditional animal husbandry in the Mediterranean require little complex technology. If animals are not kept in fenced or walled enclosures, they mainly need to be taken out each day to grazing areas and guarded to protect them from predators (or thieves!) and to keep them away from crops. In the mountains of central Italy today, for example, much of the technology of shepherding still consists of organic materials that would not survive archaeologically: night pens made of rope, a wooden yoke to restrain the ewe at milking and a wooden stool for the shepherd, wooden utensils for stirring the boiling milk during cheese-making, wooden frames for the cheeses and wicker baskets for the *ricotta* or curd cheese.[42]

The main workroom at Podere Tartuchino had a large rectangular hearth of beaten clay bounded on at least three sides (the fourth was damaged) by low clay walls, the whole structure reddened by fire. The hearth had been re-cut on many occasions, presumably when ashes were removed. Three small stakeholes nearby may be the traces of associated equipment such as a tripod. It may not be too fanciful to suggest that this part of the farm was where sheep's milk was heated for making *pecorino* cheese. Pottery vessels with internal ledges of a kind first manufactured in the Bronze Age are thought to have been used for boiling sheep's milk, and sherds with perforations could be from strainer vessels also associated with

37 Heron and Pollard, 1988: 430
38 Grant et al., 1992
39 Ricciardi, 1987
40 Stefani, 1922
41 Giuliani and Sommella, 1977
42 Barker and Grant, 1991

cheese-making. One of the motifs carved into the *tufo* columns of the Tomb of the Reliefs at Cerveteri has been interpreted as a wicker *ricotta* basket,[43] though it is more commonly identified as a cushion![44] The most common artefacts associated with animal husbandry from Etruscan sites are spindle whorls and loom weights. An iron billhook[45] is identical to those used by Italian peasants today to cut leaf fodder for their cattle, though it could also have been used for pruning vines.

In addition to the fixed open hearths found at Podere Tartuchino and, for example, at Acquarossa, a number of portable clay ovens and cooking stands are also known, as well as the elaborate metal braziers, griddles and firedogs from tombs.[46] Kitchen equipment represented in the Tomb of the Reliefs includes a pan suspended on a tripod, a pestle and a meat-chopper.[47]

The agricultural economy

Although the archaeological data are still limited, they demonstrate an extraordinary transformation in the scale and intensity of Etruscan agricultural systems compared with those of Villanovan times.[48] The agricultural economy that emerged from these developments consisted of three distinct but interlinked activities: increased production of staple foods to sustain the greatly increased population, both rural and urban; the production of luxury commodities to support the lifestyles of the elites and differentiate them from the rest of the population; and the creation of surplus commodities in both of the above sectors for exchange and trade.

All the major components of pre-modern Mediterranean agriculture were now exploited. Polyculture using all these resources allowed a wider range of soils and topographies than hitherto to be exploited efficiently, offering to most farmers the potential to produce more from the same land in their vicinity. There are other indications of intensification in production: the archaeobotanical evidence, for example, shows that the principle of growing cereals and legumes in rotation to maintain soil fertility was understood

43   Heurgon, 1964: 170
44   Blanck, 1987; Blanck and Proietti, 1986
45   Barbieri, 1987a: 144
46   Cristofani, 1985a; Scheffer, 1987b
47   Blanck, 1987
48   Forni, 1989

and was being practised, whilst the faunal samples indicate that greater emphasis was placed on producing secondary products from livestock in addition to meat, so that – as with the crops – the same land could be used in a more productive way.

It is extremely difficult, if not impossible, to estimate the yields achieved by Etruscan farmers. One approach often used by ancient historians has consisted simply of reading back yields obtained by farmers at the turn of this century, an exercise that has generally indicated extremely low yields for cereals of three to four times the amount of seed sown, a harvest of about three quintals per hectare.[49] As Halstead has pointed out, however,[50] such farming was often characterized by large-scale but extensive (low input/low output) systems of exploitation rather than the small-scale but intensive (high input/high output) systems that we know were often practised by small farmers in antiquity. On the evidence of the archaeobotanical data that the ancient Greeks practised cereal/legume rotation and manuring, Garnsey has argued that classical Greek farmers probably achieved cereal yields of five to six times the amount of seed sown, yielding perhaps eight to twelve quintals per hectare.[51] Given the same archaeobotanical evidence from Etruria, the figures are probably a much better guide to Etruscan yields than those cited by Ampolo, who assumed a primitive agricultural system based on fallowing.[52]

It is important to remember the dietary implications of such statements about increased efficiency and production in Etruscan cereal farming. A trace element analysis of Etruscan human skeletons has indicated an increase in vegetable foods and a decrease in animal products in the diet from the archaic to the Hellenistic periods,[53] a trend that accompanied earlier processes of urbanization and rising population levels in Egypt and Greece.[54] The teeth of some forty individuals from Tarquinia were characterized by heavy wear from poorly ground flour and dental caries indicative of a cereal-dominated diet short of the vitamins that would have been provided by vegetables and root crops.[55] Much the same was true of a hundred skeletons from Chiusi, mostly of Hellenistic date: the state of their teeth indicated that they consumed 'large mouthfuls, raw

49   Barbagallo, 1904
50   Halstead, 1987
51   Garnsey, 1992
52   Ampolo, 1980
53   Fornaciari and Mallegni, 1987
54   Hillson, 1979; Renfrew, 1972
55   Bartoli et al., 1989–90

for the most part, and requiring lengthy chewing'[56] – rather a striking insight into Etruscan table manners! Some of the skeletons from elite graves in Tarquinia, Capodimonte and Civita Castellana have teeth crowned and bridged with light gold fittings.[57] For many ordinary Etruscans, like most Roman and medieval peasants in Italy, animal protein probably had to be derived increasingly from cheese and preserved meats, religious festivals presenting a welcome opportunity to alleviate their diet with fresh meat.

Perkins and Attolini[58] used the size of the Podere Tartuchino *pithos,* together with annual production and processing figures cited by Roman writers, to calculate that the equipment used flat-out for five or six fermentations would have been able to produce between about 1500 and 2000 litres of wine a year. If ancient Etruscans drank more or less the same as modern Italian farmers (a total unquantifiable, it has to be admitted!), this would have yielded a surplus of about 1250 litres over and above the requirements of the household, which they estimate on other grounds to have consisted of about four adults. Even with only one fermentation, there would still have been a modest surplus. The recommended planting densities given by Roman agronomists suggest that the farm had the capacity to process the harvest of about 3 ha of vines.

To the above evidence for intensification in production must be added the evidence discussed in the last chapter for a substantial expansion in the zone of cultivation. The Veii, Tuscania and Albegna Valley surveys all provide evidence for a dramatic increase in the numbers of Etruscan rural sites compared with previous periods.[59] At Tuscania, too, the spreads of 'off-site' material (which, whether or not a result of manuring, is almost certainly a measure of land use) suggest that archaic Etruscan land use was not only more extensive in area but also more intensive in its techniques than that of late prehistoric times (fig. 72). It is also noteworthy that the trends noted by the archaeological surveys coincide with palynological and geomorphological evidence for increased levels of forest clearance and soil erosion at this time (see chapter 1, p. 41).

For the territory of Veii, Potter concluded from the density of Etruscan rural settlement that 'there can be no doubt that most of the land was under cultivation or grazing by the sixth century',[60]

56 Capasso, 1982: 191
57 Corrucini and Pacciani, 1991
58 Perkins and Attolini, 1992: 127–8
59 Barker et al., 1993; Perkins, 1991, and in press; Potter, 1979
60 Potter, 1979: 76

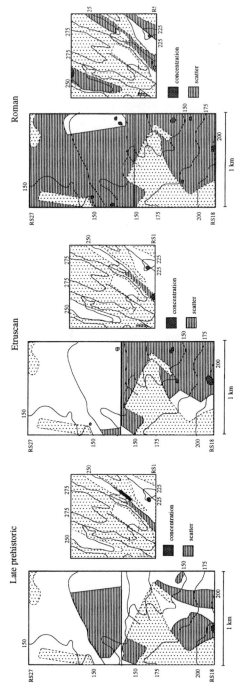

Figure 72   Changing patterns of settlement and land use in three typical square kilometres investigated by the Tuscania survey. Grey stippling covers areas that could not be walked because of dense vegetation; the white areas were walked but devoid of settlement material of the period in question; contours are in metres. (After Barker et al., 1993)

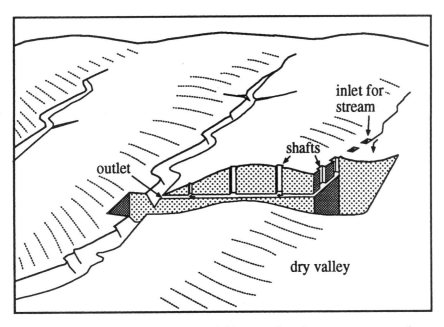

Figure 73 Diagram illustrating a field cuniculus *diverting a stream from one valley to another. (After Judson and Kahane, 1963)*

but this view is probably exaggerated. In the Albegna valley, for example, the densities of Etruscan settlement are such that each site has a theoretical maximum territory of about 120 ha, but Perkins and Attolini calculated that the Podere Tartuchino farm may only have been cultivating a tenth of that, so even allowing for the community's needs for pasture and woodland, there must still have been tracts of land between the farms that was little if at all exploited.[61]

Perhaps the most remarkable indicators of the scale of change in Etruscan farming compared with previous land use are the *cuniculi* (fig. 73). A horizontal shaft would be driven through the hillside, and a series of vertical shafts cut down to join it at intervals of 25–30 m to provide further drainage. Judson and Kahane listed more than seventy examples, many of them several hundred metres long and the longest measuring 5600 m.[62] The technology was mainly developed in the primary *tufo* area of southern Etruria and the Alban Hills south of Rome.[63] These remarkable feats of engineering

61 Perkins and Attolini, 1992
62 Judson and Kahane, 1963
63 Ravelli and Howarth, 1988

were substantial public works, and it must be significant that most
are in the vicinity of major sites like Veii. Some tunnels seem to
have been designed primarily as aqueducts to carry drinking water
to centres of population. Most, however, seem to have been cut in
order to drain waterlogged clays that would otherwise have been
difficult to cultivate, by diverting one valley's stream away from it
into another valley.

The expansion of the cultivation zone and intensification in systems of crop husbandry were probably paralleled in the pastoral
sector too. We have already seen indications of this in the faunal
evidence: although the amount of specialization should certainly not
be exaggerated, the faunal samples from the Etruscan centres discussed earlier are significantly different in their species frequencies,
age structures and butchery systems from those from Villanovan
sites and suggest the development of different systems of stock-
keeping, some geared more to producing meat and cheese, others to
wool. Long-distance transhumance is first documented for central
Italy by the Roman authors in the second and first centuries BC.
Given the scale of expansion and intensification in other aspects of
Etruscan farming, however, it is possible that this kind of specialized pastoralism also had its origins in Etruscan systems of animal
husbandry. Certainly the pollen diagrams indicate the same trends
towards more open vegetation on uplands as well as on the lowlands,[64] and Etruscan settlements in the mountains have the same evidence for substantial architecture, large fixed hearths and numbers of
spindle whorls and loom weights as the lowland farms.[65] Some of
the Etruscan and Italic 'garrison' sites identified away from the main
settlement areas on the Maremma and in the uplands[66] may well have
had a dual function, like the medieval castles that were often established beside them, in both demarcating territorial boundaries and
protecting access to the pastures and woods of the frontier zone.

It has traditionally been argued that both olives and vines were
introduced to the Etruscans by the Greeks.[67] Clearly this cannot
have been the case with the grape, and may not have been the case
with the olive – wild olives were certainly native to Italy. Whether
imported or developed locally, however, the significant fact is that
olive as well as vine cultivation became an important component of

64 Cruise, 1991
65 Vinicio Gentili, 1988
66 Bonomi Ponzi, 1985; Colonna, 1986: 462
67 Boardman, 1976; Vallet, 1962

Etruria's crop husbandry only at this time and not earlier. Olive oil was an essential commodity in classical antiquity not only for its dietary contribution but also for washing, ointment, perfume and illumination. Perfume vases and lamps for oil were being manufactured in Etruria by the end of the seventh century BC. However, the restriction of these and of large oil storage amphorae (often imported rather than locally manufactured) to the 'princely tombs' indicates the prestige value of olive oil in archaic Etruscan society. Wine, too, was obviously essential for the elite's *symposion* (see fig. 62c, chapter 5), its consumption associated with elaborate rituals that required expensive drinking vessels of metal or the highest-quality pottery. In time, the products of polyculture became more accessible to the lower sectors of Etruscan society (including the Podere Tartuchino farmers, presumably), but it is clear that their initial importance was primarily as a prestige product for the Etruscan elite.

The same was probably true of high-quality textiles, which were essential to clothe the Etruscan elite[68] – we must presume that ordinary people wore simple homespun clothing. The role of fine textiles in covering the walls and ceilings of high-status dwellings, too, is implicit in the tomb-paintings.

Hunting and fishing

There are numerous striking representations of hunting in Etruscan art.[69] Whilst they cannot be taken as simple representations of everyday life, the art serves to emphasize the social importance of blood sports, particularly deer- and boar-hunting, for young Etruscan males (see chapter 7). A model chariot in bronze from Bisenzio dated to the eighth century BC has a realistic representation of a huntsman equipped with a bow and arrow in pursuit of a boar. The fifth century BC Tomb of the Hunter at Tarquinia is taken to represent a lavishly decorated tent set up in an idealized landscape: on one wall hang the hunting trophies like deer's feet and wild ducks, whilst a fawn grazes quietly in the background. In the Tomb of Hunting and Fishing dated to about 510 BC, young nobles on horseback return from the hunt, accompanied by their dogs, servants and the game they have captured, and another scene shows line-fishing from a rowing boat in a lake or sea (see fig. 102) and fowling (bird-hunting) with a sling.

68 Bonfante, 1975
69 Camporeale, 1984

There is a famous description of Etruscan hunting methods by Aelian in his work *On Animals*, which is charming if no doubt as far from the truth as his other reporting on Etruscan habits:

they lay out nets and other snares destined to trap the beasts. Then a practised flute player arrives, who tries to give his melody the most flowing possible sound, taking the greatest pains with the harmony; he plays that music for the flute which is softest. In the calm and the silence, the sound easily ranges over hilltops, valleys and woodlands . . . into the animals' dens. When the music first reaches their ears, it stuns them and fills them with fear; then the true and invincible pleasure that the music brings seizes them, and, filled with it, they forget their young and their lairs. Although beasts seldom like to be separated from the places of their birth, in Etruria they are torn away as if by a magic enchantment, and the fascination exerted on them by the melody draws them into the nets, victims of the music.

A far cry from the Unspeakable in pursuit of the Uneatable across the English countryside!

It is difficult to judge whether or not hunting made an important contribution to the elite diet, but an analogy with Roman and medieval England may be instructive. Hunting was an important activity for English medieval nobles as for Etruscans, and the faunal samples from their castles have unusually high frequencies of game and fowl, whereas in Roman Britain (as in Roman Italy) elite diet was marked more by young domestic stock such as suckling pig and veal. Grant argues that the difference can be understood better in terms of the requirements of the overall economic system than merely in terms of fashion and taste.[70] With medieval farming visibly under strain to feed the rapidly expanding population, the rural economy could not afford to 'waste' young stock as an elite food, so the elites had to look to wild resources instead as a way of marking their status. In part at least, Etruscan elite hunting may have developed its undoubted importance in social life in a rather comparable reaction to the intensification of the agricultural system.

At the other end of the scale, the small-scale but repeated occurrences of wild foods on the domestic sites (fruits and nuts, large game like deer and small game like hare and tortoise) suggest that ordinary Etruscans made as full a use of the seasonal resources of the Etruscan countryside as present-day Italians, to break the monotony of the everyday staples. It would be nice to think that, like modern Tuscans, even the most *obesus Etruscus* went thrashing about the woods at dawn in the mushroom season.

70 Grant, 1988

Domestic technologies

Inevitably, we know least about everyday technology, which we assume was dominated by wood, leather, bark, woven basketry and the like, and most about the finest craft products in durable materials. Even the equipment represented on the walls of the Tomb of the Reliefs at Cerveteri includes wooden beds and chests, a leather satchel and purse, and a hemp rope and slings, as well as pottery and bronze crockery and bronze and iron armour, weapons and tools.[71]

Timber of all kinds and sizes was involved in house (and indeed temple) construction: cylindrical uprights (as substantial as modern telegraph poles) to make up the main frame, long squared cross beams and rafters to support the massive roof tiles, and the smaller uprights and interleaving withies for wattle and daub walls. In the countryside, the ploughs, carts, hand tools, cheese-making equipment, grain sieves and so on involved a similar range of timber. Large quantities of timber must also have been necessary for heating homes, cooking and many household crafts (quite apart from the massive needs of the major pottery and metal kilns), and the fire technology available – open hearths, closed hearths, portable ovens and cooking stands, metal braziers – shows that both firewood and prepared charcoal must have been used. We must assume that the majority of the timber required for everyday purposes was obtained in the vicinity of settlements, though it is conceivable that there were also specialist charcoal-burners to supply the major centres of population.

Another mainstay of domestic technology was clay, which was needed for floors, wall mortar, benching, ovens, cooking stands, walls and roof tiles, as well as for pottery and a wide variety of small implements like loom and net weights, spindle whorls and so on. Prodigious quantities of clay go into a wattle and daub wall or a tiled roof: Ammerman and Schaffer, for example, have calculated that some 7 tons would be needed to wall a small rectangular hut measuring just 5×3 m.[72] Most of the clay needed for building can only have been hauled short distances.

The same was probably true regarding the ordinary stone needed for most Etruscan buildings, particularly for the wall foundations. The walls of the Podere Tartuchino farm were built of stones up to 40 cm across, quarried directly from the local bedrock, termed

71 Blanck and Proietti, 1986
72 Ammerman and Schaffer, 1981

galestro. The stones were roughly faced on one side, the wall being built up of two rows of the faced stones with a rubble core. The wall foundations of the Tuscania farm were also built in the same rough and ready manner of the local bedrock, but the upper walls were built partly of squared blocks of *tufo* which was probably quarried a kilometre or so to the north.

The arrival of Italo-geometric pottery in the mid eighth century seems to have been the context in which the potter's wheel was adopted in Etruria, probably in the hands of Greek potters. However, a considerable amount of the ordinary domestic pottery (*impasto*) needed for cooking and storage continued to be produced in the traditional way, by modelling coils or slabs. The clay was mixed with temper to give added strength and help bind the clay during firing, the tempering materials including small fragments of rock such as limestone, shale, *tufo* or crystal, and ground-up potsherds. The pots were fired in open kilns, so the finished result could be very variable in shape, texture and colour. Decoration was usually minimal, restricted to the occasional cordon. At most Etruscan sites, *impasto* is by far the commonest form of pottery. A variety of vessel shapes was produced, but large jars were the most frequent type.

Etruscan coarse pottery has been poorly studied in terms of its manufacture and function, but what is clear is that there was considerable standardization in particular regions and it is unlikely that much of it was produced by individual households. The rim diameters of the storage jars from Podere Tartuchino fall into three distinct size classes, of 130, 180 and 240 mm, and, in general, the forms and fabrics of the *impasto* from the site are similar to the collections made from Etruscan sites throughout the upper Albegna valley. Although the necessary raw materials were close to hand, and local materials were used in the temper, Perkins and Attolini have argued that the *impasto* pottery was produced by a local workshop and obtained by exchange rather than being produced on site.[73] They put forward the same hypothesis for the tiles, *pithoi* and amphorae, all of which were produced in an identical fabric to the *impasto*. Similar conclusions have been reached by other studies of Etruscan and contemporary Faliscan coarse wares,[74] confirming the evidence already detected in the agricultural data for the development of an economic system in which few, if any, people lived any longer in self-sufficient isolation. Over time, production became even more centralized as major cities like Cerveteri became centres of specialist

73 Perkins and Attolini, 1992: 129
74 Bouloumié Marique, 1978; Potter, 1976

workshops for these sorts of commodities as well as for quality craft goods.

Domestic wares of medium quality were also produced. At Murlo, for example, the coarsest *impasto* was reserved for storing, cooking and serving food, whereas a better-quality ware was used for eating and drinking (fig. 74).[75] At Podere Tartuchino, too, a medium-quality ware, cream-coloured with heavy grit inclusions similar to those used in the *impasto,* was used for basins, jars and jugs. The same pottery was used at contemporary Etruscan sites throughout the upper Albegna valley and is assumed to have come from a local workshop. Similar wares, manufactured at local or regional centres, were used throughout Etruria. Tomb-paintings of kitchen scenes indicate that the basins were used in the preparation of dough for bread.[76] The community at Podere Tartuchino also used two kinds of fine ware, presumably for eating and drinking: a cream ware for cups, bowls, beakers, jars and jugs; and *bucchero* for cups, miniature bowls, chalices and jugs. The technical quality of both wares suggests that they were produced by specialist workshops, presumably at regional centres like Doganella and Saturnia.

The technology required to produce these fine wares developed as a result of contact and familiarity not only with Greek imports but also with Greek craftsmen. The similarities between several Greek and Etruscan terms for different vessel shapes emphasize the close links between the two technologies – *kothon* (Greek) and *qutum* (Etruscan) for jug, for example, or *askos* and *aska* for flask. The production of Greek black-figure pottery required sophisticated kiln technology, because both the temperature and amount of oxygen had to be altered during firing to end up with a background fired red and the figures and other decoration fired black. The first Greek potters who came to work for Etruscan masters in Etruria are thought to have originated from Euboea and the Cycladic islands.[77] After 700 BC, we can identify in cities such as Tarquinia, Caere and Vulci other groups of incoming potters from the Greek mainland or the Greek colonies of the Bay of Naples, who produced hybrid Etruscan-Greek (Italo-geometric and Etrusco-Corinthian) pottery.[78]

Soon after 700 BC, the Caere workshops began to produce *bucchero* of highly purified clay and fired it with a restricted supply of oxygen to turn the iron oxides in the clay black.[79] The style was

75 Bouloumié Marique, 1978
76 Barbieri, 1987a: 119–20
77 Williams, 1986
78 Martelli, 1987
79 Rasmussen, 1979

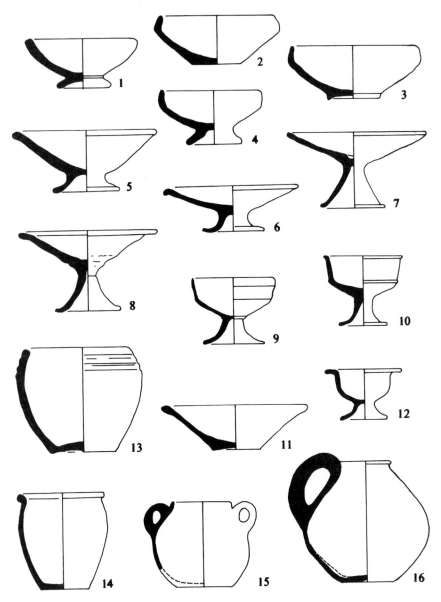

Figure 74   Domestic wheel-made pottery used at Murlo for eating (1–4) and drinking (5–13), and for storing, cooking and serving (14–16). (After Bouloumié Marique, 1978)

swiftly adopted throughout southern and central Etruria. By this time there were a number of ceramic workshops producing fine pottery of different types, though at a small scale and with variable levels of skill. In several cases, the work of individual master potters and their assistants can be recognized, such as the Bearded Sphinx Painter, who in the course of his career moved from Vulci to Caere;[80] other potters, too, may have moved from centre to centre. In the later seventh century, the scale of Etruscan pottery production expanded and more uniformity developed between the centres. Early *bucchero* was of extremely fine quality, with highly refined clay and thin walls; palaeomagnetic analysis shows that over time, as production expanded, the clay became less refined.

Metallurgy is cited repeatedly as the foundation of Etruscan wealth, but there is still little direct evidence for the industrial processes behind the superb metalwork of the cemeteries.[81] Central Etruria was certainly rich in mineral wealth, including deposits of copper and iron on the island of Elba, copper, tin, iron, lead, silver, antimony and zinc in the Colline Metallifere, and copper, iron, lead and zinc in the Tolfa hills.[82] Some of the copper ores would probably have been visible as surface veins, and could have been exploited by surface trenching, whereas others needed mining from depth. After extraction, the copper-bearing rocks had to be smashed up into rubble, mixed up with charcoal and smelted in an open bowl furnace at temperatures of just over 1000°C (a process that requires the use of bellows) to produce lumps of relatively pure copper. These then had to be re-heated in a lengthy process to get rid of impurities, at which point the copper (or bronze when tin was added) was in a useful form for the craftsman.

Presumably most of the primary smelting took place near the quarrying or mining areas. We assume that the ores were intensively exploited, despite the fact that many of the putative 'Etruscan mines' – simple shafts cut into the rock – are undated and probably undateable. One such group, below the medieval village of Rocca San Silvestro, has been shown conclusively to be contemporary with the village,[83] though most of the 300 or so pits around Serrabottini are thought to be Etruscan,[84] and galleries 40 m deep and 100 m

---

80 Martelli, 1987; Szilágyi, 1992
81 Craddock, 1980
82 Cristofani, 1981; Minto, 1954
83 Frankovich, pers. comm.
84 Cristofani, 1986: 122

long at Cornacchino on Monte Amiata are also reasonable candidates as Etruscan mines.[85] It remains uncertain whether or not the main tin deposit near Campiglia Marittima was exploited. It is also an entirely open question whether there were specialist full-time mining communities, or (more likely) communities who lived by a mixture of farming and mining like the people of Rocca San Silvestro in the medieval period. This was probably the case in the Tolfa hills.[86] In late Etruscan times, it is possible that slaves were involved in mining and the ancillary tasks like wood-cutting and haulage.

The earliest iron objects in Italy date to the end of the Bronze Age, but iron remained a rarity for many centuries. By the seventh century, iron was still a luxury, an important indicator of wealth and prestige, but production then expanded dramatically as iron replaced bronze in everyday metal technology. Much of the smelting probably remained local and small scale, but the purity of the Elba iron ores made their transport to centralized smelting sites feasible. The Elba ores began to be exploited systematically in the second half of the sixth century BC, coinciding with the development of extensive slag deposits around Populonia:[87] it has been estimated that the total weight of iron slag deposited around the town in antiquity was in the region of some ten to twelve million tons.[88] A kiln excavated by Minto at Val Fulcinaia near Campiglia Marittima is also cited as an early example of Etruscan iron-smelting technology;[89] it might equally have been a pottery kiln, though it is in a mining area and finds in the vicinity included crude lamps unlike normal domestic lamps that might have been used to illuminate mine shafts.[90]

The metallurgical activity of the Etruscans was the most intense in all of the central Mediterranean. Etruscan smiths produced high-quality domestic utensils, agricultural tools, weapons and luxury goods, with techniques far more advanced than those used by their contemporaries in, for example, Sardinia or Spain, with leaded bronze being particularly favoured.[91] Whereas there had been broad homogeneity in Villanovan metalworking, from about 750 BC onwards we can discern increasing regionalization and competition between cen-

85 Zifferero, 1991
86 Naso et al., 1989; Zifferero, 1991
87 Cristofani and Martelli, 1979
88 Craddock, 1980
89 Minto, 1937, 1940
90 Cristofani, 1985c: 137, 146
91 Craddock, 1976, 1977, 1978, 1986

tres in the scale of production, with the metal industries concentrated especially on the coastal zone, first at cities such as Tarquinia, Vulci and Vetulonia, then Caere, then Vulci.[92] Schools of craftsmen operating at the luxury end of the market can be distinguished: Perugia, for example, produced superb tripods and objects in bronze and iron, while Vulci produced tripods, candelabra and weapons.

Relatively common items like engraved bronze mirrors and inlaid bronze jugs were produced to the highest standards, and an astonishing level of skill was achieved in the masterpieces of Etruscan bronzeworking like the Capitoline Museum she-wolf, the Todi Mars, the Loeb tripods and, perhaps most remarkable of all, the fifth century BC Arezzo Chimaera (see fig. 84, chapter 7).[93] The study of a series of bronze incense-burners in the British Museum (fig. 75) clearly showed the craft of an Etruscan bronze-smith: first the spool, shoulder of the crown and plinth were cast together, then the branches of the crown were cast onto it, and finally a statuette that had been cast separately was soldered onto the top.[94] Moreover, the analysis of the metal content showed conclusively that 'they were made from one stock of metal, that is, one workshop, and the product of craft industry and not mass production'.[95] Presumably artefacts like sickles and ploughshares were not produced in the same way by such specialized workshops in the major centres, but studies of everyday Etruscan metallurgy do not provide useful insights into how its production was organized.

Materials like gold and silver, exotic woods, glass, bone, ivory and ostrich shell were turned into beautiful ornaments for the wealthy by the same kind of craft specialist that produced the finest pottery and metalwork. The faunal sample from Populonia showed how carcasses were butchered systematically to separate the meatbearing parts from the best pieces for boneworking, and the Cerveteri material included refuse discarded by a bone craftsperson who was working cattle metapodials and horn cores and red deer antler.[96] Williams argued that a number of striking similarities between particular classes of pottery, glasswork and bronze vessels suggests a close rapport between different workshops in the same centre, though whether this took the form of collaboration or competition we cannot tell.[97]

92 Torelli, 1987: 48
93 Briguet, 1986; Haynes, 1985
94 Macnamara, 1986
95 Craddock and Hockey, 1986: 90
96 Clark, 1994
97 Williams, 1986

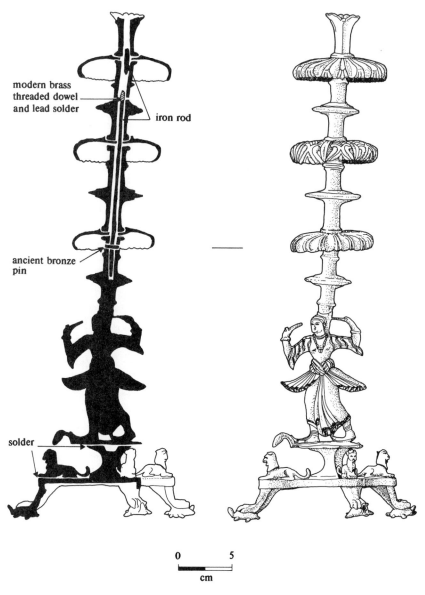

modern brass
threaded dowel
and lead solder

iron rod

ancient bronze
pin

solder

0   5

cm

Figure 75   Details of the construction of an Etruscan bronze incense-burner.
(After Macnamara, 1986)

The level of skill involved in many of the most famous pieces of Etruscan jewellery is simply astounding.[98] The techniques of Etruscan goldsmiths, for example, combined beating out the thinnest sheets, drawing wires of extreme thinness (filigree) and soldering on tiny balls (granulation) to produce ornaments of exquisite delicacy. The balls produced in granulation can be as small as 0.02 mm across, produced with a regularity that can be appreciated today only with the aid of a microscope. A gold fibula from Chiusi of the seventh century BC has decoration and a long inscription picked out in granulation, and a gold clasp from the Bernadini Tomb at Palestrina (of similar antiquity) has its surface covered with tiny lions and mythological creatures worked in repoussé and decorated with delicate threads of granulation. The same tomb has a superb plain gold goblet decorated with a sphinx on each handle.

Another distinct craft group must have been the skilled stone-masons who operated at a wide variety of scales, from the substantial architecture of city gates like Volterra and complex tomb groups to smaller carvings like the sixth century BC centaur and lion from Vulci now in the Villa Giulia Museum in Rome. Terracotta work likewise involved the elaborate carvings of the temple antefixes, and masterpieces like the horses that decorated the temple at Tarquinia (see fig. 109, chapter 8) and the statues which decorated the roof of the Portonaccio temple at Veii (see fig. 80, chapter 7). Studies of these statues indicate, once more, the existence of a distinct and highly specialized school of craftsmen.[99] From indications given by Pliny, the master craftsman may be identified as Vulca. Several craftsmen are known by name because objects carry inscriptions such as 'I am Lemausna's jug. Ranazu shaped me' or 'I was made by Larthuza Kulenie' – a command of literacy that is in itself an indication of the high social status such craftsmen must have enjoyed.

As with pottery and metalwork, however, we have little idea how 'middle order' production was organized. The master carpenter, for example, no doubt made the finest furniture or flute or lyre for the Etruscan noble, but who made the wooden tools, weapons like bows and arrows, or specialized agricultural equipment like barrels and cartwheels, that were in much wider circulation? How centralized were these workshops? Were there single workshops in the major (and minor?) Etruscan centres, as for the luxury goods, or were quarters given over to numbers of families producing the same

98 Cristofani and Martelli, 1983; Forte, 1995
99 Briguet, 1986

goods, like medieval guilds (or indeed like parts of backstreet Rome today), or were there scattered enterprises producing commonly used goods like kitchen pottery on a quasi-industrial scale? Similar questions can be posed, and currently must remain unanswered, for all areas of Etruscan technology.

Exchange, trade and the Etruscan economy

As this chapter has already made clear, there is a great deal of evidence for commodities being found in one location which must have been manufactured elsewhere – most obviously, the pots found in Etruscan tombs that can be definitely identified as the work of Greek craftsmen working outside Etruria, either in the Greek colonies of southern Italy or on the Greek mainland. The movement of commodities can in fact be discerned operating at the local, regional and 'international' (that is, long-distance) scale, though the social and economic mechanisms differed considerably both in space and time.

The most difficult to identify is the movement of commodities at the local scale, even though it was probably the cornerstone of the Etruscan economy. The faunal and botanical samples indicate that centres of population like Cerveteri and Populonia were supplied with foodstuffs and other agricultural products from elsewhere, and the excavation at Podere Tartuchino suggests that a farm such as this would have been producing a small surplus of the same commodities. We know that transporting bulk foodstuffs (particularly grain) overland in Roman times was extremely expensive, and Etruscan roads and transport technology (pack animals and ox carts) were even less developed, whilst few of the major centres were served by rivers navigable by anything other than very small craft. Hence we must assume that farms like Podere Tartuchino were the primary producers of foodstuffs for their local centres, like the cluster of farms around Tuscania. The evidence for what Podere Tartuchino received in return from its locality consists of the *impasto* pottery and *pithoi* with local inclusions, iron nails, a couple of soapstone beads (from a source 15 km away), the fine cream ware thought to be from a centre like Saturnia or Doganella, and two sherds of amphorae also identified as from Doganella.[100]

Given what we know of the clientship system at the heart of Etruscan society and the gift exchange networks that operated

100   Perkins and Attolini, 1992: 129

between leading families, it is commonly assumed that much local exchange would have been in the form of redistribution of the kind practised amongst many chiefdom societies in the ethnographic record. In this, a community provides the local chief and his followers with foodstuffs, other commodities and services, and he uses part of it to maintain his household (his craftsmen, for example) and redistributes any surplus back to the client community in the form of gifts, feasts and so on. Such exchange as took place outside such social obligations, prior to the development of coinage in the fifth century BC, is assumed to have been at the level of barter. In fact, barter long continued to be the main system of exchange, for not all Etruscan cities issued coins, and those that did were spasmodic in doing so;[101] only at Populonia was there a more continuous coinage tradition.[102]

Certainly in Villanovan times, much exchange was probably of this kind, and clientship systems within and between Etruscan clangroups presumably involved such exchange as well. (In many ways it continues in Italian peasant villages today in marriage festivals, when families give lavish gifts to the bride knowing that their own families will in turn be recipients on the same scale in due course.) In both the Albegna and Tuscania surveys, it has been noted that the numbers of sherds of Etruscan and imported fine pottery decline with distance from the regional centres, suggesting that hierarchical systems of gift exchange or clientship linked more and less powerful families. At the bottom of the social scale, too, it is likely that, as in ancient Greece,[103] neighbouring Etruscan communities in the countryside helped each other out in bad years with surplus foodstuffs, creating a system of mutual obligation which Halstead has termed 'social storage'. However, it is also clear that, as the Etruscan economy developed, much local exchange was of a different order.

A small sub-rectangular scrap of bronze found at Podere Tartuchino has been identified as an *aes rude* or bronze ingot. Elsewhere in the Albegna valley, similar ingots have been found at Doganella, in the cemeteries of Saturnia and in a third century BC hoard from Talamonaccio. They are thought to have been used as a medium of pre-monetary exchange in the Etruscan world: their presence in buried hoards shows that they were a useful way of accumulating wealth in life, and their presence in tombs that they served as payment

101   Tripp, 1986
102   Catalli, 1990: 41
103   Halstead, 1989; Halstead and Jones, 1989

for Charon on the journey into the underworld.[104] In addition to the *aes rude* bronze ingots, *ramo secco* bars, with an iron content so high as to preclude practical use, were also circulating in Etruria from the sixth century BC and are assumed to have been currency bars.[105] The implication is that at the local level, in addition to the transfers of goods that took place to meet social and ritual obligations, transfers were also taking place (and wealth accumulating) within a form of primitive market exchange between cities, local centres and the surrounding rural populations.

We know next to nothing of Etruscan systems of land tenure, though a second century BC boundary stone from Umbria records a territorial dispute between two powerful land-owning families,[106] and presumably over time there were winners and losers. As the Etruscan economy developed, there was probably a spectrum of social levels in the countryside, with some farmers working for themselves, some in share-cropping or renting systems, and some in quasi-feudal conditions of clientship and servitude.

A number of artefact classes demonstrate the operation of exchange at the regional scale, though again there was no single mechanism at work. At Podere Tartuchino, regional imports included *pithoi* sherds and a coarse cream ware, both with volcanic inclusions, which presumably originated in southern Etruria. The cream ware has been found distributed along the length of coastal Etruria.[107] Both commodities could equally well have been traded in their own right or acquired from itinerant potters.[108] On the other hand, the black-figure pottery produced (probably in Vulci) by the Micali Painter was clearly valued highly as a prestige item throughout southern and central Etruria and was probably exchanged between leading families (fig. 76).[109] Presumably such gift exchanges were normally in the context of occasions such as marriages and the cementing of political and military alliances rather than commercial transactions.[110] Inscriptions on other prestige artefacts like 'I am the fibula of Aranth Velavesna. Mamurke Tursikana gave it' and 'I am the fibula of Mamarce presented to Arte' testify to similar patterns of gift exchange.

104   Cattani, 198
105   Burnett et al., 1986
106   Cristofani, 1979a: 47
107   Milanesi and Mannoni, 1984
108   Perkins and Walker, 1990: 73–4
109   Spivey, 1987
110   Cristofani, 1975a

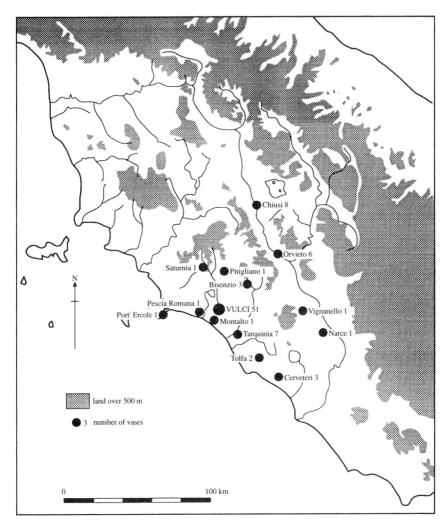

Figure 76   The distribution of vases from the workshop of the Micali Painter. (After Spivey, 1987)

The changing distributions of goods imported to the leading families of Etruria from Greece demonstrate how relations with the outside world shifted constantly in the volatile power networks of the central and eastern Mediterranean.[111] Between 625 and 550 BC, for example, Greek pottery imported into Etruria came mainly from Corinth and eastern Greece, whereas trade between 550 and 475 BC

111   *Commercio*, 1983; Martelli, 1985

was primarily with Athens, though for a short time also with Sparta. The majority of the Greek goods stayed within the sphere of the major coastal cities, far smaller quantities filtering further into the interior, though their stranglehold on this trade was less powerful in the north. Most of the trade seems to have been administered directly from Cerveteri, Tarquinia and Vulci in the eighth and early seventh centuries, and then through their ports.[112] As well as the exotic artefacts being valued in themselves, some of the pots may also have contained exotic oils and perfumes that were just as valued, and Greek oil and wine were also imported to the coastal cities.

The evidence for long-distance export from Etruria consists mainly of *bucchero*, bronzes and amphorae. Outside Italy, *bucchero* has been found in Spain, southern France, Corsica, Sardinia, Greece, Turkey, the Black Sea, the eastern Mediterranean (Cyprus and Syria) and along the north African coast in Tunisia, Libya and Egypt (see fig. 49, chapter 4). Etruscan wine amphorae have been found in Spain, southern France, Sicily and Greece. The cargo of the Etruscan ship wrecked off the island of Giglio in about 600 BC included both *bucchero* and amphorae, one of the latter containing olive stones,[113] and that of another Etruscan ship wrecked off the French coast (near Cap d'Antibes) in about 580–570 BC included *bucchero*, imitation Corinthian cups from Vulci and wine amphorae. Etruscan bronzes were prized by the Greeks, one of the most notable finds being the fragment of a Vulci tripod at Athens. Bronze jugs from Etruria were part of the drinking services that accompanied Greek wine from the Greek port of Massilia (Marseilles) to the Celtic chieftains of central France and southern Germany.[114]

It is assumed that a primary stimulus for the development of Phoenician and Greek trade with the Etruscans was the mineral wealth of Etruria – fragments of ore found at the Greek colony of Pithecusa have in fact been identified as hematite from Elba. On the other hand, the main distribution of exotic goods is in southern Etruria rather than in the region of the ores, suggesting that the southern cities controlled the sea trade. Cristofani in fact argues from later Greek and Roman descriptions of Etruscan sailors that the predominant form of Etruscan maritime trade was piracy,[115] but it is unlikely that Etruscan sea trade can be described so simply. The complexity of Mediterranean trade is demonstrated by the

112   Spivey and Stoddart, 1990
113   Bound, 1985
114   Wells, 1980
115   Cristofani, 1979a

cargo from the Giglio shipwreck, which included, in addition to the Etruscan goods, Phoenician amphorae, Corinthian and Spartan pottery, and bronzework including a superb bronze helmet identified as Corinthian.[116] We also know from inscriptions that Greek and Phoenician merchants lived in a port such as Gravisca. Etruscan maritime trade surely included a spectrum of activities from individual cargo ships plying along the coasts of the central Mediterranean to more organized expeditions, both peaceful and warlike. The most critical feature of archaic Etruscan maritime trade, however, was that it was in the hands of enterprising individuals and families rather than being 'state-directed'.

Although many of the details still elude us, it is clear that the different levels of production and exchange described in this chapter operated in response to Etruscan social institutions, above all the competing aspirations of the elite. The mineral and agricultural resources of the countryside were exploited in ways that produced materials such as wine, oil, wool, fine pottery, bronze and iron, that were essential for differentiating the lifestyles of the elites from ordinary people. They made possible the disparities in the construction, decoration and equipping of their houses, cemeteries and sanctuaries, and in their clothing and diet. They allowed the elite to maintain a social order in Etruria based on inequality and to compete with each other and with the outside world for power and prestige. Production, redistribution, exchange and trade operated within a rather sophisticated pre-monetary economy: the absence of coinage from archaic Etruria can no longer be taken as evidence of archaism and primitivism in economic structure.

116 Bound, 1990

7

Life, Cult and Afterlife

And death, to the Etruscans, was a pleasant continuance of life, with jewels and wine and flutes playing for the dance. It was neither an ecstasy of bliss, nor a purgatory of torment. It was just a natural continuance of the fullness of life. Everything was in terms of life, of living.

D.H. Lawrence (1932) *Etruscan Places*

Introduction

It is difficult to form a balanced view of Etruscan life and of Etruscan attitudes to religion and the afterlife. On the one hand, there are the written sources, mostly late in date, sometimes confused, often exaggerated in their reporting; on the other, there are the monuments themselves, which are far from easy to interpret.

The Tomb of the Baron at Tarquinia may illustrate the point (fig. 77). It is among the best preserved of the painted tombs and shows on the far wall a meeting of three figures – a man with his arm around a boy flute-player, facing a woman – flanked by riders; in the pediment above are two hippocamps (sea-horses). There are a further two pairs of riders on the side walls, but they have dismounted, and on the left wall they are joined by a woman. There is much to wonder at here: the elegant spacing of the figures, the feeling for the open air suggested by the stylized trees, the technique of the painting – one of the rare cases where paint was applied straight onto the wall surface without plaster preparation. But what are we to make of the scenes themselves? Some see in the lady with her hands raised a goddess, or a priestess. The gesture looks significant so that we seem to be on the threshold of knowing what the whole sequence means, but the enigma and ambiguity are never fully unravelled. If the lady is the deceased for whom the tomb was prepared, then it is perhaps her again on the left wall. Dennis wondered whether the riders of the right-hand wall might both be claiming the victor's garland after a race; but this is unlikely, for

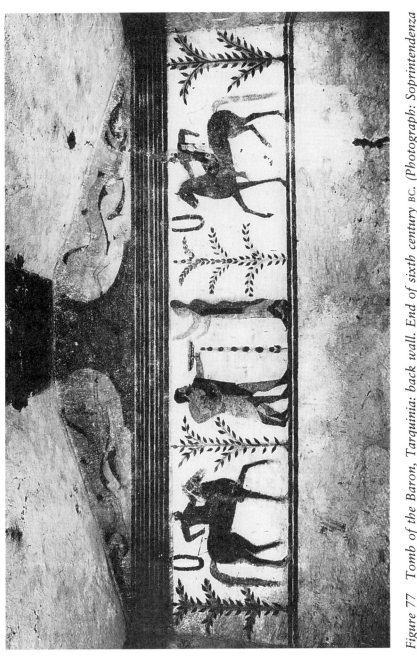

Figure 77 *Tomb of the Baron, Tarquinia: back wall. End of sixth century* BC. *(Photograph: Soprintendenza Archeologica per l'Etruria Meridionale)*

such garlands are everywhere in the painted tombs and seem to denote simply that the setting is a funerary one.[1]

If it is difficult to be sure how to interpret the figures, it can only be harder to know why they are painted on the walls of a tomb, a tomb that would rarely be re-opened after the funeral. One answer might be that they are nothing more than decorative: an artist was called in to paint some scenes for the delectation of the deceased and simply chose the first thing that came into his head. But it is an unsatisfactory answer and anyway begs the question as to why he chose these figures in these particular poses. At the other extreme, one could envisage that all the humans represented would be recognizable to whoever commissioned the work. Another possibility is that the scenes do mean something but only on a generalized level, if only showing that this is the tomb of a member of a horse-loving aristocracy.

Following Ernst Gombrich's principle that artists learn mainly from other artists' representations, and noting that the style of the work is essentially Greek-inspired, we might also consider it possible that for his figures the artist copied Greek work in other media, perhaps painted pottery or metalwork from eastern Greece. If that was the case, then other questions follow, for we can no longer be sure that what is represented reflects or corresponds to contemporary realities. The men and women are shown wearing dress that is basically Greek in style, but would the same be true of Tarquinian society? And what about the undress of the left-hand rider of the far wall? 'Heroic' nudity is a commonplace in Greek art, but did men ride around Etruria in the nude? A further consideration is that if the customs and dress illustrated were actually adopted, was it true of the urban population as a whole or only of a comparatively small elite, considering that only some 2 per cent of chamber tombs at Tarquinia were given painted decoration? Although it may seem on the surface unlikely that any decoration for a tomb would not reflect accurately the life of the community, the questions raised here can be asked not only of all tomb-painting but also of Etruscan figurative art in general.

We may take our leave of this tomb with two different interpretations. For Pallottino all the figures shown are human, representing the family of the deceased lady on the back wall, whereas for Walberg they are a mixture of human and divine.[2] The deceased

1   Dennis, 1878: 369
2   Pallottino, 1952: 57; Walberg, 1986

lady is greeted by her husband who proffers a cup in farewell. The riders are the Dioscuri, Castor and Polydeuces (Etruscan: Kastur and Pultuce). The horse-loving sons of Zeus, who spent half the year in the underworld and half with the gods on Olympos, are shown three times: alone together (right wall), in attendance at the funeral (back wall) and about to lead the woman to the underworld (left wall). This interpretation makes much sense, but there is no absolute proof that it is correct.

Where cult and religion are concerned, we have to make a particular effort today to appreciate the Etruscan, indeed the ancient Mediterranean, mentality in dealing with a world where, as the Greek philosopher Thales put it, 'everything is full of gods'. In fact to create a separate section or chapter on 'religion' is probably to miss the mark altogether and only reflects modern compartmentalized thinking. With that awareness, we might consider first the architectural backdrop.

Temples and sanctuaries

Etruscan religion did not require temples, and it is likely that these sprang up, as in Greece, for reasons of civic pride and in order to house cult statues. From Greece, too, came almost certainly the whole idea of anthropomorphic gods, and in the process some of the Greek gods became assimilated with their Etruscan counterparts. Temples in Etruria differ from Greek temples in a number of ways, especially in materials and proportions. Materials were discussed in chapter 5 (p. 153). What is known about the proportions has been gleaned mainly from the Roman architectural writer Vitruvius, who described in some detail (4.7) a 'tuscanic' style of temple probably still current in his own day but based on earlier traditions. Vitruvius' temple is almost square in plan, with columns only at the front and with a plain back wall, and either its *cella* (inner room) is divided into three chambers side by side or it has a single *cella* with *alae* (open wings) to either side. The whole building is raised on a stone podium. The tripartite arrangement of rooms is reminiscent of early monumental tombs at Caere,[3] which in turn appear to be modelled on house plans like those displayed at Acquarossa (see fig. 89b, c); it is an arrangement that fits fairly comfortably with preserved remains of actual temples. What is less

3 Colonna, 1981: 42

certain is how proportionately tall the buildings were. Vitruvius' temple clearly has a markedly lower roof than Greek temples, and archaeologists have calculated the height of excavated temples according to his prescription. This is of course a circular argument, but there is no overriding reason why what he said about height should not apply to actual temples of well before his time, especially as his additional remarks about exceptionally wide eaves are borne out by archaeological evidence.[4] However, in the end, column height was probably as much determined by the length of available timber as by close adherence to set rules. Vitruvius also mentioned the distinctive manner in which gables were treated, and this is backed up by surviving terracotta models of temples. As shown in the reconstruction of an excavated temple (fig. 78), the pediment is recessed and has no *tympanum* (back wall), nor did it normally contain sculpture.

Etruscan temples did not follow the Greek orders closely, and moreover the entablatures were lower and organized differently. On the other hand, there are Greek echoes in the columns, of which the usual type was the tuscanic as described by Vitruvius, with a plain unfluted shaft, a capital reminiscent of Doric and a moulded base – a style of column which was to continue in Roman architecture and to be revived in the Renaissance.[5] Two further interconnected characteristics exerted a major influence on Roman temples: the tall podium (fig. 79) which could be mounted only at the front, and the frontal emphasis created by the columns which did not continue round the back of the building.

The above remarks are highly generalized and do not cover the wide variety of types of temple in Etruria, which also include examples of Greek peripteral type (with a colonnade on all four sides). One of the largest temples in the Etruscan style was built on the Capitoline Hill in Rome by the Tarquin kings[6] and finally dedicated in the late sixth century to the Roman Capitoline Triad (Jupiter, Juno and Minerva). It had not only three *cellae* but also wings at the sides and three rows of columns at the front; and Roman sources tell how craftsmen from all over Etruria worked on it, including specialists in terracotta sculpture from Veii. It so happens that some of the finest surviving terracotta *akroteria* (roof sculptures) are also from Veii, from the Portonaccio sanctuary (fig. 80), and are from this same period. The arrangement of *akroteria* along the ridge-pole

4   Boëthius, 1978: 57
5   Borsi, 1985
6   Rasmussen, 1983: 15; Richardson, 1992: 221–4

Figure 78   Temple A at Pyrgi: reconstruction model, in the Museo di Antichità Etrusche e Italiche dell'Università 'La Sapienza', Rome. (After Colonna, 1986: fig. 342)

Figure 79   Marzabotto: podium of Temple D. (Photograph: T. Rasmussen)

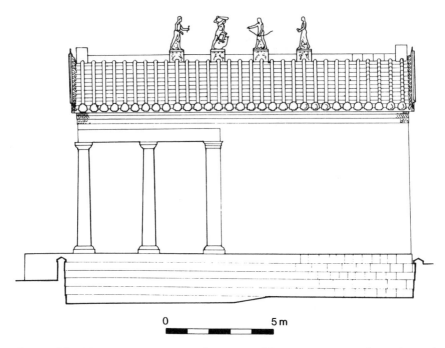

0   5 m

Figure 80   Veii: reconstruction elevation of Portonaccio temple with roof sculpture, late sixth century BC. (After Boëthius, 1978: fig. 51)

is an idea unique to Etruria and Latium. We have seen it already at Murlo (see chapter 5, p. 162), where at least some faced outwards; here they faced along the axis of the roof.

There is much that one has to reconstruct with the mind's eye when looking at the scanty remains of Etruscan temples, and even more of an effort is needed to visualize the original surroundings of the sanctuaries of which all temples were only a part, even if visually the most prominent part. Details of the majority of sanctuaries are now totally destroyed. At the Portonaccio sanctuary just mentioned (fig. 81), the provision of water seems to have been an important requirement, for close up to the temple there is a large rectangular pool (B) and a complex system for channelling the water (the purpose of which is not understood). Further away are the *tufo* altar (F) and the foundations of a small building (I) which was a treasury to house votive offerings.

Inscriptions from here make it clear that the principal deity worshipped was Menerva,[7] and presumably hers is the temple (A),

7   Colonna, 1985: 101

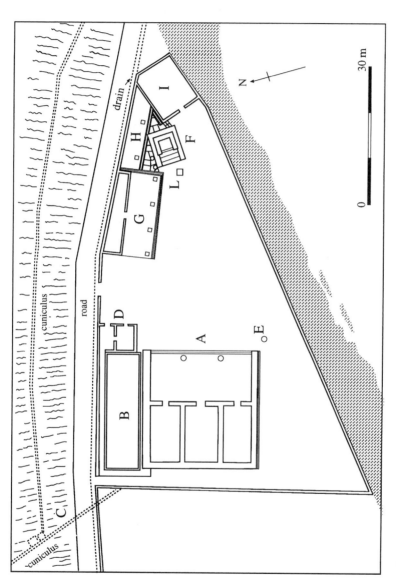

Figure 81 Veii: plan of the Portonaccio sanctuary. (After Colonna, 1985: fig. on p. 100)

which is Vitruvian in its ground-plan and is usually restored on paper with three *cellae*. The temple was probably also in part dedicated to Apollo (Aplu), and it is his deeds that are celebrated in the more than life-size terracotta roof statues (see fig. 80). A major feature of the sanctuary at Pyrgi near Caere, in which there are two substantial temples, is a long narrow building with twenty small chambers, which has been tentatively interpreted as a series of rooms for sacred prostitution in devotion to the Phoenician love goddess Astarte, who was here equated with the Etruscan divinity Uni.[8]

Gifts for the gods

Many sanctuaries did not possess monumental temples, and even when they did, the area outside around the altar was for cult purposes of greater importance. Ancient Mediterranean cult practice involved a relationship between worshipper and god from which both benefited or hoped to benefit, the former by securing the god's favour, the god by receiving payment. No-one approached the gods empty-handed, and a common form of payment was animal sacrifice or some other food offering and/or a drink libation. So the altar was the focal point of the whole sanctuary. Instead of this, or in addition, a gift might be offered in the form of a manufactured article of varying value according to the importance of the occasion or the wealth of the worshipper. The precious and more fragile objects were often stored in small treasuries, and when these became full they were taken out and buried in pits or trenches nearby. Between them, votive offerings from sanctuaries and gravegoods from the cemeteries make up the bulk of all Etruscan objects in museums.

At the Portonaccio sanctuary, as elsewhere, a common form of gift was pottery. Sculpture was also dedicated here in abundance, often in the form of small terracotta statuettes. But around 500 BC, a terracotta statue group of three quarters life-size (fig. 82) was set up possibly in one of the porticoed buildings near the altar (G, H in fig. 81). This must have been an especially expensive dedication, and it showed an appropriately grand subject: Herakles with his patron Menerva (Athena) at the moment of his apotheosis,[9] for which there are close parallels in another statue group set up earlier on a temple in Rome.

8   Colonna, 1985: 128
9   Colonna, 1987b

Figure 82   Terracotta figure of Menerva (upper part) from the Portonaccio sanctuary, Veii, late sixth century BC, *in the Villa Giulia Museum, Rome. (After Colonna, 1987b: fig. 10)*

Figure 83 Bronze solid-cast statuette of a warrior, from Monte Falterona, near the source of the Arno, late fifth century BC, *in the British Museum, London. (Photograph: copyright British Museum)*

At other sanctuaries, especially in northern Etruria, bronze sculptures were favoured for dedications. Again most of these are small-scale statuettes and figurines and of standardized types: armed warriors posing self-consciously (fig. 83), schematic sexless standing figures, and numerous others. But many were of monumental scale, of which few survive today, and among them are some of the

Figure 84   Bronze Chimaera from Arezzo, fourth century BC: *drawing of 1583, before the later restorations which included the addition of a serpent-headed tail. Original in the Museo Archeologico, Florence. (After Cristofani 1985b: fig. on p. 66)*

finest works of Etruscan art.[10] By anyone's reckoning, the Chimaera from Arezzo (fig. 84) must rank as a masterpiece; according to the inscription carved on one of the forelegs,[11] it was a dedication to Tinia (the Etruscan equivalent of Zeus). The wounded beast needs an opponent to snarl at and originally may have been complemented by an attacking Bellerophon mounted on Pegasus.

Understanding the will of the gods

If from Roman accounts (see chapter 3) the Etruscans seem obsessed with ritual and over-anxious about displeasing the gods, it may be worth recalling that in Greece the vitally important battle of Plataea of 479 BC was held up for days on end, with the Greek

10   Cristofani, 1985b
11   Bonfante and Bonfante, 1983: 115

and Persian armies in position, because on both sides the omens of repeated sacrifice were unfavourable for attack (Herodotus 9.38ff.), and that Livy's account of early Roman history is saturated with descriptions of portents of every kind. The Etruscans' preoccupations with securing divine aid in reading the future were those of the ancient Mediterranean as a whole, but in this area they stand out on two counts: they were regarded by other peoples as especially skilled, and they themselves regarded these skills as a revealed religion, centred around the figure of Tages, the mythical teacher.

It is not difficult to appreciate that the most powerful gods were those of the sky. The sky is unpredictable: it can produce hail, rain, lightning, wind seemingly out of nowhere; and as it was thought to be the abode of many gods, such sudden events could be read as indications of pleasure and displeasure on their part. In Roman terms, a person skilled in interpreting such signs was an *augur*. There were other happenings in the air to look out for, too, that might be sent from the gods, and an augur would also know what significance to attach to flights of birds. In all cases, it mattered a great deal where in the sky events happened and from what direction they appeared, for the gods of the western heavens (for example) were of a very different nature from those of the eastern. An augur might carry a curved stick or *lituus* as a kind of staff of office, but not all men represented with curved sticks are necessarily augurs. It is from a common tendency to see priests as dominant everywhere in Etruscan society that such a figure depicted in the Tomb of the Augurs (fig. 85) gave its name to the tomb. In fact he and his companion are more likely to be umpires of the games that are taking place around them; and the birds that fly towards him are there to fill space elegantly, as they do on other walls.

Another method of learning the will of the gods involved animal sacrifice, after which the entrails were inspected, with special attention given to the liver. A man with this knowledge was called by the Romans a *haruspex*, by the Etruscans a *netsvis;* but in Latin *augur* and *haruspex* are often interchangeable. The liver, rather than the heart, was regarded as the seat of life, being the largest organ in the body and containing more blood than any other. The health of the liver of an animal that had been vowed to the gods was thought to mirror the health of the enquirer, and by extension the health or viability of the enterprise about to be undertaken. This was a difficult procedure and required long instruction and apprenticeship. A mirror from Tuscania shows it in progress in mythological terms (fig. 86): holding the liver and bent over it is Pava Tarchies (= Tages?), and listening intently is Avle Tarchunus, whom Pallottino

Figure 85   Tomb of the Augurs, Tarquinia: umpire and wrestlers, c.520 BC, watercolour reproduction. (After Becatti and Magi, 1955: fig. 10)

takes for Tarchon, legendary founder of Tarquinia and first Etruscan haruspex.[12] Cristofani argues that the man is more probably a son of Tarchon, and that the significance of the event portrayed is emphasized by the figures placed above and below, who are divinities of the upper regions (the dawn goddess in her chariot) and the lower.[13]

Originally it was probably sufficient simply to check the liver for general defects and signs of disease; later the surface of the liver was viewed as if it were the sky above in microcosm, so that it became in effect another means of consulting the sky gods. This required much higher precision, and it mattered greatly how the organ was held in relation to the sky and where on its surface any irregularities were located. On the famous bronze model of a sheep's liver from Piacenza (fig. 87), the surface is divided into numerous compartments, each, like the sky itself, 'inhabited' by a god whose name is incised.[14] It is thought by some to have been a teaching aid, but the whole system was so complex that even a trained haruspex might have needed a crib of this sort by him fairly constantly.

It is clear that the general idea of examining entrails is in origin a Babylonian one. Model livers incised with interpretations of blemishes

12   Pallottino, 1930
13   Cristofani, 1987b
14   van der Meer, 1987

Figure 86   Engraved bronze mirror from Tuscania: mythological scene of haruspication. Third century BC, *in the Museo Archeologico, Florence. (After Cristofani, 1987b, fig. 1)*

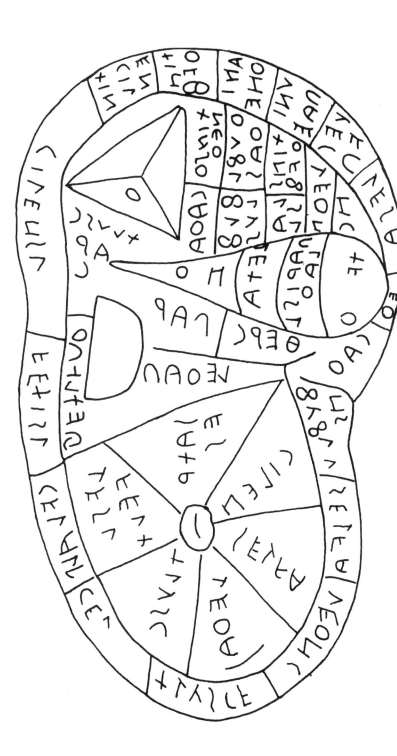

Figure 87 Inscribed bronze model of sheep's liver, found near Piacenza, now in Museo Civico, Piacenza. (After van der Meer, 1979: fig. 2)

are known from here from as early as the beginning of the second millennium BC, while an incised terracotta sheep's lung was excavated at Nimrud in Assyria.[15] What the Etruscans seem to have added to the art is the notion of the microcosm of the internal organ as an accurate reflection of the macrocosm of the heavens. It is worth noting that at about the time the Piacenza liver was made in the third century BC, the haruspices were at last beginning to pay similar attention to the heart (Pliny 11.186).

Death and the afterlife

According to the Greek geographer Strabo (17.1.10), there was a suburb with a cemetery in ancient Alexandria called Necropolis. This is the first appearance in literature of the word ('city of the dead'), which is often used by modern archaeologists for any early cemetery but is especially suited to the extensive burial grounds of Etruria. Their sheer size comes as overwhelming to many who visit them and has contributed to a common perception that, rather like the Egyptians, the Etruscans must have been greatly preoccupied with death. There are, however, distorting factors to bear in mind: modern western soceties tend to go to the opposite extreme and hide their dead and their cemeteries away; there are special geological conditions in southern Etruria which may help to explain the predilection for rock-cut and built *tufo* tombs (see chapter 1); and the size of many of the larger necropolises is the result of steady growth over many centuries – five in the case of the Banditaccia at Cerveteri (fig. 88). The fact remains that the Etruscans, looking out from their towns or travelling on the roads immediately beyond, would have been constantly aware of the dead around them, and one can but wonder to what extent their lives and thinking were coloured by it.

The early circular tombs of cemeteries such as the Banditaccia look like giant versions of old-fashioned bee-hives, their upper parts built of ashlar masonry covering one or more chambers cut into the rock. The standard layout of a burial chamber consisted of an entrance vestibule, two small rooms leading off it on either side and a main room at the end, carved with a sloping roof imitating (we assume) the inside of an above-ground house roof with details of the ridge-beam and rafters. Chamber doorways were often picked out with imitation frames and lintels, and some chambers were 'supported' by columns or pillars. More elaborate tombs had numbers

15   Mallowan, 1966: 274

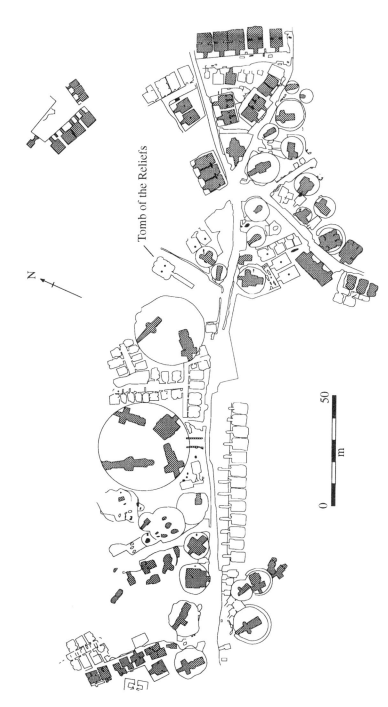

N

Tomb of the Reliefs

0 50 m

Figure 88   The Banditaccia necropolis, Cerveteri. (After Prayon, 1975a)

of chambers. The dead were laid on couches which were also cut out of the living rock, including a pillow or sloping support with a semi-circular section cut out for the head. Particularly rich tombs had further intricate carving – the detail in the Tomb of the Reliefs at Cerveteri, as mentioned previously, included cushions on the couches and body armour and other personal equipment hanging on the walls. Poorer burials around the tumuli included free-standing stone sarcophagi or simple grave slots cut into the bedrock covered with stone slabs.

There was considerable variation in tomb types from region to region in Etruria:[16] at Tarquinia, for example, the sixth and fifth century BC tumuli were much like those of Cerveteri in terms of their above- and below-ground architecture (though most of the mounds have disappeared today), but many chambers were plastered and painted. Nevertheless, certain trends can be detected in terms of overall tomb development. Later Etruscan tombs were commonly cut in rows into vertical rock faces, like terraced housing; the rock face was often decorated in ways that we assume imitated the exteriors of domestic houses. Whereas the earlier tumuli were placed at random, these later burials were often ordered in groups in a kind of 'town plan', most famously at Orvieto (see fig. 46, chapter 4). The increasing use of continuous stone benches rather than individual couches in the chambers suggests that, over time, tombs were used for larger groups of people, perhaps clan members, rather than individual families as before. Poorer burials continued to be simple trenches cut into the bedrock. After Romanization, the ordinary form of burial was usually a simple earth grave, with the body laid out not in a coffin but under under a ridged tent-like structure of roof tiles (*cappuccina*). Beyond the major and minor centres, there was also a large number of small cemeteries and individual graves in the countryside, though the graves have rarely been mapped systematically.

It is commonly assumed that the architecture and decoration of Etruscan cemeteries must echo Etruscan domestic architecture. As figure 89 shows, the plans of the major types of tomb in a necropolis such as Cerveteri certainly have many parallels with plans of many of the houses found in the major and minor Etruscan settlements. To this comparison must now be added the parallels between rural settlement and burial forms: the simplest graves in the Tuscania countryside, for example – single square chambers cut into cliff faces, devoid of any extraneous carving – parallel the

16　Colonna, 1967, 1974

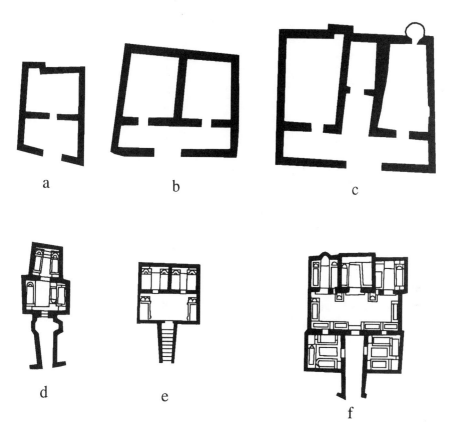

a   b   c

d   e

f

Figure 89   Etruscan tomb types, compared with Etruscan house plans. (a), (b) and (c) are plans of typical sixth century buildings, while (d), (e) and (f) show typical arrangements of chambers in tombs at Cerveteri. (After Cristofani, 1979a: 30)

cottage-like structure of the farm we excavated.[17] One roofing technique implied from tomb architecture is corbelling – laying overlapping blocks of stone horizontally to create pitched ceilings where the blocks are cut to form straight lines (fig. 90 (above)), or steps in reverse (fig. 90 (below)), or to create false domes;[18] but there is no evidence yet for its use in the houses of the living.

In the Chiusi museum is a clay cinerary urn (fig. 91) surmounted by a large figure of the deceased[19] or more probably a mourner,[20] with smaller attached mourners below alternating with griffin heads.

17   Grant et al., 1992
18   Boitani et al., 1975: 36, 108
19   Brendel, 1995: 106
20   Sprenger and Bartoloni, 1983: 79

Figure 91   Clay cinerary urn ('Paolozzi urn') from Chiusi, seventh century
BC, *in the Museo Etrusco, Chiusi. (Photograph: Alinari)*

Figure 90   (opposite) Techniques of corbelling. Above: Orvieto, Crocefisso
del Tufo necropolis, corbelled tomb under restoration. Below: Cortona,
Melone di Camucia, corbelling Tomb B. (Photographs: T. Rasmussen)

The monstrous heads with their gaping mouths are a feature borrowed from Greek and Oriental metal cauldrons, but here their long necks spring from male genitalia. Chiusi has produced several such urns, and what they appear to convey is an unsophisticated message of re-birth, of a generative power released at death. Further south, a somewhat similar idea of renewed life is suggested by some of the painted tombs, for example the Tombs of the Lionesses, Leopards, and Shields, where banqueters are shown holding out an egg.[21] It has been suggested that this simply shows the stage in the feasting that the banqueters have reached;[22] but the egg, which began with the potential for new life inside it, probably signifies more. These images have a wide geographical and chronological spread: the Chiusi urns are late seventh century, the Tarquinian painted tombs are of the sixth and late fourth.

The dead lived on after death and may have become the subject of ancestor worship. In Greece there were many cults of the heroized dead, and, according to Pausanias, those who died fighting at Marathon were still worshipped as heroes in his own day, more than six centuries after the battle. In Etruria, we have already met with possible ancestor cults (see chapter 4, p. 128), most notably in the Tomb of the Five Chairs at Cerveteri. Such a cult has been invoked to explain a roofed shrine-like building uncovered a few years ago next to the Cuccumelletta tumulus at Vulci.[23] But perhaps the most spectacular example is at Cortona, where recent work on the largest of the burial mounds, the Sodo II Tumulus (64 m in diameter), has uncovered a grand altar attached to the tumulus and of the same period in the sixth century as its largest chamber tomb.[24] A flight of steps leads up to the platform, flanked by large reliefs of a struggle between a monstrous beast (a sphinx?) and a male human figure who thrusts his sword into her flank. Significantly, the altar faces east towards the Etruscan hill town, over which the honoured dead were perhaps thought for a long time to have a controlling influence.

Visions of the underworld

If the dead lived on, what sort of life was envisaged for them? To attempt an answer it is necessary to turn to the funerary imagery, most of which is Greek-inspired, and once again one is confronted

21   Steingräber, 1986: plates 101, 105, 146
22   Small, 1994: 86
23   Sgubini Moretti, 1994
24   Zamarchi Grassi, 1992

by the problem of whether the images reflect contemporary thought and belief or were chosen to parade familiarity with Greek culture (without sharing its convictions), or whether some of them are merely conventional or decorative; and there was probably a blurring of all three possibilities on many occasions. To the Greeks the dead body had obviously lost something – what they called *psyche* and we translate as 'soul'. The most obviously tangible thing missing was breath, and this is probably how most Greeks thought of psyche. In Greek art the soul is sometimes pictured as a small winged human shape fleeing from the body at death. A fifth century Athenian funerary oil-flask shows little winged souls flitting around the figure of Charon, ferryman of the underworld, who has come to transport a deceased lady across the water.[25] Flying souls are rare in Etruscan art, but there are wingless examples in a painted Tarquinian tomb (the Tomb of Orcus II) who swing about on the shrubbery like Victorian fairies (fig. 92), though to either side the figures of the deceased Greek heroes Teiresias (Teriasa) and Agamemnon (Achmemrun) are full-size.

Death is a journey, but once the body or cremated remains are in the tomb, that is not the journey's end. There is a contradiction here: the tomb was house-like for the deceased's accommodation, and everything was made comfortable for the soul including provision of a set of metalware or crockery. But it seems that the soul, rather than staying put in the tomb for eternity, went off somewhere else, off in fact to the underworld – which was not the tomb itself, though the entrance to it might be shown as a door in some tombs (fig. 93). Yet one didn't just step through the walls of the tomb to the underworld next door: a journey was involved, and judging by the number of sea-creatures featured in funerary contexts (see figs 34 and 77), it is possible that a voyage across the sea was sometimes envisaged.

Representations of underworld scenes are not common and are late in date – of the fourth century and later. The visions are essentially Greek, of a world presided over by Hades (Aita) and Persephone (Phersipnei), and their ultimate source is *Odyssey*, Book 11, though usually there are Etruscan demons also present. It has often been said that the Etruscans became more pessimistic about the afterlife in the later centuries, and this is primarily because the atmosphere of gaiety that permeates many of the archaic painted tombs is rarely seen later. But the first death demons appear already in the fifth

25 Boardman, 1989: fig. 255

Figure 92　Tomb of Orcus II, Tarquinia: souls in the underworld. Late fourth century BC. *(Photograph: Soprintendenza Archeologica per l'Etruria Meridionale)*

century. Principal among them is Charun (or Charu), whose name is clearly that of the harmless Greek ferryman Charon, but who has no boat and instead threatens the dead with a heavy hammer (fig. 94). As Pallottino observed,[26] his iconography seems in part to be taken from another Greek character, a demon called Eurynomos mentioned once by Pausanias (10.28.4) when describing a famous painting of *The Underworld* by Polygnotos at Delphi: 'a demonic spirit in Hades . . . who eats away the flesh of the dead and leaves only their bones. . . . His flesh is between blue and black, like the flies that settle on meat, and he shows his teeth.' The complexion and description fit very accurately some of the Etruscan depictions, such as in the François Tomb of Vulci[27] and other painted tombs at Tarquinia.[28]

26　Pallottino, 1952: 102
27　Buranelli, 1987: 94
28　For example, Steingräber, 1986: plate 61

Figure 93   Tomb of the Augurs, Tarquinia: back wall showing door and mourners. c.520 BC, watercolour reproduction. (After Becatti and Magi, 1955: fig. 3)

Figure 94   Querciola II Tomb, Tarquinia: scene with two figures of Charun. The inscription reads: 'Anes Arnth, son of Velthur, died aged 50'. Third/second century BC. (After Pfiffig, 1975: fig. 97)

It would seem the Etruscans knew or cared little about the Greek Charon, but he does appear once in the Tomb of the Blue Demons, discovered at Tarquinia in 1985, where he ferries the dead to an underworld terrorized by demons of various colours, not just blue (fig. 95).[29] This is not just an interesting juxtaposition – a Greek-style Charon acting in concert with Etruscan agents of death – but also a fifth century vision that marks an intermediate stage between early and late funerary iconography.

Charun appears often in scenes of death, sometimes twice as in figure 94. There may be other demons with him, some, like the female Vanth, less threatening than he. There are indeed many demons in the Etruscan underworld, but apart from Charun and Vanth they are rarely named. Most horrific of them is Tuchulcha, who occurs rarely and is named only once, on the walls of the Tomb of Orcus II already mentioned (fig. 96), where she stands before the Greek hero Theseus (These). This is a composite creation that makes one think again of ghastly creatures like Eurynomos; only here the inspiration may have come from further afield than Greece. In the Epic of Gilgamesh, the most widely recited narrative of the ancient Near East, the hero Enkidu has a dream of the underworld before he dies.

I stood before an awful being, the sombre-faced man-bird. His was a vampire face, his foot was a lion's foot, his hand was an eagle's talon. He fell on me and his claws were in my hair, he held me fast, and I smothered . . . and he led me away to the palace of the Queen of Darkness . . . down the road from which there is no coming back.[30]

Not all the details fit by any means, and some of Tuchulcha's features are those of another Near Eastern underworld figure, the demoness Lamashtu[31] – notably the ass's ears (which Charun also sports) and hand-held snakes. Such conceptions appear to have been part of an undercurrent of popular belief concerning the afterlife that was held right across the ancient Mediterranean. They spread ultimately from Mesopotamia, surfacing very occasionally in Greek art, rather more frequently in Etruscan.

29 Cataldi Dini, 1987, 1989
30 Sandars, 1972: 92
31 Black and Green, 1992: 116; de Ruyt, 1934: 238–40

Figure 95 Tomb of the Blue Demons, Cerveteri, right wall: Charon and the underworld. Fifth century BC. (After Cataldi Dini, 1989: fig. 110)

Figure 96   Tomb of Orcus II, Tarquinia: Tuchulcha. (After Martha, 1889: fig. 268)

Funerary art and daily life

A late archaic stone *cippus* from Chiusi displays a very fine relief of a group of women holding up – sorting? examining? – long draperies.[32] The scene may be one of preparation for a wedding (one of the seated figures is possibly a man); but given that *cippi* are tomb-markers, it is more than likely that the women are not handling garments for the living but shrouds for the deceased. It is a kind of problem of interpretation that is ever-present in the study of a society for which the principal visual evidence is funerary art.

Among the more common subjects that occur on *cippi* and tomb-paintings are sporting scenes, banquets and dancing. To an aristocratic society, these are agreeable enough leisure pursuits, and all are treated as 'diversions' by Heurgon; but again such scenes, given

32 Jannot, 1984: fig. 319

their funerary context, do not necessarily provide a transparent window onto everyday Etruscan activities.[33] The most interesting question is not so much what information about such pursuits is offered by the scenes, as why they were chosen to enhance the environment of the tomb. There are many possibilities. The first is that they provide a kind of pictorial record of the highlights of the life that is no more, a vision of the past. But they can equally be taken as a vision of the future, an attempt to perpetuate the good things of life, offering glimpses of a hoped-for afterlife of energetic and carefree living. A somewhat related possibility is that the images – as in Egyptian funerary art – were thought to possess the magical power of helping to reactivate the soul of the deceased.[34] More commonly held is the view that the scenes document the rites that took place at burial, so the feasts are funeral feasts, the sports are athletic competitions that actually took place – or that the deceased's family would have wished to take place – to honour the dead. Nor need any one of these interpretations exclude any of the others. Finally, an extreme sceptic might argue that the scenes are taken direct from Greek art (especially vase-painting) and need not have anything to say about Etruscan practice or belief.

Sports

Greek art is full of sporting scenes, but the context is different: the association is more with daily life and especially with the great four-yearly athletic festivals, to which the Etruscans were barred by virtue of being 'barbarian'. But a passage from Pindar (*Pyth.* 8.88–96) might, if the sentiment expressed were held across the Mediterranean, help to explain both why many Greek sculptures portray the deceased as athletes and why sport might feature so prominently in tomb decoration. The Greek poet's ode is for a boy who won in the wrestling event at Delphi, and juxtaposes death and athletic prowess in a striking and poignant way: 'He who wins, of a sudden, some noble prize in the rich years of youth . . . has in his heart what is better than wealth. . . . But brief is the time of man's delight. . . . Creature of a day! . . . Such is man: a shadow in a dream.'

In Etruria, the connection between death and sporting events is often explicit, as in the painted Tomb of the Inscriptions at Tarquinia, where the events are physically interrupted by depictions of the

33 'Diversions': Heurgon, 1964: 183ff; on the ambiguities of Etruscan funerary art: d'Agostino, 1983, 1989
34 Jannot, 1984: 413

Figure 97   Tomb of the Augurs, Tarquinia: Phersu. (After Moretti, 1974: fig. 15)

door to the underworld (or to the tomb itself).[35] In the Tomb of the Augurs, on the adjoining wall to that with the scene of wrestling, two mourners stand either side of a similar door (see fig. 93). Out in the open air, as suggested by the plants underfoot, the funeral games take place (see fig. 85), among them the grim contest directed by the masked actor labelled Phersu. It is an unequal struggle: the victim, though armed, has a bag over his head; the dog is urged on to maul him (fig. 97).

The Phersu character turns up in two other tomb-paintings, both directing the same game (Tomb of the Olympic Games) and dancing alone (Tomba della Pulcinella). One might imagine that all these were visions of a kind of proto-Charun master-minding underworld tortures, especially as there seem to be etymological correspondences between Phersu and infernal beings such as Phersipnei/Persephone.[36] But it has been argued recently that *phersu* is more likely to mean 'mask' rather than 'masked man', and that actors of this type can also be seen in contexts of burlesque. So on the left wall of the Tomb of the Augurs, a Phersu character appears to be mimicking the boxers next to him[37] – though he has also been

35 Thuillier, 1985: 419ff
36 Croon, 1955
37 Jannot, 1993a: 311

interpreted as running away from a victim who has beaten the dog and broken free. There seems every reason to believe that the blind-fold game, of pitting one's wits against the gods of death, is as much a sport as any of the others shown in the tomb (boxing, wrestling and a gruesome kind of tug-of-war) and that the scenes are not intrusive or pulled from some Near Eastern context, as implied by Åkerström.[38]

The game with the dog is a bloody one, as are some other sports detailed in the tombs. But these are funeral games, and it was probably part of their ritual nature that the outcome should entail a flow of blood, for the primitive belief was that blood would assuage and nourish the dead. The atmosphere is very much that of the games for Patroklos in *Iliad*, Book 23, where in the boxing match the loser ends up senseless and spitting clots of blood, and of the games for Anchises in Virgil (*Aeneid* 5), where the same sport has an equally horrific climax. Etruscan boxers, like their Greek counterparts, performed with gloves, which were not, as in modern practice, for the protection of both contestants: they were thongs of ox-hide to inflict greater damage. Other sports, such as discus-throwing, were also taken from Greek usage, but in chariot-racing a novel feature was the dangerous practice of tying the reins be-hind the charioteer's back, which must on occasion have resulted in death or serious injury.[39]

There were other larger-scale occasions for games, too, for which the evidence is mainly literary. According to Herodotus, to expi-ate the crime of stoning the Phocaean prisoners after the battle of Alalia, the Caeretans were instructed by Delphi to hold a regular festival of athletic and equestrian events. From Livy (1.35.9) we learn that already at the end of the seventh century, Etruscan 'boxers and horses' were being supplied to Rome for the Roman Games, and (5.1.4) that a couple of centuries later the leader of Veii, in a fit of pique, withdrew his troupe of performers from the pan-Etruscan festival held regularly at Fanum Voltumnae. Livy's word for per-former is *artifex*, meaning someone with any special expertise which might range from sporting ability to skill at some of the sideshow turns, such as juggling and clowning, which we see staged for the benefit of the deceased in a number of painted tombs. A full range of sporting and sideshow activities, including climbing a (greasy?) pole, is shown on a black-figure amphora in the British Museum

38 Åkerström, 1981: 13, 31
39 Bronson, 1965

(see fig. 100), and the context may be some kind of Dionysiac festival.[40] Of the mainstream events, equestrian races are the most frequently illustrated outside of a funerary context, notably on architectural frieze plaques (see fig. 62d, chapter 5).[41] Aside from funeral games, the main big sporting celebrations seem to have been staged, as in Greece, for the honour of the gods at their sanctuaries.

Banqueting

Again it is necessary to bear in mind the funerary bias of the evidence. In early Etruria, it seems to have been customary to take meals seated, as shown on a well known cinerary urn from Montescudaio near Volterra.[42] Reclining at banquet was a feature of Near Eastern living,[43] practised by Assyrian kings, condemned by Amos (6.4–6) in the Old Testament. In Greece, the first signs of its use are illustrations on Corinthian pottery of around 600 BC, and it appears in Etruria soon afterwards. The Greeks called a banqueting couch a *kline*, but the same word also meant a bed for sleeping on (or for dying in), and this dual function of the *kline* is equally apparent in Etruria, where the dead are often shown in the guise of reclining banqueters. One of the great showpieces of the Villa Giulia in Rome is the archaic terracotta sculpture from Caere of a married couple reclining on a *kline* which served as a container for their cremated remains.[44]

Cinerary urns of rather similar form, but in stone, are known from the Chiusi region, where the deceased may have at their elbow a figure of the female death demon Vanth.[45] To show the dead as asleep is comparatively uncommon and is best known from two series of sarcophagi with single figures, in stone from Cerveteri[46] and in terracotta from Tuscania,[47] and from a couple of striking examples from Vulci, now in Boston, which show the marriage bed with couples lying in permanent embrace.[48] But these are heavily outnumbered by banqueting dead on cinerary urns of the Hellenistic period.

40   van der Meer, 1986
41   Root, 1973
42   Sprenger and Bartoloni, 1983: plate 17
43   Boardman, 1990
44   Brendel, 1995: fig. 159
45   Cristofani, 1975b
46   Sprenger and Bartoloni, 1983: plate 202
47   Cristofani, 1985a: 329
48   Brendel, 1995: figs. 299, 300

The ambiguity of the *kline* extends into the tombs themselves where, in southern Etruria, rock-cut couches for the dead frequently line the walls, and it is likely as not that these were viewed as banqueting couches. Carbonized food remains found in some tombs suggest that a final funeral meal was consumed in which the dead were thought to participate and could then continue to dine from the crockery sealed away with them. Just as the *kline* itself originated in the Near East, so did the idea of the permanent funerary *kline*, which is seen to best effect in western and southern Anatolia. Perhaps closest of all to what we see in Etruscan cemeteries are the tomb interiors of the Phrygian highlands of Turkey around Midas Şehri, where everything is rock-cut: pitched roofs to the chambers with relief ceiling beams, and couches around the walls with raised head-rests and with legs in relief.[49] The tombs that provide closest parallels with Etruria are of the sixth century and later, but there is continuous development of architectural form here from the late eighth century on. Geologically it is not surprising that this is another extensive *tufo* area.

Most Greek banqueting scenes, on painted cups and the like, are illustrations of the *symposion* or symposium, the wine-drinking and discourse that went on after the consumption of food, a thoroughly Greek institution with set rules and entertainments, as recent scholarly 'symposia' on the Greek symposium have made clear.[50] There is an emphasis on drinking, too, in Etruscan representations (see fig. 62c), and the atmosphere is similarly aristocratic, but there are also differences. Most obvious is that Greek symposiasts are always male, whereas in Etruria women are participators in banquets from the later sixth century onwards.[51] Moreover, the women are free-born wives and family members, as context and inscriptions make clear, whereas the only women admitted to Greek symposia were entertainers and prostitutes.

Etruscan banquets were occasions for displaying the status and influence of the most powerful families in the community, whose elaborately dressed and bejewelled members are often carefully distinguished from the servants and lower orders by clear differences of scale, as in the painted pediment of the Tomb of Hunting and Fishing at Tarquinia (fig. 98). But although these were not symposia in the Greek sense, the equipment used was almost identical: couches

49 For example, Haspels, 1970: figs. 56, 542 (3,5,6)
50 For example, Murray and Tecuşan, 1995
51 Cristofani, 1987a

Figure 98 Tomb of Hunting and Fishing, Tarquinia: pediment of rear chamber showing banquet. End of sixth century BC. (After Weber-Lehmann, 1985: plate 5.4)

with embroidered coverlets and pillows, Greek-style drinking cups, jugs and bowls for wine, garlands for the hair of the participants. Even some symposium games reached Etruria, such as *kottabos*, in which players attempted to hit a target with the last dregs of their wine.[52]

Few, if any, of the portrayals are scenes of everyday banquets. In some later tomb-paintings, the setting is the underworld itself, which is most clearly seen in the Golini I Tomb at Orvieto, where previous generations of the family are shown at the feast which the deceased is about to join. In other cases, it is probably the funeral feast that we see, food scraps having been found in some tombs, as already noted. Judging by the small dimensions of many tomb interiors, the meal is hardly likely to have been held within the tomb, but rather outside, where some representations (for example, in the Tomb of the Lionesses) suggest that special marquees were set up.[53] The dead needed sustenance, but not necessarily fresh food: remains of the meal would presumably suffice.

As with sporting scenes, banquets are also illustrated on architectural terracottas from several sites, where the context may be ceremonial or connected with cult. In the case of Murlo (see fig. 62c) and Acquarossa,[54] suggestions were made soon after their excavation that both series of plaques may have decorated formal dining-rooms.[55]

Dance, music and sex

Another series of Acquarossa plaques from the same building shows a troupe of dancers and musicians, including an acrobat performing a handstand.[56] Dance is one of the more popular motifs in Etruscan art; many varieties and contexts are shown.

The male dance in armour is among the first to appear. In Greece, a similar dance was known as the *pyrrhic*, a term which Aristotle (fr. 519) derived from the Greek *pyra*, 'funeral pyre'. The etymology may be dubious, but an original connection with funerals may well have been widely made. In this connection, it is interesting that one of the first manifestations in Etruria of the dance has a

52 Rasmussen, 1995
53 Golini I: Steingräber, 1986: 278; food scraps from tombs: Barbieri, 1987b: nos. 51, 53; marquees: Holloway, 1965: 344
54 Strandberg Olofsson, 1985: 58
55 Rathje, 1990: 286
56 Strandberg Olofsson, 1985: 58

Figure 99   Bronze cinerary urn from Bisenzio: warriors and a ploughman parade and dance around a chained beast. Second half of the eighth century BC, *in the Villa Giulia Museum, Rome. (Photograph: Soprintendenza Archeologica per l'Etruria Meridionale)*

funerary context. The object concerned is a large bronze container of the late eighth century from Bisenzio on Lake Bolsena, now in the Villa Giulia Museum in Rome; on its lid are a number of figurines, including men brandishing shields and weapons (fig. 99). The vessel is itself a cinerary urn, and so a procession of dancing warriors seems entirely appropriate. On painted pottery the armed dance takes many forms: feigned combats, processions, sometimes with musicians present. It is unclear whether they all fulfilled similar functions.[57]

The Micali Painter's black-figure amphora in the British Museum, mentioned already for its sporting scenes, also shows groups of

57   Spivey, 1988

Figure 100 Etruscan black-figure amphora attributed to the Micali Painter: sporting scenes. Later sixth century BC, *in the British Museum, London. (Photograph: copyright British Museum)*

dancing figures (fig. 100): one group, fully human, gyrates with castanets; the other consists of 'three pairs of exultant, dancing nude ithyphallic hooved satyrs'.[58] Dancing, and participants dressed as satyrs, are components of early Roman festivals as well,[59] possibly through Etruscan influence, and we hear that Etruria was again the provider of specialist entertainers to Rome when, in 364 BC, Etruscan dancers were sent there for a performance, with flute

58 van der Meer, 1986
59 Szilágyi, 1981

accompaniment, that was staged to avert plague. Livy (7.2.6) calls them *histriones* ('performers', 'actors'), and as with the *artifices* discussed earlier, these look to be professionals of intermediate or lower status in the social hierarchy.

Satyrs (or 'silens') occasionally stray onto the walls of painted Tarquinian tombs as well: dancing around their patron god in the now lost Tomb of Dionysus and the Silens; reclining in a pediment of the Tomb of the Inscriptions; up and mobile again in Tomb 1999. There is also a Dionsysiac 'feel' to a number of other dancing scenes in these tombs, with their prominent display of ivy wreaths, wine bowls and the like.

In primitive societies, dancing may serve many purposes: to avert evil and placate the gods; to promote fertility; and, by pounding on the ground, to communicate with those who dwell below it – the dead and those who rule over them. Scenes of dancing shown in tomb-paintings and on other funerary monuments have some like-lihood of being connected with the funeral celebrations themselves. Music is provided by the double-flute (which may accompany many other energetic activities such as sports) and the lyre, and sometimes the musicians join in with footwork of their own (as in the case of the Tomb of the Triclinium). Women play an important part, but otherwise many details are taken from the practices of Greek after-dinner dancing (the *komos*), in particular the vase-dance, where performers gesticulate with cups and other vessels as they cavort.[60]

How do we explain the occasional appearance of erotic scenes? The Tarquinian Tomb of the Whipping is so called from the depic-tion of a prone woman being flogged by two naked men; on the other side of the same wall is a sexual encounter between two men and a woman. Two more erotic groups feature in the Tomb of the Bulls, one homosexual, the other acrobatically heterosexual, in a narrow frieze which is difficult to connect with the main scene of Troilos ambushed by Achilles. Some Etruscans collected Greek erotica, and many of the most explicit sexual scenes on Greek vases are from Etruscan tombs. But in Etruscan art, such portrayals are rare, so it is all the more surprising to find them as tomb decoration. In both tombs, there are elements of unreality, as if these are not everyday encounters: in one, the scenes are interrupted by a large painted door to the underworld of a kind we have seen before; in the other, they are accompanied by two bulls (one with a human face) which give the tomb its name.

60 Rasmussen, 1995

Several explanations are possible. Towards the end of the Greek symposium, the drinking often led to sexual pleasures, sometimes to sexual gymnastics, even to sadism. The tomb-painter might have simply copied the groups off Greek symposium vases which illustrated such activities, which could explain why the two flagellators have their hair garlanded as if for a party. The scenes might also be symbolic, like the urn with griffin heads from Chiusi discussed earlier, illustrating the sexual power released at death, a power that enabled life to be prolonged, even regenerated. This is perhaps the reason why a relief scene of fellatio and copulation between satyrs and maenads was chosen for a stone sarcophagus from Chiusi,[61] why a large flying winged phallus figures prominently in the painted decoration of the Tomb of the Mouse at Tarquinia,[62] and why the dancing warriors on the bronze cinerary urn from Bisenzio (see fig. 99) are in a state of sexual excitement. Finally such images can also be viewed in a different symbolic light as apotropaic (warding off evil), a view advocated most recently by Holloway.[63] In the Greek and Roman worlds, the image of the phallus as a protective emblem could be seen everywhere, especially at Athens where everyone had a herm (pillar-statue) with erect phallus by their gateway.[64] Some Etruscans may have thought one needed protection in the afterlife as much as in life, especially perhaps for the journey from one to the other.

The sexual organs are also exposed during defecation, and an unusual image in the Tomb of the Jugglers of a man defecating has also been interpreted as apotropaic, here protecting the name of the tomb-painter inscribed next to it.[65] There seems little symbolic, however, about the incidental, everyday setting of the sexual scenes depicted in the painted Tomb of the Chariots, where homosexual groups are squeezed in almost as space-fillers under the grandstands of spectators watching the sporting events.[66]

The shedding of blood, animal and human

Suggestions have already been made, in connection with sporting scenes, as to why there should be such an emphasis on blood-letting

61 Jannot, 1984: plate 107
62 Steingräber, 1986: plate 156
63 Holloway, 1986
64 Johns, 1982: 61ff
65 Colonna, 1975: 185
66 Steingräber, 1986: 290–1

Figure 101   Leg-in-mouth beasts: detail of incised frieze on impasto *vessel made at Capena. c.600 BC, in the Manchester Museum. (Drawing: courtesy of A.J.N.W. Prag)*

in Etruscan art – in funerary art in particular. Scenes of animals drawing blood (animal against animal) are common not only in the Orientalizing and archaic periods, when they are prolific in Greece too, but also later when the Greeks had lost their taste for it, as illustrated in the small animal frieze of the fourth century François Tomb at Vulci where quadrupeds are mauled by predators of various kinds.[67] In Etruria, the goriness is often taken a degree or two further. So the minor Orientalizing motif in Greek art of a lion devouring a human or part of a human becomes a dominant theme in archaic Etruria, and everywhere (especially on pottery) there are lions with human legs dangling from their jaws. One artist of incised *impasto*, working at Capena outside Etruria but in the Etruscan tradition (fig. 101), seems to have been interested in almost no other subject.[68]

As for representing the shedding of human blood, there was plenty of scope in the many depictions of battle, whether real, imaginary or mythological. Here, too, there are scenes of the macabre that seem peculiarly Etruscan, especially some painted by an Etrusco-Corinthian vase-painter known as the Pittore dei Caduti (alias the Carnage Painter), which show dead soldiers being decapitated by their victors while vultures peck at other parts of their anatomy.[69] An Assyrian from Nineveh might have cast an admiring glance at these pots; a Greek, though relishing such details in Homer, would

67   Buranelli, 1987: 104–5
68   Rasmussen and Horie, 1988
69   Szilágyi, 1981: plates 107–8

have been less likely to. A similar taste for blood and sudden death is revealed in the choice of Greek myths that decorate the sides of many of the sarcophagi and ash-urns. Whether the scene is from the Amazon or Theban cycles or from the fall of the house of Atreus, the artist unerringly focuses on the point of maximum horror.

From these myths, scenes of human sacrifice are sometimes shown, such as Achilles' slaughter of the Trojan prisoners on the painted walls of the François Tomb at Vulci and elsewhere, or the sacrifice of Iphigenia on cinerary urns and on painted pottery. The question has also been seriously raised of whether the Etruscans actually practised ritual human sacrifice, either at funerals or on other more public occasions.[70] Examination of the bones of an adult male corpse recently discovered in an early context in a sanctuary at Tarquinia suggests that they did,[71] and one or two funerary reliefs seem to point in the same direction, but there is no evidence that it was a regular occurrence. Even the Romans felt driven to this expedient in isolated situations of extreme crisis.

Male pursuits: hunting and warfare

Driving through the countryside, one gets a clear message, from the many large tracts of wooded terrain signposted *riserva di caccia*, that hunting figures prominently in modern Italy. It provides both food for the table (hare for the *pappardelle alla lepre*) and in many cases camaraderie for the well heeled, expensively armed hunting fraternities. These two functions of hunting have invariably gone hand-in-hand (see chapter 6, p. 200), and Etruscan Italy was no exception. Because it involved ownership of equipment, possession of horses and skill in handling them, together with rights or control over terrain, large-scale hunting (especially of large quadrupeds such as boar and deer) was a prerogative of the few, the rich. Though others might also be employed, it was the aristocracy who could dictate terms.

Most hunt representations decorate funerary monuments, as Camporeale notes, briefly wondering whether the subject itself has funerary significance.[72] They show men pursuing a variety of game, on foot, with dogs and on horseback, or a return from the hunt with the victims slung on poles. Plants and shrubs may indicate the

70 Bonfante, 1984, 1986b: 262
71 Bonghi Jovino et al., forthcoming
72 Camporeale, 1984: 187

Figure 102   Tomb of Hunting and Fishing, Tarquinia: rear chamber showing fishing boat. (Photograph: Soprintendenza Archeologica per l'Etruria Meridionale)

open air, but there is rarely any indication of terrain, a fact that makes the far chamber of the Tomb of Hunting and Fishing at Tarquinia (fig. 102) – at once the best known and most atypical of all the painted tombs – all the more remarkable for its close observation of natural setting. It has been suggested that these rocky waterscapes show glimpses of the sea nearby.[73] But where exactly? There is no flatter stretch of coast than around Tarquinia, nor does the landscape depicted fit any of the neighbouring crater lakes. It fits far better the coastline of the Aegean, and bears an uncanny resemblance to the rock formations displayed in the bronze age frescoes from Thera.[74] The inclusion of fishing from boats also has an eastern Mediterranean look about it, for it is featured in the contemporary Lycian painted tomb at Elmali (see above, p. 136).[75] And who are the energetic little figures who seem a world apart

73 Holloway, 1965: 347
74 Hood, 1978: fig. 36
75 Mellink, 1970: plate 59

from the huge stately banqueters crammed into the pediment space above (fig. 98)? They are carefully observed: the steersman of the fourman boat is bald, and their dress consists of close-fitting vests or short tunics.

One interpretation of the paintings focuses on the amatory embrace of the banqueting pair (he has his arm over her shoulder) and stresses the link between hunting and erotic pursuit. To the left of the boat shown in figure 102 a youth dives into the water, and in a later and smaller-scale tomb-painting in Greek style, at Paestum south of Naples, the themes of diving and amorous approach (but here homoerotic) are also combined. But there are many elements in the Tomb of Hunting and Fishing – the marked differences of scale, the subject-matter, stylistic details of poses – that find their closest parallels in Egyptian painting, though the figure-drawing is both less precise and more lively. The whole chamber can even be 'read' in a straightforwardly Egyptian way, except that in Egyptian tombs it is usually the tombowner who is shown fishing and fowling. Here at Tarquinia in the pediment of the first chamber, we see noblemen returning from the hunt on horseback; but in the far chamber, it is perhaps through the ceaseless labour of their servants and retainers (who are, though, allowed time off for diving practice) that the noble aristocratic dead will continue to be served with game in the next world. At neighbouring Caere, there is sufficient evidence to argue that the Greek vase-painters who set up the workshop of the Caeretan hydriai came to Etruria via a short sojourn in Egypt. So, too, it is not inconceivable that the painter who founded the workshop responsible for decorating this tomb (most likely an Ionian Greek) had picked up some Egyptian conventions in a similar manner.[76]

Feasting, hunting, fighting: clearly in the aristocratic echelons of society all three were important, but the evidence relating to warfare requires careful weighing. In early iron age graves, the importance of fighting can be gauged by the numerous finds of round shields, spear-heads and crested helmets, all of bronze.[77] The problems proliferate in the seventh century, when armour becomes both subject to influences from abroad, especially from Greece, and also scarcer in the archaeological record. Greek hoplite armour was introduced into Italy at this time – round shield held at the rim, helmet covering the sides of the face and neck, bronze corselet and

76 Eroticism in Tomb of Hunting and Fishing: Cerchiai, 1987; Caeretan hydriai and Egypt: Hemelrijk, 1984: 160
77 Fugazzola Delpino, 1984: 31ff

greaves, long spear – but not to the exclusion of pre-existing forms. In Greece, the new type of armour is usually associated with far-reaching reforms both in style of fighting and on the socio-political front. The hoplite panoply was designed for massed ranks of men standing shoulder to shoulder with shields overlapping, presenting an unbroken barrier. The strategy demanded large numbers of soldiers who had sufficient vested interest in their home territory to be willing to risk their lives in its service. In other words, it implies a degree of democratization.

Where Etruria is concerned, there is disagreement between those who believe that the appearance of hoplite armour carries with it the introduction of the new fighting strategy[78] and those who see warfare continuing to be conducted in the old way with small armed groups raised by individual clans and fighting in a less disciplined fashion.[79] The latter view gets some support from finds of hoplite armour in tombs, which appears to be restricted to men of high rank.[80] Anyone looking to representations of warfare in Etruscan art to decide the issue would be disappointed (and indeed there are very few depictions of hoplites fighting in formation in Greek art). But the subsequent history of military conflict with Rome suggests that the Etruscans never adopted the Greek system in any thoroughgoing way, whereas the Romans did, and Rome's large citizen army fighting in compact formation was inevitably superior.

From the foregoing it should be clear that there was never an Etruscan 'national' army, only those of individual city states (as in Greece) or – more likely than not – of individual family groups within the city states. The same must have been true of sea-power, which was clearly strong into the fifth century; the earliest illustrations of warships go back to the seventh.[81] Presumably only the coastal cities were involved here. Caere seems to have been heavily involved in the naval operation against the Phocaeans of Alalia, for it was allotted the majority of the Greek prisoners afterwards (Herodotus 1.166). At some unspecified date, a Tarquinian commander, Velthur Spurinna, led an army to Sicily (for which he presumably needed ships), 'the first to do so', as recorded in a late inscription.[82]

78   Stary, 1979
79   Spivey and Stoddart, 1990: 127
80   d'Agostino, 1990
81   Cristofani, 1983a: 28
82   Torelli, 1975: 43

Although in early iron age graves the cinerary urns for men are often anthropomorphized to resemble warriors by the addition of a helmet of bronze or clay, only seldom does subsequent funerary art depict the deceased as fighters or show scenes of non-mythological warfare. True, there are well known examples that are often illustrated, such as the *stele* (tombstone) of Avle Feluske from Vetulonia in Florence,[83] but it is interesting to compare the few instances of scenes of soldiers or fighting in Etruscan tomb-painting with the proliferation of such images in that other great body of contemporary funerary painting from Italy, from Lucanian Paestum.[84] Where war imagery is more common is on the *stelai* from the northern fringes of the Etruscan world, in the Apennine region from Fiesole to Felsina/ Bologna and beyond, where there were threats to be faced from belligerent Gauls. Sometimes a military interest is shown in a more muted way by the representation of armour alone: examples include the painted Moretti Tomb at Tarquinia, and the reliefs of the Tomb of the Shields and Thrones and of the Tomb of the Reliefs at Cerveteri. Otherwise, apart from the scene of battling Etruscan heroes in the François Tomb at Vulci, there are many funerary reliefs of Greek mythological battles showing victors with whom the deceased would perhaps have identified – though some of them decorate the sarcophagi and ash-urns of women.

One final point about the evidence from tombs is made by Spivey and Stoddart:[85] that the military equipment deposited as gravegoods seems rarely to have been that which was actually used for fighting. The armour is often beautifully made of thin embossed bronze and seems rather to be ornamental and ceremonial or made especially for the tomb.[86] Although no doubt bearing a resemblance to what was put in tombs, real armour may have been of different materials altogether such as leather. In the case of chariots, these occur (rarely) in female as well as male burials – in Latium at any rate (for example, at Acqua Acetosa-Laurentina)[87] – and it is not clear whether they were ever used in battle. Chariot burials in central Italy may have more to say about burial customs and the status of the deceased than about military practice.

---

83 Sprenger and Bartoloni, 1983: fig. 24
84 Pontrandolfo and Rouveret, 1992
85 Spivey and Stoddart, 1990: 129
86 Strøm, 1971: 19
87 Bartoloni and Grottanelli, 1989: 61

8

Romanization

The Etruscans, as everyone knows, were the people who occupied the middle of Italy in early Roman days and whom the Romans, in their usual neighbourly fashion, wiped out entirely to make room for Rome with a very big R.

D.H. Lawrence (1932) *Etruscan Places*

Cosa and Roman colonization

In 273 BC a substantial body of Roman colonists, drawn from Rome itself and from towns subject to Rome in Latium and further afield, took up residence in the territory of Vulci. Their new home was Cosa, on a hill later to be called Ansedonia, overlooking the sea. Like all Roman *coloniae*, it was laid out like a small but more regularized version of Rome itself, with a forum area surrounded by public buildings and with a temple to the Roman state gods, the Capitolium. The precise number of original colonists is not known – one informed guess puts it at 2500 adult males, which together with all family members would make a total figure of about 9000.[1] But Cosa itself is too small a site to have accommodated all of them: some would have been settled on farms allocated to them in the surrounding area, the Ager Cosanus.

For the Romans, colonization was a highly effective method of land redistribution. In Latin, *colonus* means 'farmer', and that is essentially what colonists were; but they were also fighters and had obligations to serve in the local garrison. The landless poor were in this way enabled to make a new start with an allotment of land, but only at the expense of the recently vanquished, in this case the Etruscans of the Maremma. Vulci had suffered military defeat in 280 BC by an army led by the consul T. Coruncianus. An immediate punishment meted out, typical of the settlements imposed by Rome

---

1 Brown, 1980: 16

on defeated enemies, was the confiscation of part – in this case a third – of its territory. The area concerned was to the northwest of the city, adjacent to the coast and encompassing the plains and river valleys eastwards to the hills of the interior.

The normal method of parcelling out such territory was by centuriation – from the Latin *centuria*, meaning a regular division of land of standard area. In this way large tracts of land were measured out, very similar to the chequerboard plans of towns (such as Cosa itself) but using much bigger units.[2] Vestiges of centuriation, in the form of boundary stones marking out the grid plan, and of continuity of field layout, have been found in many parts of the Roman world. In the territory of Vulci, which has been extensively surveyed and field-walked in recent times, centuriation has been plotted in detail not only adjacent to Cosa (fig. 103) but also around the later (second century BC?) inland *colonia* of Heba[3] and elsewhere.

The foundation of a colony with its concomitant *territorium* was clearly a major imposition on the native population. In the Ager Cosanus, some of the plots closest to the town were probably farmed by those who lived in the town, those further out by families living where they farmed, and perhaps not all Etruscans were displaced from the area but instead farmed on plots that were leased to them. Whatever the arrangements of the settlement were in detail, there must have been great resentment at the time, and it is therefore not surprising that among the first projects undertaken at Cosa was the erecting of stout town walls. Their construction greatly impressed George Dennis, who ascribed to them pre-Roman, even pre-Etruscan, origins.[4] A still impressive sight today, they are built of large close-fitting polygonal blocks, similar in technique to the Etruscan walls of Orbetello and closely matched by those of other early colonies in Etruria such as Saturnia and Pyrgi. What is unique about them – and this was for greater defence – is the incorporation of towers in the polygonal circuit.

There is no evidence of earlier settlement on the hill of Cosa, but the nearest Etruscan town was only a short distance away at Orbetello opposite Monte Argentario. The modern town overlies it, but finds from cemeteries on the neck of the peninsula show that it was a flourishing centre from the Early Iron Age onwards. It is very likely that its Etruscan name was Cusi[5] and that Roman Cosa

2   Salmon, 1969: 21
3   Carandini, 1985: fig. 149
4   Dennis, 1878: II, 257
5   Cristofani, 1985c: 195; Pallottino, 1937: 724

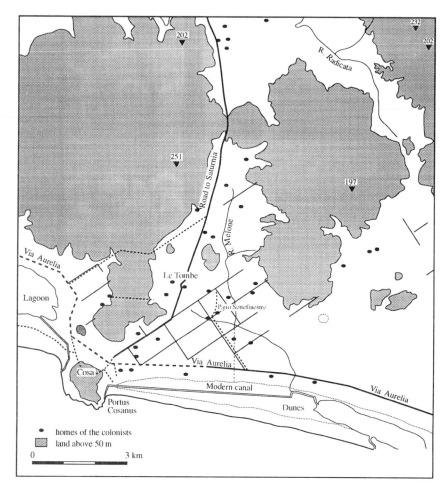

Figure 103   Centuriation around Cosa. (After Carandini, 1985: fig. 111)

derived its name from it. It, too, has remains of polygonal walls, here without the addition of towers, which were presumably put up earlier than Cosa's, when Rome was posing a threat to the whole area. The status of its inhabitants after the Roman takeover is quite unknown.

There were other impositions, too, suffered by Vulci after the defeat of 280. The destruction of Doganella may date to then or just before, but that of the smaller site of Ghiaccio Forte higher up the Albegna valley seems more certainly a direct consequence. Further inland, two towns were created *praefecturae* (native towns under

Roman jurisdiction) at Saturnia and Statonia, the latter located probably at Poggio Buco or Castro, and in 183 BC a *colonia* was planted at the former. Livy (39.55.9) implies an injection of 2000 colonists, and the resulting centuriation around the town has been partially traced. It is probable that by this time or soon afterwards, a great swathe of land stretching from the Tyrrhenian Sea eastwards as far as Lake Bolsena had been taken out of Etruscan control altogether.[6]

The status of Vulci itself after the conquest is problematic. Settlement continues into the Roman period, but excavation has not been systematic and the city is scarcely mentioned in literary sources. However, the fate of its territory was similar to that of other parts of Etruria further south. Although of all the Etruscan states Caere had been on friendliest terms with Rome, this did not prevent it eventually falling foul of its more powerful neighbour and having to cede half its territory, an event that may have happened in 273, the same year as the foundation of Cosa. The way was then open for the planting of further maritime colonies at Castrum Novum (just north of Santa Marinella), Pyrgi, Alsium (at Palo) and Fregenae. Tarquinia was made to suffer with confiscations around the same time in the third century, although it was not until 181 that the colony of Graviscae came into being.

Rome's colonization policy was masterly, if brutal, in its efficient application of a stranglehold on Etruscan means to retaliate. By the settlement of the coastal plains, much of the prime agricultural land was taken out of Etruscan control. By the establishment of colonies at the old ports which had provided so much wealth in the past, any continuing Etruscan aspiration to sea-power and to independent foreign policy was squashed.

Military disasters

The Romans were enabled to carry out their settlement of Etruria as a result of their relentless military successes, which began with the defeat of Veii only 15 km from Rome. Down to 400 BC, Etruria remained strong and intact, and in the fifth century Veii even notched up some victories in skirmishes against the Romans. But that is the last we hear of Etruscan superiority in the field. The destruction of Veii, after a seige much embroidered by Livy and others so as to resemble the epic Trojan War, is usually dated to 396 BC.

6 Harris, 1971: 151

The immediate upshot was that the whole territory around it, the Ager Veientanus, estimated at some 562 km²,[7] became annexed to Rome's, and shortly afterwards Capena and Falerii, both Latin-speaking but culturally Etruscan and solid allies of Veii, were also forced into submission. To help secure these areas, two colonies were planted at Sutrium (Sutri) and Nepet (Nepi), both probably in 383 BC.

Even when Etruscan forces allied themselves with the Gauls of northern Italy, who sporadically swept south to confront Rome (and succeeded in forcing entry into the city in 390), they were no more successful and could not prevent the eventual loss of independence of their city states. Sometimes the outcome included wholesale destruction of the city: as at Veii in 396; as at Volsinii in 264, from where the inhabitants – having called in the Romans to quell an internal dispute (see above, p. 101) – were forcibly moved to the new site of Bolsena; and as at Falerii, which rebelled against Rome in 241, whereupon the population was transferred to the less inaccessible site of Falerii Novi (now Santa Maria di Falleri).

On the whole, the Etruscans of northern Etruria fared rather better. There were no Roman colonies between the territory of Vulci and the river Arno before the first century BC. Although we hear in Livy of fighting either side of 300 BC between the Romans and many of the northern cities, Roman policy seems to have been to forge (or rather to force) individual treaties of varying degrees of subservience and dependency with the oligarchic powers of each state, and these arrangements remained fairly stable. But real deprivation lay ahead. In the Roman civil war of the 80s, much of the conflict centred on this area, and a number of Etruscan cities sided with Marius and were severely punished by Sulla. Populonia was besieged, and Volterra, where the Marians had taken refuge, was reduced after a long siege. Thousands of Sulla's veteran soldiers were rewarded with land allotments in this region, and Sullan colonies were established at Fiesole, Arezzo, Chiusi and Volterra. A great many Etruscans must have been dispossessed; some left the area and even went abroad, as Strabo (5.2.6) tells of the survivors of Volterra.

It is perhaps to this historical context that a very remarkable group of monuments belongs, consisting of three boundary stones inscribed in a late north Etruscan script which were found in the valley of the Oued Miliane south of Tunis.[8] The leader who set

7   Cornell, 1989: 295
8   Cristofani, 1985a: 392–3

them up was one Marce, whose family name Unata is known from inscriptions from Chiusi.[9] In fleeing Italy, his band of exiles was hoping to establish a community that would have a famous future before it: the texts on the stones designate the place as Dardania, an alternative name for Troy. As it turned out, the site was to vanish almost without trace.

The Roman road system

Before the Roman era, the Etruscans had their own roads linking one Etruscan centre with the next.[10] For the Romans, this system had to suffice for some time; consequently when colonists were sent out to the early colonies of Cosa, Sutrium and Nepet, they drove and walked northwards to their destination along Etruscan roads. When later the Romans organized their own system of roads (fig. 104), they made use of the Etruscan roads as and where necessary. Among the first of the paved Roman roads was the Via Amerina, cutting through Faliscan territory to southern Umbria, which was laid out soon after the destruction of Falerii in 241 BC. But this road started from a junction of what was to be the Via Cassia, the southern part of which must therefore have had a precursor.

There are possibilities for dispute about the chronology of all of the consular roads in Etruria, but of the four that ran in a northerly direction from Rome, the most easterly, the Via Flaminia, was probably laid out in 220. The Via Aurelia was possibly begun even somewhat earlier, though Harris argues for 144 and dates the Clodia and Cassia in the first half of the second century BC.[11] The roads were of course constructed to suit Roman needs, which were primarily military: to enable armies to move as quickly as possible into Etruria and beyond, to the still unpacified areas of Liguria and the Gallic Po valley. There was little attempt to service the old Etruscan towns, so the Via Aurelia served admirably to link up the new colonies along the coast but bypassed the old centres of Caere, Tarquinia, Vulci and even Populonia, which therefore had to be approached from it via side-roads or *diverticula*. The Via Clodia, running to the colony of Saturnia, did in fact join up a number of small Etruscan settlements such as Norchia and Tuscania, and so is more likely to have followed earlier roads more closely. But the Via

9 Colonna, 1980
10 Quilici, 1985; and see chapter 5
11 Harris, 1971: 165

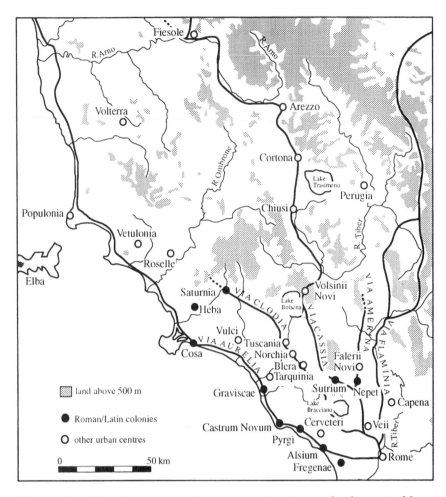

*Figure 104   The Roman road system in Etruria in the late republican
period. (Adapted from Camporeale, 1992: fig. on p. 103)*

Cassia swept north, completely avoiding the Etruscan city nearest
Rome: Veii had been built up again after its destruction to become
a small town under the late Republic and early Empire, but it was
sidestepped by the Roman road system and left as something of a
backwater.

The countryside in transition

Although the picture painted so far of Etruscan life after the Roman
conquest is a bleak one, conditions varied in different parts of the

country. In gauging them, the data obtained from the various field surveys that have taken place in southern Etruria are of special importance, the evidence being primarily based on changes in the pottery tradition: pre-Roman Etruscan sites are characterized by finds of Etruscan coarse wares and *bucchero*, sites of the republican period by black-glazed wares. Although this aspect of fieldwork has its detractors,[12] its usefulness for mapping settlement sequences in the countryside is widely acknowledged, especially when it is combined with other kinds of archaeological enquiry.

The South Etruria survey, for example, demonstrated that in the territory of Falerii, the Ager Faliscus, more than half of the farms were abandoned after the defeat of 241 BC; only some time later were new farms established on new sites, some of them presumably by settlers from Rome.[13] The countryside north of Veii, however, showed a survival ratio of two thirds for the farms after the annexation of the Ager Veientanus, and a later study has put it even higher.[14] In this connection it is worth bearing in mind that, according to Livy, those Veientes who came over to the Roman side during the conflict were granted Roman citizenship, which would have enabled them to remain owners of their land.[15] Finally, in the survey of the area south of Bracciano, the survival ratio for farms was even higher.

Further north, three other recent surveys help to build a picture for the territories of Tarquinia and Vulci. Around San Giovenale, more than half the farm sites continued into the third century, a third of them into the second.[16] In the Ager Cosanus and Albegna valley, maximum disruption was caused by the appropriation and centuriation of land around the newly planted colonies.[17] Figure 105 shows the situation in the second century after the foundation of Heba and its centuriation, which extended to the coast around Telamon. Around Cosa the centuriation was carried out in the third century, but most of the centuriated plots acquired farm buildings only in the following century, presumably after a new influx of colonists recorded by Livy for 197 BC. Higher up the Albegna valley, in the environs of Saturnia, there seems to have been greater continuity in the local population, even though the one Etruscan farm excavated here, at Podere Tartuchino, did not survive into the

12 For example, Torelli, 1989: 397
13 Potter, 1979
14 Liverani, 1984: 38
15 Cornell, 1989: 329
16 Hemphill, 1993: 49
17 Attolini et al., 1991

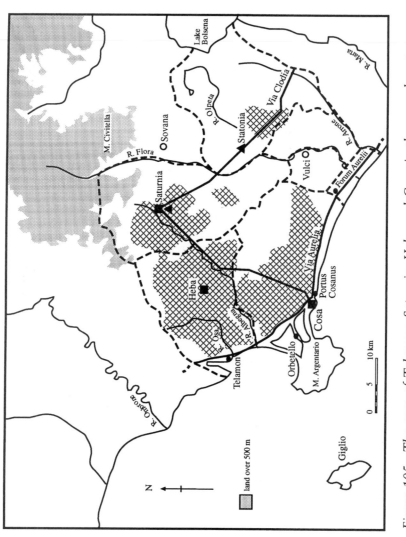

Figure 105　The area of Telamon, Saturnia, Heba and Cosa in the second century BC. Cross-hatching shows centuriation. Square: colonia. Triangle: praefectura. (After Carandini, 1985: fig. 35)

third century.[18] Inscriptional evidence shows that here a local Etruscan aristocracy continued in existence into the late Republic and that some of its members succeeded in making the transition to a villa-owning lifestyle. But from an agricultural point of view, this is marginal hill country, where the economy was more one of subsistence, unlike the rich farmlands towards the coast.

The Tuscania survey, centred on a part of the territory of Tarquinia that was well inland, shows that there were areas that remained comparatively unaffected.[19] The continuity is remarkable: the majority of the many farm sites in this very fertile region persist from the Etruscan into the republican period and even into the later Empire without a break (fig. 106). They are most numerous, and there seems to have been greatest prosperity, in the third and second centuries BC. The better communications provided by the Roman road network, especially by the Via Clodia, and the new markets this may have provided for local produce may have been contributing factors. The one farm site excavated revealed uninterrupted occupation from the sixth to the second centuries.[20]

Some of the cemeteries surrounding Tuscania, especially along the right bank of the river Marta to the south, also reach their apogee in this period. The three chamber tombs of the Curuna family, excavated in 1967–70, contained a series of depositions from the middle of the fourth to the end of second century, and both the earlier sculpted sarcophagi and the gravegoods accompanying them are of impressive quality.[21] Another famous tomb with sculpted sarcophagi, nearer the town but the precise location now lost, was the resting-place for five generations of the Vipinana family which extended into the middle of the second century.[22] There is a number of other wealthy families known from the same period, including the Statlane and Treptie, which shows clearly that the old aristocracy remained in place and retained its possessions for a considerable time. The same is true at nearby Norchia, where inscribed sarcophagi were placed in the family tombs of the Smurina in the third century and of the Tetatru in the second.[23]

At Tuscania, there is very little evidence of farms merging to form large villa estates. In the period of the Republic and the early Empire,

18 Perkins, 1991
19 Barker and Rasmussen, 1988; Barker et al., 1993; Rasmussen, 1991
20 Grant et al., 1993
21 Moretti and Sgubini Moretti, 1983; Sgubini Moretti, 1991
22 Colonna, 1978
23 Colonna di Paolo and Colonna, 1978: 408

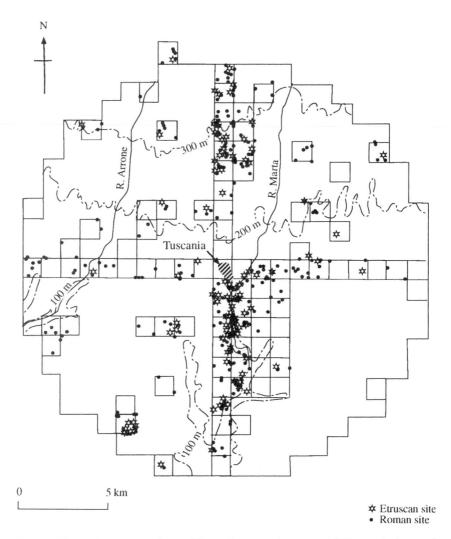

*Figure 106   Etruscan and republican Roman sites around Tuscania located
by field-walking in the square kilometres marked.*

the farms are almost invariably larger than in the Etruscan, but
even so they are spread evenly across the countryside at fairly close
intervals, and there are hardly any that approach the scale of those
that developed along the coast northwest of Vulci. There, the small
plots in which the land had been divided were gradually bought up
by the wealthy in a process that succeeded in both ousting the
original smallholders and creating huge properties, some of which
were owned by the senatorial class of Rome, such as the Domitii

Ahenobarbi who controlled estates around Monte Argentario.[24] The picture is one that is familiar from Gaius Gracchus' description of the journey across coastal Etruria made in 135 BC by his brother Tiberius, the Roman tribune, through countryside denuded of inhabitants and farmed by imported barbarian slaves (Plutarch, *T. Gracchus* 8).

However, Carandini has pointed out that the great villas of the Ager Cosanus were developments of the following century, and suggested that the reason several of them were fortified with defensive walls and turrets (as in the case of Settefinestre, the major excavated site) was for protection against the unrest and lawlessness following on from the terror of the Civil War and Sulla's proscriptions; it is more likely (he reasoned) that Gracchus wrote with the territory of Tarquinia or Caere in mind.[25] Here, along the coastlands of Caere, there are at any rate literary references to large Roman-owned estates from the later second century onwards.[26] Two things seem fairly certain. First, *latifundia*, the vast slave-run ranches and estates, appeared on the scene late in Etruria:[27] the one that is best known from excavation, Settefinestre, was not up and running before the mid first century BC. Second, in southern Etruria, such large-scale establishments cannot anyway have been common except in the coastal plains: elsewhere, as Potter has remarked, the bulk of the terrain is too broken and rugged to suit them.[28]

The cities in decline

As we mentioned in chapter 5, Etruscan archaeology is noted for its dearth of excavation on the major urban sites, and although the balance has begun to be redressed with recent campaigns at Populonia, Cerveteri and Tarquinia, it is still very difficult to plot in physical detail the development of any of the cities – even at their acme, let alone in the period of their decline as centres of power. Nevertheless, useful indications can be obtained by a study of defensive walls and by field-walking.

Many of the wall circuits – whether of ashlar masonry or (rarely) of mud-brick – were thrown up just prior to the period of Romanization. Walls of the Orientalizing and archaic periods, as at

24 Carandini, 1985: 153
25 Carandini, 1985: 145
26 Enei, 1995: 73
27 Potter, 1991a: 199
28 Potter, 1979: 125

Roselle (see above, p. 151), are so far not common. Those of Veii are of the second half of the fifth century[29] and must have been raised during the Rome/Veii wars of this period. At Cerveteri, the walls problably date to the fourth century, as also the fine circuit at Tarquinia, originally some 8 km long, which may have been built to replace an earlier wall encompassing a smaller area.[30]

It is conceivable that some of these defences were put up to protect against aggression from other Etruscan states, and such hostility is indeed recorded in the *elogia* of Tarquinia, which detail events such as Tarquinian military involvement in the affairs of Caere and Arezzo.[31] But the most likely reason for concerted wall-building on this scale is provided by Rome's policy of expansion. Etruscan inter-state rivalry is likely to have occurred at all periods, as the paintings in the François Tomb at Vulci attest for the archaic period, but before the fifth century, many cities and smaller settlements seem to have relied for defence mainly on the natural configuration of the landscape in which they were sited. When most of the final wall circuits were constructed, the days of independence were already numbered.

In some cases, it is possible to plot the density of settlement in successive periods by means of field survey, where best results are achieved on sites that are now entirely given over to arable cultivation. By this means, it has been shown that Doganella (where much land within the walls was never settled) did not survive beyond the third century;[32] that it was actually destroyed is confirmed by excavation.[33] At Veii, the considerable amount of black-glazed pottery recovered by field-walking has shown that the site was by no means totally abandoned between the destruction of 396 BC and the creation of an Augustan town on the site some time before 1 BC.[34] At Cerveteri, although there are substantial visible remains of late republican and early imperial date, this is also precisely the time – the first centuries BC and AD – of severe contraction of settlement.[35]

At Roselle, neighbour to Vetulonia, a more concerted effort at urban excavation has been made than at most of the town sites. However, there has been no final publication, only preliminary

29   Ward-Perkins, 1961: 36
30   Edlund, 1987: 67
31   Cornell, 1978; Torelli, 1975: 39
32   Perkins and Walker, 1990: 77
33   Michelucci, 1985
34   Ward-Perkins, 1961: 55–6
35   Merlino and Mirenda, 1990: 45, 54

accounts published through the 1960s and summarized in the catalogue to the permanent exhibition set up in the Museo Nazionale della Maremma in Grosseto.[36] From the Orientalizing and archaic periods are the impressive town walls (see fig. 55, chapter 5) and a number of chamber tombs, at which time settlement seems to have extended over both the north and south hills of the site. In the saddle between the two are the most important excavated buildings (of mud-brick) of this era, adjacent to and partly underlying the later Roman forum.

It is possible to see in some detail at Roselle the kind of development that Veii must have undergone, but at the latter site nothing is any longer visible. The town was captured by the Romans in 294 BC, when, according to Livy (10.4.5,37), two thousand inhabitants were slain and a further two thousand taken prisoner. As at Veii, however, there was a recovery, and to an even greater extent: blackglazed pottery is abundant, and there are considerable remains of houses of this period as well as evidence of a temple decorated with figurative terracottas.[37] A certain level of prosperity is even suggested by Roselle's ability in 205 BC to contribute 'timber for shipbuilding and a great quantity of grain' to aid Scipio's campaigns in North Africa (Livy 38.45.13). In the early first century BC, there is evidence of widespread destruction, presumably a result of the Sullan terror.[38] Then later a *colonia* was planted with all its trappings of a forum and other amenities, probably in the time of Augustus, but this is confined to the saddle and north hill. Today, the path up to the excavations runs alongside a paved Roman road (fig. 107) which leads up to the forum area and on to the small amphitheatre at the top of the hill. As so often in Etruria, it is the remains of a minor Roman settlement that dominate a site which had been very powerful in pre-Roman times.

Most Etruscan towns of southern Etruria were abandoned well before the end of the Roman era, though their easily defended positions tended to attract settlement again in unsettled medieval times. In contrast, many of the northern cities, of which Arezzo and Volterra are good examples, continued always to remain important centres. In respect of its later history Roselle is rather like a city of the south. There are remains of a Christian basilica and a medieval defensive tower, and there are further medieval fortifications on the

36 *Roselle*, 1975
37 *Roselle*, 1975: 90
38 Bocci Pacini, 1981: 12

Figure 107   Roman road at Roselle. (Photograph: T. Rasmussen)

nearby hill of Moscona. But the ultimate future lay elsewhere: like
Tuscania in the south, it was the seat of a bishopric, but in 1138
this was moved to a more accessible location down on the river
plain at Grosseto, after which the site was soon abandoned.

Sanctuaries

One other focus of archaeological attention on town sites has been
the temples and sanctuaries. They have long attracted excavators

(and plunderers), partly because their substantial remains are often easy to locate and partly for their rich votive deposits. It is analysis of the latter that can offer further revelations about continuity of life, making it clear that – presumably through the strength of religious tradition – the sanctuaries were sometimes the last areas to be abandoned. So the sanctuary in the Cannicella necropolis at Orvieto (destroyed in 264 BC) continued to be frequented and embellished even into Roman times,[39] and at Falerii (sacked in 241) the temple at Lo Scasato was in use until the first century BC.[40] The Portonaccio sanctuary at Veii received gifts long after 396, including a few inscribed in Latin.

The period during and after the conflict with Rome witnessed some of the most ambitious temple-building in Etruria's history. Two of the largest structures, one at Vulci and the Ara della Regina at Tarquinia, date from the fourth century BC, and extensive remains of their stone foundations are still visible (fig. 108). The latter may have been dedicated to Artumes, and there is evidence that it was remodelled some generations later.[41] The splendid terracotta plaque (fig. 109) decorated either the end of its ridge-beam or one of the side beams; the composition originally included a chariot for the winged horses to pull. Another temple of this period, at Telamon, was rebuilt in the second century and given a pediment composition some 9 m in width.[42] The possible reasons for such an extensive renovation at this time and for the subject chosen – episodes from the Greek myth of the Seven against Thebes – have been widely and inconclusively discussed, but the iconography has much in common with the reliefs on contemporary cinerary urns from Chiusi and Volterra.[43] Meanwhile, in the same century, Volterra itself could boast two new temples on its acropolis, and to the previous one belongs the temple at Fiesole.

From the later fourth century onwards there is a new element in the nature of the votive deposits. Many consist entirely, others at least partly, of parts of the human body in terracotta. The material may include full statues, heads, half-heads (where only one profile is shown), hands, feet, eyes, ears, genitals, even intestines, and swaddled babies and toddlers crouching on the ground. Clearly the cults concerned are of healing and fertility, but what is rarely clear

39   Stopponi, 1985b: 117
40   Comella, 1986: 200
41   Bonghi Jovino, 1986a: 355
42   von Vacano, 1992
43   *Talamone*, 1982; von Freytag gen. Löringhoff, 1986

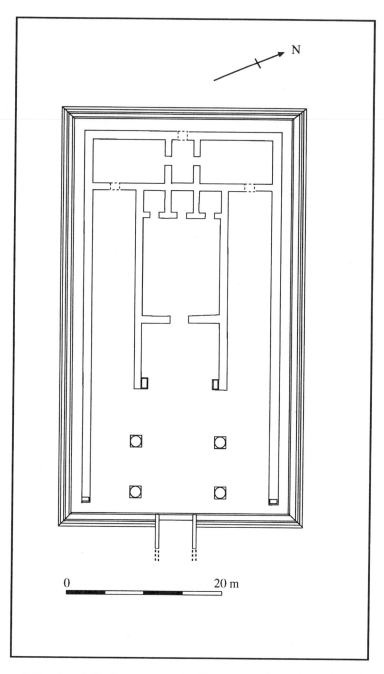

N

0   20 m

Figure 108   Ara della Regina temple, Tarquinia: plan of fourth century BC
phase. (After Colonna, 1985: fig. on p. 73)

Figure 109   Terracotta relief plaque with winged horses, from the Ara della Regina temple, Tarquinia. (Photograph: T. Rasmussen, courtesy of Soprintendenza Archeologica per l'Etruria Meridionale)

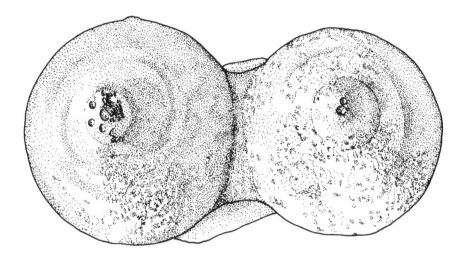

Figure 110   Terracotta female breasts from Punta della Vipera, in the Museo Archeologico, Civitavecchia. (After Stopponi, 1985c: fig. B13)

is whether the votive gifts were made in thanks for, or in anticipation of, a successful cure or childbirth. The heads and statues are especially ambiguous: a few no doubt represent the god of the sanctuary; but most of the heads, which were mass-produced from moulds and then in some cases retouched to give a more individual appearance, were probably bought and dedicated by worshippers as representations of themselves.[44]

The bodily parts may display considerable anatomical knowledge[45] but rarely indicate disease or injury. One exception comes not from an urban sanctuary but from an apparently isolated shrine dedicated to Menerva on the coast at Punta della Vipera near Santa Marinella.[46] It is a pair of female breasts, one clearly enlarged and with damage to the area of the areola indicated by incision (fig. 110).

Dedication of anatomical votives was widespread in the ancient Mediterranean world, as in more modern times, and in Italy was especially prevalent in Etruria, Latium and Campania.[47] Greece has also produced many assemblages,[48] but usually in more expensive materials such as marble and gold, and they are often associated

44   Steingräber, 1981b
45   Turfa, 1994
46   Edlund, 1987: 77; Stopponi, 1985c: 153
47   Fenelli, 1975; Potter, 1985
48   van Straten, 1981

with shrines of the healing god Asclepius. His cult was introduced into Rome early in the third century BC, and it is very possible that it was from here that the tradition of making these kinds of dedications spread into adjacent regions.[49]

Monuments of late Etruria

The Etruscans' political independence was lost long before the individuality of their visual and material culture was finally extinguished in the first century BC. Many aspects of the latter have been mentioned in passing in previous chapters. So, for example, whereas mirror-engraving shows a steady loss of vigour, the making of bronze vessels continued unabated and at an impressive level of skill, while the monumental art of embellishing temples with terracotta decorations reached new heights with compositions to fill Greek-style pediments, as at Talamone and at Lo Scasato, Falerii (the latter grandly displayed in the Villa Giulia Museum in Rome[50]). In many spheres of activity there is no loss of vitality and no lack of invention, and, as in previous periods, a strong regionalism persists, especially between northern and southern Etruria, characterized by craftsmen exploiting local materials in ways to suit local tastes. The discussion that follows will focus briefly on two kinds of monument, façade tombs and sculpted burial containers, both of which are especially typical of the period and have a conspicuous presence either in the Etruscan landscape or in museum displays.

Façade tombs and late funerary architecture

In many parts of southern Etruria, especially in the rugged areas between Viterbo and the coast[51] but also further north to the east of Lake Bolsena around Sovana,[52] the principal tomb type is the cube tomb or *tomba a dado*. Its origins go back to the sixth century BC, when it is first seen in the cemeteries of Cerveteri[53] and at other sites such as Tuscania. There are several varieties. The full cube tomb, seen at Cerveteri, is usually at least partly built with blocks

49 Turfa, 1986: 207
50 Proietti, 1980: fig. 348
51 Colonna di Paolo, 1981
52 Maggiani, 1978
53 Colonna, 1974: 257

rather than entirely rock-cut, and a related type is standard at Orvieto. But in the rock-cut tomb areas mentioned above, the tombs are precisely that: they are, with few exceptions, *tombe rupestre* cut from the rock face. Most of them are not laboriously cut into full cubes; instead, they are either half-cubes (with only the front and sides isolated from the cliff) or false cubes (front only). But in any case, the emphasis is always very much on the front, which is given a more decorative treatment, with far more delicate upper mouldings, than is seen at Cerveteri and Orvieto.

To wander on foot through the rock tomb regions is a dramatic experience even today, and must have been far more so in antiquity. But why restrict tombs to cliff faces? Why not utilize the plateaux as at Cerveteri? The answer is not clear. It cannot have been simply to leave as much land free for cultivation near the towns as possible, for that ought to apply to Cerveteri, too, where the cliffs are left mainly untouched. There does seem, however, an element of sheer opportunism in their siting: the tombs are carved where the cliffs are most vertical and sometimes on more than one level where the stream-cut gorges are deepest.

Of all the sites, it is the tombs of Castel d'Asso and Norchia that are perhaps most rewarding to study, partly because of their good preservation but also because of their meticulous publication.[54] The cube tombs here are of the kind which have a false door with hooked or undercut architrave carved in relief on the façade (fig. 111); the actual tomb-chamber is approached underneath by means of a sloping passage or *dromos*. Earlier cube tombs at other sites have the real entrance to the chamber carved in the façade itself, and the reason why the later scheme was adopted may perhaps again be one of opportunism. For what was felt to be important about the façade was clearly the door and the crowning mouldings; physically divorcing these elements from the entrance to the burial chamber meant that a suitable vertical surface could be chosen for the carved façade display even if, due to the lie of the land, it had to be some distance above or to the side of the dromos entrance.[55] On a more symbolic level, however, the false door, often elevated now to a position of visual prominence, almost certainly came to stand for the door to the underworld, representations of which are a feature of many earlier painted tombs at Tarquinia. As if to make the association quite clear, one Norchia tomb had a

54 Colonna di Paolo and Colonna, 1970, 1978
55 Oleson, 1976: 213

Figure 111   Castel d'Asso: façade tombs. (Photograph: T. Rasmussen)

standing figure of Charun carved in relief above the door, now weather-beaten and half missing, but still grimly carrying his heavy hammer.[56]

Most of the tombs do not have chambers as such, but merely rough-hewn spaces for the dead. Funerary rites must have taken place outside, sometimes on the flat top of the cube reached by external steps, or in a projecting lower porch which – along with its pillars – would also be rock cut. These are false porches for they lead nowhere, and they are also featured in the Acqualta necropolis at Norchia in the two tombs built to resemble temple façades (fig. 112). Here, the pillars have worn away to reveal on one of the back walls scant traces of a procession of human figures carved in low relief, mirroring the funerary processions that once must actually have been staged. The pediments contain in both cases fighting figures, again in relief and only slightly less worn, possibly scenes from Greek mythology.

Such atypical rock-cut tombs, that depart radically from the standard façade (cube) and chamber types, seem to be products mainly of the second century BC. At Sovana, two examples on a monumental

56 Colonna di Paolo and Colonna, 1978: plate 324

Figure 112   Norchia: pedimented tombs. (Photograph: T. Rasmussen)

scale, the Pola and Ildebranda Tombs, feature elaborate columnar
fronts; the former (now badly ruined) had a pediment above like
the Norchia pair. Also at Sovana is the less extravagant Tomb of
the Siren (fig. 113) – so called, though the figure in the centre of the
crowning relief is actually a Scylla clutching her paddle, a snakey-
legged monster who also turns up on contemporary ash-urns as well
as in the earlier Tomb of the Reliefs at Cerveteri. The false door is
here a big arched recess, within which was originally a sculpted
banqueter reclining on a couch (at some later date carved away to
form a kind of altar), the whole composition somewhat reminiscent
of later Roman *arcosolium* tombs. The symbolism of the door again
seems clear and is confirmed by excavations in front of the façade
which have shown that the arched recess was flanked on both sides
by a demon Vanth carved in relief.[57]

The tombs discussed so far have been rock-cut. But in northern
Etruria of this same period, around Chiusi and Perugia, there are
small clutches of carefully built barrel-vaulted chamber tombs, most
of them built into low hillsides so that externally their construction
was not visible. There is also the remarkable Tanella di Pitagora

57   Carter, 1974

Figure 113   Sovana: Tomb of the Siren. (Photograph: T. Rasmussen)

(Den of Pythagoras) at Cortona, a vaulted single-chamber tomb roofed by means of extended voussoir slabs that run the length of the chamber and rest on large semi-circular supports at either end. Barrel-vaulted tombs of this period are also a phenomenon of Greece and Asia Minor, and the only close parallel to the Cortona tomb is in Phrygia.[58]

58   Oleson, 1982: 87

Late tombs and local aristocracies

The tombs of the fourth century BC and later show considerable inventiveness, and even grandness and opulence. Many were built for repeated use over generations for the same extended family or clan, unlike the tombs for small nuclear families of the archaic period. With the façade tombs of the south, the display element is confined to the outside; there is generally no chamber as such. So in the Orioli Tomb at Castel d'Asso, close to the tombs of figure 111, the dead were placed below in a rough-hewn passage 17 m long with space on either side for a total of sixty-two corpses.[59]

The contemporary family tombs of Cerveteri and Tarquinia, being built on or cut out of the plateaux, have no exterior display but internally possess properly proportioned large chambers. A few at Tarquinia have painted decoration, but those at Cerveteri are fairly plain, apart from the exceptional Tomb of the Reliefs of the Matuna family, where all manner of homely household goods and military equipment is vividly represented in painted relief on the walls and pillars.[60] We know a number of the names of these aristocratic families from tomb inscriptions, including the Matuna, Tamsnie and Tarchna at Cerveteri, and the Spurina, Velcha and Pulena at Tarquinia.

The sudden increase in the number of monumental tombs has induced many to think in terms of an economic revival in the later fourth century following on from a stagnation or crisis in the fifth.[61] But the crisis may turn out to be somewhat illusory (see above, p. 131). In southern Etruria, so few monumental tombs, or tombs of any description for that matter, are datable to the fifth century that either there was a drastic reduction in population, which is unlikely, or many of the tombs of this period either have not been located or have been misdated. At Tuscania, for example, there is a wealth of archaic tombs, of which some of the more recently discovered are especially elaborate,[62] and then a series of rich burials begins again in the fourth century. But the Tuscania survey has found no obvious fifth century gap in the sequence of rural sites: many of them were first settled in the archaic period and continued

59 Colonna di Paolo, 1981: fig. 103
60 Blanck and Proietti, 1986
61 For example, Torelli, 1986a: 69
62 Sgubini Moretti, 1989

in operation into the full Roman period.[63] Another interesting case is Castel d'Asso, where a preliminary spatial analysis of the surface sherds suggests that the town site was spread over a larger area before the fourth century and later dwindled in size.[64] Yet almost all the surrounding tombs belong to the later period. Where were the pre-fourth century dead buried?

There is no single explanation that neatly accounts for the sudden rise of the great family tombs described above. It is as if, no longer having the means to exert real political power (which was now increasingly in Roman hands), the aristocracy could resort only to self-glorification by building extravagant funerary monuments and – equally important for building up self-esteem – often by displaying a careful inscribed record of the genealogies of the deceased. Above all, the tombs display wealth, and what is certain is that the continued prosperity of the great families was part of the Roman plan for Etruria. Here it is worth bearing in mind how little colonization took place in Etruria as a whole, even though the earlier part of this chapter has dwelt on the harshness to local inhabitants where it did occur. In most of the country, the Romans relied on maintaining good relations with local oligarchs who in turn ensured that the towns under their control paid their dues under treaty to Rome. So, whenever Rome did intervene in the internal affairs of Etruscan cities, it was to bring military support to the ruling aristocracy.

By this means, the status quo was maintained throughout Etruria, and the established families benefited, whether they were in small centres like the Curuna of Tuscania, or in the great cities of the north, such as the Velimna/Volumnii of Perugia, the Cilnii of Arezzo or the Ceicna/Caecinae of Volterra. Of the latter clan two tombs were long ago found at Volterra, each containing many inscribed ash-urns covering a number of generations. The family had close connections with Rome and enjoyed the professional support and personal friendship of Cicero. One begins to taste the flavour of complete Romanization when, at the end of the first century BC, two of its members paid for the construction of a Roman-style theatre to embellish their city and had their names inscribed on it.[65]

---

63 See also Colonna, 1990: 14–15
64 Colonna di Paolo and Colonna, 1970: 52
65 Fiumi, 1955: 123

Sarcophagi and ash-urns

Many of the big tombs belonging to the great families of the late period have very plain interiors, and it seems that, as they became plainer, so the taste grew for elaboration in the burial containers which were placed in them. Among the plainest of the tombs are those of the Volterra region, consisting simply of large rough-hewn circular spaces; most of them no longer exist, though one (the Inghirami Tomb) has been reconstructed in the garden of Florence Archaeological Museum. In it the ash-urns were placed on a rock-cut shelf which runs round the circular area, and this positioning of the containers around the perimeter of the room on one or more shelves is common throughout Etruria, though often the arrangement is more random. The main regional difference is that, as in earlier periods, in the north cremation is the norm and in the south inhumation; and the one demands ash-urns (usually about 60 cm in length), the other sarcophagi (about 2 m). Even so, some centres do not follow one practice exclusively. The changing style of, and inscriptions on, the burial containers show that some of the big tombs – the Ceicna Tombs at Volterra, the Volumnii and the recently discovered Cutu Tomb at Perugia, the Curuna and Vipinana at Tuscania, the Calisna Sepu near Monteriggioni, to list just a few – were in use for many generations, even for a couple of hundred years and more. The last mentioned contained more than a hundred burials; more than twenty-five is not uncommon.

The containers come in many forms and in many degrees of elaboration. Many are not much more than plain chests with simple gabled lids, but the most interesting are those with representations of the deceased on the lid and with relief decoration on the chest, especially when they carry inscriptions as well. Various aspects of these monuments have already been remarked on; here it is necessary only to draw attention briefly to the strength of the varying traditions of their local manufacture.

At Volterra the medium is generally stone. The earliest of the great series of urns are in a calcareous *tufo*, but after the middle of the third century those of alabaster are rather more numerous. Terracotta was used rarely, but occasionally to great effect. It is much more common at Chiusi, especially for urns, and the few Chiusine terracotta sarcophagi are of high quality (see fig. 36). Here the type of stone used for urns and sarcophagi varies: alabaster, and limestones including travertine. The latter, not the easiest material for carving detail, is the local stone used for the urns of Perugia (where terracotta was of less importance), which are generally of an inferior quality, with the exception of the outstanding examples placed in the Cutu and Volumnii Tombs.[66] In the south, there are fine fourth century stone sarcophagi from Vulci and Cerveteri, but later stone (*tufo* and limestone) examples are most numerous from Tarquinia and its territory, including Tuscania, where there is also a long series of sarcophagi in terracotta made in two or more pieces.

The terracotta work at Tuscania seems to have been produced locally, the most striking piece being what is probably the upper part of an urn showing the deceased in the guise of a dying Adonis.[67] In the course of the second century, however, the figures on the sarcophagus lids become progressively attenuated and summarily executed, ending up with their bodies almost totally embedded in the lid itself.[68] For most of its stone sarcophagi, Tuscania, along with neighbouring small towns such as Norchia and Musarna, seems to have been supplied by Tarquinia, either directly or by artists based in the city who were prepared to travel out locally to fulfil commissions on the spot. Such seems to have been the case also in the north, with Volterran artists meeting the needs not only of the city but also of at least some of the smaller communities in the vicinity, while others of these such as San Gimignano developed relatively independent traditions.[69] Chiusi, too, supplied urns over a wide area extending as far as Cortona.

Making containers for the dead was an industry, and many thousands of these monuments survive. They vary not only in materials but also in quality of execution, and many must have been aimed at a wider population spectrum than the aristocratic families alone. One can sense this especially at Chiusi, where many of the terracotta urns were mass-produced in moulds repeating the same relief compositions on their fronts, and where a number of inscribed urns belonged to the *lautni* class, which was not the most privileged section of society (see above, p. 101). As for the craftsmen who made them, clearly there was considerable interchange of ideas

66 Dareggi, 1972
67 Sprenger and Bartoloni, 1983: fig. 273
68 Gentili, 1994: plates 5, 73
69 Nielsen, 1985: 65

Figure 114   Front of alabaster urn made at Volterra showing journey by wagon, second century BC, *in the British Museum, London. (Photograph: copyright British Museum)*

between the main centres: so, for example, scenes from the Theban myth cycle are equally common at Chiusi and Volterra. But they also worked in accordance with local tastes, which must explain why the theme of Greeks fighting Amazons is especially popular at Tarquinia and Tuscania, the journey to the underworld by muledrawn cart (fig. 114) is a favoured theme on Volterran urns, while scenes of Alexander the Great fighting the Persians are confined to Perugia.

Last but not least, there are the figures of the deceased portrayed on the lids. Like the reliefs on the chests, they were originally coloured. They are shown either recumbent, with head barely raised if at all (these are mostly early in the period), or propped up on one elbow as if reclining at banquet. The banqueting theme is further alluded to by the form of some of the urns and sarcophagi which are in the shape of banqueting couches overlaid with fine coverlets, and by the figures themselves which are wreathed and garlanded for the party. The women are fully draped; the men may be in heroic semi-nudity. To show their status, a few of the men are shown holding scrolls; more often, with their free right hand the men hold a cup or a drinking horn (*rhyton*) and the women a leaf-shaped fan or a mirror (usually with a hinged lid). But the most commonly held object (especially by men) is a cup of a special kind, round and handleless with a raised navel in the centre, the *phiale mesomphalos*. It is a vessel which in Greece was used especially for pouring libations to the gods, and it is likely that the association with the undying gods is the reason for its presence here.

In all these works the focal point is the head of the deceased. Often rather little attention is given by the craftsman to the body, and on many of the urns the body is shortened and compressed in anatomically impossible ways. Contemplating these heads today in the museums, we inevitably ask ourselves: are we standing before individual Etruscans as they actually looked? The answer is likely in most cases to be a negative one. These are representations made in type series rather than portraits made to order. Moreover, many of the types are Greek-inspired: early on, it is possible to detect strong reflections from images of Greek Hellenistic rulers; later, there are still noticeable Greek traits, but as interpreted by artists working at Rome. Many figures, especially of women, are clearly idealized. When, towards the end of the second century BC, realism took firm root, it was not because the inhabitants of Volterra and Perugia suddenly developed deep furrows on their cheeks and heavy lines on their brows, but because such details had become fashionable in the art of Greece and Rome.

Nevertheless, there does seem on occasion to have been a degree of special commissioning. So, a very few lid figures are shown clutching in their hand an artist's measuring rod, presumably indicating the profession of the deceased, while two urns from Perugia, one of stone, the other (probably made at Chiusi) of terracotta, display rare duos of husband and wife on the lids which were also perhaps specifically ordered. Very occasionally, too, on very careful and elaborate monuments, there may be considerable individualization of the features suggesting some degree of portraiture. With lid figures such as Laris Pulenas at Tarquinia (see fig. 33, chapter 3), Volterra Guarnacci Museum inv. 291 and a handful of others, we may be given a real indication of individual Etruscan features; in the case of Seianti Hanunia Tlesnasa from Chiusi (see fig. 36) this is further suggested by the scientific reconstruction of the skull found in her sarcophagus.[70]

70 Volterra inv. 291: Maggiani, 1985: no.77; Seianti: Prag and Neave, 1997: 198

Figure 115   Mosaic at Musarna, with name of member of the Alethna family, late second century BC. *(Photograph: courtesy of V. Jolivet)*

The Etruscan legacy

Around 100 BC, as noted earlier (see above, p. 100), the small town of Musarna near Tuscania was embellished with a bath-building funded by members of two local families. It included a Roman-style hot room (*caldarium*) complete with tessellated mosaic floor (fig. 115) which bore along its border their names in Etruscan letters: Alethna and Hulchnie, written in tesserae.[71] There could be no clearer example of the adoption of Roman lifestyle and values which must have occurred throughout Etruria in this period. At around the same time, in 89 BC, the whole of Etruria was given Roman citizenship, and for bureaucratic and voting purposes all Etruscans were registered in Roman tribes. Tarquinia was subsumed in the Roman tribe Stellatina (probably along with Musarna), Volterra in Sabatina, and so forth. Etruria no longer existed as a separate entity: politically it was now but a small part of the vast and growing area of the Roman state. The language for conducting the business of the state was Latin, and any Etruscan who was in any way ambitious

71   Barbieri, 1987c

needed to gain close familiarity with it. A hundred years after the Musarna mosaic was laid, the Etruscan family who dedicated the theatre at Volterra (see above, p. 287) had their names inscribed on it in Latin: Caecinae, not Ceicna. Funerary inscriptions of the last generations BC are full of Etruscan names becoming Latinized in form and script: Cutu into Cutius, Velimna into Volumnius, Alfni into Alfius. The last Etruscan inscriptions are of the age of Augustus;[72] as Rome entered its long era of empire, so Etruscan traditions were being rapidly forgotten.

What about influence in the other direction? What Etruscan contributions were there to Roman culture? Some have been mentioned in passing in previous chapters and this is no place for an exhaustive discussion. They range from the trivial to the important. One obvious case, which might be placed by different people in either category, is the symbols of Roman state office: among them, the *fasces* and the curule chair (of folding stool type), mentioned by various ancient authors as of Etruscan origin, and to which Etruscan material remains provide convincing forerunners.[73] Of greater significance were Etruscan attitudes to, and practices in, divination which for a very long time permeated Roman consciousness.[74]

There is also the important matter of the alphabet. It was shown long ago that the Latin alphabet is derived ultimately from the Greek, but as (at least partly) mediated through the Etruscan, the argument centring on the Greek gamma and the phonetic value given to it in Etruscan.[75] The very thought of such a crucial contribution to western culture provoked a memorable remark from an eminent Hellenic scholar of a previous generation, Sir Ellis Minns:[76] 'To those who, like me, dislike the Etruscans, it is a grief that we should have got our alphabet through them; for myself I think it would have been better without their share in it.'

The Etruscans borrowed a number of items of vocabulary from the Greeks, and it would be surprising if the Romans in turn did not pick up some words from their northern neighbours. The standard survey in this field remains that of Ernout.[77] In fact a few Etruscan words passed through Latin and into present-day usage: 'histrionic' is derived from *histrio* ('performer'); 'persona' goes back to *phersu*

---

72 Bruun, 1975: 479
73 Jannot, 1993b
74 Ogilvie, 1969: 65–7
75 Bonfante, 1981: 124
76 In his preface to Diringer, 1947
77 Ernout, 1930

('mask'). Bonfante has made out a case for 'triumph', the Romans taking from the Etruscans not only the word itself but also many of the complex rituals of the Roman military triumph.[78] From the musical world come more terms, but which have no post-Roman existence: *lituus*, a curved trumpet (also an augur's curved staff), and *subulo*, 'flute-player'.

In matters of dress the Romans borrowed much, not least the toga, which is derived from the Etruscan curved mantle (see above, p. 108).[79] That they borrowed ideas for their public sporting events is also very probable. We hear of the first laying out of the Circus Maximus at Rome in the period of the Tarquins, along with the first public games, for which some of the sporting participants were imported from Etruria (Livy, 1.35.7–9). Several features of Roman chariot-racing practice are Etruscan in origin, including charioteers' dress and the use of three-horse teams.[80] Etruria has also been credited by many, including ancient authors, with introducing gladiatorial performances, but the evidence is very weak: Etruscan monuments that display one-to-one combats are very late in date, and in most cases a mythological context cannot be excluded. It is now generally agreed that the origin of gladiatorial displays is to be found in Campania (where admittedly there was an Etruscan element in the population) and southern Italy.[81] However, that even grislier spectacle often staged to amuse the Roman public, of a more or less defenceless human victim confronted by a wild beast, has a clear forerunner in the blind-man-against-dog game of archaic Tarquinia (see fig. 97, chapter 7).

Concerning Etruscan contributions to Roman art, architecture and engineering, it must suffice here to mention just a few points. Etruscan ash-urns and sarcophagi are a very possible inspiration behind the standard type of Roman imperial sarcophagus with relief mythological scenes on three sides, whether the lid is simply gabled or carries reclining figures of the deceased.[82] There is actually a gap of some generations between the Etruscan and Roman series, and absolute proof of a direct connection is lacking. A more clear-cut connection is that between the disposition of Etruscan and Roman temples, in particular their frontality and the way they are raised above the ground by means of a tall podium (see above, p. 220).

78   Bonfante, 1981: 93
79   Bonfante, 1975: 91, 93
80   Humphrey, 1986: 16–17
81   Thuillier, 1985: 589; Ville, 1981: 8
82   Strong, 1988: 190; S. Walker, 1985: 26

Figure 116   Falerii Novi: Porta di Giove. (Photograph: T. Rasmussen)

Then there is the matter of the first use of the arch and barrel vault. It used to be thought that in monumental arched gates the Etruscans had priority, but it has long been accepted that none of them need be earlier than the Roman gate that leads into Falerii Novi, built soon after 241 BC (fig. 116). A fourth century tomb at Ripa Sant'Angelo, Cerveteri, roofed with a two-skinned barrel vault, has more recently been brought into the debate,[83] but already by 600 BC

83   Cristofani and Nardi, 1988: 99

the Etruscans were feeling their way towards the principle of the arch with the Campana Tomb at Veii.[84] In Rome, small-scale vaults, covering cisterns and drains and the like, are known from the late sixth century BC onwards.[85]

Finally, both peoples were extremely adept at controlling the landscape and making it more suited to habitation, agriculturally more productive, and easier for communication and transport. In this field the Romans could have learned much from the Etruscans.[86] Prior to the Roman network, the Etruscan road system was the most extensive in Italy (see p. 172). The earliest proper drainage of the centre of Rome, according to Livy, goes back to the period of the Etruscan kings. In the countryside, large-scale Etruscan drainage schemes, designed to improve its cultivation (see fig. 73, chapter 6) and demanding high levels of engineering skill, may prefigure many later ambitious projects of the Romans.

84 Naso, 1991: plate 2.4
85 Cifani, 1994: 194
86 Ward-Perkins, 1962

Appendix

Etruscan Places – a Rough Guide

> *There is a queer stillness and a curious peaceful repose about the Etruscan places I have been to.*
>
> D.H. Lawrence (1932) *Etruscan Places*

Introduction

There are a number of useful guidebooks to Etruria. Torelli[1] is very good but needs to be supplemented by others in the same series, such as Gaggiotti et al.,[2] for those areas beyond Tuscany and northern Lazio. Steingräber[3] is more comprehensive, as is Carnabuci and Palombi,[4] which includes a thematic 1:275,000 map. Also of value, though of bulky size, is Boitani et al.,[5] while to Dennis's descriptions Hemphill adds very helpful comments on sixteen sites.[6] For guides to single sites and areas in southern Etruria, there are two good series, one published by De Agostini,[7] the other by Quasar;[8] the *Antiche Strade: Lazio* volumes cover wider areas.[9] Some of these books can sometimes be obtained on site, or at the bookshop in the Villa Giulia Museum in Rome.

Locating Etruscan sites on the ground can be a frustrating business even for the experienced and well read. The purpose of this appendix is essentially practical, and the emphasis is on Etruria proper, between the Arno and Tiber rivers and the coast. Even here, comprehensiveness is not attempted, nor can every aspect of each

1 Torelli, 1993
2 Gaggiotti et al., 1993
3 Steingräber, 1981a
4 Carnabuci and Palombi, 1993
5 Boitani et al., 1975
6 Hemphill, 1985
7 For example, Moretti, 1983
8 For example, Sgubini Moretti, 1991
9 For example, Giacobelli, 1991

site be mentioned. The object is to point the way to a majority of the interesting places, including some of the remote and little visited; and it is perhaps worth remarking that there may be as much insight into the Etruscans to be gained from noting a fragment of wall on an obscure wooded hillside as from jostling with the crowds in some monumental necropolis. But what is unlikely to emerge from the brief notes and dry route directions that follow is the sheer beauty and variety of the Etrurian countryside.

Although many sites are today signposted with yellow tourist road signs, their use is intermittent and rarely do they show distances. Moreover, the physical state of sites is constantly changing: those that were cleared a few years ago may now be overgrown, and vice versa. On the whole the authorities seem to be winning, thanks in large measure to the cooperation of local volunteer organizations. Consequently, new archaeological parks and trails are being opened up all the time; their maintenance will be a test of sustained effort and dedication.

A decent road map is essential, such as the Touring Club Italiano 1:200,000 series. Unless otherwise stated, roads can be assumed to be tarmacked. For the rougher roads (in descending order: *strada bianca* or gravel road, stabilized road, [farm] track), provided they are reasonably dry, small size of vehicle is more important than four-wheel drive: Italian farmers get everywhere they need to in their Fiat Pandas and Unos. For walking in Etruria, it is advisable to wear strong shoes or boots and to take a pocket torch for the tomb interiors. A compass and/or car-compass is also very useful. Visiting sites on dry winter days can be equally pleasant as in summer, except that the countryside may have to be shared with armed hunters blasting away at everything that moves, and tomb-chambers are liable to be flooded.

Opening times vary for museums and sites which charge for entry, but the usual day of closure is Monday. Unattended sites may still be fenced in, but often there is an obvious means of entry, through a hole or a deliberate gap. Such enclosures are designed to exclude farm animals rather than people; but to be forced into some serious climbing means that it is better not to. Finally, readers of this book should hardly require warning that archaeological sites can be dangerous places for the unwary or clumsy, that it is all too easy to damage sites (particularly where excavation is ongoing), that the removal of antiquities is forbidden by law and liable to harsh fines and/or imprisonment, and that agricultural and other private land needs to be treated with the greatest respect.

Numbers in brackets after each site name refer to the locations on figure 117.

Acquarossa (28)

Urban site excavated by the Swedish Institute at Rome. At 6 km on the road north from Viterbo to Bagnoregio, turn right for Bagnaia. At 500 m after crossing the Acquarossa stream at the valley bottom, walk up the rough track on the left which leads (500 m) to the courtyard complex of Zone F (fig. 60), under roofed protection – virtually the only part of the excavations still visible. On the other side of it is the ancient road that led off the plateau. From Zone F the habitation site extends several hundred metres to the south. The town was abandoned/destroyed in the second half of the sixth century BC.

Arezzo (54)   Latin name: Arretium

The Etruscan town was centred on the upper part of the hill, but there are very few remains of the Etruscan walls. The **Museo Archeologico Mecenate,** housed in a monastic complex built on the curve of the Roman amphitheatre, contains not only Etruscan material (not all of local provenance) and Greek vases, but also a fine display of Arretine pottery and moulds.

Bisenzio (42)   Latin name: Visentium

A prominent hill (Monte Bisenzo) on the shore of Lake Bolsena (fig. 3), occupied from the Late Bronze Age to the sixth century BC and again in the Roman period, a landmark on the road between Capodimonte and Valentano. From here a small road runs to the left of the hill (and continues around the western shore of the lake). After 500 m a track/path to the right winds up to the summit. The site is known chiefly from the many tomb finds (for example, fig. 99) in the vicinity. Although excavations have located remains of late bronze age buildings near the summit, nothing survives above ground either of the early settlement or of the later Roman town founded here.

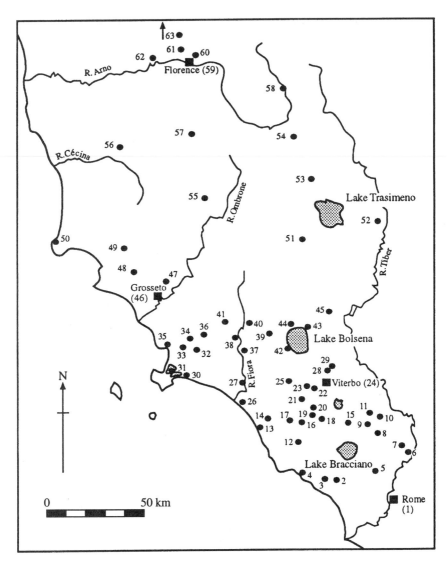

Figure 117 Site location map: 1 Rome; 2 Ceri; 3 Cerveteri; 4 Pyrgi;
5 Veio; 6 Lucus Feroniae; 7 Capena; 8 Narce; 9 Nepi; 10 Civita Castellana; 11 Falerii Novi; 12 Tolfa; 13 Graviscae; 14 Tarquinia; 15 Sutri;
16 San Giovenale; 17 Luni sul Mignone; 18 San Giuliano; 19 Blera;
20 Grotta Porcina; 21 Norchia; 22 Castel d'Asso; 23 Musarna; 24 Viterbo;
25 Tuscania; 26 Regisvilla; 27 Vulci 28 Acquarossa; 29 Ferento; 30 Cosa;
31 Orbetello; 32 Marsiliana; 33 Doganella; 34 Magliano in Toscana;
35 Talamone; 36 Ghiaccio Forte; 37 Castro; 38 Poggio Buco; 39 Sorgenti
della Nova; 40 Sovana; 41 Saturnia; 42 Bisenzio; 43 Bolsena; 44 Pianezze;
45 Orvieto; 46 Grosseto; 47 Roselle; 48 Vetulonia; 49 Lago dell'Accesa;
50 Populonia; 51 Chiusi; 52 Perugia; 53 Cortona; 54 Arezzo; 55 Murlo
(Poggio Civitate); 56 Volterra; 57 Castellina in Chianti; 58 Pieve Socana;
59 Florence; 60 Fiesole; 61 Quinto Fiorentino; 62 Comeana; 63 Marzabotto.
The major museums with Etruscan collections (squares) are: Rome (1);
Viterbo (24); Grosseto (46); and Florence (59).

Blera (19)   Medieval name: Bieda

A small medieval town with long narrow streets, on the site of an Etruscan town. Lining the valleys facing the settlement plateau there are many necropolises of the sixth to fourth centuries BC, the predominant tomb type being the cube with real (as opposed to false) door. Early this century a German mission calculated the total number of tombs at more than a thousand. From the modern bridge across the gorge towards Monte Romano one can view far below the three-arched Roman bridge (Ponte del Diavolo) that carried the Via Clodia across the Biedano. Beyond the arched gate at the other end of the town a narrow track (best walked) swings round to the right hugging the side of the settlement plateau with the Biedano below, finally reaching a Roman one-arched bridge (Ponte della Rocca) by which the Clodia exited the town over a tributary of the same river. Immediately beyond is the Pian del Vescovo, the most extensive of the rock-cut necropolises.

Bolsena (43)   Latin name: Volsinii (Novi)

The remains of the extensive site to the northeast of modern Bolsena belong to the period after the Roman destruction of Volsinii (Orvieto) in 264 BC, when the surviving inhabitants were moved here. A tall remnant of the ancient town wall can be seen just below the Rocca, some of the blocks bearing masons' marks. Further up along the same road is a big gate on the left leading to the excavations. Following the path straight brings one to the Roman forum area and, beyond, to remains of houses with interior decorations. Sculptural finds suggest that a subterranean room belonging to one of these contained a shrine sacred to the mysteries of Dionysus, a cult which, according to Livy, was especially widespread in Etruria (and was suppressed by Rome for its sexual and other excesses in 186 BC). The settlement extended many hundreds of metres up the hill to the northeast. Near the top are the scant remains of two sanctuaries of Hellenistic date, the earliest structures within the walls.

For the earlier site (sixth to fourth centuries BC) of La Civica/La Civita del Fosso di Arlena, also excavated by the French School at Rome, take the road south from Bolsena for 4.5 km, turning left onto the very small road for Parco di Turona for nearly a kilometre. Park by the tiny chapel, from where a woodland path takes one on an hour's circular walk with the Civita hill at the furthest point. The site was defended by walls which take advantage of the rock outcrops. Among the remains of buildings is a squarish temple sited near a deep natural fissure in the rock. A kilometre to the northeast from here is the hill of Capriola, another defended settlement but of the Apennine Bronze Age and also the site of numerous early iron age burials. The latter are contemporary with the prehistoric village discovered beneath the edge of the lake at Gran Carro 6 km south of Bolsena. Finds from these sites and from Etrusco-Roman Bolsena are exhibited in the **Museo Territoriale del Lago di Bolsena** housed in the Rocca Monaldeschi della Cervara.

Capena   (7)

Centre of the Capenate peoples, Latin-speaking but allies of Veii. Ancient Capena lies 3 km north of the modern town of the same name, which gave up its medieval name of Leprignano only recently. Situated on the hill of Civitucola, the site is best approached from the Lucus Feroniae side. From here take the road for Morlupo, then just before modern Capena turn right for 'Fiano, Le Piani'. After 1 km ignore the road to Fiano to the right, continuing for a further 3.3 km (finally on a *strada bianca*). Park at the fork and walk the track to the left, shortly bearing right up to the top of the plateau. At the highest point is the Castellaccio ruin, a tall Roman building of uncertain function (perhaps a temple, then a church) with a narrow inserted medieval window near the top. The town site was protected by walls of which there are very few visible traces, but a couple of stone courses remain below the brow of the plateau near Castellaccio on the far (northern) side. On either side of the plateau are necropolis hills: San Martino to the north, to the south the densely wooded Monte Cornazzano (finds in the Pigorini Museum and the Villa Giulia, Rome).

Castel d'Asso (22)   Latin name: Axia

Signposted at 3 km along the Viterbo–Tuscania road. The tombs (of semi- and false cube type with carved false doors) are fourth to second century BC, but the town site was occupied already in the sixth century. The descending approach track follows an ancient road, with branches feeding in from the right, and as it swings towards the valley bottom there are tombs on both sides (fig. 111) and for a good way along the side of the valley. Opposite is the urban plateau with a medieval *castello* at the end, and there is a good view of it from the Tomba Grande about 100 m along the valley to the left (then a stepped path up). From the eastern side the settlement was without natural defences, so at 800 m from the *castello* there is a big defensive ditch (*fossato*) across the plateau, and – rather oddly – a similar ditch 500 m closer to the *castello*. Later, in the medieval period, a third ditch was dug up against the castle itself. The settlement site is inaccessible from the necropolis side. [To reach it, take the road back, at 4 km turn right, at 2.5 km right again, then after 300 m take a very poor track to the right for about 3 km.]

Castellina in Chianti   (57)

North of Siena. The huge Orientalizing tumulus at Montecalvario (200 m along the road to Radda) is unusual in being sited at virtually the highest point in the area, and in the positioning of its four tombs at the cardinal points of the compass. All the chambers have corbelled roofs, and in the southern tomb the main square chamber has the beginnings of a corbelled dome. There is a two-stepped tumulus drum. The nearest settlement site was on the nearby hill of Castellina Vecchia.

To the southeast, off the Siena road to the left, is the Fonterutoli necropolis. Before Fonterutoli village, take the *strada bianca* signed to Vagliagli for 1.8 km. The small tumuli extend for about 200 m along the top of a pine-covered ridge, each containing a single tomb of one or more chambers constructed with large stone slabs or ashlar masonry.

Castro   (37)

Etruscan centre, with rich tomb finds of the seventh and sixth centuries BC; the site also of a later town. Turn left off the Ischia di Castro–Pitigliano road towards Manciano and almost immediately left again onto a track leading (1 km) to a church, the Chiesa del Crocifisso. Opposite is a large rock-cut Etruscan altar (?) which is divided into three roofed segments, the central one with pitched ceiling; at the back the upper blocks are given a single cushion moulding.

To the right of the church a poor track leads (0.7 km) to an even poorer track to the right, at the bottom of which is a roofed enclosure protecting the large rock-cut Tomba della Biga. Its interest lies not so much in its architecture as in the sixth century two-wheeled chariot found in it, which is displayed restored in the Villa Giulia in Rome.

From the junction of the tracks there is a view across to two wooded plateaux. The one to the right is the town site, and one reaches it across the field passing the modern farm building. Nothing is visible of its Etruscan origins; but here was also the medieval and Renaissance town of Castro, destroyed in 1649 in a papal war. It is now a ruin-field of architectural fragments amid thick undergrowth.

Etruscan finds from the area, including animal-head sculptures from the rock-cut altar, can be seen in the **Museo Civico** at Ischia di Castro.

Ceri (2)

A medieval hill village (*borgo*) perched on a *tufo* rock east of Cerveteri, on the presumed site of an Etruscan settlement of which there are no remains except for the tombs around. The Tomb of the Statues of the early seventh century (actually they are two very worn high reliefs: fig. 43) is 500 m up the road to Bracciano, on the right overlooking the road but screened by thick prickly vegetation. This is an ancient road, for there are rock-cut tombs on both sides.

Cerveteri (3)   Etruscan name: Cisra; Latin name: Caere

The older part of the present town occupies the western corner of the area of the ancient city (now mainly given over to cultivation but currently under excavation at various points) which extended over the central of three parallel plateaux. The other two are Monte Abatone to the southeast and Banditaccia to the northwest, both of them sites of extensive necropolises (fig. 88). Soon after the entrance to the latter the path leads past the tombs of the great Tumuli 1 and 2 and the Tomb of the Reliefs. At the very far end of it, beyond the fence, is the funerary way (Via degli Inferi, usually very overgrown) which leads down to the foot of the city plateau. To the southwest of the ancient city is the Sorbo, the earliest of the cemeteries and the site of the Regolini-Galassi Tomb (about 300 m up the Bracciano road, on the right, on private property). The **Museo Nazionale**

Cerite is housed in the Castello Ruspoli in the old centre of the town and has a fine display of gravegoods from the area, among which the Etruscan pottery is outstanding.

For Monte Abatone, cross the Mola stream and take the road for Ceri. After 500 m a track on the left leads to the top, which now has few ancient features, but the big seventh century Campana tumulus is visible to the far left. On the very edge of the plateau, its two tombs (one with a monumental hewn *dromos* or entrance passage) faced the Etruscan city and were originally quite separate. For the now tree-covered Montetosto tumulus, take the road for Sasso from the main square. At 3.5 km turn left onto the Via della Tomba. A hundred metres southwest of the tumulus is the site of a large sanctuary (sixth century and later, now backfilled). Between the two ran the Etruscan road from the city to Pyrgi.

Chiusi (51)   Etruscan name: Clevsi(?); Latin name: Clusium/Camars

There are scant traces of this major Etruscan city, and it is best to head straight for the **Museo Etrusco Nazionale** which has a wide range of artefacts in the distinctive local styles (for example, fig. 91). It is here that one can arrange to visit several painted tombs in the neighbourhood, but they are mostly in poor condition.

Civita Castellana (10)   Latin name: Falerii Veteres

53 km north of Rome along the Via Flaminia; chief town of the Faliscan peoples, and dramatically situated on a *tufo* plateau isolated by deep river gorges. Immediately to the northeast is the hill of Vignale, now deserted, which was also part of the settlement, in fact the earliest part, for it was occupied already in the Final Bronze Age. On the main plateau the medieval and modern town has obliterated most traces of earlier occupation, but stretches of fortification wall (fifth century BC?) are visible on the northern side to the east of the Ponte Clementino and in the garden of the church of Santa Maria del Carmine (locked and guarded, however, by a closed order of nuns), and evidence has recently come to light that Vignale also had stone walls of the same period.

Most of Falerii's temples – at Scosato, Sassi Caduti, two on Vignale – have left few visible traces *in situ*. For the extra-urban sanctuary at Celle with its cult of Juno Curitis celebrated by Ovid, proceed down the hill towards the Via Flaminia. Just where the city plateau and the Vignale hill almost meet, at a bend to the right, a path off to the left drops down abruptly. At the bottom take the left path over a stone bridge, of medieval or earlier date, which leads to the enclosure below the light-coloured cliff of Celle. Within is a confusion of foundation walls, now thought to belong to a single monumental temple (rather than two side by side) of fourth century BC date, preceded by a small archaic shrine set at right-angles to it higher up the slope. Lower down are ruins of a medieval church with traces of vaulting. For the architectural terracottas from all these temples, many of the highest quality, one must go to the Villa Giulia in Rome.

At the western end of town the massive Forte Sangallo (*c.*AD 1500) contains the **Museo Archeologico dell'Agro Falisco,** with displays of mainly tomb material not only from Falerii but also other Faliscan centres such as Narce. Locally produced pottery includes incised *impasto* with figurative decoration, and some ambitious red-figure of the fourth century BC.

Comeana   (62)

A village west of Florence and north of the Arno, the location of two big Orientalizing tumuli. That at Boschetti is by the modern cemetery; little remains of the tumulus itself, but the small tomb-chamber and its vestibule with paved floor are still visible. For the larger Montefortini tumulus, continue up the road from the cemetery, then left. The tomb here, too, is larger, and there is a 'shelf' around the main chamber at the point from which the corbelled vault springs.

The principal habitation site seems to have been on the nearby hilltop at Artimino, where finds from the area are collected in the private *museo archeologico* housed in the grand Villa Medicea. On the slopes of the hill are more (smaller) tumuli, for example at Prato di Rosello.

Cortona (53)   Etruscan name: Curtun(?)

Of particular interest are the town wall, the museum and several monumental tombs lower down the hill. Stretches of the Etruscan wall of massive blocks are incorporated in the medieval town wall, and there are clearly visible sections either side of the Porta Santa

Maria (Via Roma) facing towards the plain below. From the same gate it is 2 km (follow the wall down, take the first right and then the road signed to Arezzo) to the better preserved of the two Hellenistic tombs known as *tanelle* ('dens'). This is the Tanella di Pitagora, a tomb built on a circular stone base, with a vault of unique construction (see p. 284); the circumference of the earth tumulus that originally covered it is also visible. From here, down the same road it is a further 2 km to the main Perugia–Arezzo road. On the other side of it, at about 100 m, are the Sodo 'melons', two big tree-covered tumuli of the sixth century and later. Within view of each other, they are sited either side of a canalized stream. Melone del Sodo I, on the left, contains a single multi-chamber tomb, of fine masonry with modern restorations in brick. Melone II has two tombs, and excavations continue on the monumental altar on its eastern side (see p. 238). The great masonry drum is also visible at this point. Of similar date is the Melone di Camucia (detail: fig. 90b), which is reached from here on the main road towards Perugia. At 2.5 km take the Via Lauretana to the right. The tumulus is on the right of this road and takes up much of the triangle formed by it, the Via dell'Ipogeo and the little Via Etruria. Beneath the mound, which is partly natural, are two tomb complexes, the more complete one discovered by François in 1842.

Material from the *meloni* is partly in Florence Archaeological Museum and partly (especially for Sodo II) in Cortona in the **Museo dell'Accademia Etrusca** (off the Piazza Signorelli). This museum, one of the oldest of its kind, also has casts of the sculptures from the altar of Sodo II, as well as the famous monumental bronze lamp – displayed in a *tempietto* setting.

Cosa (30)   Medieval name: Ansedonia

Roman colony (founded 273 BC), perched on a hill between the Via Aurelia and the sea. On the Aurelia take the northern of the two Ansedonia turn-offs. Standing remains include the walls of polygonal masonry, the temples on the arx (acropolis), and public buildings around the forum. *Antiquarium* at site entrance.

Doganella   (33)

Major urban site of the sixth to third centuries BC (fig. 57); signposted on the road that runs south from Magliano in Toscana (towards

Albinia). The excavated area with its protective roofing is visible from the road and close to a substantial farm. It consists of footings of houses either side of a road of stone and broken tile. This is a tiny part of a town site that was spread over a large low plateau (the definition of which is most clearly visible from the east beyond the farm). The stone footings of the town walls, originally 6 km long, were removed in the nineteenth century for road building.

Falerii Novi (11)

A town founded after 241 BC for the inhabitants of Falerii (Civita Castellana) after its destruction by the Romans. The circuit of walls survives remarkably complete, and is visible from the road from Civita Castellana to Fabrica di Roma. Where the walls are closest to the road the site of the amphitheatre is just a few metres from it, marked by a line of trees. To enter the walls take the road that leads towards them from the centre of the modern one-street Falerii Novi, then walk the track that leads left from this towards a gate of the town, the Porta di Giove (fig. 116). Within, the scene is dominated by the church of Santa Maria di Falleri and a big farm attached to it (with unfriendly dogs).

Ferento (29)   Latin name: Ferentium

A Roman town with origins in the fourth century BC on a plateau immediately north of Acquarossa, taking over the role of the latter as the chief centre of population. Set off as for Acquarossa, continue on the Bagnoregio road 1 km further, then turn right. The site has a large bath-building, a well preserved/restored theatre, with paved *decumanus* running behind. Tomb finds are in the Museo Civico at Viterbo.

Fiesole (60)   Latin name: Faesulae

North of the Arno above Florence. The urban site as excavated is mainly Roman (the big piazza perhaps marks the area of the Roman forum), but the well preserved temple and the town wall date back to the third century BC. The longest and most impressive stretches of the latter are on the north side. Of a similar period are the two stone-built tombs to the east (in the Via del Bargellino), of which the larger has internal steps for cinerary urns. Of earlier date (late archaic) are the tombstones with relief scenes (*stele fiesolane*) from the town and neighbouring areas, of which there is a good example in the *museum* at the site entrance and more in Florence Archaeological Museum.

Florence (59)

The **Museo Archeologico** (Via della Colonna) is the prime repository for material from the Tuscan area of Etruria, but its collections extend much further.

Ghiaccio Forte (36)

Town site of the sixth to third centuries BC in a commanding position on a hill overlooking the Albegna valley, excavated by the University of California. On the Manciano–Scansano road continue past the Pomonte turn-off and take the asphalt road to the left signed for Aquilaia. After 4.6 km continue straight onto a *strada bianca* for 1.6 km. At the private road walk through the field to the right. The site is of a large irregular figure-of-eight shape. It was defended by stone walls, their line clearly traceable. Excavated remains include the northwest and southeast gates and, in the centre, footings of buildings.

Gravisca (13) Latin name: Graviscae

Site of the port and coastal emporium of Etruscan Tarquinia and later (181 BC) of the Roman colony. Just before the road from Tarquinia to the coast curves left to the Saline, two small roads branch off right: the first to the Lido (signed), the second leads after a few metres to a beach and to the Mole Clementino (a vestige of the medieval and later harbour of Corneto). Between the two roads, on the other side of the original road, are the remains of the Roman colony, of which the lines of the axially planned streets can be made out. A road cuts through it, and after about 200 m the area of the archaic emporium becomes visible to the right under protective cover. Although of great importance for early trading contacts with Greece, the site, which preserves an area of small shrines to various Greek and Etruscan deities, now looks insignificant behind a coastal swamp.

Grosseto   (46)

The location of an important provincial museum, the **Museo Nazionale della Maremma**, with extensive displays concerning Roselle, Poggio Buco and many other sites in the region. At the time of writing, the building is closed for complete renovation.

Grotta Porcina   (20)

Near Vetralla. The name says it all, 'cave for pigs', and could be applied to many other necropolises which have later periods of re-use for housing farm animals. The site is signposted at 2 km along the Vetralla–Monte Romano road, lying 4 km off the main road. Turn left off this, then right, then left onto a *strada bianca*. Drive as far as you can, then take the path ahead. The grandest monument here is a large archaic rock tumulus completely cut away from the cliff except for a *tufo* bridge. It has external mouldings like those at Cerveteri. Inside there are big interconnected chambers with many cuttings for animal pens. One of the ceilings (matched elsewhere in the necropolis) has a carved pattern imitating intersecting beams.

Down the hill, enclosed and under roofed protection, is an archaic circular altar at the end of a spur wall with traces of reliefs, including the lower parts of domestic animals (led to sacrifice?). The monument seems to have been at the centre of a stepped area for spectators.

Lago dell'Accesa   (49)

Archaic settlement on the southeastern side of the little lake south of Massa Marittima. This is in the heart of the 'metal-bearing hills' (the Colline Metallifere), and the dwellings may have been inhabited by mine-owners or overseers. A path runs from La Pesta to the site, of which there are three areas. Area A is on the lower slope of the hill. Another area of similar houses, but now rather overgrown, is higher up, a further kilometre's walk along the original path (bearing left where possible). A third zone, near the lakeside further to the north, is currently under excavation by the University of Florence. The standard house type is of two or more squarish rooms in a single row. The footings are of stone, which would have supported walls of mud-brick and tiled roofs. Finds from the domestic quarters and from adjacent tombs are on display in the **Museo Civico** at Massa Marittima.

Lucus Feroniae   (6)

The 'Grove of Feronia', originally a sanctuary on an open site in the Tiber plain frequented by Capenates, Sabines, Latins and others. It is very close to the *Autostrada del Sole* but is accessible just off the Via Tiberina south of Fiano Romano. Sacked by Hannibal in 211 BC, it was later to grow into a Roman town, its population boosted by the planting of a Roman colony in the first century BC. There is a notable forum and basilica complex and an unusual circular amphitheatre. The original shrine is immediately to the east of the forum. Votive material from it goes back to the fourth century. There is an *antiquarium* on site.

Luni sul Mignone   (17)

Habitation site extending from the Late Bronze Age to Etruscan and later. Not to be tackled towards the end of the the day: few sites offer such ample scope for seriously losing one's way in wild and wooded country. At 8.3 km along the Monte Romano–Barbarano road, turn right onto a stabilized but rough road, just before the old Civitella Cesi station building. (Luni will seem rather less desolate in the future with the revivification of the railway line for industrial use, which passes beneath the western tip of the site.) At 5.5 km (a gate may have to be opened on the way) there is a crossroads of poor tracks at the bottom of an incline. Continue on foot straight ahead up the hill, walking westwards for 2 km. The track skirts the right side of a field and fetches up at the edge of a much larger field. Walk along the field edge (from here you can see the grassy plateau you are making for, ahead and slightly to the left) until you reach a fence that can be stepped over. On the other side, continue to the right as far as a cutting that takes you down the plateau (a natural feature probably enlarged for a route in Etruscan times). The rocky plateau now ahead is Monte Fornicchio, with rock-cut tombs in its cliff-face; like Luni it was occupied in the Late Bronze Age and can be regarded as an extension of it. To the left of it a winding path through the brambles leads to the larger plateau adjacent, taking you between the two through a boulder field consisting partly of *tufo* blocks fallen from the Etruscan defences above, and up through a rock-cut gateway on Luni's northeastern side. Below is the Vesca/ Mignone on the south, the line of the railway on the north.

Swedish excavations in the 1960s revealed traces of huts of the neolithic and Copper Age at Tre Erici immediately below the eastern end of the plateau. There are substantial visible remain thought by the excavator to date to the Late and Final Bronze Ages (see p. 52): first, towards the western end, the foundations of three long habitations in a row, their lower parts rock-cut, the longest of them some 40 m long; then, at the western extremity, a large rectangular building, again partially excavated in the bedrock and completed with drystone walls. The southern half of this was later converted for sanctuary use, later still into a church, and there are Christian graves cut into the rock behind. To the Etruscan period belongs the big rock-cut ditch, which runs close to and parallel with the row of longhouses and which isolated the western end of the plateau for defensive purposes, and also the remains of fortifications at the eastern end.

Magliano in Toscana (34)   Latin name: Heba

The Etruscan centre lay to the southeast of the present town but is known only from its Orientalizing and archaic rock-tomb necropolises, among them Santa Maria in Borraccia and San Bruzio (the former should be approached from the piazza in front of the old town). In the sixth century it seems to have been eclipsed by neighbouring Doganella. Of the Roman colony of Heba later planted here, there are very few remains, and its extent has had to be gauged by field survey and air photography.

Marsiliana (32)

Etruscan centre known only from its very rich Orientalizing grave-goods (now in Florence Archaeological Museum). As one leaves the

Via Aurelia at Albinia and drives east, Marsiliana makes a striking landmark in the distance: a tower on top of a hill jutting into the Albegna plain. The hill with its *borgo* may well be the site of the settlement, but even in the surrounding cemetery areas the Etruscan presence is today virtually invisible. The decline in the late seventh century may be due to the rise of Magliano nearby.

Marzabotto   (63)

Southwest of Bologna on the road towards Pistoia. This regularly planned town (fig. 58), laid out *c.*500 BC, is on a terrace above the river Reno which has eroded away much of the site on the south-west. At the far southeast, immediately beyond the eastern gate, is a necropolis (fig. 59) of tombs lined with stone slabs and capped with stone markers (*cippi*). A similar and larger necropolis to the north is reached through a gate on the far side of the main road. The gravegoods in the site *museum* show that most of the burials were of well-to-do folk (but all the gold jewellery was stolen in 1911). Adjacent to the car-park are the scant remains of a sanctuary which has yielded numerous votive offerings, especially of crude bronze human figurines – probably cast in the foundry area at the bottom of the main north–south street where it is cut by the course of the river. The acropolis, with remains of several temples (fig. 79) and shrines, is on a height above the town and is now approached from it by a wooden bridge across the road.

Murlo (Poggio Civitate)   (55)

Seventh to sixth century BC centre south of Siena (fig. 61). Poggio Civitate is the long wooded hill visible to the southeast from the upper windows of the well laid-out **Antiquarium di Poggio Civitate** at Murlo, the right-hand extremity being Monte Aguzzo, the necro-polis area. Because the main site was deliberately and thoroughly destroyed in antiquity, leaving only the terracotta roofing and dec-orations which have been entirely removed, all that was ever visible were the trenches of the Bryn Mawr College excavations, now mainly in deep thickets. [To reach the location, take the road for Buon-convento, at 400 m take the poor track to the right up the hill for 600 m, then the path to the left along the spine of the hill until it begins gently to descend at about 600 m.]

Musarna   (23)

Late Etruscan town site. At 8 km on the Viterbo–Tuscania road
there is a lay-by on the left created by a curve of the old road. From
here a stabilized road runs 2.5 km to the Casale della Macchia del
Conte; 200 m beyond this farm, take the track to the right. Excavations by the French School at Rome continue in a number of areas
including the impressive rock-cut entrance-way. Finds from the
necropolises are in the Museo Civico at Viterbo.

Narce   (8)

Faliscan settlement. At 2.5 km on the Mazzano Romano–Calcata
road there is a bridge across the river Treia. Narce is the hill to the
left. A few metres further on is another bridge across a stream
which, on the right, separates the hills of Pizzo Piede and Monte Li
Santi. All three hills possessed ancient settlements, but that on Narce
was earliest: at its foot immediately by the first bridge the British
School at Rome excavated a settlement stratigraphy running from
the Apennine Bronze Age to the Roman conquest of the area.[10]
From this bridge a path runs along the right bank of the Treia towards Mazzano. At 300 m there are remains of a recently excavated
sanctuary that continued in use into the second century BC and has
produced terracotta votives of babies and anatomical features.

Nepi (9)   Latin name: Nepet(e)

A small town in Faliscan territory, site of a Roman colony founded
contemporaneously with Sutri in the fourth century BC. The earliest
visible remains are parts of the (fifth century?) wall circuit by the
medieval *castello*, but recent Bristol University excavations within
the medieval/modern town have uncovered an occupation sequence
stretching back into the seventh century.

Norchia (21)   Etruscan/Latin name: Orcla(?)

Etruscan town site with associated necropolises, mainly of the third
and second centuries BC but beginning in the sixth century. The

10   Potter, 1976

approach is from the Vetralla–Monte Romano road. Beyond the parking area the path runs between fields and plunges down the Fosso Pile ravine, on the way passing rock tombs on many levels. The most elaborate kind, found here especially, has a false door façade, a projecting porch below with columns or pillars at the front (all rock-cut), and below that again the entrance to the tomb proper; the flat roof above the façade is accessed by a staircase at the side.

Below, beneath the *castello* opposite, there is a flimsy bridge across the stream and, beyond, a steep path leading up onto the narrowest part of the settlement plateau. Here is one of four medieval *fossati* (ditches) connected with the castle defences. Turning right (north) – through one of several late medieval habitation grottoes beneath the *castello* – brings one eventually to the elegant ruins of the early medieval church of San Pietro. However, 500 m south of the *castello* is the most obvious sign of Etruscan presence: the great ditch, 25 m across, the largest of all Etruscan *fossati,* here giving added protection on the north with a surmounting ashlar defensive/retaining wall.

For the pedimented tombs (fig. 112) of the Acqualta necropolis, walk north along the valley bottom beyond the end of the San Pietro spur, cross the stream by another flimsy bridge, then turn right along the valley but keeping well up to the foot of the cliffs on the left.

Orbetello (31)   Etruscan name: Cusi(?)

The Etruscan settlement (beneath the modern town) lay at the end of a pensinsula; the causeway to Monte Argentario is modern. It also probably had direct access to the sea, for the northern (Giannella) sandbar is thought to have been then incomplete. The (third century?) town walls of polygonal masonry are most easily seen from the causeway; the circuit is still complete except on the landward side. The *comune* opposite the Duomo houses a permanent display of the figured terracotta pediment from the temple at Talamone.

Orvieto (45)   Etruscan name: Velzna; Latin name: Volsinii

The most dramatic approach is from the Bolsena road (fig. 50). Later occupation of the *tufo* outcrop has obliterated most traces of the Etruscan city, of which the best preserved remains are those of the fifth century BC Belvedere Temple, on the left of the road as one enters from Orvieto Scalo, just before the funicular terminus. Most of Orvieto's tombs are at the foot of the rock. Back down the same road is the archaic, rigorously planned Crocefisso del Tufo necropolis (fig. 46). Currently a necropolis of similar kind and period, together with an associated sanctuary, is under excavation by the University of Perugia on the south side at Cannicella.

Opposite the Duomo is the **Museo Civico Claudio Faina**, where the Etruscan material includes the figurative terracottas from the Belvedere Temple. To the right of the Duomo is the **Museo Archeologico Nazionale**, with tomb-goods from the Crocefisso del Tufo and elsewhere. It also houses paintings detached from the two Golini tombs 6 km to the south. In the same zone, outside Porano, is the painted Hescanas Tomb (the family name is incised on an urn still in the tomb), also of the fourth century, which may be visited through arrangement with the museum.

Perugia (52)   Latin name: Perusia

A major urban centre, especially in the third century BC and later. Many stretches of the Hellenistic town wall survive along with a number of gateways, of which the two most substantial are the Porta Marzia on the southeast and the elaborate Arco di Augusto on the north, the latter surmounted by a Renaissance loggia. The **Museo Archeologico Nazionale dell'Umbria** is arranged around the cloister of San Domenico; its prehistoric section is second only to the Museo Pigorini in Rome in comprehensive coverage for central Italy. On the outskirts of the town are two important tombs. The second century BC Ipogeo dei Volumni is about 5 km from the Porta Santa Costanza (near San Domenico) towards Assisi, complete with its urns of the Velimna/Volumnii family. There is also a collection of ash-urns here from other parts of the Palazzone necropolis. The rather earlier Ipogeo di San Manno, resting place of the Precu family and roofed with a travertine barrel-vault, is by the church of the same name beyond the railway station towards Arezzo.

Pianezze   (44)

Archaic rock-cut necropolis north of Lake Bolsena, on the road between the lake and Grotte di Castro. Most tombs are multi-chamber with no exterior detailing except for the single-step recessed door. Some have carved interior ridge-beams, and one tomb has ceiling rafters simply painted in red (without relief). The habitation site on a nearby hill is unexplored.

Pieve Socana   (58)

A village by the Arno north of Arezzo. Outside the medieval church, just beyond the apse, are the remains of a sanctuary of fourth/third century BC date which include an exceptionally well preserved altar with fine cushion mouldings. It stood in front of a temple which is now under the church.

Poggio Buco   (38)

Immediately after the bridge across the Fiora, on the Pitigliano–Manciano road, turn left onto a track, bearing left after a few metres, along the valley and up. At 1.5 km a track joins from the left, just before a two-chamber tomb. Walk down this track, passing an abandoned farmhouse. This was the western approach to the ancient town, and there are chamber tombs on both sides, many adapted for later agricultural use. Ahead is the cliff of the town plateau which stretches down towards the Fiora to the east. Necropolises abound in the vicinity, especially around the lower plateau nearest the river. Little is known of the town itself, except for scanty temple remains, which have yielded figurative architectural terracottas of the archaic period.

Populonia (50)   Etruscan name: Pupluna

Ancient Etruria's centre of heavy industry, situated by an idyllic bay well out of sight of its modern counterpart at Piombino only a few kilometres to the south. The short road from the coast to where the guided tours begin runs between the San Cerbone and Porcareccia necropolises, notable for their Orientalizing and archaic tumuli and built tombs with pitched roofs. This area was later given over to metallurgical processing, and at Porcareccia there is a small excavated industrial complex of workshops, dwellings and furnaces (in use from the later sixth century to the third century). The headland site was defended by a system of inner and outer walls. A stretch of the former is visible from the road leading to the top of the hill, just before it reaches the *castello* area, which was the site of the ancient acropolis. To the left of the parking area there are the foundations of a complex of monumental buildings, including part of a second century temple. Within the castle complex is the small **Museo Etrusco** with old-fashioned displays of necropolis material (the rest is in the Museo Archeologico at Florence).

Pyrgi (4)   Medieval name: Santa Severa

The site of one of Caere's ports. The coast today is dominated by the medieval *castello* of Santa Severa, itself built within the walls of the Roman colony, which are best seen on the side facing towards Civitavecchia. Some 300 m down-coast is the site of one of Etruria's most important sanctuaries, centred around a fertility cult. The place was sacked in 384 BC by Greeks from Syracuse and never fully recovered. The finds from Rome University's excavations are divided between the Villa Giulia in Rome and the *antiquarium* here. The latter is by the parking area and contains reconstructions of the rich terracotta decorations of the two temples and other site documentation. Also on display are the famous inscribed gold plaques – in facsimile (the originals are kept in a bank vault). To the south of the main sanctuary is another sanctuary area of small shrines to Etruscan deities, currently under excavation.

Quinto Fiorentino   (61)

West of Florence. Two monumental seventh century BC tombs are visible here; a third is long since demolished. On the eastern outskirts of Sesto Fiorentino, where the main road from Florence has become the Via Gramsci, take the small Via degli Strozzi to the right, then first left and left again. This brings one to the splendid Montagnola tumulus, with its tomb of three chambers of which the largest is circular with a corbelled dome and central pillar. The stone is alberese limestone. For the Mula tumulus take the same Via degli Strozzi, ignore the left turn and continue straight for a few metres. This, too, has a circular chamber, but much larger and without the central pillar. On top of the mound is a substantial villa.

Regisvilla (26)   Latin name: Regae; modern name: Le Murelle

One of Vulci's trading ports (fig. 63) and a site potentially on the same level of importance as Pyrgi and Graviscae. The excavations of the 1970s have been backfilled and the area fenced in. [To reach the location, the Via delle Murelle is 3 km south along the Via Aurelia from the Marina di Montalto turn-off, and the site is to the right of it, 500 m before the beach.]

Rome   (1)

There are three outstanding museums. The **Museo Nazionale di Villa Giulia** (Viale delle Belle Arti) houses, in a fine Renaissance building, extensive collections from southern Etruria and Latium partly arranged in a topographical sequence. The **Museo Gregoriano Etrusco** (in the Vatican Museums) has, among other treasures, the Regolini-Galassi Tomb material from Cerveteri and the Guglielmi collection (mainly from Vulci). The **Museo Preistorico ed Etnografico Luigi Pigorini** in the EUR (Esposizione Universale di Rome) district outside Rome displays early iron age material from major Etruscan sites and is important for the prehistory of the whole peninsula.

Roselle (47)   Latin name: Rusellae

The line of the walls can be seen from the Grosseto–Siena road. The approach road passes a zone of Orientalizing/archaic chamber tombs and tumuli (on the left), and at a short distance to the right of the parking area there is a stretch of the massive town wall. The most impressive lengths of it are at the top of the hill beyond the amphitheatre. Immediately to the northeast of the amphitheatre are remains of the sixth century BC House of the Impluvium (fenced in). For further details, see p. 274.

San Giovenale   (16)

Clearly signposted from the Monte Romano–Blera road. This is a settlement site extensively investigated by the Swedish Institute at Rome (fig. 60). There was occupation in the Middle and Late Bronze

Age, and in the Early Iron Age much of the plateau was covered by oval huts. Two areas of early Etruscan buildings (seventh to sixth centuries BC) are visible and protected by roofing: an area of houses and workshops on the 'Borgo' at the east, and a smaller housing complex at mid plateau. Between the two is the late medieval *castello* and, beyond it, the remains of the early medieval church of San Giovenale. Further west is the Etruscan *fossato*, the defensive transverse ditch, marked by a line of trees. On the north in front of the *castello* a section of the Etruscan town wall has been exposed, revealing seven courses of massive squared blocks.

Of the many surrounding necropolises, closest is the Casale Vignale, right up against the Borgo. This begins with a group of tombs arranged in a piazza, with, on the left, a tomb that is midway between a tumulus and a cube (that is, the front is cut back flat). Opposite is a fully developed cube tomb, its flat roof reached by a staircase to the left. Further on is a stretch of rock-cut road lined with tombs along one side, and beyond this an area of monumental tumuli.

San Giuliano   (18)

An unexplored settlement in a woodland setting with necropolises of the seventh to the fourth centuries BC and of a variety of tomb types, the site offers a particular blend of Etruscan and medieval which this part of Etruria can provide in abundance but rarely on such an intimate scale. Nearly 2 km from Barbarano towards Vetralla, a path (signed) leads directly from the road up to the big Tomba Cima. The earliest of the many tombs of this tumulus is also the largest (seventh century) and has a huge dromos like that of the Campana Tomb at Cerveteri, with which it can also be compared for interior architectural detail. The curious structure adjacent to it, with its rows of rock-cut bases, has been interpreted as an elaborate altar. The path continues steeply down with tombs on all sides. Ahead is the settlement plateau; immediately above, part of its defensive wall has been consolidated. Across the stream the path branches. To the left is the way up onto the plateau, in the centre of which is the small ruined medieval church of San Giuliano. To the right, one is led down across another stream to more tombs, some of monumental dimensions such as the double cube of the Tomba della Regina, and then up onto the Pian di Caiolo, where there are more early tumuli, especially along the edge of the plateau facing the town site. Their rich contents are in the Villa Giulia Museum in Rome.

Saturnia (41)   Etruscan name: Urina(?)

Nothing remains of the Etruscan town, and little of the Roman colony of 183 – a notable exception being the Porta Romana near the Duomo, a Roman gateway for the Via Clodia to enter through the polygonal walls. There are many Etruscan necropolises, however. That at Puntone is close by, but 7 km by road (starting off towards Semproniano). The tumuli here, of the seventh century and later, are distinctive of the area: each has a tomb of one or two stone-built chambers lined with thin slabs, which are also laid horizontally for the ceiling.

Sorgenti della Nova   (39)

Late bronze age settlement, east of Pitigliano at the 'source of the Nova'. From Pitigliano take the Albinia road, turn left for Farnese, but after 200 m keep straight ahead towards San Quirico. After 500 m take the road to the right, which changes to a *strada bianca* and then a poor track. Keep to the main track. After 4.7 km turn right at the T-junction, and after 1 km bear left downhill to (600 m) a ford. Stop 200 m beyond the ford, where a farm track joins from the left. Across the field beyond the gate is the whitish cliff of the hill.

Sorgenti is a long ridge of a hill, very narrow along the top, steep and slippery on the sides. It is crowned by a medieval tower towards the eastern end. Traces of prehistoric huts of various sizes are visible on the long sides, cut into the rock at their back (fig. 23). More huts were sited along the top of the ridge, but traces of some of these were partially obliterated by medieval re-occupation. Excavations by Milan University continue. A permanent display relating to the site can be seen in the **Museo di Preistoria e Protostoria della Valle del Fiume Fiora** at Manciano, and further material is currently under re-organization at the *museum* at Farnese.

Sovana (40)   Latin name: Suana

The modern (medieval) village occupies only a small part of the Etruscan settlement plateau which, judging by the surrounding tombs, was at a peak of prosperity in the later fourth to second centuries BC. Parts of the lower courses of the outer wall of the Rocca Aldobrandeschi are the Etruscan town wall. Façade tombs – here with complex crowning elements – with false doors are plentiful, and there is a good series at the Torrente Folonia necropolis (take the path from the foot of the plateau near the Rocca). But there are also tombs which architecturally and sculpturally display more flamboyant designs, among them the Tomb of the Siren (fig. 113; just past the road-tunnel, heading towards Saturnia), the Pola and Ildebranda Tombs (further along the same road), and the Tomb of the Typhon (path opposite the Ildebranda Tomb). The track between the Ildebranda and the path to the Typhon leads up to a *via cava*, an Etruscan rock-cut road of great depth, of which Sovana offers several examples; there is a far bigger one (a *cavone*) further along the track beneath the Typhon Tomb.

For the Tomb of the Silen (Monte Rosello necropolis), walk the road east for Sorano; after a few metres take the path to the left, branching off through a small-holding on the right and crossing the little Fosso della Valle Bona. Turn right and the tomb is 150 m along the valley beneath the lip of the plateau. Above the chamber is a (much ruined) cylindrical drum with attached semi-columns, a design first seen in the fourth century Lysicrates Monument at Athens. Originally it was embellished with a frieze of silen/satyr masks.

Sutri (15)   Latin name: Sutrium

A small town north of Rome by the Via Cassia, on the Etruscan/Faliscan border, on the site of the fourth century BC Roman colony. Nothing remains of the pre-Roman settlement and very little of the Roman. To the south just off the Cassia is the amphitheatre, one of the very few that are totally rock-cut. The rock-cut tombs and niches in this area are mainly of Roman date.

Talamone (35)   Etruscan name: Tlamu;
Greek/Latin name: Telamon

The ancient site is east of the modern/medieval town of Talamone, around the bay on the wooded hill of Talamonaccio, overlooking the Via Aurelia where the river Osa reaches the sea. The only visible remains are the foundations (overgrown and enclosed) of the fourth century BC temple on the hilltop (fig. 6), refurbished in the second century with an ambitious terracotta pediment (see: Orbetello). Settlement also extended over the hill of Bengodi to the north which has produced archaic finds. To reach the temple site, approaching on the Aurelia from the north, continue past the Talamone turn-off to where the Aurelia curves left under Talamonaccio, where there is a raised lay-by; immediately after this a small unmarked road leads off and up the hill. Approaching from the south, take the Talamone exit, turn left at the village of Fonteblanda and back up onto the Aurelia; after a few metres take the small road to the right as above.

Tarquinia (14)   Etruscan name: Tarch(u)na; Latin name: Tarquinii; medieval name: Corneto

The towers of medieval Tarquinia begin to dominate the skyline as one drives north from Civitavecchia along the Via Aurelia. But this was not the site of the Etruscan city, which was on the parallel plateau further inland, the Pian di Civita. Immediately within the medieval walls of Tarquinia is the **Museo Nazionale**, housed in the imposing fourteenth century Palazzo Vitelleschi and containing a wealth of material from the Civita (fig. 109) and the surrounding necropolises, including paintings detached from some of the painted tombs. To see tomb-painting *in situ*, head southeast of the town to the Monterozzi ridge, where the main area of painted tombs is fenced off. Only a handful of tombs is normally open on any one day.

To reach the Pian di Civita continue along the Monterozzi road, turning left onto the road to Vetralla. Passing the remains of an impressive acqueduct serving Renaissance Corneto, one glimpses on the left the course of the Etruscan city walls, marked by a line of scrubby bushes. Soon afterwards, a track leads left off the Vetralla road up onto the top of the fennel-covered plateau where, to the left, a very rough track branches off to the Ara della Regina, the great fourth century temple (fig. 108), of which the lower parts are still visible; while to the right one can walk to a well preserved section of the city walls. Further to the west is the area of the Milan University excavations, which have uncovered a sanctuary area extending back to the ninth century.

Tolfa   (12)

In the hill country around Tolfa, the Gruppo Archeologico Romano has in recent years investigated many settlements and associated necropolises. For orientation one should see the display in the **Museo Civico**. The Pian della Conserva necropolis of archaic tumuli (of Caeretan type) is 5 km from Tolfa towards Rota. It is on top of the hillside, just out of view, on the left of the road immediately opposite a large farm. Follow the left side of the field straight up; there is a steep climb towards the end. Some of the tombs are still under excavation; others illustrate well just how completely the modern plough can obliterate a rock tumulus. In the field to the furthest left a rock-cut funerary way leads down off the plateau, lined with tombs like the Via degli Inferi at Cerveteri.

Tuscania   (25)   Latin name: Tuscana;
medieval name: Toscanella

The centre of Etruscan settlement was on the hill now dominated by the medieval church of San Pietro; recent survey has shown that the site also extended into the valley below on the right bank of the river Marta. Of Roman Tuscania, excavations have uncovered part of the settlement on the hill, part of a bath-building below it to the north, and near this a short stretch of the Via Clodia.

There are extensive necropolises, especially to the east and south. Among the more notable are: (1) the Tomba della Regina complex of the Hellenistic era. (Take the road south to the Madonna dell'Olivo, turn left immediately before the church.) From here came the great series of sarcophagi of the Curuna family. A custodian on site will unlock the gate to the Regina itself with its very intricate series of chambers. (2) The Ara del Tufo complex, a cluster of archaic tumulus tombs. (A further 1.5 km past the Madonna dell'Olivo, then left onto a *strada bianca*. Halfway down the slope the tombs are visible in the field on the right.) (3) The Peschiera necropolis. (Take the road north for Marta; turn right before the modern cemetery, then left, then right. After 500 m there is a small parking area on the right. Across the field is a low cliff with chamber tombs. Walk round it keeping it on your left.) The sixth century BC Peschiera Tomb is shaped like a rectangular house with pitched roof, entered on the long side. Within is a central hall with chambers to either side, their couches with legs carved in relief. From the tomb there is a view across the valley to the necropolis hill of

Pian di Mole and to a group of monumental tombs currently under excavation/conservation by the Superintendency.

Tuscania's necropolis material is well displayed in the **Museo Nazionale Archeologico** arranged around the cloister of the Madonna del Riposo. Many stone sarcophagi and figured lids are also laid out in the aisles of San Pietro, and crowning the walls of the Piazza del Comune.

Veio (5)   Latin name: Veii

The area of the ancient city (fig. 26) is set in deep countryside and gives little indication of being only 15 km north of Rome. After La Storta on the Via Cassia, a small road runs off to the right to Isola Farnese, a hill village that became the main population centre when Veii was abandoned after the Roman period. But before the village, where the road is at its lowest point, a lane leads off left at a hairpin angle down to the Piordo stream. This has to be crossed on foot by the waterfall, and the path continues up and to the right, finally becoming a paved Roman road that leads (beyond the gate) to the Portonaccio sanctuary with its Etruscan temple and associated foundations (fig. 81).

Back past the gate, the main track leads off to the right up onto the city plateau, here dominated by the extensive remains of a large Roman villa. From here the Ponte Sodo is just over 1 km to the northeast at the foot of the other side of the plateau. This ancient work of engineering, probably of the fifth century BC or earlier,[11] consists of a large 70 m-long tunnel through a bluff of the plateau, providing an artificial channel for the Valchetta stream and preventing it from flooding the surrounding area. It can only be observed from the level of the stream. In the area beyond the stream are a number of *cuniculi*. Half a kilometre downstream (east) from the Ponte Sodo is the monumental Campana Tomb of Orientalizing date, its painted walls long since faded and its entrance blocked by a gate.

Vetulonia (48)   Etruscan name: Vetluna; medieval name: Colonna

One of the chief centres of power in northern Etruria in the Orientalizing period, on a hilltop site now overlooking the plain of Grosseto – which was in Etruscan times an inlet of the sea. The

11   Ward-Perkins, 1961: 50

most substantial remains of the acropolis wall, built with large squared blocks, are at the very top of the village behind the church. In the village centre a new *museum* is about to be opened. Further down, on the outskirts, a Hellenistic quarter has been excavated, with buildings by the side of a (Roman) road. Below this a road to the right bears downhill to the northeast to two famous seventh century tumuli, the Diavolino 2 (a fine example of a corbelled dome surmounting a square chamber) and the Pietrera (containing two tombs superimposed). Much material is in Florence Archaeological Museum, including the human-figure sculptures from the latter and the complete Diavolino 1 tumulus – restored in the museum garden.

Viterbo   (24)

A medieval walled town and busy provincial capital with two archaeological museums. The **Museo Civico**, adjacent to the convent of Santa Maria della Verità on the main road just outside the walls to the east, houses material from various parts of the region. The cloister displays sarcophagi, dominated by those of the Alethna family from Musarna. The **Museo Nazionale** at the Rocca Albornoz, the austere medieval building that adjoins the Porta Fiorentina to the north, contains material and architectural reconstructions connected with the Swedish excavations at Acquarossa and San Giovenale. There are plans to extend this museum to include other sites.

Volterra (56)   Etruscan name: Velathri;
Latin name: Volaterrae

D.H. Lawrence took against Volterra for various reasons including the chill wind; but as a great centre of power in northern Etruria (especially from the fourth century on) and with its commanding hilltop location, it is worth spending more time here than he gave it. The fourth century walls, of sandstone, were more than 7 km long, enclosing an area more than four times greater than the medieval circuit. Long stretches remain, including two gates of Hellenistic date: the famous Porta dell'Arco on the south decorated with three heads (of protective deities?) and the Portone (or Porta di Diana) on the north. Immediately beyond the latter is the Portone necropolis, from which many of the urns in the museum came, but where there are only a few chambers now open. An earlier circuit of walls had enclosed the acropolis in the southeast part of the town (including the area around the fortress/prison), but very little of it survives. The **Museo Etrusco Guarnacci** (Via Don Minzoni) is better heated than in Lawrence's day, but even his numbed attention was enthusiastically drawn to the vast collection of funerary urns; here, too, are many examples of the distinctive Volterran red-figure vases (kraters) of the fourth and third centuries BC.

In the acropolis area west of the prison there are remains of a sanctuary with two temples of the third and second centuries BC. Further north, through the Porta Fiorentina of the medieval walls, is a substantial Roman theatre with a square portico behind (like the theatre at Ostia) and a bath-building.

Vulci (27)   Etruscan name: Velc-

The chief landmark, as one heads north from the Via Aurelia, is the medieval Castello dell'Abbadia, Dennis's 'dark castle standing in lonely pomp'. Especially picturesque is the juxtaposition of the castle with the adjoining stone bridge arching high over the river Fiora. The castle is now the *museum*, containing well arranged displays of funerary and votive material from the ancient site. The foundations of the bridge are Etruscan, but the arch is Roman and the topmost part is medieval. The bridge carried an aqueduct as well as a footpath, and the seepage of water with high mineral content is responsible for the huge stalactites on one side of it.

The site of the Etruscan city lies 1 km to the south. It is best reached by re-tracking down the road to the Aurelia and taking the first track on the left. Beyond the entrance is a paved Roman road, the *decumanus*, some way down it on the left are the remains of a vast Etruscan temple (the *tempio grande*), and further along are those of a large Roman house with mosaic floors and an underground vaulted corridor (*cryptoportico*). This is one of the best examples in Etruria of a late republican house of Pompeian plan. Prominent on the site are the lofty ruins of two Roman apsed buildings of uncertain function.

The city was surrounded by necropolises on all sides. To reach the François Tomb, turn right out of the *castello* cul-de-sac, then right at the crossroads (towards Montalto di Castro) and right again after 1.5 km onto a track that leads eventually past the Cuccumella tumulus (on the left), one of the largest of the burial mounds, to a parking area below the brow of the plateau. The tomb is open during museum opening hours. Although the detached figured paintings (detail: fig. 38) lie faded and inaccessible in the Villa Torlonia in Rome, much of the painted decorative scheme of the tomb complex still remains. From the entrance there are views across the Fiora to the city site beyond. A steep path leads down to the river and (slightly to the left) to the scanty remains of the ancient bridge across it (the Ponte Rotto).

Bibliography

N.B. *for an overview of the literature on the Etruscans, see the Selected Reading at the end of the Bibliography.*

Agostini, S., de Grossi Mazzorin, J., and d'Ercole, V. (1991–2) Economia e territoria in Abruzzo durante la media età del bronzo. *Rassegna di Archeologia* 10: 419–26.

Åkerström, Å. (1981) Etruscan tomb painting, an art of many faces. *Opuscula Romana* 13: 7–34.

Alessio, M., Allegri, L., Bella, F., Calderoni, G., Cortesi, C., Dai Pra, G., de Rita, D., Esu, D., Follieri, M., Improta, S., Magri, D., Narcisi, B., Petrone, V., and Sadori, L. (1986) 14C dating, geochemical features, faunistic and pollen analyses of the uppermost 10 m core from Valle di Castiglione (Rome, Italy). *Geologica Romana* 25: 287–308.

Alfieri, N. (1979) *Spina. Museo archeologico di Ferrara 1.* Bologna, Calderini.

Alvarez, W. (1972) The Treia valley north of Rome: volcanic stratigraphy, topographic evolution and geological influence on human settlement. *Geologica Romana* 11: 153–76.

Alvarez, W. (1973) The ancient course of the Tiber river near Rome: an introduction to the middle Pleistocene volcanic stratigraphy of central Italy. *Bulletin of the Geological Society of America* 84: 749–58.

Ammerman, A.J., and Schaffer, G.D. (1981) Neolithic settlement patterns in Calabria. *Current Anthropology* 22: 430–40.

Ampolo, C. (1980) Le condizioni materiali della produzione: agricoltura e paesaggio agrario. *Dialoghi di Archeologia* 2: 15–46.

Ampolo, C. (1987) Per uno studio dell'alimentazione dell'Etruria e di Roma arcaica. In G. Barbieri (ed.) *L'alimentazione nel mondo antico: gli etruschi*: 9–13. Rome, Istituto Poligrafico e Zecca dello Stato.

Anati, E. (1981) *Le statue-stele della Lunigiana.* Milan, Jaca Book.

Andersen, H.D. (1993) The Etruscan ancestral cult: its origins and development and the importance of anthropomorphization. *Analecta Romana Instituti Danici* 21: 7–66.

Angle, M., Gianni, A., and Guidi, A. (1982) Gli insediamenti montani di sommità nell'Italia centrale: il caso dei monti Lucretili. *Dialoghi di Archeologia* 2: 80–98.

Anzidei, A.P. (1987) Il processo di neolitizzazione nell'area centro-meridionale del Lazio: dati e problemi. *Il neolitico d'Italia: Atti della XXVI Riunione Scientifica del'Istituto Italiano di Preistoria e Protostoria*: 273–85. Florence, IIPP.

Anzidei, A.P., Bietti-Sestieri, A.M., and de Santis, A. (1985) *Roma e il Lazio dall'età della pietra alla formazione della città*. Rome, Quasar.

Attema, P. (1992) Measuring landscape perception in archaeology: a model for the Pontine Region (southern Lazio). *Caeculus* 1: 3–10.

Attolini, I., Cambi, F., Castagna, M., Celuzza, M., Fentress, E., Perkins, P., and Regoli, E. (1991) Political geography and productive geography between the valleys of the Albegna and Fiora in northern Etruria. In G. Barker and J. Lloyd (eds.) *Roman Landscapes: Archaeological Survey in the Mediterranean Region*: 142–52. London, British School at Rome, Archaeological Monographs 2.

Bagnasco Gianni, G. (1986) Le epigrafi. In M. Bonghi Jovino (ed.) *Gli etruschi di Tarquinia*: 172–8. Modena, Edizioni Panini.

Baker, J.R. (1984) The study of animal diseases with regard to agricultural practices and man's attitude to his animals. In C. Grigson and J. Clutton-Brock (eds.) *Animals and Archaeology 4. Husbandry in Europe*: 253–7. Oxford, British Archaeological Reports, International Series 227.

Balista, C., Carancini, G.L., and Guerzoni, R.P. (1991–2) Insediamenti nell'area della conca velina (Province di Terni e Rieti). *Rassegna di Archeologia* 10: 403–10.

Barbagallo, C. (1904) La produzione media relativa dei cereali e della vite nella Grecia, nella Sicilia e nell'Italia antica. *Rivista di Storia Antica* 8: 477–504.

Barbieri, G. (ed.) (1987a) *L'alimentazione nel mondo antico: gli etruschi*. Rome, Istituto Poligrafico e Zecca dello Stato.

Barbieri, G. (1987b) Catalogo. In G. Barbieri (ed.) *L'alimentazione nel mondo antico: gli etruschi*: 143–79. Rome, Istituto Poligrafico e Zecca dello Stato.

Barbieri, G. (1987c) Musarna 2. Note in margine al restauro dei mosaici. *Bollettino d'Arte* 41: 61–70.

Barfield, L.H. (1977) The beaker culture in Italy. In R. Mercer (ed.) *Beakers in Britain and Europe: Four Studies*: 27–49. Oxford, British Archaeological Reports, Supplementary Series 26.

Barker, G. (1976) Animal husbandry at Narce. In T.W. Potter (ed.) *A Faliscan Town in South Etruria, Excavations at Narce 1966–71*: 295–307. London, British School at Rome.

Barker, G. (1981) *Landscape and Society: Prehistoric Central Italy*. London, Academic Press.

Barker, G. (1985) *Prehistoric Farming in Europe*. Cambridge, Cambridge University Press.

Barker, G. (1988) Archaeology and the Etruscan countryside. *Antiquity* 62 (237): 772–85.

Barker, G. (1989) The archaeology of the Italian shepherd. *Proceedings of the Cambridge Philological Society* 215: 1–19.

Barker, G. (1995) *A Mediterranean Valley: Landscape Archaeology and Annales History in the Biferno Valley, Italy.* London, Leicester University Press.

Barker, G., and Gamble, C.S. (eds.) (1985) *Beyond Domestication in Prehistoric Europe: Investigations in Subsistence Archaeology and Social Complexity.* London, Academic Press.

Barker, G., and Grant, A. (eds.) (1991) Ancient and modern pastoralism in central Italy: an interdisciplinary study in the Cicolano mountains. *Papers of the British School at Rome* 59: 15–88.

Barker, G., and Lloyd, J.A. (eds.) (1991) *Roman Landscapes: Archaeological Survey in the Mediterranean Region.* London, British School at Rome, Archaeological Monographs 2.

Barker, G., and Rasmussen, T. (1988) The archaeology of an Etruscan *polis*: a preliminary report on the Tuscania Project (1986 and 1987 seasons). *Papers of the British School at Rome* 56: 25–42.

Barker, G., and Slater, E.A. (1971) The development of prehistoric copper and bronze age metallurgy in Italy, in the light of the metal analyses from the Pigorini Museum, Rome. *Bullettino di Paletnologia Italiana* 80, n.s.22: 12–44.

Barker, G., and Stallibrass, S. (1987) La fauna. In P. Meloni and D. Whitehouse (eds.) *La rocca posteriore sul Monte Ingino di Gubbio (campagne di scavo 1975–1977)*: 277–312. Florence, La Nuova Italia.

Barker, G., and Stoddart, S. (1994) The Bronze Age of central Italy: c.2000–900 BC. In C. Mathers and S. Stoddart (eds.) *Development and Decline in the Mediterranean Bronze Age*: 145–65. Sheffield, Sheffield University, Sheffield Archaeology Monographs 8.

Barker, G., and Symonds, J. (1984) The Montarrenti survey, 1982–3. *Archeologia Medievale* 11: 278–89.

Barker, G., Grant, A., and Rasmussen, T. (1993) Approaches to the Etruscan landscape: the development of the Tuscania Survey. In P. Bogucki (ed.) *Case Studies in European Prehistory*: 229–57. Boca Raton, CRC Press.

Barker, G., Coccia, S., Jones, D.A., and Sitzia, J. (1986) The Montarrenti survey, 1985: problems of integrating archaeological, environmental and historical data. *Archeologia Medievale* 13: 291–320.

Bartoli, F., Mallegni, F., and Vitiello, A. (1989–90) Indagini nutrizionali e odontostomatologiche per una definizione della dietà alimentare in un gruppo umano a cultura etrusca: gli inumati della necropoli dei Monterozzi di Tarqunia (VI–II sec. a.C.). *Studi Etruschi* 56: 255–69.

Bartoloni, G. (1987) Le comunità dell'Italia centrale tirrenica a la colonizzazione greca in Campania. In M. Cristofani (ed.) *Etruria e Lazio arcaico*: 37–53. Rome, Consiglio Nazionale delle Ricerche.

Bartoloni, G. (1989a) *La cultura villanoviana.* Rome, Nuova Italia Scientifica.

Bartoloni, G. (1989b) Marriage, sale and gift. A proposito di alcuni corredi femminili dalle necropoli populoniesi della prima età del ferro. In A. Rallo (ed.) *Le donne in Etruria*: 35–54. Rome, 'L'Erma' di Bretschneider.

Bartoloni, G. (1991) Populonia: characteristic features of a port community in Italy during the First Iron Age. In E. Herring, R. Whitehouse and J. Wilkins (eds.) *Papers of the Fourth Conference of Italian Archaeology: The Archaeology of Power Part 2*: 101–16. London, Accordia Research Centre.

Bartoloni, G., and Grottanelli, C. (1989) I carri a due ruote nelle tombe femminili del Lazio e dell'Etruria. In A. Rallo (ed.) *Le donne in Etruria*: 55–73. Rome, 'L'Erma' di Bretschneider.

Becatti, G., and Magi, F. (1955) *Monumenti della pittura antica scoperti in Italia. Sezione prima: la pittura etrusca. Tarquinii fasc. III–IV: Le pitture delle tombe degli Auguri e del Pulcinella.* Rome, Libreria dello Stato.

Bender, B. (1978) Gatherer-hunter to farmer: a social perspective. *World Archaeology* 10: 204–22.

Berti, F., Baldacci, E., and Alderighi, L. (1985) *L'abitato etrusco di Montereggi. Scavi 1982–1985.* Capraia, Quaderni del Museo della Ceramica e del Territorio di Montelupo No. 2.

Bianchi Bandinelli, R. (1925) Clusium. Ricerche archeologiche e topografiche su Chiusi e il suo territorio in età etrusca. *Monumenti Antichi* 30: 210–551.

Biancofiore, E., and Toti, O. (1973) Monte Rovello. Testimonianze dei Micenei nel Lazio. *Incunabula Graeca* 53: 7–78.

Bietti Sestieri, A.M. (1973) The metal industry of continental Italy, 13th to the 11th century BC, and its connection with the Aegean. *Proceedings of the Prehistoric Society* 39: 383–424.

Bietti Sestieri, A.M. (1976) Contributo allo studio delle forme di scambio della tarda età del bronzo nell'Italia continentale. *Dialoghi di Archeologia* 9–10 (1–2): 201–41.

Bietti Sestieri, A.M. (ed.) (1979) *Ricerca su una comunità del Lazio protostorico.* Rome, De Luca.

Bietti Sestieri, A.M. (ed.) (1984a) *Preistoria e protostoria nel territorio di Roma.* Rome, De Luca.

Bietti Sestieri, A.M. (1984b) Central and southern Italy in the Late Bronze Age. In T. Hackens, N.D. Holloway and R.R. Holloway (eds.) *Crossroads of the Mediterranean*: 55–122. Louvain, Université Catholique de Louvain/Providence (Rhode Island), Brown University, Center for Old World Archaeology and Art.

Bietti Sestieri, A.M. (1992a) *La necropoli laziale di Osteria dell'Osa.* Rome, Quasar.

Bietti Sestieri, A.M. (1992b) *The Iron Age Community of Osteria dell'Osa.* Cambridge, Cambridge University Press.

Bietti Sestieri, A.M., and de Santis, A. (1985) Indicatori archeologici di cambiamento nella struttura delle communità laziali nell' 8 sec. a.C. *Dialoghi di Archeologia* 1: 35–45.

Bietti Sestieri, A.M., Belardelli, C., Capoferri, B., Moscetta, M.P., and Saltini, A.C. (1991–2) La media età del bronzo nel territorio di Roma. *Rassegna di Archeologia* 10: 439–54.

Bintliff, J.L. (1982) Settlement patterns, land tenure and social structure: a diachronic model. In C. Renfrew and S.J. Shennan (eds.) *Ranking, Resource and Exchange*: 106–11. Cambridge, Cambridge University Press.

Bintliff, J.L., and Snodgrass, A.M. (1988) Off-site pottery distributions: a regional and inter-regional perspective. *Current Anthropology* 29: 506–13.

Black, J., and Green, A. (1992) *Gods, Demons and Symbols of Ancient Mesopotamia*. London, British Museum Publications.

Blakeway, A. (1935). Demaratus: a study in some aspects of the earliest Hellenisation of Latium and Etruria. *Journal of Roman Studies* 25: 129–49.

Blanck, H. (1987) La Tomba dei Rilievi di Cerveteri. In G. Barbieri (ed.) *L'alimentazione nel mondo antico: gli etruschi*: 114–15. Rome, Istituto Poligrafico e Zecca dello Stato.

Blanck, H., and Proietti, G. (1986) *La Tomba dei Rilievi di Cerveteri*. Rome, De Luca.

Bloch, R. (1958) *The Etruscans*. London, Thames and Hudson.

Bloch, R. (1972) *Recherches archéologiques en territoire volsinien de la protohistoire à la civilisation étrusque*. Paris, Boccard.

Boardman, J. (1976) The olive in the Mediterranean: its culture and use. *Philosophical Transactions of the Royal Society of London* Ser. B, 275: 187–96.

Boardman, J. (1980) *The Greeks Overseas: Their Early Colonies and Trade*. London, Thames and Hudson, 3rd edition.

Boardman, J. (1989) *Athenian Red Figure Vases: The Classical Period*. London, Thames and Hudson.

Boardman, J. (1990) Symposion furniture. In O. Murray (ed.) *Sympotica*: 122–31. Oxford, Oxford University Press.

Bocci Pacini, P. (1981) Roselle. In M. Cristofani (ed.) *Gli etruschi in Maremma*: 115–29. Milan, Electa.

Boëthius, A. (1978) *Etruscan and Early Roman Architecture*. Harmondsworth, Penguin.

Boitani, F. (1982) Veio: nuovi ritrovamenti nella necropoli di Monte Michele. In G.B. Caporali and A.M. Sgubini Moretti (eds.) *Archeologia nella Tuscia*: 95–103. Rome, Consiglio Nazionale delle Ricerche.

Boitani, F. (1983) Veio: la tomba 'principesca' della necropoli di Monte Michele. *Studi Etruschi* 51: 535–56.

Boitani, F., Cataldi, M., and Pasquinucci, M. (1975) *Etruscan Cities*. London, Cassell.

Boitani, F., Deriu, A., and Ridgway, D. (1985a) Provenance and firing techniques of geometric pottery from Veii: a Mossbauer investigation. *Annual of the British School at Athens* 80: 139–50.

Boitani, F., Cristofani, M., Moscati, P., and Nardi, G. (1985b) *Strade degli etrusche: vie e mezzi di comunicazione nell'antica Etruria*. Rome, Autostrade S.p.A.

Bonatti, E. (1961) I sedimenti del Lago di Monterosi. *Experientia* 17 (252): 1–4.

Bonatti, E. (1963) Stratigrafia pollinica dei sedimenti postglaciali di Baccano, lago craterico del Lazio. *Atti della Società Toscana di Scienze Naturali* Ser. A, 70: 40–8.

Bonatti, E. (1966) North Mediterranean climate during the late Würm glaciation. *Nature* 209: 984–5.

Bonatti, E. (1970) Pollen sequence in the lake sediments. In G.E. Hutchinson (ed.) Ianula: an account of the history and development of the Lago di Monterosi, Latium: 26–31. *Transactions of the American Philosophical Society* 60: 5–175.

Bonfante, G., and Bonfante, L. (1983) *The Etruscan Language. An Introduction*. Manchester, Manchester University Press.

Bonfante, L. (1973) The women of Etruria. *Arethusa* 6: 91–101.

Bonfante, L. (1975) *Etruscan Dress*. Baltimore, John Hopkins University Press.

Bonfante, L. (1978) Historical art: Etruscan and early Roman. *American Journal of Ancient History* 3: 136–62.

Bonfante, L. (1981) *Out of Etruria: Etruscan Influence North and South*. Oxford, British Archaeological Reports, International Series 103.

Bonfante, L. (1984) Human sacrifice on an Etruscan urn in New York. *American Journal of Archaeology* 88: 531–9.

Bonfante, L. (ed.) (1986a) *Etruscan Life and Afterlife*. Detroit, Wayne State University Press.

Bonfante, L. (1986b) Daily life and afterlife. In L. Bonfante (ed.) *Etruscan Life and Afterlife*: 232–78. Detroit, Wayne State University Press.

Bonfante, L. (1990) *Reading the Past: Etruscan*. London, British Museum.

Bonghi Jovino, M. (ed.) (1986a) *Gli etruschi di Tarquinia*. Modena, Edizioni Panini.

Bonghi Jovino, M. (1986b) Gli scavi della Università degli Studi di Milano (campagne 1982–1985) sul Pian di Civita. L'orizzonte protovillanoviano. In M. Bonghi Jovino (ed.) *Gli Etruschi di Tarquinia*: 83–6. Modena, Panini.

Bonghi Jovino, M. (ed.) (1993) *Produzione artigianale ed esportazione nel mondo antico. Il bucchero etrusco*. Milan, Edizioni ET.

Bonghi Jovino, M., Mallegni, F., and Usai, L. (forthcoming) Una morte violenta: appunti e considerazioni biologiche relative ad una sepoltura villanoviana nel 'complesso' della Civita di Tarquinia. *Atti del XIX Convegno di Studi Etruschi e Italici, Volterra*.

Bonomi Ponzi, L. (1985) Topographic survey of the Colfiorito di Foligno plateau: a contribution towards the study of the population in the territory of the Plestini. In C. Malone and S. Stoddart (eds.) *Papers in Italian Archaeology IV. Vol. 1: The Human Landscape*: 201–38. Oxford, British Archaeological Reports, International Series 245.

Borsi, F. (1985) La fortuna del toscanico nel rinascimento europeo. In F. Borsi (ed.) *Fortuna degli etruschi*: 44–52. Milan, Electa.

Bottema, S. (1974) Implications of a pollen diagram from the Adriatic sea. *Geologie en Mijnbouw* 53 (6): 401–5.

Bouloumié, B. (1982) *L'Épave étrusque d'Antibes et le commerce en Méditerranée occidentale au VI siècle av. J-C.* Mainz, Kleine Schriften Marburg 10.

Bouloumié Marique, A. (1978) La céramique comune de Murlo (Poggio Civitate). *Mélanges de l'École Française de Rome. Antiquité* 90: 51–112.

Bound, M. (1985) Una nave mercantile di età arcaica all'Isola del Giglio. In *Il commercio etrusco arcaico*: 65–70. Rome, Consiglio Nazionale delle Ricerche (Quaderni del Centro di Studio per l'Archeologia Etrusco-Italica).

Bound, M. (1990) In search of an Etruscan wreck. *Minerva* 1.1: 3–6.

Braudel, F. (1972) *The Mediterranean and the Mediterranean World in the Age of Philip II.* London, Fontana.

Brendel, O. (1995) *Etruscan Art.* New Haven and London, Yale University Press, 2nd edition.

Briguet, M.-F. (1986) Art. In L. Bonfante (ed.) *Etruscan Life and Afterlife*: 92–173. Detroit, Wayne State University Press.

Bronson, R.C. (1965) Chariot racing in Etruria. In *Studi in onore di L. Banti*: 89–106. Rome, 'L'Erma' di Bretschneider.

Brown, A.G., and Ellis, C. (1995) People, climate and alluviation: theory, research design and new sedimentological and stratigraphic data from Etruria, Italy. *Papers of the British School at Rome* 63: 45–73.

Brown, F.E. (1980) *Cosa. The Making of a Roman Town.* Ann Arbor, University of Michigan Press.

Brown, W.L. (1960) *The Etruscan Lion.* Oxford, Oxford University Press.

Bruckner, H. (1986) Man's impact on the evolution of the physical environment in the Mediterranean region in historical times. *GeoJournal* 13: 7–17.

Bruun, P. (1975) Conclusion: the Roman census and Romanization under Augustus. In P. Bruun, P. Hohti, J. Kaimio, E. Michelsen, M. Nielsen, and E. Ruoff-Väänänen, *Studies in the Romanization of Etruria*: 435–505. Rome, Acta Instituti Romani Finlandiae 5.

Buchner, G. (1979) Early Orientalizing: aspects of the Euboean connection. In D. Ridgway and F. Ridgway (eds.) *Italy Before the Romans*: 129–44. London, Academic Press.

Buranelli, F. (ed.) (1987) *La Tomba François di Vulci.* Rome, Quasar.

Burnett, A., Craddock, P.T., and Meeks, N. (1986) Italian currency bars. In J. Swaddling (ed.) *Italian Iron Age Artefacts in the British Museum*: 127–30. London, British Museum Publications.

Butzer, K.W. (1982) *Archaeology as Human Ecology*. Cambridge, Cambridge University Press.

Caloi, L., and Palombo, M.R. (1981) Analisi dei resti ossei. In N. Negroni Catacchio (ed.) *Sorgenti della Nova: una comunità protostorica e il suo territorio nell'Etruria meridionale*: 269–77. Rome, Consiglio Nazionale delle Ricerche.

Caloi, L., Palombo, M.R., and Romei, C. (1988) La fauna e l'allevamento. In G. Colonna, C. Bettini and R.A. Staccioli (eds.) *Etruria meridionale. Conoscenza, conservazione, fruizione*: 51–7. Rome, Quasar.

Calvi Rezia, G. (1972) I resti dell'insediamento neolitico di Pienza. *Atti della XIV Riunione Scientifica dell'Istituto Italiano di Preistoria e Protostoria in Puglia*: 285–99. Florence, IIPP.

Calvi Rezia, G. (1973) I resti dell'insediamento neolitico di Pienza. *Atti della XV Riunione Scientifica dell'Istituto Italiano di Preistoria e Protostoria Verona-Trento*: 169–79. Florence, IIPP.

Cambi, L. (1958–9) I metalli dei cimeli della grotta tombale di Monte Bradoni (Volterra). *Bullettino di Paletnologia Italiana* 67–8 (ns 12): 137–45.

Camporeale, G. (1984) *La caccia in Etruria*. Rome, G. Bretschneider.

Camporeale, G. (ed.) (1985) *L'Etruria mineraria*. Milan, Electa.

Camporeale, G. (1986) Vita privata. In G.P. Carratelli (ed.) *Rasenna. Storia e civiltà degli etruschi*: 241–308. Milan, Libri Scheiwiller (Credito Italiano).

Camporeale, G. (1992) La romanisation. In *Les Étrusques et l'Europe*: 102–9. Paris, Réunion des Musées Nationaux.

Canocchi, D. (1980) Roselle excavations. *Studi Etruschi* 48: 31–50.

Capasso, A. (1982) Dental pathology and alimentary habits: reconstruction of Etruscan populations. *Studi Etruschi* 50: 177–91.

Carancini, G.L. (1991–2) L'Italia centro-meridionale. *Rassegna di Archeologia* 10: 235–54.

Carancini, G.L., Massetti, S., and Posi, F. (1986) L'area tra Umbria meridionale e Sabina alla fine della protostoria. *Dialoghi di Archeologia* 3 (2): 37–56.

Carandini, A. (ed.) (1985) *La romanizzazione dell'Etruria: il territorio di Vulci*. Milan, Electa.

Cardarelli, A. (1992) Le età dei metalli nell'Italia settentrionale. In A. Guidi and M. Piperno (eds.) *Italia preistorica*: 366–419. Rome, Laterza.

Cardarelli, A., di Gennaro, F., Guidi, A., and Pacciarelli, M. (1980) Le ricerche di topografia protostorica nel Lazio. In R. Peroni (ed.) *Il bronzo finale in Italia*: 91–103. Bari, De Donato.

Cardini, L. (1980) La necropoli mesolitica della Caverna delle Arene Candide. *Memorie dell'Istituto Italiano di Paletnologia Umana* 3: 9–31.

Carnabuci, E., and Palombi, D. (1993) *Guida ai luoghi etruschi*. Novara, De Agostini.

Carpino, A. (1996) Greek mythology in Etruria: an iconographic analysis of three Etruscan relief mirrors. In J.F. Hall (ed.) *Etruscan Italy*: 65–91. Provo, Utah, Museum of Art, Brigham Young University.

Carratelli, G.P. (ed.) (1986) *Rasenna. Storia e civiltà degli etruschi*. Milan, Libri Scheiwiller (Credito Italiano).

Carta del utilizzazione del suolo d'Italia (1959) Milan, Touring Club Italiano and Consiglio Nazionale delle Ricerche (Centro Studi di Geografia Economica).

Carter, J.C. (1974) The Tomb of the Siren. *American Journal of Archaeology* 78: 131–9.

Cassano, M., and Manfredini, A. (1978) Torrionaccio (Viterbo). Scavo di un abitato protostorico. *Notizie degli Scavi* 32: 1–382.

Castelletti, L. (1974–5) Rapporto preliminare sui resti vegetali macroscopici della serie neolitico-bronzo di Pienza (Siena). *Rivista Archeologica dell'Antica Provincia e Diocesi di Como* 156–7: 243–51.

Cataldi Dini, M. (1987) La Tomba dei Demoni Azzurri. In M. Bonghi Jovino and C. C. Treré (eds.) *Tarquinia: ricerche, scavi e prospettive*: 37–42. Milan, Edizioni ET.

Cataldi Dini, M. (1989) La Tomba dei Demoni Azzurri. In M.A. Rizzo (ed.) *Pittura etrusca al Museo di Villa Giulia*: 151–3. Rome, Studi di Archeologia pubblicati dalla Soprintendenza Archeologica per l'Etruria Meridionale 6.

Catalli, F. (1990) *Monete etrusche*. Rome, Libreria dello Stato.

Cattani, M. (1987) Aes rude. In R. de Marinis (ed.) *Gli etruschi a nord del Po*: 204–10. Mantua, Regione Lombardia.

Cavagnaro Vanoni, L. (1989) Intervento alla Civita di Tarquinia della Fondazione Lerici. *Atti del Secondo Congresso Internazionale Etrusco*: 341–5. Rome, G. Bretschneider.

Cavinato, G. (1964) *Giacimenti minerali*. Rome.

Cerchiai, L. (1987) Sulle tombe 'del Tuffatore' e 'della Caccia e Pesca': proposta di lettura iconologica. *Dialoghi di Archeologia* Ser. 3, 5.2: 113–23.

Champion, T., Gamble, C., Shennan, S., and Whittle, A. (1984) *Prehistoric Europe*. London, Academic Press.

Chapman, R., Kinnes, I., and Randsborg, K. (eds.) (1981) *The Archaeology of Death*. Cambridge, Cambridge University Press.

Cherkauer, D. (1976) The stratigraphy and chronology of the River Treia alluvial deposits. In T.W. Potter (ed.) *A Faliscan Town in South Etruria: Excavations at Narce 1966–71*: 106–20. London, British School at Rome.

Chiarugi, A. (1939) La vegetazione dell'Appennino nei suoi aspetti d'ambiente e di storia del popolamento umano. *Società Italiana per il Progresso delle Scienze* 27: 9–45.

Chisholm, M. (1968) *Rural Settlement and Land Use*. London, Hutchinson University Library.

Ciampoltrini, G., Rendini, P., and Wilkens, B. (1989–90) L'alimentazione nell'abitato etrusco di Montecatino in Val Freddana (Lucca). *Studi Etruschi* 56: 271–84.

CIE – *Corpus Inscriptionum Etruscarum*. (1970) Florence, Consiglio Nazionale delle Ricerche.

Cifani, G. (1994) Aspetti dell'edilizia romana arcaica. *Studi Etruschi* 60: 185–226.

Cinelli, F. (1993) Shedding light on Etruscan origins: mitochondrial DNA studies launched. *Amici di Spannocchia Newsletter* 13: 5.

Cipolloni, M. (1971) Insediamento protovillanoviano sulla Vetta di Monte Cetona. *Origini* 5: 149–91.

Clark, G. (1994) A group of animal bones from Cerveteri. *Studi Etruschi* 59: 253–69.

Clark, M. (1984) *Modern Italy 1871–1982*. London, Longman.

Clementi, A. (1984) La transumanza nell'alto medioevo. *Bullettino della Deputazione Abruzzese di Storia Patria* 74: 31–47.

Close-Brooks, J. (1965) Quattro Fontanili: proposta per una suddivisione in fase. *Notizie degli Scavi*: 53–64.

Cocchi Genick, D., and Grifoni Cremonesi, R. (1985) *L'età dei metalli nella Toscana nord-occidentale*. Pisa, Pacini.

Coldstream, N. (1993) Mixed marriages on the frontiers of the Greek world. *Oxford Journal of Archaeology* 12: 89–107.

Coles, G.M., Gilbertson, D.D., and Hunt, C.O. (1984) Soil erosion and soil genesis in the Tuscan landscape: 1. Morphological sequences of carbonate induration in slope deposits. *Archeologia Medievale* 11: 289–95.

Colonna, G. (1967) L'Etruria meridionale interna dal villanoviano alle tombe rupestri. *Studi Etruschi* 35: 3–30.

Colonna, G. (1970) Una nuova iscrizione etrusca del VII secolo e appunti sull'epigrafia ceretana dell'epoca. *Mélanges d'Archéologie et d'Histoire de l'École Française de Rome* 82: 637–72.

Colonna, G. (1973–4) Nomi etruschi di vasi. *Archeologia Classica* 25–6: 132–50.

Colonna, G. (1974) La cultura dell'Etruria meridionale interna con particolare riguardo alle necropoli rupestri. *Atti dell' VIII Convegno Nazionale di Studi Etruschi e Italici, Orvieto 1972*: 253–67. Florence, Olschki.

Colonna, G. (1975) Firme arcaiche di artefici nell'Italia centrale. *Römische Mitteilungen* 82: 181–92.

Colonna, G. (1976) Il sistema alfabetico. *Atti del Colloquio sul Tema l'Etrusco Arcaico*: 7–24. Florence, Istituto di Studi Etruschi ed Italici.

Colonna, G. (1978) Archeologia dell'età romantica in Etruria: i Campanari di Toscanella e la tomba dei Vipinana. *Studi Etruschi* 46: 81–117.

Colonna, G. (1980) Virgilio, Cortona, e la leggenda etrusca di Dardano. *Archeologia Classica* 32: 1–15.

Colonna, G. (1981) Tarquinio Prisco e il tempio di Giove Capitolino. *La Parola del Passato* 36: 41–59.

Colonna, G. (ed.) (1985) *Santuari d'Etruria*. Milan, Electa.

Colonna, G. (1986) Urbanistica e architettura. In G.P. Carratelli (ed.) *Rasenna. Storia e civiltà degli etruschi*: 369–530. Milan, Credito Italiano.

Colonna, G. (1987a) Pyrgi. In G. Barbieri (ed.) *L'alimentazione nel mondo antico: gli etruschi*: 77–81. Rome, Istituto Poligrafico e Zecca dello Stato.

Colonna, G. (1987b) Il maestro dell'Ercole e della Minerva. Nuova luce sull'attività dell'officina veiente. *Opuscula Romana* 16: 7–41.

Colonna, G. (1990) Città e territorio nell'Etruria meridionale del V secolo. In *Crise e transformation des societés archaiques de l'Italie au Ve siècle av. J-C.*: 7–21. Rome, Collection de l'École Française de Rome 137.

Colonna, G., and von Hase, F.W. (1984) Alle origini della statuaria etrusca: la Tomba delle Statue presso Ceri. *Studi Etruschi* 52: 13–59.

Colonna di Paolo, E. (1981) *Necropoli rupestri del Viterbese*. Novara, De Agostini.

Colonna di Paolo, E., and Colonna, G. (1970) *Castel d'Asso*. Rome, Consiglio Nazionale delle Ricerche.

Colonna di Paolo, E., and Colonna, G. (1978) *Norchia I*. Rome, Consiglio Nazionale delle Ricerche.

Comella, A. (1986) *I materiali votivi di Falerii*. Rome, G. Bretschneider.

Commercio (1985) *Il commercio etrusco arcaico*. Rome, Consiglio Nazionale delle Ricerche (Quaderni del Centro di Studio per l'Archeologia Etrusco-Italica).

Cornell, T.J. (1978) *Principes* of Tarquinia (M. Torelli, *Elogia tarquiniensia*). *Journal of Roman Studies* 68: 167–73.

Cornell, T.J. (1989) Rome and Latium to 390 BC. *Cambridge Ancient History* vol. 7.2: 243–308. Cambridge, Cambridge University Press, 2nd edition.

Cornell, T.J. (1991) The tyranny of the evidence: a discussion of possible uses of literacy in Etruria and Latium in the archaic age. In M. Beard, A.K. Bowman, M. Corbier, T. Cornell, J.L. Franklin Jr., A. Hanson, K. Hopkins and N. Horsfall, *Literacy in the Roman World*: 7–33. Ann Arbor, Journal of Roman Archaeology Supplementary Series 3.

Cornell, T.J. (1995) *The Beginnings of Rome. Italy and Rome from the Bronze Age to the Punic Wars (c.1000–264 BC)*. London, Routledge.

Corrain, C., and Capitanio, M. (1975) I resti umani della necropoli eneolitica di S. Antonio. In R.R. Holloway (ed.) *Buccino: The Eneolithic Necropolis of S. Antonio*: 40–108. Rome, De Luca.

Corruccini, R., and Pacciani, E. (1991) Ortodonzia e occlusione dentale negli Etruschi. *Studi Etruschi* 57: 189–94.

Costantini, L., and Costantini Biasini, L. (1987) Bolsena – Gran Carro: i resti vegetali. In G. Barbieri (ed.) *L'alimentazione nel mondo antico: gli etruschi*: 61–7. Rome, Istituto Poligrafico e Zecca dello Stato.

Costantini, L., and Giorgi, J.A. (1987) I resti vegetali (di Blera). In G. Barbieri (ed.) *L'alimentazione nel mondo antico: gli etruschi*: 83–6. Rome, Istituto Poligrafico e Zecca dello Stato.

Craddock, P. (1984) The metallurgy and composition of Etruscan bronze. *Studi Etruschi* 52: 211–71.

Craddock, P.T. (1976) The composition of the copper alloys used by the Greek, Etruscan and Roman civilisations I. *Journal of Archaeological Science* 3: 93–113.

Craddock, P.T. (1977) The composition of the copper alloys used by the Greek, Etruscan and Roman civilisations II. *Journal of Archaeological Science* 4: 103–23.

Craddock, P.T. (1978) The composition of the copper alloys used by the Greek, Etruscan and Roman civilisations III. *Journal of Archaeological Science* 5: 1–16.

Craddock, P.T. (ed.) (1980) *Aspects of Early Mining and Etruscan Metallurgy*. London, British Museum Occasional Paper 20.

Craddock, P.T. (1986) The metallurgy of Italic and Sardinian bronzes. In J. Swaddling (ed.) *Italian Iron Age Artefacts in the British Museum*: 143–50. London, British Museum Publications.

Craddock, P.T., and Hockey, M.I. (1986) Appendix: technical examination and analysis, in E.F. Macnamara. The construction of some Etruscan incense-burners and candelabra. In J. Swaddling (ed.) *Italian Iron Age Artefacts in the British Museum*: 81–98 (88–90). London, British Museum Publications.

Cremonesi, G. (1978) L'eneolitico e l'età del bronzo in basilicata. *Atti della XX Riunione Scientifica dell'Istituto Italiano per la Preistoria e Protostoria*: 63–86. Florence, Parenti.

Cristofani, M. (1967) Ricerche sulle pitture della Tomba François di Vulci: i fregi decorativi. *Dialoghi di Archeologia* 1: 186–219.

Cristofani, M. (1974) Diffusione dell'alfabeto e onomastica arcaica nell'Etruria interna settentrionale. *Atti dell' VIII Convegno Nazionale di Studi Etruschi e Italici, Orvieto 1972*: 307–24. Florence, Olschki.

Cristofani, M. (1975a) Il 'dono' nell'Etruria arcaica. *La Parola del Passato* 30: 132–52.

Cristofani, M. (1975b) *Statue-cinerario chiusine di età classica*. Rome, G. Bretschneider.

Cristofani, M. (1976a) Storia dell'arte e acculturazione: le pitture tombali arcaiche di Tarquinia. *Prospettiva* 7: 2–9.

Cristofani, M. (1976b) Il sistema onomastico. *Atti del Colloquio sul Tema l'Etrusco Arcaico*: 92–109. Florence, Istituto di Studi Etruschi ed Italici.

Cristofani, M. (1976c) *Città e campagne nell'Etruria settentrionale*. Florence, Banca Populare dell'Etruria.

Cristofani, M. (1978) *L'arte degli etruschi*. Turin, Einaudi.

Cristofani, M. (1979a) *The Etruscans. A New Investigation*. London, Orbis.

Cristofani, M. (1979b) Recent advances in Etruscan epigraphy and language. In D. Ridgway and F. Ridgway (eds.) *Italy Before the Romans*: 373–412. London, Academic Press.

Cristofani, M. (1981) *Gli etruschi in Maremma*. Milan, Electa.

Cristofani, M. (1983a) *Gli etruschi del mare*. Milan, Longanesi.

Cristofani, M. (1983b) I greci in Etruria. In *Forme di contatto e processi di trasformazione nelle società antiche*: 235–54. Rome, École Française de Rome.

Cristofani, M. (ed.) (1985a) *La civiltà degli etruschi*. Milan, Electa.

Cristofani, M. (1985b) *Bronzi etruschi: la plastica votiva*. Novara, De Agostini.

Cristofani, M. (ed.) (1985c) *Dizionario della civiltà etrusca*. Florence, Giunti Martello.

Cristofani, M. (1985d) Le attività produttive. In M. Cristofani (ed.) *La civiltà degli etruschi*: 137–74. Milan, Electa.

Cristofani, M. (1986) Economia e società. In G.P. Carratelli (ed.) *Rasenna. Storia e civiltà degli etruschi*: 80–156. Milan, Libri Scheiwiller (Credito Italiano).

Cristofani, M. (1987a) Il banchetto in Etruria. In G. Barbieri (ed.) *L'alimentazione nel mondo antico: gli etruschi*: 123–32. Rome, Istituto Poligrafico e Zecca dello Stato.

Cristofani, M. (1987b) Ancora sul cosidetto specchio di Tarchon. *Prospettiva* 51: 46–8.

Cristofani, M. (1988) Processi di trasformazione socio-economica nell'Etruria Padana fra VI e V secolo a.C. In G.A. Mansuelli (ed.) *La formazione della città preromana in Emilia Romagna*: 45–59. Bologna, Istituto per la Storia di Bologna.

Cristofani, M. (ed.) (1989–90) Rivista di epigrafia etrusca. *Studi Etruschi* 56: 289–368.

Cristofani, M. (ed.) (1990) *La grande Roma dei Tarquini*. Rome, 'L'Erma' di Bretschneider.

Cristofani, M. (1991a) *Introduzione allo studio dell'etrusco*. Florence, Olschki, 2nd edition.

Cristofani, M. (1991b) Gli etruschi e i fenici nel mediterraneo. *Atti del II Congresso Internazionale di Studi Fenici e Punici*: 67–75. Rome, Consiglio Nazionale delle Ricerche.

Cristofani, M. (ed.) (1992/3) *Caere 3. 1–2. Lo scarico arcaico della vigna parrocchiale*. Rome, Consiglio Nazionale delle Ricerche.

Cristofani, M. (1995) Novità sul commercio etrusco arcaico. Dal relitto del Giglio al contratto di Pech Maho. In J. Swaddling, S. Walker and P. Roberts (eds.) *Italy in Europe. Economic Relations 700 BC–AD 50*: 131–7. London, British Museum.

Cristofani, M., and Martelli, M. (1979) Ricerche archaeologiche nella zona 'industriale' di Populonia. *Prospettiva* 16: 74–6.

Cristofani, M., and Martelli, M. (1983) *L'oro degli etruschi*. Novara, De Agostini.

Cristofani, M., and Nardi, G. (1988) *Caere I*. Rome, Consiglio Nazionale delle Ricerche.

Croon, J.H. (1955) The mask of the underworld daemon. *Journal of Hellenic Studies* 75: 9–16.

Cruise, G.M. (1991) Environmental change and human impact in the upper mountain zone of the Ligurian Apennines: the last 5000 years. In R. Maggi, R. Nisbet and G. Barker (eds.) *Archaeologia della pastorizia nell'Europe meridionale* II: 169–94. Bordighera, Istituto Internazionale di Studi Liguri.

Cucini, C. (1985) Topografia del territorio delle valli del Pecora e dell'Alma. In R. Francovich (ed.) *Scarlino I. Storia e territorio*: 147–335. Florence, Insegna del Giglio.

d'Achiardi, A. (1872) *Mineralogia della Toscana*. Pisa, Nistri (2 vols.).

d'Agostino, B. (1983) L'immagine, la pittura e la tomba nell'Etruria arcaica. *Prospettiva* 32: 2–11.

d'Agostino, B. (1989) Image and society in archaic Etruria. *Journal of Roman Studies* 89: 1–10.

d'Agostino, B. (1990) Military organisation and social structure in archaic Etruria. In O. Murray and S. Price (eds.) *The Greek City from Homer to Alexander*: 59–82. Oxford, Clarendon Press.

Dareggi, G. (1972) *Urne del territorio perugino*. Perugia, Quaderni dell'Istituto di Archeologia dell'Università di Perugia 1.

Davidson, D.A. (1980) Erosion in Greece during the first and second millennia BC. In R.A. Cullingford, D.A. Davidson and J. Lewin (eds.) *Timescales in Geomorphology*: 143–58. New York, John Wiley.

de Beer, G. (1955) *The Origin of the Etruscans*. Text of BBC Third Programme talk, 25 October 1955.

de Casanove, O., and Jolivet, V. (1983) Musarna. *Studi Etruschi* 51: 398–401.

de Grossi Mazzorin, J. (1985a) I resti faunistici dell'insediamento protostorico di Pitigliano-Mulino Rossi (GR). In E. Pellegrini (ed.) *L'insediamento protostorico di Pitigliano – campagne di scavo 1982–83*: 77–92. Pitigliano.

de Grossi Mazzorin, J. (1985b) Reperti faunistici dall'acropoli di Populonia: testimonianze di allevamento e caccia nel III secolo a.C. *Rassegna di Archeologia* 5: 131–71.

de Grossi Mazzorin, J. (1987) Populonia: reperti faunistici dall'acropoli. In G. Barbieri (ed.) *L'alimentazione nel mondo antico: gli etruschi*: 89–93. Rome, Istituto Poligrafico e Zecca dello Stato.

de Grossi Mazzorin, J. (1995) Economie di allevamento in Italia centrale dalla media età del bronzo alla fine dell'età del ferro. In N. Christie (ed.)

Settlement and Economy in Italy 1500 BC to AD 1500. Papers of the Fifth Conference of Italian Archaeology: 167–77. Oxford, Oxbow.

de Grummond, N. (ed.) (1982) *A Guide to Etruscan Mirrors*. Tallahassee, Archaeological News Inc.

de la Genière, J. (1979) The Iron Age in southern Italy. In D. Ridgway and F. Ridgway (eds.) *Italy Before the Romans*: 59–93. London, Academic Press.

Delpino, F. (1977) Aspetti e problemi della prima età del ferro nell'Etruria settentrionale marittima. *L'Etruria mineraria*: 265–98. Florence, Olschki.

Delpino, F. (1982) Saggi di scavo sul Monte Bisenzo. *Archeologia nella Tuscia* 1: 153–63.

Delpino, F. (1984) Sulla presenza di oggetti 'enotri' in Etruria: la tomba Poggio Impiccato 6 di Tarquinia. In *Studi in onore di G. Maetske*: 257–71. Rome, G. Bretschneider.

Delpino, F. (1986) Rapporti e scambi nell'Etruria meridionale villanoviana con particolare riferimento al mezzogiorno. *Archeologia nella Tuscia* 2: 167–76.

Delpino, F. (1987) Etruria e Lazio prima dei Tarquini. Le fasi protostoriche. In M. Cristofani (ed.) *Etruria e Lazio arcaico*: 9–36. Rome, Consiglio Nazionale delle Ricerche.

de Maria, S. (1991) Bologna and the Reno valley. In G. Barker and J.A. Lloyd (eds.) *Roman Landscapes: Archaeological Survey in the Mediterranean Region*: 96–105. London, British School at Rome, Archaeological Monographs 2.

de Marinis, S. (ed.) (1988) *Gli etruschi a nord del Po*. Udine, Campanotto Editore.

Dennis, G. (1878) *Cities and Cemeteries of Etruria*. London, John Murray, 2nd edition.

Dennis, G. (1883) *The Cities and Cemeteries of Etruria*. London, John Murray, 3rd edition.

de Rosa, P.A., and Trastulli, P.E. (1988) *I pittori Coleman*. Rome, Studio Ottocento.

de Ruyt, F. (1934) *Charun: démon étrusque de la mort*. Rome, Institut Historique Belge.

Descoeudres, J.P., and Kearsley, R. (1983) Greek pottery at Veii: another look. *Annual of the British School at Athens* 78: 9–53.

de Simone, C. (1994) I tirreni a Lemnos: l'alfabeto. *Studi Etruschi* 60: 145–63.

di Gennaro, F. (1982) Organizzazione del territorio nell'Etruria meridionale protostorica: applicazione di un modello grafico. *Dialoghi di Archeologia* 2: 102–12.

di Gennaro, F. (1986) *Forme di insediamento tra Tevere e Fiora dal bronzo finale al principio dell'età del ferro*. Florence, Olschki.

di Gennaro, F. (1988) Il popolamento dell'Etruria meridionale e le caratteristiche degli insediamenti tra l'età del bronzo e l'età del ferro. In

G. Colonna, C. Bettini and R.A. Staccioli (eds.) *Etruria meridionale. Conoscenza, conservazione, fruizione*: 59–82. Rome, Quasar.

di Gennaro, F. (1990) Aspetti delle ricerche sull'assetto territoriale dell'area mediotirrenica in età protostorico. In F.M. Andraschko and W.-R. Teegen (eds.) *Gedenkschrift für Jürgen Driehaus*: 203–24. Mainz am Rhein, Philipp von Zabern.

di Gennaro, F. (1991–2) Insediamento e territorio. *Rassegna di Archeologia* 10: 197–205.

di Gennaro, F., and Pennacchioni, M. (1988) Aspetti insediativi dell'età del rame nel Lazio settentrionale. *Rassegna di Archeologia* 7: 583–4.

Diringer, D. (1947) *The Alphabet*. London, Hutchinson.

Donahue, R.E. (1988) Microwear analysis and site function of Paglicci Cave level 4a. *World Archaeology* 19: 357–75.

Donahue, R.E., Burroni, D.B., Coles, G.M., Colten, R.H., and Hunt, C.O. (1993) Petriolo III South: implications for the transition to agriculture in Tuscany, Italy. *Current Anthropology* 33: 328–31.

Donati, L. (1994) *La Casa dell'Impluvium. Architettura etrusca a Roselle*. Rome, G. Bretschneider.

Duncan, G.C. (1958) Sutri (Sutrium). *Papers of the British School at Rome* 26: 63–134.

Edlund, I.E.M. (1987) *The Gods and the Place. Location and Function of Sanctuaries in the Countryside of Etruria and Magna Graecia 700–400* BC. Rome, Skrifter utgivna av Svenska Institutet i Rom 43.

Edlund-Berry, I.E.M. (1991) Power and religion: how social change affected the emergence and collapse of power structures in central Italy. In E. Herring, R. Whitehouse and J. Wilkins (eds.) *Papers of the Fourth Conference of Italian Archaeology: The Archaeology of Power* 2: 161–72. London, Accordia Research Centre.

Edlund-Berry, I.E.M. (1992) *The Seated and Standing Statue Akroteria from Poggio Civitate (Murlo)*. Rome, G. Bretschneider.

Eisner, W., Kamermans, H., and Wymstra, A.T. (1986) The Agro Pontino survey: results from a first pollen core. *Dialoghi di Archeologia* 2: 145–53.

Enei, F. (1995) Ricognizioni archeologiche nell'Ager Caeretanus 1990–1992. In N. Christie (ed.) *Settlement and Economy in Italy 1500* BC *to* AD *1500. Papers of the Fifth Conference of Italian Archaeology*: 63–79. Oxford, Oxbow.

Ernout, A. (1930) Les élements étrusques du vocabulaire latin. *Bulletin de la Societé de Linguistique de Paris* 30: 82–124.

Fedeli, F. (1983) *Populonia. Storia e territorio*. Florence, Insegna del Giglio.

Fedeli, F. (1984) Ricerche e materiali per la carta archeologica del comprensorio di Piombino: la protostoria. *Rassegna di Archeologia* 4: 301–18.

Fenelli, M. (1975) Contributo per lo studio del votivo anatomico: i votivi anatomici di Lavinio. *Archeologia Classica* 27: 206–52.

Ferrarini, A., and Marraccini, L. (1978) Pollini fossili in depositi lacustri della valle della Farma (Toscana meridionale). *Atti della Società Toscana di Scienze Naturale* Memorie Ser. B, 85: 29–34.

Fiumi, E. (1955) Volterra: scavi nell'area del teatro romano 1950–3. *Notizie degli Scavi*: 114–50.

Follieri, M. (1981) Significato dei resti vegetali macroscopici. In N. Negroni Catacchio (ed.) *Sorgenti della Nova: una comunità protostorica e il suo territorio nell'Etruria meridionale*: 261–8. Rome, Consiglio Nazionale delle Ricerche.

Follieri, M., Magri, M., and Sadori, L. (1988) 250,000-year pollen record from the Valle di Castiglione (Roma). *Pollen et Spores* 30 (3–4): 329–56.

Fornaciari, G., and Mallegni, F. (1987) Indagini paleonutrizionali su campioni di popolazioni a cultura etrusca. In G. Barbieri (ed.) *L'alimentazione nel mondo antico: gli etruschi*: 135–9. Rome, Istituto Poligrafico e Zecca dello Stato.

Forni, G. (1989) Questioni di storia agraria pre-romana: le quattro fasi dell'agricoltura etrusca. *Secondo Congresso Internazionale Etrusco III*: 1501–15. Rome, 'L'Erma' di Bretschneider.

Forte, M. (ed.) (1995) *Il dono delle eliadi: ambre e oreficerie dei principi etruschi di Verucchio*. Bologna, Soprintendenza Archaeologica dell'Emilia Romagna.

Frank, A.H.E. (1969) Pollen stratigraphy from the Lake of Vico (central Italy). *Palaeogeography, Palaeoclimatology and Palaeoecology* 6: 67–85.

Frankenstein, S., and Rowlands, M.J. (1978) The internal structure and regional context of early iron age society in southwestern Germany. *Institute of Archaeology Bulletin* 15: 73–112.

Frederiksen, M. (1979) The Etruscans in Campania. In D. Ridgway and F. Ridgway (eds.) *Italy Before the Romans*: 277–311. London, Academic Press.

Frederiksen, M. (1984) *Campania*. London, British School at Rome.

Frederiksen, M., and Ward-Perkins, J.B. (1957) The ancient road systems of the central and northern Ager Faliscus. *Papers of the British School at Rome* 25: 67–208.

Fugazzola Delpino, M.A. (1982) Rapporto preliminare sulle ricerche condotte dalla Soprintendenza Archeologica dell'Etruria Meridionale nei bacini lacustri dell'apparato vulcanico sabatino. *Bollettino d'Arte* Supplemento 4: 123–49.

Fugazzola Delpino, M.A. (1984) *La cultura villanoviana*. Rome, Edizioni dell'Ateneo.

Fugazzola Delpino, M.A. (1987) Il neolitico nel Lazio settentrionale. *Il neolitico d'Italia: Atti della XXVI Riunione Scientifica del'Istituto Italiano di Preistoria e Protostoria*: 253–71. Florence, IIPP.

Fugazzola Delpino, M.A., and Delpino, F. (1979) Il bronzo finale del Lazio settentrionale. *Il bronzo finale: Atti della XXI Riunione Scientifica dell'Istituto Italiano di Preistoria e Protostoria*: 275–316. Florence, IIPP.

Gabba, E. (1985) La transumanza nell'Italia romana. Evidenze e problemi. Qualche prospettiva per l'età altomedievale. *XXXI Settimana di Studio sull'Alto Medioevo, Spoleto 1985*: 373–400. Spoleto, Centro Italiano di Studi sull'Alto Medioevo.

Gabba, E. (1988) La pastorizia nell'età tardo-imperiale in Italia. In C.R. Whitaker (ed.) *Pastoral Economies in Classical Antiquity*: 196–209. Cambridge, Cambridge Philological Society, Supplementary Volume 14.

Gaggiotti, M., Manconi, D., Mercando, L., and Verzár M. (1993) *Umbria, Marche*. Rome-Bari, Laterza, 2nd edition.

Gamble, C.S. (1982) Interaction and alliance in palaeolithic society. *Man* 17: 92–107.

Gantz, T.N. (1971) Divine triads on an archaic Etruscan frieze plaque from Poggio Civitate (Murlo). *Studi Etruschi* 39: 3–24.

Gantz, T.N. (1974) The procession frieze from the Etruscan sanctuary at Poggio Civitate. *Römische Mitteilungen* 81: 1–14.

Garnsey, P. (1992) Yield of the land. In B. Wells (ed.) *Agriculture in Ancient Greece*: 147–53. Stockholm, Skrifter utgivna av Svenska Institutet i Athen 4, 42.

Gejvall, N.G. (1967) Esame del materiale osteologico, in C.E. Östenberg, Luni sul Mignone e problemi della preistoria d'Italia. *Acta Instituti Romani Regni Sueciae* 4, 25: 1–306 (263–76).

Gejvall, N.G. (1982) Animal remains from Zone A in Acquarossa. In M.B. Lundgren and L. Wendt (eds.) *Acquarossa III: Zone A*: 68–70. Stockholm, Skrifter utgivna av Svenska Institutet i Rom 4, 38 (3).

Gempeler, R.D. (1974) *Die etruskischen Kanopen*. Einsiedeln, Benziger A.G.

Gentili, M.D. (1994) *I sarcofagi etruschi in terracotta di età recente*. Rome, G. Bretschneider.

Giacobelli, M. (1991) *Antiche strade, Lazio: Via Clodia*. Rome, Libreria dello Stato.

Giardino, C. (1984) Insediamenti e sfruttamento minerario del territorio durante la media e tarda età del bronzo nel Lazio: ipotesi e considerazioni. *Nuova Bullettino Archeologico Sardo* 1: 123–41.

Giardino, C., Belardelli, C., and Malizia, A. (1991) Power and the individual in funerary ideology: the emergence of the aristocracy in the Villanovan period in the Bologna region. In E. Herring, R. Whitehouse and J. Wilkins (eds.) *Papers of the Fourth Conference of Italian Archaeology: The Archaeology of Power Part 2*: 9–19. London, Accordia Research Centre.

Gilbertson, D.D., Holyoak, D.H., Hunt, C.O., and Paget, F.N. (1983) Palaeoecology of Late Quaternary floodplain deposits in Tuscany: the Feccia Valley at Frosini. *Archeologia Medievale* 10: 340–50.

Gilbertson, D.D., Hunt, C.O., Donahue, R.E., Harkness, D.D., and Mills, C.M. (1992) Towards a palaeoecology of the medieval and post-medieval landscape of Tuscany. In M. Bernardi (ed.) *Archeologia del paesaggio*: 205–48. Florence, Insegna del Giglio.

Gill, D.W.J. (1994) Positivism, pots and long-distance trade. In I. Morris (ed.) *Classical Greece: Ancient Histories and Modern Ideologies*: 49–107. Cambridge, Cambridge University Press.

Gilman, A. (1981) The development of social stratification in bronze age Europe. *Current Anthropology* 22 (1): 1–8.

Gimbutas, M. (1965) *Bronze Age Cultures in Central and Eastern Europe*. The Hague, Mouton.

Giuffrida Ientile, M. (1983) *La pirateria tirrenica*. Rome, G. Bretschneider.

Giuliani, C.F., and Sommella, P. (1977) Lavinium: compendio dei documenti archeologici. *La Parola del Passato* 32: 356–72.

Gran Aymerich, J.M.J. (1979) Bucchero, impasto e les tumuli Banditaccia 1 e 2 à Cerveteri. *Latomus* 38: 579–636.

Grant, A. (1988) Animal resources. In G. Astill and A. Grant (eds.) *The Countryside of Medieval England*: 149–87. Oxford, Blackwell.

Grant, A. (1989) Animals in Roman Britain. In M. Todd (ed.) *Research on Roman Britain*: 135–46. London, Society for the Promotion of Roman Studies, Britannia Monograph Series 11.

Grant, A., Rasmussen, T., and Barker, G. (1993) Tuscania: excavation of an Etruscan rural building. *Studi Etruschi* 58: 566–70.

Grant, M. (1980) *The Etruscans*. London, Weidenfeld and Nicolson.

Gras, M. (1976) La piraterie tyrrhenienne en mer égée: mythe ou realité? In *Mélanges offerts à Jacques Heurgon: L'Italie préromaine et la Rome républicaine*: 342–70. Rome, École Française de Rome.

Gras, M. (1985) *Trafics tyrrheniens archaiques*. Rome, École Française de Rome.

Greene, K. (1986) *The Archaeology of the Roman Economy*. London, Batsford.

Grifon Cremonesi, R. (1987) Il neolitico della Toscana e dell'Umbria. *Il neolitico d'Italia: Atti della XXVI Riunione Scientifica del'Istituto Italiano di Preistoria e Protostoria*: 239–51. Florence, IIPP.

Grüger, E. (1977) Pollenanalytische Untersuchung zur würmzeitlichen Vegetationgeschichte von Kalabrien (Suditalien). *Flora* 166: 475–89.

Guaitoli, M. (1982) Notizie preliminari su recenti ricognizioni svolte in seminari dell'Istituto. *Quaderni dell'Istituto di Topografia Antica dell'Università di Roma* 9: 79–87.

Gualandi, L. (1990) Strade, viaggi, trasporti e servizi postali. In S. Settis (ed.) *La civiltà dei romani: la città, il territorio, l'impero*: 199–214. Milan, Electa.

Guerreschi, A. (1992) La fine del pleistocene e gli inizi dell'olocene. In A. Guidi and M. Piperno (eds.) *Italia preistorica*: 198–237. Rome, Laterza.

Guidi, A. (1985) An application of the rank size rule to protohistoric settlements in the middle Tyrrhenian area. In C. Malone and S. Stoddart (eds.) *Papers in Italian Archaeology IV. Vol. 3: Patterns in Protohistory*: 217–42. Oxford, British Archaeological Reports, International Series 245.

Guidi, A. (1992) Le età dei metalli nell'Italia centrale e in Sardegna. In A. Guidi and M. Piperno (eds.) *Italia preistorica*: 420–40. Rome, Laterza.

Halstead, P. (1987) Traditional and ancient rural economy in Mediterranean Europe: plus ça change? *Journal of Hellenic Studies* 107: 77–87.

Halstead, P. (1989) The economy has a normal surplus: economic stability and social change among early farming communities of Thessaly, Greece. In P. Halstead and J. O'Shea (eds.) *Bad Year Economics: Cultural Responses to Risk and Uncertainty*: 68–80. Cambridge, Cambridge University Press.

Halstead, P., and Jones, G. (1989) Agrarian ecology in the Greek islands: time stress, scale and risk. *Journal of Hellenic Studies* 109: 41–55.

Halstead, P., and O'Shea, J. (1982) A friend in need is a friend indeed: social storage and the rise of the Minoan palace. In C. Renfrew and S.J. Shennan (1982) *Ranking, Resource and Exchange*: 92–9. Cambridge, Cambridge University Press.

Hanell, K. (1962) The excavations of the Swedish Institute in Rome in San Giovenale and its environs. In A. Boëthius (ed.) *Etruscan Culture, Land and People*: 277–358. Malmö, Alhem Publishing House.

Hare, A.J.C. (1875) *Days near Rome*. London, Dalby Isbister and Co.

Harris, W.V. (1971) *Rome in Etruria and Umbria*. Oxford, Clarendon.

Haspels, E. (1970) *The Highlands of Phrygia*. Princeton, Princeton University Press.

Haynes, S. (1971) *Etruscan Sculpture*. London, British Museum Publications.

Haynes, S. (1985) *Etruscan Bronzes*. London, Sotheby's.

Helbaek, H. (1953) The plant remains. In E. Gjerstad (ed.) *Early Rome I*: 355–7. Lund, Skrifter utgivna av Svenska Institutet i Rom 4, 17 (1).

Helbaek, H. (1956) Vegetables in the funerary meals of pre-urban Rome. In E. Gjerstad (ed.) *Early Rome II*: 286. Lund, Skrifter utgivna av Svenska Institutet i Rom 4, 17 (2).

Helbaek, H. (1960) Carbonized plant remains from the Pozzo di Vesta, Rome. In E. Gjerstad (ed.) *Early Rome III*: 464. Lund, Skrifter utgivna av Svenska Institutet i Rom 4, 17 (3).

Hemelrijk, J. (1984) *Caeretan Hydriai*. Mainz, Philipp von Zabern.

Hemphill, P. (1975) The Cassia-Clodia survey. *Papers of the British School at Rome* 43: 118–72.

Hemphill, P. (ed.) (1985) *G. Dennis: Cities and Cemeteries of Etruria*. Princeton, Princeton University Press, abridged edition.

Hemphill, P. (1993) The Romans and the San Giovenale area. *Opuscula Romana* 19: 45–53.

Hencken, H. (1968a) *Tarquinia, Villanovans and Early Etruscans*. Cambridge, Peabody Museum, American School of Prehistoric Research, Bulletin No. 23.

Hencken, H. (1968b) *Tarquinia and Etruscan Origins.* London, Thames and Hudson.

Herbig, R. (1965) *Götter und Dämonen der Etrusker.* Mainz, Philipp von Zabern.

Heron, C., and Pollard, A.M. (1988) The analysis of natural resinous materials from Roman amphoras. In E.A. Slater and J.O. Tate (eds.) *Science and Archaeology, Glasgow 1987*: 429–47. Oxford, British Archaeological Reports, British Series 196.

Heurgon, J. (1961) *La Vie quotidienne chez les etrusques.* Paris, Librairie Hachette.

Heurgon, J. (1964) *Daily Life of the Etruscans.* London, Weidenfeld and Nicolson.

Heurgon, J. (1989) À propos de l'inscription tyrrhenienne de Lemnos. *Atti del Secondo Congresso Internazionale Etrusco*: 93–102. Rome, G. Bretschneider.

Hillson, S. (1979) Diet and dental disease. *World Archaeology* 11: 147–62.

Hjelmqvist, H. (1989) *A Cereal Find from Old Etruria.* Partille, Paul Åströms Forlag (Studies in Mediterranean Archaeology and Literature, Pocket-Book 86).

Hoffmann, H. (1988) Why did the Greeks need imagery? An anthropological approach to the study of Greek vase-painting. *Hephaistos* 9: 143–61.

Holloway, R.R. (1965) Conventions of Etruscan painting in the Tomb of Hunting and Fishing at Tarquinia. *American Journal of Archaeology* 69: 341–7.

Holloway, R.R. (ed.) (1975) Buccino: the early bronze age site of Tufariello. *Journal of Field Archaeology* 2: 11–81.

Holloway, R.R. (1986) The bulls in the Tomb of the Bulls at Tarquinia. *American Journal of Archaeology* 90: 447–52.

Holloway, R.R. (1994) *The Archaeology of Early Latium and Rome.* London, Routledge.

Holloway, R.R., and Holloway, N.D. (1993) Where did the Greeks learn to write? *Archaeological News* 18: 1–5.

Hood, S. (1963) *Pebbles from my Skull.* London, Hutchinson.

Hood, S. (1978) *The Arts in Prehistoric Greece.* Harmondsworth, Penguin.

Humphrey, J. (1986) *Roman Circuses: Arenas for Chariot Racing.* London, Batsford.

Hunt, C.O. (1988) Environmental studies, in G. Barker and T. Rasmussen, The archaeology of an Etruscan *polis*: a preliminary report on the Tuscania Project (1986 and 1987 seasons). *Papers of the British School at Rome* 56: 25–42 (34–7).

Hunt, C.O. (1995) The natural landscape and its evolution. In G. Barker, *A Mediterranean Valley: Landscape Archaeology and* Annales *History in the Biferno Valley, Italy*: 62–83. London, Leicester University Press.

Hunt, C.O., and Eisner, W.R. (1991) Palynology of the Mezzaluna core. In A. Voorrips, S.H. Loving, and H. Kamermans (eds.) *The Agro Pontino Survey Project*: 49–59. Amsterdam, Studies in Prae- en Protohistorie 6.

Hunt, C.O., Malone, C., Sevink, J., and Stoddart, S. (1990) Environment, soils and early agriculture in Apennine Central Italy. *World Archaeology* 22, 1: 33–44.

Hus, A. (1961) *The Etruscans*. London, Evergreen Books.

Hutton, E. (1909) *Rome*. London, Methuen.

Jannot, J.-R. (1984) *Les Reliefs archaiques de Chiusi*. Rome, École Française de Rome.

Jannot, J.-R. (1993a) Phersu, phersuna, persona. In *Spectacles sportifs et sceniques dans le monde etrusco-italique*: 281–320. Rome, Collection de l'École Française de Rome 172.

Jannot, J.-R. (1993b) Insignia Potestatis. Les signes du pouvoir dans l'iconographie de Chiusi. *La civiltà di Chiusi e del suo territorio. Atti del XVII Convegno di Studi Etruschi ed Italici*: 217–37. Florence, Olschki.

Jarman, H.N. (1976) The plant remains. In T.W. Potter (ed.) *A Faliscan Town in South Etruria: Excavations at Narce 1966–71*: 308–10. London, British School at Rome.

Jehasse, J., and Jehasse, L. (1979) The Etruscans and Corsica. In D. Ridgway and F. Ridgway (eds.) *Italy Before the Romans*: 313–51. London, Academic Press.

Johns, C. (1982) *Sex or Symbol? Erotic Images of Greece and Rome*. London, British Museum Publications.

Johnston, A. (1972) The rehabilitation of Sostratos. *La Parola del Passato* 27: 416–23.

Johnston, A. (1991) Greek vases in the market-place. In T. Rasmussen and N. Spivey (eds.) *Looking at Greek Vases*: 203–31. Cambridge, Cambridge University Press.

Jones, G.D.B. (1962) Capena and the Ager Capenas, Part I. *Papers of the British School at Rome* 30: 116–207.

Jones, G.D.B. (1963) Capena and the Ager Capenas, Part II. *Papers of the British School at Rome* 31: 100–58.

Jones, M. (1985) I paesaggi nella Valle d'Oro. In A. Carandini (ed.) *Settefinestre, una villa schiavistica nell'Etruria romana*: 31–9. Milan, Electa.

Judson, S. (1963) Erosion and deposition of Italian stream valleys during historic time. *Science* 140 (3569): 898–9.

Judson, S., and Hemphill, P. (1981) Sizes of settlements in southern Etruria, 6th-5th centuries BC. *Studi Etruschi* 49: 193–202.

Judson, S., and Kahane, A. (1963) Underground drainageways in southern Etruria and northern Latium. *Papers of the British School at Rome* 31: 74–99.

Kelly, M.G., and Huntley, B. (1991) An 11,000-year record of vegetation and environment from Lago di Martignano, Latium, Italy. *Journal of Quaternary Science* 6 (3): 209–24.

Kezich, G. (1986) Lawrence in Etruria: *Etruscan Places* in context. In D.H. Lawrence, *Etruscan Places*: 159–70. London, Olive Press.

Lambrechts, R. (1959) *Essai sur les magistratures des républiques etrusques.* Rome, L'Institute Historique Belge de Rome.

Lawrence, D.H. (1932) *Etruscan Places.* London, Secker (1986 edition published by Nuova Immagine Editrice, Siena).

Levi, C. (1947) *Christ Stopped at Eboli.* New York, Farrar Strauss and Co.

Lewthwaite, J. (1982) Ambiguous first impressions: a survey of recent work on the early neolithic of the West Mediterranean. *Journal of Mediterranean Anthropology and Archaeology* 1(2): 297–307.

Lewthwaite, J. (1985) From precocity to involution: the neolithic of Corsica in its West Mediterranean and French contexts. *Oxford Journal of Archaeology* 4, 1: 47–68.

Lewthwaite, J. (1986) The transition to food production: a Mediterranean perspective. In M. Zvelebil (ed.) *Hunters in Transition: Mesolithic Societies of Temperate Eurasia and their Transition to Farming*: 53–66. Cambridge, Cambridge University Press.

Lewthwaite, J. (1987) Three steps to leaven: applicazione del modello di disponibilità al neolitico italiano. *Il neolitico d'Italia: Atti della XXVI Riunione Scientifica dell'Istituto Italiano di Preistoria e Protostoria*: 89–102. Florence, IIPP.

Linington, R.E. (1980) *Lo scavo nella zona Laghetto della necropoli della Banditaccia a Cerveteri.* Milan, Museo Civico.

Linington, R.E. (1982) Tarquinia, località Calvario: recenti interventi nella zona del abitato protostorico. In G.B. Caporali and A.M. Sgubini Moretti (eds.) *Archeologia nella Tuscia*: 117–23. Rome, Consiglio Nazionale delle Ricerche.

Liverani, P. (1984) L'ager veientanus in età repubblicana. *Papers of the British School at Rome* 52: 36–48.

Loney, H. (1996) The Development of Apennine Ceramic Manufacture. Philadelphia, University of Pennsylvania (unpublished Ph.D. thesis).

MacIver, R. (1927) *The Etruscans.* Oxford, Clarendon Press.

MacIver, R. (1928) *Italy Before the Romans.* Oxford, Clarendon.

Macnamara, E.F. (1986) The construction of some Etruscan incense-burners and candelabra. In J. Swaddling (ed.) *Italian Iron Age Artefacts in the British Museum*: 81–98. London, British Museum Publications.

Macnamara, E.F. (1990) *The Etruscans.* London, British Museum Publications.

Maffi, A., and Nastasi, F. (eds.) (1990) *Caere e il suo territorio da Agylla a Centumcellae.* Rome, Istituto Poligrafico e Zecca dello Stato.

Maggiani, A. (1978) Le tombe a dado di Sovana. *Prospettiva* 14: 15–31.

Maggiani, A. (ed.) (1985) *Artigianato artistico in Etruria.* Milan, Electa.

Mallegni, F. (1991) Un caso di perostosi frontale interna in uno scheletro umano di Tarquinia del III secolo a.C. *Studi Etruschi* 57: 195–200.

Mallowan, M. (1966) *Nimrud and its Remains*. London, Collins.

Malone, C. (1985) Pots, prestige and ritual in neolithic southern Italy. In C. Malone and S. Stoddart (eds.) *Papers in Italian Archaeology IV. Vol. 2: Prehistory:* 118–51. Oxford, British Archaeological Reports, International Series 244.

Malone, C., and Stoddart, S. (1984) Settlement nucleation in the Late Bronze Age of Umbria. *Antiquity* 58: 56–8.

Malone, C., and Stoddart, S. (1986) The Gubbio Project: the study of the development of an intermontane polity. *Dialoghi di Archeologia* 4: 201–8.

Malone, C., and Stoddart, S. (eds.) (1992) The neolithic site of San Marco, Gubbio (Perugia), Umbria: survey and excavation 1985–7. *Papers of the British School at Rome* 60: 1–69.

Malone, C., and Stoddart, S. (1994) *Territory, Time and State: The Archaeological Development of the Gubbio Basin*. Cambridge, Cambridge University Press.

Mangani, E. (1985) Castelnuovo Berardenga. In S. Stopponi (ed.) *Case e palazzi d'Etruria:* 155–63. Milan, Electa.

Mansuelli, G.A. (1972) Marzabotto: dix années de fouilles et de recherches. *Mélanges de l'École Française de Rome. Antiquité* 84: 111–44.

Marazzi, M., and Tusa, S. (1976) Interrelazioni dei centri siciliani e peninsulari durante la penetrazione micenea. *Sicilia Archeologica* 9: 49–90.

Martelli, M. (1985) I luoghi e prodotti dello scambio. In M. Cristofani (ed.) *La civiltà degli etruschi:* 175–81. Milan, Electa.

Martelli, M. (ed.) (1987) *La ceramica degli etruschi: la pittura vascolare*. Novara, De Agostini.

Martha, J. (1889) *L'Art étrusque*. Paris, Librairie de Firmin-Didot.

Martinelli, T., and Scott, V. (eds.) (1986) *Thomas Ashby: un archeologo fotografa la campagna romana tra '800 e '900*. Rome, De Luca.

Mazzanti, R., Grifoni Cremonesi, R., Pasquinucci, M., and Pult Quaglia, A.M. (eds.) (1986) *Terre e paduli: reperti cocumenti immagini per la storia di Coltano*. Pontedera, Bandecchi and Vivaldi.

McCarter, P.K. (1975) *The Antiquity of the Greek Alphabet and the Early Phoenician Scripts*. Missoula (Montana), Scholars Press.

Mellink, M. (1970) The painted tomb near Elmali. *American Journal of Archaeology* 74: 251–3.

Merlino, M., and Mirenda T. (1990) Caere. In A. Maffi and F. Nastasi (eds.) *Caere e il suo territorio da Agylla a Centumcellae:* 4–56. Rome, Istituto Poligrafico e Zecca dello Stato.

Miari, M. (1987) La documentazione dei siti archeologici dei bacini del Fiora e dell'Albegna: criteri di classificazione e analisi dei modelli di insediamento dell'età del bronzo. *Padusa* 23: 113–45.

Michelucci, M. (1985) Doganella-Kalousion. In A. Carandini (ed.) *La romanizzazione dell'Etruria: il territorio di Vulci:* 110–14. Milan, Electa.

Milanesi, M., and Mannoni, T. (1984) Gli etruschi a Genova e il commercio mediterraneo. *Studi Etruschi* 52: 117–46.

Minto, A. (1937) I materiali archeologici. *Studi Etruschi* 11: 335–41.

Minto, A. (1940) Le ricerche archeologico-mineraria in Val Fucinaia. *Studi Etruschi* 14: 315–20.

Minto, A. (1954) L'antica industria mineraria in Etruria e il porto di Populonia. *Studi Etruschi* 23: 291–319.

Mithen, S. (1990) *Thoughtful Foragers. A Study in Prehistoric Decision-Making*. Cambridge, Cambridge University Press.

Moretti, M. (1974) *Pittura etrusca in Tarqunia*. Milan, Silvana Editoriale.

Moretti, M. (1983) *Cerveteri*. Novara, De Agostini.

Moretti, M., and Sgubini Moretti, A.M. (1983) *I Curunas di Tuscania*. Rome, De Luca.

Morigi Govi, C. (1971) Il tintinnabulo della 'Tomba degli Ori' dell'Arsenale Militare di Bologna. *Archeologica Classica* 23: 211–35.

Morris, I. (1987) *Burial and Ancient Society: The Rise of the Greek City-State*. Cambridge, Cambridge University Press.

Morris, I. (1991) The early *polis* as city and state. In J. Rich and A. Wallace-Hadrill (eds.) *City and Country in the Ancient World*: 25–57. London, Routledge.

Morris, I. (1992) *Death-Ritual and Social Structure in Classical Antiquity*. Cambridge, Cambridge University Press.

Moscati, S. (1987) Fonti letterarie. In G. Barbieri (ed.) *L'alimentazione nel mondo antico: gli etruschi*: 41–6. Rome, Istituto Poligrafico e Zecca dello Stato.

Murray, O. (ed.) (1990) *Sympotica*. Oxford, Clarendon.

Murray, O., and Tecuşan, M. (eds.) (1995) *In Vino Veritas*. London, British School at Rome.

Musti, D. (1989) L'immagine degli etruschi nella storiografia antica. *Atti del Secondo Congresso Internazionale Etrusco*: 19–39. Rome, 'L'Erma' di Bretschneider.

Nardi, G. (1985) La viabilità di una metropoli: il caso di Caere. In F. Boitani, M. Cristofani, P. Moscati and G. Nardi, *Strade degli etrusche: vie e mezzi di comunicazione nell'antica Etruria*: 155–213. Rome, Autostrade S.p.A.

Nash, S. (1979) Thin Section Analysis of Bronze Age Pottery in Molise, Central Italy. Sheffield, Sheffield University, Department of Archaeology and Prehistory (unpublished BA thesis).

Naso, A. (1991) *La Tomba dei Denti di Lupo*. Florence, Olschki.

Naso, A., Rendeli, M., and Zifferero, A. (1989) Note sul popolamento e sull'economia etrusca in due zone campione degli entroterra vulcente e ceretano. *Secondo Congresso Internazionale Etrusco* I: 537–72. Rome, Bretschneider.

Neboit, R. (1984) Erosion des sols et colonisation grecque en Sicile et en Grand Grèce. *Bulletin, Association des Géographes Français* 499: 5–13.

Negroni Catacchio, N. (ed.) (1981) *Sorgenti della Nova: una comunità protostorica e il suo territorio nell'Etruria meridionale*. Rome, Consiglio Nazionale delle Ricerche.

Negroni Catacchio, N. (1986) Sorgenti della Nova. In *Alle radici della civiltà etrusca: una comunità protostorica e il suo territorio nell'Etruria meridionale*. Viterbo, Provincia di Viterbo, Assessorato della Cultura (exhibition pamphlet guide).

Negroni Catacchio, N. (1987) Aspetti e problemi del neolitico nella valle del fiume Fiora. *Il Neolitico d'Italia: Atti della XXVI Riunione Scientifica dell'Istituto Italiano di Preistoria e Protostoria*: 655–69. Florence, IIPP.

Negroni Catacchio, N. (1988) La cultura di Rinaldone. *Rassegna di Archeologia* 7: 348–63.

Negroni Catacchio, N. (1989) L'abitato del bronzo finale di Sorgenti della Nova (VT). Possibilità di confronti con i modelli abitativi dei centri villanoviani. *Atti del Secondo Convegno Internazionale Etrusco*: 271–83. Florence, Istituto di Studi Etruschi.

Negroni Catacchio, N., and Domanico, L. (1986) I modelli abitativi dell'Etruria protostorica. *Annali Benacensi. XI Convegno Archeologico Benacense Simposio Internazionale 1986*: 515–85.

Negroni Catacchio, N., and Miari, M. (1991–2) L'area tra Fiora e Albegna: nuovi dati su paesaggio e popolamento. *Rassegna di Archeologia* 10: 393–402.

Newby, E. (1971) *Love and War in the Apennines*. London, Hodder and Stoughton.

Nicosia, M. (1966) Duo nuovi cippi fiesolani. *Studi Etruschi* 34: 149–64.

Nielsen, E. (1987) Some preliminary thoughts on new and old terracottas. *Opuscula Romana* 16: 92–119.

Nielsen, E. (1991) Excavations at Poggio Civitate. *Studi e Materiali* 6: 245–59. Rome, 'L'Erma' di Bretschneider.

Nielsen, E., and Phillips, K.M. (1974) Bryn Mawr College excavations in Tuscany, 1972. *American Journal of Archeology* 78: 265–78.

Nielsen, E., and Phillips, K.M. (1985) Poggio Civitate (Murlo). In S. Stopponi (ed.) *Case e palazzi d'Etruria*: 64–9. Milan, Electa.

Nielsen, M. (1985) Le produzioni locali nel territorio volterrano. In A. Maggiani (ed.) *Artigianato artistico in Etruria*: 65–6. Milan, Electa.

Nielsen, M. (1989) Women and family in a changing society: a quantitative approach to late Etruscan burials. *Analecta Romana Instituti Danici* 17–18: 53–98.

Nietzsche, F. (1956) *The Birth of Tragedy* (trans. F. Golffing). New York, Doubleday Anchor.

Noël des Vergers, A. (1862–4) *L'Étrurie et les Étrusques*. Paris, Librairie de Firmin-Didot.

Ogilvie, R.M. (1965) *A Commentary on Livy, Books 1–5*. Oxford, Clarendon Press.

Ogilvie, R.M. (1969) *The Romans and Their Gods*. London, Chatto and Windus.

Oleson, J.P. (1976) Regulatory planning and individual site development in Etruscan necropoleis. *Journal of the Society of Architectural Historians* 35: 204–18.

Oleson, J.P. (1982) *The Sources of Innovation in Later Etruscan Tomb Design*. Rome, G. Bretschneider.

Onions, C.T. (ed.) (1973) *The Shorter Oxford English Dictionary*. Oxford, Clarendon Press.

Östenberg, C.E. (1967) Luni sul Mignone e problemi della preistoria d'Italia. *Acta Instituti Romani Regni Sueciae* 4, 25: 1–306.

Östenberg, C.E. (1975) *Case etrusche di Acquarossa*. Rome, Comitato per le Attività Archeologiche nella Tuscia.

Pacciarelli, M. (1982) Economia e organizzazione del territorio in Etruria meridionale nell'età del bronzo media e recente. *Dialoghi di Archeologia* 2: 69–79.

Pacciarelli, M. (1989–90) Ricerche topografiche a Vulci: dati e problemi relative all'origine delle città medio-tirreniche. *Studi Etruschi* 56: 11–48.

Pallottino, M. (1930) Uno specchio di Tuscania e la leggenda etrusca di Tarchon. *Rendiconti dell'Accademia Nazionale dei Lincei* 6: 49–87.

Pallottino, M. (1937a) Nomi etruschi di città. In *Scritti in onore di B. Nogara*: 341–58. Rome, G. Bretschneider.

Pallottino, M. (1937b) Tarquinia. *Monumenti Antichi* 36: 5–594.

Pallottino, M. (1952) *Etruscan Painting*. Geneva, Skira.

Pallottino, M. (1957) *La necropoli di Cerveteri*. Rome, Poligrafico dello Stato.

Pallottino, M. (1975) *The Etruscans*. Harmondsworth, Penguin.

Pallottino, M. (1991) *A History of Earliest Italy*. London, Routledge.

Pandolfini, M. (1988) Le iscrizioni etrusche del Mantovano. In R. de Marinis (ed.) *Gli etruschi a nord del Po I*: 116–23. Udine, Camponotto Editore.

Pannuti, S. (1969) Gli scavi di Grotta a Male presso L'Aquila. *Bullettino di Paletnologia Italiana* 78, n.s. 20: 147–67.

Pardini, E., and Mannucci, P. (1981) Gli etruschi di Selvaccia (Siena). *Studi Etruschi* 49: 303–15.

Pasquinucci, M. (1979) La transumanza nell'Italia romana. In E. Gabba and M. Pasquinucci, *Strutture agrarie e allevamento transumante nell'Italia romana*: 79–182. Pisa, Giardini.

Pellegrini, E. (1992) L'età dei metalli nell'Italia meridionale e in Sicilia. In A. Guidi and M. Piperno (eds.) *Italia preistorica*: 471–516. Rome, Laterza.

Peretto, C. (1992) Il paleolitico medio. In A. Guidi and M. Piperno (eds.) *Italia preistorica*: 170–97. Rome, Laterza.

Peretto, C., Terzani, C., and Cremaschi, M. (eds.) (1983) *Isernia La Pineta: un accampamento più antico di 700.000 anni*. Bologna, Calderini.

Perkins, P. (1991) Cities, cemeteries and rural settlements of the Albegna valley and the Ager Cosanus in the Orientalising and archaic periods. In

E. Herring, R. Whitehouse and J. Wilkins (eds.) *Papers of the Fourth Conference of Italian Archaeology: The Archaeology of Power 1*: 135–44. London, Accordia Research Centre.

Perkins, P. (in press) Reconstructing the population history of the Albegna valley and the Ager Cosanus, Tuscany, Italy, between the seventh and the second centuries BC. In D.J. Mattingly and J. van Dalen (eds.) *Issues in Mediterranean Landscape Archaeology: The Contribution of GIS*. Oxford, Oxbow.

Perkins, P., and Attolini, I. (1992) An Etruscan farm at Podere Tartuchino. *Papers of the British School at Rome* 60: 71–134.

Perkins, P., and Walker, L. (1990) Survey of an Etruscan city at Doganella in the Albegna valley. *Papers of the British School at Rome* 58: 1–143.

Peroni, R. (1971) *L'età del bronzo nella penisula italiana. I: L'antica età del bronzo*. Florence, Parenti.

Pfiffig, A.J. (1975) *Religio etrusca*. Graz, Akademische Druck.

Phillips, K.M. (1973) Bryn Mawr College excavations in Tuscany, 1972. *American Journal of Archaeology* 77: 319–26.

Phillips, K.M. (1993) *In the Hills of Tuscany: Recent Excavations at the Etruscan Site of Poggio Civitate*. Philadelphia, University Museum.

Pianu, G. (1996) Etruscan: major periods. In J. Turner (ed.) *The Dictionary of Art* 10: 587–8. London, Macmillan.

Piggott, S. (1965) *Ancient Europe*. Edinburgh, Edinburgh University Press.

Piperno, M. (1992) Il paleolitico inferiore. In A. Guidi and M. Piperno (eds.) *Italia preistorica*: 139–69. Rome, Laterza.

Pitti, C., and Tozzi, C. (1976) Gli scavi nel villaggio neolitico di Catignano (Pescara). *Rivista Scienze Preistoriche* 31: 87–107.

Placidi, C. (1978) Fauna, in S.M. Cassano and A. Manfredini (eds.) Torrionaccio (Viterbo). Scavo di un abitato protostorico. *Notizie degli Scavi* 32: 1–382 (270).

Poggio Civitate (1970) *Poggio Civitate (Murlo, Siena). Il santuario arcaico*. Florence, Olschki.

Pohl, I. (1987) San Giovenale. In G. Barbieri (ed.) *L'alimentazione nel mondo antico: gli etruschi*: 71–3. Rome, Istituto Poligrafico e Zecca dello Stato.

Pontrandolfo, A., and Rouveret, A. (1992) *Le tombe dipinte di Paestum*. Modena, Panini.

Pope, K.O., and van Andel, Tj.H. (1984) Late Quaternary alluviation and soil formation in the southern Argolid: its history, causes and archaeological implications. *Journal of Archaeological Science* 11: 281–306.

Potter, T.W. (1976) *A Faliscan Town in South Etruria. Excavations at Narce 1966–71*. London, British School at Rome.

Potter, T.W. (1979) *The Changing Landscape of South Etruria*. London, Elek.

Potter, T.W. (1985) A republican healing sanctuary at Ponte di Nona near Rome and the classical tradition of votive medicine. *Journal of the British Archaeological Association* 138: 23–47.

Potter, T.W. (1991a) Towns and territories in Southern Etruria. In J. Rich and A. Wallace-Hadrill (eds.) *Town and Country in the Ancient World*: 191–209. London, Routledge.

Potter, T.W. (1991b) Power, politics and territory in southern Etruria. In E. Herring, R. Whitehouse and J. Wilkins (eds.) *Papers of the Fourth Conference of Italian Archaeology: The Archaeology of Power 2*: 173–84. London, Accordia Research Centre.

Prag, J., and Neave, R. (1997) *Making Faces. Using Forensic and Archaeological Evidence*. London, British Museum Press.

Prayon, F. (1975a) *Frühetruskische Grab- und Hausarchitektur*. Heidelberg, F.H. Kerle.

Prayon, F. (1975b) Zur Datierung der drei frühetruskischen Sitzstatuetten aus Cerveteri. *Mitteilungen des deutschen Archäologischen Instituts. Römische Abteilung* 82: 165–79.

Prayon, F. (1986) Architecture. In L. Bonfante (ed.) *Etruscan Life and Afterlife*: 174–201. Detroit, Wayne State University Press.

Proietti, G. (1980) *Il Museo di Villa Giulia*. Rome, Quasar.

QF (1970) (various authors) Quattro Fontanili. *Notizie degli Scavi*: 178–329.

Quilici, L. (1985) Le antiche vie dell'Etruria. *Atti del Secondo Congresso Internazionale Etrusco*: 451–506. Rome, G. Bretschneider.

Quilici Gigli, S. (1970) *Tuscania (Forma Italiae, Regio VII, Vol. II)*. Rome, Consiglio Nazionale delle Ricerche.

Radmilli, A.M. (1951–2) Notizie preliminari sulla grotta sepolcrale 'Patrizi' di Sasso-Furbara. *Bullettino di Paletnologia Italiana* 8 (4): 100–4.

Radmilli, A.M. (1953) Attività del Museo Nazionale Preistorico 'L. Pigorini' – anno 1952. *Bullettino di Paletnologia Italiana* 8 (5): 37–48.

Raison, L. (1983) *Tuscany: An Anthology*. London, Cadogan Books.

Rallo, A. (1989) Classi sociali e mano d'opera femminile. In A. Rallo (ed.) *Le donne in Etruria*: 147–56. Rome, 'L'Erma' di Bretschneider.

Randall-McIver, D. (1924) *Villanovans and Early Etruscans*. Oxford, Clarendon.

Randsborg, K. (1991) *The First Millennium AD in Europe and the Mediterranean: An Archaeological Essay*. Cambridge, Cambridge University Press.

Rasmussen, T. (1979) *Bucchero Pottery from Southern Etruria*. Cambridge, Cambridge University Press.

Rasmussen, T. (1983) Early Roman art. In M. Henig (ed.) *A Handbook of Roman Art*: 13–25. Oxford, Phaidon.

Rasmussen, T. (1985) Etruscan shapes in Attic pottery. *Antike Kunst* 28.1: 33–9.

Rasmussen, T. (1986a) Archaeology in Etruria 1980–85. *Archaeological Reports* 32: 102–22.

Rasmussen, T. (1986b) Campanian *bucchero*. In J. Swaddling (ed.) *Italian Iron Age Artefacts in the British Museum*: 273–81. London, British Museum Publications.

Rasmussen, T. (1991) Tuscania and its territory. In G. Barker and J.A. Lloyd (eds.) *Roman Landscapes: Archaeological Survey in the Mediterranean Region*: 106–14. London, British School at Rome, Archaeological Monographs 2.

Rasmussen, T. (1995) Rattling among the Etruscans and Greeks. In J. Swaddling, S. Walker and P. Roberts (eds.) *Italy in Europe: Economic Relations 700 BC–AD 50*: 195–203. London, British Museum.

Rasmussen, T. (1996) Archaeology in Etruria 1985–95. *Archaeological Reports* 42: 45–58.

Rasmussen, T. (1997) The Tarquins and 'Etruscan Rome'. In T. Cornell and K. Lomas (eds.) *Gender and Ethnicity in Ancient Italy*: 23–30. London, Accordia.

Rasmussen, T., and Horie, V. (1988) Italic incised *impasto*: a case of partial authenticity. In J. Christiansen and T. Melander (eds.) *Proceedings of the Third Symposium on Ancient Greek and Related Pottery*: 478–85. Copenhagen, Ny Carlsberg Glyptotek and Thorvaldsen Museum.

Rathje, A. (1979) Oriental imports in Etruria. In D. Ridgway and F. Ridgway (eds.) *Italy Before the Romans*: 145–83. London, Academic Press.

Rathje, A. (1983) A banquet service from the Latin city of Ficana. *Analecta Romana Istituti Danici* 12: 7–29.

Rathje, A. (1990) The adoption of the Homeric banquet in central Italy in the Orientalizing period. In O. Murray (ed.) *Sympotica*: 279–88. Oxford, Clarendon.

Ravelli, F., and Howarth, P. (1988) I cuniculi etrusco-latini: tunnel per la captazione di acqua pura. *Irrigazione e Drenaggio* 35: 57–70.

Rendeli, M. (1993) *Città aperte: ambiente e paesaggio rurale organizzato nell'Etruria meridionale costiera durante l'età orientalizzante e arcaica*. Rome, Gruppo Editoriale Internazionale.

Renfrew, C. (1972) *The Emergence of Civilisation*. London, Methuen.

Renfrew, C. (1973) Monuments, mobilisation and social organisation in neolithic Wessex. In C. Renfrew (ed.) *The Explanation of Culture Change: Models in Prehistory*: 539–58. London, Duckworth.

Renfrew, C. (1987) *Archaeology and Language: The Puzzle of Indo-European Origins*. London, Jonathan Cape.

Renfrew, C. (1992) Archaeology, genetics and linguistic diversity. *Man* 27 (3): 445–78.

Renfrew, C., and Cherry, J. (eds.) (1986) *Peer Polity Interaction and Socio-Political Change*. Cambridge, Cambridge University Press.

Ricciardi, L. (1987) Blera. In G. Barbieri (ed.) *L'alimentazione nel mondo antico: gli etruschi*: 83–7. Rome, Istituto Poligrafico e Zecca dello Stato.

Richardson, E. (1983) *Etruscan Votive Bronzes. Geometric, Orientalizing, Archaic*. Mainz, Philipp von Zabern.

Richardson, L. (1992) *A New Topographical Dictionary of Ancient Rome*. Baltimore and London, John Hopkins University Press.

Ridgway, B.S. (1981) *Fifth Century Styles in Greek Sculpture*. Princeton, Princeton University Press.

Ridgway, D. (1973) The first western Greeks: Campanian coasts and southern Etruria. In C.F.C. Hawkes and S. Hawkes (eds.) *Greeks, Celts, and Romans*: 5–36. London, Dent.

Ridgway, D. (1988a) The Etruscans. In *Cambridge Ancient History* vol. 4: 634–75. Cambridge, Cambridge University Press, second edition.

Ridgway, D. (1988b) Western geometric pottery: new light on interactions in Italy. In J. Christiansen and T. Melander (eds.) *Proceedings of the Third Symposium on Ancient Greek and Related Pottery*: 489–505. Copenhagen, Ny Carlsberg Glyptotek and Thorvaldsen Museum.

Ridgway, D. (1992) *The First Western Greeks*. Cambridge, Cambridge University Press.

Ridgway, D. (1994) Phoenicians and Greeks in the west: a view from Pithekoussai. In G.R. Tsetskhladze and F. de Angelis (eds.) *The Archaeology of Greek Colonization. Essays Dedicated to Sir John Boardman*: 35–46. Oxford, Oxford University Committee for Archaeology.

Ridgway, D., and Ridgway, F.R. (1994) Demaratus and the archaeologists. In R. de Puma and J.P. Small (eds.) *Murlo and the Etruscans*: 6–15. Wisconsin, University of Wisconsin Press.

Rizzo, M.A. (ed.) (1988) *Un artista etrusco e il suo mondo: il pittore di Micali*. Rome, De Luca.

Rizzo, M.A. (1989) Cerveteri: il tumulo di Montetosto. *Atti del Secondo Congresso Etrusco*: 153–61. Rome, G. Bretschneider.

Robb, J. (1994) The neolithic of peninsular Italy: anthropological synthesis and critique. *Bullettino di Paletnologia Italiana* 85: 189–214.

Romer, E. (1984) *The Tuscan Year: Life and Food in an Italian Valley*. London, Weidenfeld and Nicolson.

Roncalli, F. (ed.) (1985) *Scrivere etrusco*. Milan, Electa.

Roncalli, F. (1986) L'arte. In G.P. Carratelli (ed.) *Rasenna. Storia e civiltà degli etruschi*: 80–156. Milan, Libri Scheiwiller (Credito Italiano).

Root, M.C. (1973) An Etruscan horse race from Poggio Civitate. *American Journal of Archaeology* 77: 121–38.

Roselle (1975) *Roselle. Gli scavi e la mostra*. Pisa, Pacini Editore (Soprintendenza Archeologica della Toscana).

Rowley-Conwy, P. (1981) Mesolithic Danish bacon: permanent and temporary sites in the Danish mesolithic. In A. Sheridan and G. Bailey (eds.) *Economic Archaeology*: 51–5. Oxford, British Archaeological Reports, International Series 96.

Rystedt, E. (1983) *Early Etruscan Akroteria from Acquarossa and Poggio Civitate (Murlo)*. Rome, Skrifter utgivna av Svenska Institutet i Rom 38: 4.

Salmon, E.T. (1969) *Roman Colonization under the Republic*. London, Thames and Hudson.

Saloi, F. (1981) Pontecagnano e l'Etruria: analisi statistica di un confronto craniologico. *Studi Etruschi* 44: 185–210.

Sandars, N.K. (1972) *The Epic of Gilgamesh*. London, Penguin.

San Giovenale (1969–72) *San Giovenale. Results of Excavations Conducted by the Swedish Institute of Classical Studies at Rome*. Rome, Skrifter utgivna av Svenska Institutet i Rom 26: 1.

Sassatelli, G. (1989) *La città etrusca di Marzabotto*. Bologna, Grafis.

Scali, S. (1987) Bolsena-Gran Carro: i resti faunistici. In G. Barbieri (ed.) *L'alimentazione nel mondo antico: gli etruschi*: 67–70. Rome, Istituto Poligrafico e Zecca dello Stato.

Scheffer, C. (1987a) Acquarossa. In G. Barbieri (ed.) *L'alimentazione nel mondo antico: gli etruschi*: 53–67. Rome, Istituto Poligrafico e Zecca dello Stato.

Scheffer, C. (1987b) Forni e fornelli Etruschi in età arcaica. In G. Barbieri (ed.) *L'alimentazione nel mondo antico: gli etruschi*: 97–105. Rome, Istituto Poligrafico e Zecca dello Stato.

Scullard, H.H. (1967) *The Etruscan Cities and Rome*. London, Thames and Hudson.

Service, E.R. (1962) *Primitive Social Organisation*. New York, Random House.

Settis, S. (ed.) (1985) *La terra degli etruschi*. Florence, Scala.

Sgubini Moretti, A.M. (1982) Tuscania. Necropoli in località Ara del Tufo. I campagna di scavo: relazione preliminare. *Archeologia nella Tuscia* 1: 133.

Sgubini Moretti, A.M. (1989) Tomba a casa con portico nella necropoli di Pian di Mole a Tuscania. *Atti del Secondo Congresso Internazionale Etrusco*: 321–35. Rome, G. Bretschneider.

Sgubini Moretti, A.M. (1991) *Tuscania: il Museo Archeologico*. Rome, Quasar.

Sgubini Moretti, A.M. (1994) Ricerche archeologiche a Vulci 1985–90. In M. Cristofani Martelli (ed.) *Tyrrhenoi philotechnoi*: 9–49. Rome, Gruppo Editoriale Internazionale.

Sherratt, S., and Sherratt, A. (1993) The growth of the Mediterranean economy in the early first millennium BC. *World Archaeology* 24 (3): 361–78.

Skeates, R. (1991) Caves, cult and children in neolithic Abruzzo, central Italy. In P. Garwood, D. Jennings, R. Skeates and J. Toms (eds.) *Sacred and Profane*: 50–64. Oxford, Oxford University Committee for Archaeology, Monograph No.32.

Small, J.P. (1971) The Banquet Frieze from Poggio Civitate (Murlo). *Studi Etruschi* 39: 25–61.

Small, J.P. (1981) *Studies Relating to the Theban Cycle on Late Etruscan Urns*. Rome, G. Bretschneider.

Small, J.P. (1986) Cacu and the Porsennae. In J. Swaddling (ed.) *Italian Iron Age Artefacts in the British Museum*: 459–62. London, British Museum Publications.

Small, J.P. (1987) Left, right and center: direction in Etruscan art. *Opuscula Romana* 16: 125–35.

Small, J.P. (1994) Eat, drink and be merry: Etruscan banquets. In R. de Puma and J.P. Small (eds.) *Murlo and the Etruscans*: 85–94. Wisconsin, University of Wisconsin Press.

Snodgrass, A.M. (1977) *Archaeology and the Rise of the Greek State*. Cambridge, Cambridge University Press.

Snodgrass, A.M. (1986) Interaction by design: the Greek city state. In C. Renfrew and J. Cherry (eds.) *Peer Polity Interaction and Socio-Political Change*: 47–58. Cambridge, Cambridge University Press.

Sordi, M. (1989) Storiografia e cultura etrusca nell'impero romano. *Atti del Secondo Congresso Internazonale Etrusco*: 41–51. Rome, G. Bretschneider.

Sorrentino, C. (1981a) La fauna. In E. Berggren and K. Berggren (eds.) *San Giovenale II. 2. Excavations in Area B, 1957–1960*: 58–64. Rome, Skrifter utgivna av Svenska Institutet i Rom 4, 26 (2.2).

Sorrentino, C. (1981b) Appendix. In E. Berggren and K. Berggren (eds.) *San Giovenale II. 4. The Subterranean Building in Area B*: 85–9. Rome, Skrifter utgivna av Svenska Institutet i Rom 4, 26 (2.4).

Spivey, N. (1987) *The Micali Painter and His Followers*. Oxford, Oxford University Press.

Spivey, N. (1988) The armed dance on Etruscan vases. In J. Christiansen and T. Melander (eds.) *Proceedings of the Third Symposium on Ancient Greek and Related Pottery*: 592–603. Copenhagen, Ny Carlsberg Glyptotek and Thorvaldsen Museum.

Spivey, N. (1991a) Greek vases in Etruria. In T. Rasmussen and N. Spivey (eds.) *Looking at Greek Vases*: 131–50. Cambridge, Cambridge University Press.

Spivey, N. (1991b) The power of women in Etruscan society. *Accordia Research Papers* 2: 55–67.

Spivey, N. (1997) *Etruscan Art*. London, Thames and Hudson.

Spivey, N., and Rasmussen, T. (1986) Dioniso e i pirati nel Museum of Art di Toledo. *Prospettiva* 44: 2–8.

Spivey, N., and Stoddart, S. (1990) *Etruscan Italy: An Archaeological History*. London, Batsford.

Sprengel, U. (1975) La pastorizia transumante nell'Italia centro-meridionale. *Annali del Mezzogiorno* 15: 271–327.

Sprenger, M., and Bartoloni, G. (1983) *The Etruscans. Their History, Art and Architecture*. New York, Abrams.

Stary, P.F. (1979) Foreign elements in Etruscan arms and armour: 8th to 3rd centuries BC. *Proceedings of the Prehistoric Society* 45: 179–206.

Stefani, E. (1922) Veio: esplorazioni dentro l'area dell'antica citta. *Notizie degli Scavi*: 379–404.

Stefani. E. (1944) Scavi archeologici a Veio in contrada Piazza d'Armi. *Monumenti Antichi dei Lincei* 40: 178–290.

Stefani, E. (1953) Veio: tempio detto dell'Apollo – esplorazione e sistemazione del santuario. *Notizie degli Scavi* 102: 29–112.

Steingräber, S. (1981a) *Etrurien: Städte, Heiligtümer, Nekropolen.* Munich, Hirmer.

Steingräber, S. (1981b) Zur Phänomen der etruskisch-italischen Votivköpfe. *Römische Mitteilungen* 87.2: 216–53.

Steingräber, S. (ed.) (1986) *Etruscan Painting. Catalogue Raisonné of Etruscan Wall Paintings.* New York, Harcourt Brace Jovanovich.

Stoddart, S. (1987) Complex Polity Formation in Central Italy in the First Millennium BC. Cambridge, Cambridge University (unpublished Ph.D. thesis).

Stoddart, S. (1988) Divergent trajectories in central Italy, 1200–500 BC. In T. Champion (ed.) *Centre and Periphery: Comparative Studies in Archaeology:* 88–101. London, Allen and Unwin.

Stoddart, S. (1990) The political landscape of Etruria. *Accordia Research Papers* 1: 39–51.

Stoddart, S., and Whitley, J. (1988) The social context of literacy in archaic Greece and Etruria. *Antiquity* 62: 761–72.

Stopponi, S. (ed.) (1985a) *Case e palazzi d'Etruria.* Milan, Electa.

Stopponi, S. (1985b) Il santuario di Cannicella. In G. Colonna (ed.) *Santuari d'Etruria:* 116–20. Milan, Electa.

Stopponi, S. (1985c) Il santuario di Punta della Vipera. In G. Colonna (ed.) *Santuari d'Etruria:* 159–63. Milan, Electa.

Strandberg Olofsson, M. (1985) Acquarossa Zona K: la ricostruzione del complesso monumentale. In S. Stopponi (ed.) *Case e palazzi d'Etruria:* 54–8. Milan, Electa.

Strøm, I. (1971) *Problems Concerning the Origin and Early Development of the Etruscan Orientalizing Style.* Odense, Odense University Press.

Strøm, I. (1990) Relations between Etruria and Campania around 700 BC. In J.-P. Descoeudres (ed.) *Greek Colonists and Native Populations:* 87–97. Oxford, Clarendon.

Strong, D. (1988) *Roman Art.* Harmondsworth, Penguin, 2nd edition.

Szilágyi, J.G. (1981) Impletae modis saturae. *Prospettiva* 24: 2–23.

Szilágyi, J.G. (1992) *Ceramica etrusco-corinzia figurata I.* Florence, Olschki.

Talamone (1982) *Talamone. Il mito dei sette a Tebe.* Florence, Edizioni il David.

Tamburini, P. (1986) Il villaggio del Gran Carro: conoscenze attuali e proposte di ricerca. In G.L. Carancini (ed.) *Atti dell'incontro di Acquasparta 1985. Gli insediamenti perilacustri dell'età del bronzo e della prima età del ferro: il caso dell'Antico Lacus Velinus:* 213–38. Perugia, University of Perugia, Istituto di Archeologia.

Teegen, W.R. (1995) Grave dimensions as a diagnostic tool for palaeodemography and social ranking: the example of Quattro Fontanili. In N. Christie (ed.) *Settlement and Economy in Italy, 1500 BC–AD 1500:* 261–71. Oxford, Oxbow (Oxbow Monograph 41).

Thuillier, J.-P. (1985) *Les Jeux athlétiques dans la civilization etrusque.* Rome, École Française de Rome.

TLE (1968) M. Pallottino, *Testimonia linguae etruscae.* Florence, Nuova Italia, 2nd edition.

Toms, J. (1986) The relative chronology of the Villanovan cemetery of Quattro Fontanili at Veii. *Archeologia e Storia Antica* 8: 41–97.

Torelli, M. (1975) *Elogia tarquiniensia.* Florence, Sansoni.

Torelli, M. (1982) Il commercio greco in Etruria tra l'VIII e il V secolo a.C. In *Il commercio greco nel Tirreno in età arcaica*: 67–82. Salerno, Università degli Studi di Salerno, Istituto do Storia Antica e Archeologia.

Torelli, M. (1986a) La storia. In G.P. Carratelli (ed.) *Rasenna. Storia e civiltà degli etruschi*: 15–76. Milan, Libri Scheiwiller.

Torelli, M. (1986b) History: land and people. In L. Bonfante (ed.) *Etruscan Life and Afterlife*: 47–56. Detroit, Wayne State University Press.

Torelli, M. (1987) *La società etrusca.* Rome, Nuova Italia Scientifica.

Torelli, M. (1989) Problemi di romanizzazione. *Atti del Secondo Congresso Internazionale Etrusco*: 393–403. Rome, G. Bretschneider.

Torelli, M. (1993) *Etruria.* Rome-Bari, Laterza, 4th edition.

Torelli, M., and Boitani, F. (1971) Gravisca. Scavi nella città etrusca e romana. Campagne 1969 e 1970. *Notizie degli Scavi*: 195–299.

Tortorici, A. (1981) Regisvilla. *Quaderni dell'Istituto di Topografia Antica dell'Università di Roma* 9: 151–64.

Tozzi, C. (1982) La transition du néolithique ancien au néolithique moyen dans la côte adriatique (Abruzzo-Marche). In *Le Néolithique Ancien Mediterranéen*: 319–25. Montpellier, CNRS.

Tracchi, A. (1978) *Dal Chianti al Valdarno.* Rome, Consiglio Nazionale delle Ricerche.

Tripp, D.E. (1986) Coinage. In L. Bonfante (ed.) *Etruscan Life and Afterlife*: 202–14. Detroit, Wayne State University Press.

Trump, D.H. (1966) *Central and Southern Italy Before Rome.* London, Thames and Hudson.

Tuck, A.S. (1994) The Etruscan seated banquet in Villanovan ritual and Etruscan iconography. *American Journal of Archaeology* 98: 617–28.

Turfa J.M. (1994) Anatomical votives and Italian medical conditions. In R. de Puma and J.P. Small (eds.) *Murlo and the Etruscans*: 224–40. Wisconsin, University of Wisconsin Press.

Turfa, J.M. (1986) Anatomical votive terracottas from Etruscan and Italic sanctuaries. In J. Swaddling (ed.) *Italian Iron Age Artefacts in the British Museum*: 205–13. London, British Museum Publications.

Ucko, P. (1969) Ethnography and archaeological interpretation of funerary remains. *World Archaeology* 1: 262–80.

Vallet, G. (1962) L'introduction de l'olivier en Italie centrale. In M. Rennard (ed.) *Hommage à Albert Grenier*: 154–63. Brussels, Collection Latomus 58.

van Andel, Tj.H., and Runnels, C. (1987) *Beyond the Acropolis: The Archaeology of the Greek Countryside*. Stanford, Stanford University Press.

van Andel, Tj.H., Runnels, C.N., and Pope, K.O. (1985) Five thousand years of land use and abuse in the southern Argolid, Greece. *Hesperia* 55: 103–28.

van der Meer, L.B. (1977–8) Etruscan urns from Volterra. Studies in mythological representation. *Bulletin Antieke Beschaving* 52–3: 57–131.

van der Meer, L.B. (1979) Iecur Placentinum and the orientation of the Etruscan haruspex. *Bulletin Antieke Beschaving* 54: 49–64.

van der Meer, L.B. (1986) Greek and local elements in a sporting scene by the Micali Painter. In J. Swaddling (ed.) *Italian Iron Age Artefacts in the British Museum*: 439–45. London, British Museum Publications.

van der Meer, L.B. (1987) *The Bronze Liver of Piacenza*. Amsterdam, J.C. Gieben.

van der Meer, L.B. (1995) *Interpretatio Etrusco. Greek Myths on Etruscan Mirrors*. Amsterdam, J.C. Gieben.

Vanni, V.F. (1962) Resti ossei umani di Grotta Patrizi. *Archivio per l'Antropologia e l'Etnologia* 92: 403–10.

van Straten, F.T. (1981) Gifts for the gods. In H.S. Versnel (ed.) *Faith, Hope and Worship. Aspects of Religious Mentality in the Ancient World*: 64–151. Leiden, E.J. Brill.

Verney, J. (1955) *Going to the Wars*. London, Collins.

Vickers, M. (1985–6) Imaginary Etruscans: changing perceptions of Etruria since the fifteenth century. *Hephaistos* 7–8: 153–68.

Ville, G. (1981) *La Gladiature en Occident des origins à la mort de Domitien*. Rome, École Française de Rome.

Vinicio Gentili, (1988) Testimonianze dell'abitato villanoviano ed 'etruscoide' di Verucchio. In G.A. Mansuelli (ed.) *La formazione della città preromana in Emilia Romagna*: 79–103. Bologna, Istituto per la Storia di Bologna.

Vita-Finzi, C. (1969) *The Mediterranean Valleys. Geological Changes in Historical Times*. Cambridge, Cambridge University Press.

Vitali, D. (1988) Monte Bibele: criteri distributivi nell'abitato ed aspetti del territorio bolognese dal IV al II secolo a.C. In G.A. Mansuelli (ed.) *La formazione della città preromana in Emilia Romagna*: 105–42. Bologna, Istituto per la Storia di Bologna.

von Freytag gen. Löringhoff, B. (1986) *Das Giebelrelief von Telamon (Römische Mitteilungen, Ergänzungsheft 21)*. Mainz, Philipp von Zabern.

von Hase, F.W. (1969) Die Trensen der Früheisenzeit in Italien. *Prähistorische Bronzefunde* 16, 1. Munich, Beck.

von Hase, F.W. (1989) Der etruskische Bucchero aus Karthago. *Jahrbuch des Römisch-Germanischen Zentralmuseums* 36: 327–410.

von Vacano, O.W. (1992) Osservazioni riguardanti la storia edilizia del tempio di Talamonaccio. *La coroplastica templare etrusca fra il IV e il II Secolo a.C. Atti del XVI Convegno di Studi Etruschi ed Italici*: 57–68. Florence, Olschki.

Wagstaff, J.M. (1981) Buried assumptions: some problems in the interpretation of the 'Younger Fill' raised by recent data from Greece. *Journal of Archaeological Science* 8: 247–64.

Walberg, G. (1986) The Tomb of the Baron reconsidered. *Studi Etruschi* 54: 51–9.

Walker, L. (1985) The site at Doganella in the Albegna valley: spatial patterns in an Etruscan landscape. In S. Stoddart and C. Malone (eds.) *Papers in Italian Archaeology IV. Vol. 3: Patterns in Protohistory*: 243–54. Oxford, British Archaeological Reports, International Series 245.

Walker, S. (1985) *Memorials to the Roman Dead*. London, British Museum Publications.

Wallace-Hadrill, A. (1988) The social structure of the Roman house. *Papers of the British School at Rome* 56: 43–97.

Ward-Perkins, J.B. (1959) Excavations beside the north-west gate of Veii, 1957–8. *Papers of the British School at Rome* 27: 38–79.

Ward-Perkins, J.B. (1961) Veii: the historical topography of the ancient city. *Papers of the British School at Rome* 29.

Ward-Perkins, J.B. (1962) Etruscan engineering: road-building, water-supply and drainage. In M. Renard (ed.), *Hommages à Albert Grenier*: 136–43. Brussels, Latomus.

Ward-Perkins, J.B., Kahane, A., and Murray Threipland, L. (1968a) The Ager Veientanus survey north and east of Veii. *Papers of the British School at Rome* 36: 1–218.

Ward-Perkins, J.B., Ridgway, D., and Close-Brooks, J. (1968b) Scavo della necropoli di Quattro Fontanili a Veio: appunti preliminari. *Studi Etruschi* 35: 307–29.

Watts, W.A. (1985) A long pollen record from Laghi di Monticchio, southern Italy. *Journal of the Geological Society* 142: 491–9.

Weber-Lehmann, C. (1985) Spätarchaische Gelagebilder in Tarquinia. *Mitteilungen des deutschen Archäologischen Instituts. Römische Abteilung* 92: 19–44.

Webster, G.S. (1990) Labor control and emergent stratification in prehistoric Europe. *Current Anthropology* 31: 337–66.

Wells, P. (1980) *Culture Contact and Culture Change: Early Iron Age Central Europe and the Mediterranean World*. Cambridge, Cambridge University Press.

West, M.L. (1966) *Hesiod: Theogony*. Oxford, Clarendon Press.

White, K.D. (1970) *Roman Farming*. London, Thames and Hudson.

Whitehouse, R. (1968) Settlement and economy in southern Italy in the neothermal period. *Proceedings of the Prehistoric Period* 34: 332–67.

Whitehouse, R. (1990) Caves and cult in neolithic southern Italy. *Accordia Research Papers* 1: 19–37.

Whitehouse, R. (1992) *Underground Religion: Cult and Culture in Prehistoric Italy*. London, University of London, Accordia Research Centre.

Whitley, J. (1991) *Style and Society in Dark Age Greece: The Changing Face of a Preliterate Society 1100–700* BC. Cambridge, Cambridge University Press.

Wickham, C. (1982) *Studi sulla Società degli Appennini nell'Alto Medioevo: contadini, signori e insediamento nel territorio de Valva (Sulmona).* Bologna, CLUEB.

Wikander, C. (1981) *Acquarossa 1.1: The Painted Architectural Terracottas. Catalogue and Architectural Context.* Rome, Skrifter utgivna av Svenska Institutet i Rom 38.1, 1.

Wikander, C. (1988) *Acquarossa 1.2: The Painted Architectural Terracottas. Typological and Decorative Analysis.* Rome, Skrifter utgivna av Svenska Intsitutet i Rom 38.1, 2.

Wikander, Ö. (1993) *Acquarossa 6.2: The Roof-tiles. Typology and Technical Features.* Rome, Skrifter utgivna av Svenska Institutet i Rom 38.6, 2.

Wikander, Ö, and Roos, P. (1986) *Architettura etrusca nel Viterbese. Catalogo della mostra.* Rome, De Luca.

Wilkens, B. (1987) Il passaggio dal mesolitico al neolitico attraverso lo studio delle faune di alcuni siti dell'Italia centro-meridionale. Pisa, Pisa University (unpublished Ph.D. thesis).

Wilkens, B. (1991) Il ruolo della pastorizia nelle economie preistoriche dell'Italia centro-meridionale. In R. Maggi, R. Nisbet and G. Barker (eds.) *Archaeologia della pastorizia nell'Europe meridionale* II: 81–94. Bordighera, Istituto Internazionale di Studi Liguri.

Wilkens, B. (1991–2) I resti faunistici di alcuni insediamenti dell'età del bronzo nell'Italia centro-meridionale. *Rassegna di Archeologia* 10: 463–9.

Wilkins, J.B. (1990) Nation and language in ancient Italy: problems of the linguistic evidence. *Accordia Research Papers* 1: 53–72.

Williams, D. (1986) Greek potters and their descendants in Campania and Southern Etruria, *c.*720–630 BC. In J. Swaddling (ed.) *Italian Iron Age Artefacts in the British Museum:* 295–304. London, British Museum.

Zamarchi Grassi, P. (ed.) (1992) *La Cortona dei principes.* Cortona, Calosci.

Zecchini, M. (1968) Lo sfruttamento minerario dall'eneolitico all'età del ferro e la problematica dei tempi protostorici all'isola d'Elba. *Archivio per l'Antropologia e l'Etnologia* 98: 199–206.

Zevi, F., Cataldi Dini, M., and Bartoloni, G. (1975) Castel di Decima: la necropoli arcaica. *Notizie degli Scavi:* 233–408.

Zifferero, A. (1991) Miniere e metallurgia estrattiva in Etruria meridionale: per una lettura critica di alcuni dati archeologici e minerari. *Studi Etruschi* 57: 201–41.

Zifferero, A. (1993) Economia, divinità e frontiera: sul ruolo di alcuni santuari di confine in Etruria meridionale. In *CS im Ostraka:* 1–18.

Zvelebil, M., and Rowley-Conwy, P. (1984) The transition to farming in northern Europe: a hunter-gatherer perspective. *Norwegian Archaeological Review* 17, 2: 104–28.

Selected Reading

Pallottino (1975) remains the standard overview of Etruscan culture (the last updated Italian edition is 1984); and for the wider Italian setting there is Pallottino (1991). The most recent treatments in English are Spivey and Stoddart (1990), which focuses on archaeology, and Macnamara (1990), which is a brief account based around the British Museum collections. Bonfante (1986a) is multi-authored and covers many aspects including historiography (de Grummond) and coinage (Tripp). Grant (1980) takes a region-by-region approach. Ridgway (1988a) is a concise outline, Carratelli (1986) a large and beautifully illustrated compendium by the most author-itative Italian scholars. Cristofani (1985c) is in handy encyclopaedia format, useful for quick reference. Among the guide books, Torelli (1993) is the best. For learning about what is no longer visible, Dennis (1883, and other edns.), and the abridged version by Hemphill (1985), is compelling reading.

Earlier prehistory is summarized by Barker (1981), and Potter (1979) provides a stimulating and readable summary of Villanovan and Etruscan settlement in southern Etruria. Villanovan material is well illustrated by Bartoloni (1989a), whilst Bietti Sestieri's (1992b) account of the Osteria dell'Osa cemetery excavation, though outside Etruria proper, is an excel-lent example of how modern cemetery analysis informs on iron age soci-ety. For reports on recent excavations of Etruscan sites, see Rasmussen (1986a; 1996), and *Studi Etruschi* 58 (1992) 477–655; the first lists the catalogues to the extensive series of exhibitions held in Italy in 1985, the 'Year of the Etruscans', of which the largest is Cristofani (1985a). Archae-ological aspects of settlement and territory are summarized by Spivey and Stoddart (1990), and there is a useful series of papers on Etruscan diet and agriculture in Barbieri (1987a).

Etruscan art is discussed by Spivey (1997); it is treated in greater detail by Brendel (1995), where the Additional Bibliography (pp. 485–513) by F.R. Serra Ridgway is important for all aspects of material culture. The best collection of illustrations is in Sprenger and Bartoloni (1983). For bronze sculpture, see Cristofani (1985b), Haynes (1985) and Richardson (1983). Tomb-painting is comprehensively catalogued by Steingräber (1986); for painted pottery, there is Martelli (1987), and for the significance of Greek pottery in Etruria, Spivey (1991a). Architecture is surveyed by Boëthius (1978) and, with fine illustrations, by Colonna (1986). Etruscan language is explained by Bonfante and Bonfante (1983) and more briefly by Bonfante (1990). See also Cristofani (1991a) and the chapters on language in Pallottino (1975).

The Etruscans have two dedicated journals: *Studi Etruschi* (1927-) and, on a more popular level, *Etruscan Studies* (1994-). But they feature regularly in many others, especially: *Accordia Research Papers, American Journal of Archaeology, Archeologia Classica, Journal of Roman Studies* and *Papers of the British School at Rome.*

Index

Page numbers in **bold** type indicate main references to the topic; page numbers in *italic* type refer to pages on which figures occur.

Abruzzo, 30, 33
Achilles, 254, 257
Acqua Acetosa-Laurentina (Latium), 261
Acquarossa, 143, 158, *160*, 161–2, 176; destruction, 100; economy, 184, 186, 193; house plans, 161, 219; plaques, 251
Adonis, 289
Adria, 140
Aegean, 68, 81, 94, *95*, 96, 132, 258
Aelian, 200
aes rude, *see* coinage
afterlife, 232–44; *see also* underworld
Agamemnon (Achmemrun), 106, 239
Ager Cosanus, *see* Cosa
Ager Faliscus, 269
Ager Veientanus, 269; *see also* Veii
agriculture: animal husbandry, 27, 30, 31, *32*–6, 37, 46, 47, 52, 56, 58, 73, 74, 80, 182, **185–9**, 192, 193, 197, 198; crop husbandry, 26–8, 30, 37, 40–1, 46–7, 52, 73, 80, **182–5**, 190, 193–4, 198, 199, 203, 204; fallowing, 194; implements, 47, *189*, 193, 201, 206, 209; *latifundia*, 273; manuring, 31, 47, 63, 74, 147, 195; origins, 46, 81; ploughs, 26, 27, 30, 36, 80, 181, 189–90,

201, 207, *252*; polyculture (*coltura promiscua*), 26–9, 193, 199; rotation, 193–4; technology, 189–93; yields, 194, *195*; *see also* butchery, farming
Agylla (Caere), 136; *see also* Cerveteri
Åkerström, Å., 247
akroteria, 162, 164, *165*, 220, 228; *see also* temples
Alalia (Aléria), 137, 247, 260; *see also* Corsica
Alban hills, 12, 21, 24, 197
Albegna valley, 52, 63, 153, 202, 203, 264, 269; survey, 147–9, 167, 177–8, 182, 195–7, 211
alphabet, *see* literacy
Alsium, 265
Amazon cycle, 257, 290
Amelia (Umbria), 149, *150*
Ampolo, C., 182, 194
animal bones, *see* archaeozoology
animal husbandry, *see* agriculture
antefix, 153, 161; *see also* temples
Apennines, 11, *12*, 16, 20, *21*, 23, 25, 30, 40, 61, 82, 156, 172, 261
Apollo (Apulu), *106*, 224
apotropaism, 255
aqueducts, *see* drainage
Arath Velavesna, 124, 212

archaeobotany, 182, 183–5, 193;
see also archaeological techniques,
pollen analysis
archaeological techniques: DNA
analysis, 82; Geographical
Information Systems, 178;
geophysical survey, 68, 152;
paleomagnetic analysis, 205;
radiocarbon dating, 39, 40, 41,
46; skeletal analysis, 72, 83,
194–5, 257; Thiessen polygons,
55, 61, 175; thin section analysis,
52; x-ray analysis, 52; see also
archaeobotany, archaeozoology,
field survey, metallurgy,
metalwork
archaeozoology, 45, 182–3, **185–8,
189–92**; faunal samples, 45, 47,
50, 73, 74, 194, 200, 207, 210
Ardea (Latium), 35
Arezzo (Arretium), 15, 16, 20, 22, 65,
100, 101, 143, 176, 189–90,
227, 266, 275; Chimaera, 207,
227; Cilnii family, 101, 287;
Tarquinian involvement in, 274
Aricia (Latium), 140
Arimnestos, 90
aristocracy, 100, 101, 107, 118, 123,
124, 141, 177, 180, 257, 259,
271, 286, 287, 289; see also
elites
Aristonothos, 76
Aristotle, 89, 90, 251
armour, 77, 78, 181, 215, 234, 251,
259–60, 261; see also weaponry
Arnobius, 92
Artumes, 277
Asciano, 111
ash-urns, see urns
Ashby, T., 34, 35
Assyria, 119, 232
Astarte (Uni), 90, 97, 111, 224
Athens, 6, 91, 92, 95, 134, 214
Attolini, I., 195, 197, 202
Augustus, 6, 92, 275, 293
Avle Feluske, 261
Avle Vipinas, see Vibenna brothers

Baccano, 14, 38, 40
Bagnolo San Vito, 140, 143

banquets, see symposium
Bartoloni, G., 68, 74, 75
Bay of Naples, 12, 75, 81, 203
Bearded Sphinx Painter, see pottery,
Etruscan
Berenson, B., 36–7
Biferno valley, 27
Bisenzio, 14, 56, 76, 145, 252, 255
Blera, 184, 190, 192
Bologna (Felsina), 2, 40, 143–4;
burials, 72; Greek contacts, 76–7;
metalwork, 74–5; stele, 261;
Tomba degli Ori, 110
Bolsena (Volsinii), 23, 55, 62, 91,
115, 176, 266, 301; Lake, 12,
14, 15, 16, 19, 21, 69, 76, 176,
252, 265, 281
Bonfante, L., 294
Bracciano, Lake, 14, 15, 19, 21, 23,
143, 269
British School at Rome, 70, 144
bronze: agricultural implements, 58,
71, 189–90; armour, 201,
259–60, 261; in Bronze Age, 52;
exported, 214; in graves, 77, 78,
110, 120, 128, 183, 252;
production, 206–8; sculpture,
199, 207, 226–7; smiths, 74,
207; tin-bronze, 49, 58
Bronze Age: Early and Middle, 5,
6, 40, 51–3, 54, 56, 82; Greek,
59; Late, 6, 44, 53–60, 64, 83,
84
bucchero, see pottery, Etruscan
burial: early bronze age, 51, 52;
chariot, 79, 124, 261; female,
72, 75, 104, 111; neolithic and
copper age, 45–6, 47–9;
'princely', 91, 97, 118, 120–5,
187, 199; slave, 101; Villanovan,
70–3, 177; see also cremation,
inhumation, ritual, tombs
butchery, 187–8, 198, 207; see also
agriculture: animal husbandry
butteri (herdsmen), 33–4

Cacu, 113, 115
Caere, see Cerveteri
Caile Vipinas, see Vibenna brothers
Campagna plain, 21, 32, 33, 34

Campania, 118, 124, 139, 140, 280, 294
Campiglia Marittima, 206
Camporeale, G., 257
Canina, L., 3
Cap d'Antibes shipwreck, 137, 214
Capena, 144, 256, 266, 302
Capriola, 302
Capua, 139–40
Carandini, A., 273
Carte della Utilizzazione del Suolo, 26
Carthage, 2, 90, 119, 137, 180
Casalecchio di Reno, 143, 149
Casentino, 19
Castel d'Asso, 143, 145, 286, 287; tombs, 282, 283, 302–3
Castel di Decima (Latium), 118, 124
Castellina in Chianti, 303
Castelluccio, 23
Castelnuovo Berardenga, 124
Castro, 265; Tomba della Biga, 304
Castrum Novum, 265
Cato, 30, 92
Catullus, 180
Cecina, river, 16
cemeteries: faunal samples, 187; mesolithic, 45; Orientalizing, 117–18; regular planning, 158; social stratification, 130–1, 177; Villanovan, 60, 64, 68–73, 76–7; *see also* tombs
Censorinus, 93, 112
centuriation, 263, 264, 265, 269
Ceri, Tomb of the Statues, 126–7
Cerveteri (Caere, Agylla), 15, 56, 61–2, 63, 67, 68, 136, 143, 173, 235, 273; cemeteries and tombs: Banditaccia, 122, 131, 158, 232–3, Monte Abatone, 133, Montetosto, 120, 123, 166, Regolini-Galassi, 120, 123–4, Ripa Sant'Angelo, 295, Tomb of the Five Chairs, 127, 238, Tomb of the Greek Vases, 105, 121, 122, 161, Tomb of the Olives, 183, Tomb of the Reliefs, 193, 201, 234, 261, 284, 286, Tomb of the Shields and Thrones, 261, Tumulus 2, 121, 122; families: Matuna, 286, Tamsnie, 286,

Tarchna, 286; faunal samples, 185–7, 210; festival, 247; king, 100; pottery production, 102, 134, 136, 203–5, 259; sarcophagi, 248, 289; walls, 274; wine, 182
chalcolithic, *see* Copper Age
charcoal burners (*carbonari*), 25, 30, 38, 172, 201
chariot, 79, 187, 229, 277; model of, 199; racing, 247, 294; team, 124; *see also* burial
Charon, 212, 239, 240, 242–3, 246, 283
Charu(n), *see* demons
cheese, 30, 36, 74, 195; production, 47, 51, 80, 192–3, 198, 201
Chianti, 16, 23, 30, 33
Chiarugi, 39
chiefdoms, 5, **53–60**, 72, 79, 83–4, **120–5**, 211; *see also* elites
Chimaera, 227
Chiusi (Clusium), 15, 65, 143, 305; barrel-vaulted chamber tombs, 284; *cippus*, 244; cremation, 122; sarcophagi, 108–9, 255, 288; skeletons, 194; territory, 100, 101, 176; urns, 112, 116, 128, 235, 237, 248, 255, 277, 289–90; *see also* painted tombs
Cicero, 92, 287
cippus, *see* Chiusi
Cisra (Caere), 90
cities: Etruscan, 100, 143, 147, **149–58**, 273–6; medieval, 156; *see also* urbanization
city state: Etruscan, 5, 84, 99–101, 149, 175, 177, 266; Greek, 5, 84, 149, 175; *see also* urbanization
Civita Castellana, *see* Falerii [Veteres]
Claudius, 93, 112
clientship, 79–80, 175, 177, 210–11, 212; *see also* elites
climate, 25, 45; change, 10, 39, 41; warming, 39, 40
Close-Brooks, J., 70
clothing, 49, 58, 108, 199, 215, 218, 294
Clusium, *see* Chiusi

Cneve Tarchunies, *114*
coinage, 124, 211, 215; currency bars, 212; ingot (*aes rude*), 211–12; *ramo secco* bars, 212
Coleman, C., *34*
Coleman, H., *32*
Colline Metallifere, 16, *48*, 49, 74, 76, 205
colonia, colonization, Roman, 136, 262, 265, 267, 275
Colonna, G., 128
Columella, 26, 30, 182, 192
Comeana, 306
copper, *48*, 76, 124, 205; artefacts, 49; coppersmiths, 49
Copper Age, **47–50**, 51, 82
corbelling, *see* tombs
Corchiano, 173
Corinth, 87, 131, 132, 213
Cornacchino, Monte Amiata, 206
Cornell, T.J., 131, 139
Corsica, 2, 75, 90, 137, 214; *see also* Alalia
Cortona, *15*, 131, 143, 289; Melone di Camucia, *236*, 307; Melone del Sodo II, 238; Tanella di Pitagora, 284–5, 307
Cosa, 177, 262–5, 267–9, *270*, 273
craft: *bucchero* workshops, 140; in clay, 87; household, 155, 161–2; specialization, 59, 207–10; *see also* technology
cremation, 58, 60, 72, 77, 122–3, 125–6, 288; *see also* burial
Cristofani, M., 83, 214, 229
crop husbandry, *see* agriculture
cube tombs, *see* tombs
cult, 219, 224; ancestor, 238; fertility, 277; healing, 277–81; Greek and Roman, 92; *see also* symbolism
Cumae, 6, 75, 125, 135, 140; Artiaco tomb, 125
cuniculi, *see* drainage
Cyprus, 74, 214

dance, 107, 110–11, **251–4**; *komos*, 254
death, 232–8
deer, *see* hunting and fishing

defence systems, 151, 274, 275; late bronze age, 53; earthen rampart, 151; *glacis*, 151; *see also* walling
Delphi, 240, 245, 247
Demaratus, 86, 87
demons, 239–40, *243*; Charu(n), *104*, 240, *241*, 242, 246, 283; Greek, 240; Near Eastern, 242; Tulchulcha, 242; Vanth, *104*, 242, 248, 284
Dempster, T., 3
Dennis, G., 3, 151, 216, 263
dental evidence and appliances, 194–5
di Gennaro, F., 53, 61
diet, 36, 45, 46, 47, 73, 74, 82, **182–9**, 194–5, 200, 215
Diodorus Siculus, 108, 180, 182
Dionysius of Halicarnassus, 43, 89, 91
Dionysus (Fufluns), 86, *106*, 301
Doganella, *155*, 178; amphora production, 155; bronze, 211; Romanization, 264; walls, 274, 307
drainage, 156, 158, 161, 169, 172, 182, 197, 296; aqueducts, 173, 198; *cuniculi*, 197

Edlund-Berry, I.E.M., 176
Egypt, 79, 214, 232, 259
Elba, 2, *15*, 16, 49, 64, 76, 205, 206, 214
elites, 7–8, 47, 50, 59–60, 72–3, 76–7, 100, 184, 187, 193, 201; *see also* aristocracy, chiefdoms, clientship
emporia, *see* trade
Ernout, A., 293
etera, 102
etrusca disciplina, 92
Etruscan League, 90
Euboea(n): alphabet, 87; colonization, 75; potters, 203; settlers, 125
exchange, 47, 58, 59, 68, 74–5, 77, 84, **210–15**; *see also* trade

Falerii Novi (Santa Maria di Falleri), 266, 308; Porta di Giove, *295*

Falerii [Veteres], 6, 134, 143, 173, 266, 269; Celle sanctuary, 305–6; Lo Scasato temple, 277, 281
family, 46, 68, 102–3; kin groups, 49, 72, 79, 82; rural, 169, 177; urban, 177; *see also* kinship
Fanum Voltumnae, 90, 91, 247
farming, **182–9**; *see also* agriculture, Cosa, Podere Tartuchino, Tuscania
faunal samples, *see* archaeozoology
Felsnas, 102
Ferento, 308
fibula, 71–2, 74, 109, 212; gold, 123, 124, 209; *see also* jewellery
Ficana (Latium), *135*
field survey (field-walking), 54, 65, **144–9**, 263, **269–73**; sampling strategies, 146–7, 183–4
Fiesole (Faesulae), *15*, 143, 169, 261, 266, 277, 308
flint, 45, 46, 47, 49, 51, 52
Florence, *2*, *13*, 309
forest, 26, 28, 37–9, 40, 46; clearance, 41, 51, 52, 195
France (southern), 45, 75, 137, 214
Fratte, 139
Fregenae, 265

games (sports), 107, **245–8**, 251, 294; funerary, 124; gladiatorial, 294
Gauls, 140, 261, 266
Geographical Information Systems, *see* archaeological techniques
Ghiaccio Forte, 264, 309
Giglio, shipwreck, 135, 136, 214
Gilgamesh, 242
gold, 79, 89, 90, 94, 118, 119, 167, 207, 209; dental, 195; Homeric, 124; votives, 280; *see also* jewellery
Gori, A.F., 3
Gracchus, Gaius, 273
Gran Carro, 69, 73, 74, 184, 312
Gras, M., 89
Gravisca (Graviscae), 87, 182, 191, 215, 309; *colonia*, 136, 265, 309
Grosseto, 310
Grotta Patrizi, 47

Grotta Porcina, 310
Gubbio (Umbria), *15*, *20*, 23, 56, 149

Hades (Aita), 239
haruspex (*haruspices*), 92, 93, 228–9, 232
hearth, 46, 52, 56, 70, 172, 192, 193, 198, 201
Heba, *colonia*, 263, *270*, 312
Herakles, 161, 224
Herodotus, 43, 87, 94, 137, 228, 247, 260
Hesiod, 85, 86, 93
Heurgon, J., 112
hoards, 52, 59, 74, 211
Holloway, R.R., 255
Holocene, 39
Homer: *Iliad*, 86, 119, 123–4, 247, 256; *Odyssey*, 123–4, 239
Hood, S., 30, 33
Horace, 182
houses: construction, 69–70, 156, 161; decoration, 162–4; huts, 33, 35, 52, 56, 58, 68, 69, 156, 161; longhouses, 52; rectangular, 47, 167; tombs imitating, 234–5
hunting and fishing, 45, 46, 181, 187, 199–200, 258–9

inhumation, 72, 121–3, 288; *see also* burial
inscriptions, *see* literacy
Ionia, 91, 108, 136
Iphigenia, 257
iron, 76, 118, 120, 181, 189, 201, 205, 206, 207, 210, 212, 215; *see also* metallurgy, metalwork
Iron Age (Villanovan), 5, 6, 44, **60–75**, 83, 140; graves, 96; hut urns, 164; physical types, 82
Ischia (Pithekoussai), *2*, 75, 87, 96, 119, 125, 214; graves, 125; Phoenician inscriptions, 76
ivory, 90, 118, 119, 120, 166, 207

jewellery, 79, 109; filigree, 209; gold, 109, 207, 209; granulation, 123, 124, 209; repoussé, 123, 209; *see also* fibula
Judson, S., 197

Kahane, A., 197
kings (kingship), **87–91**
kinship, 79, 82; *see also* family, society
kottabos, 251

La Civita del Fosso di Arlena, 301
La Piana, 184
Laconia, 132
Lagaccione di Mezzano, 38
Lago dell'Accesa, 190, 310
landscape, **10–25**, 27, 29, **37–42**,
    143–9; of power, **175–8**;
    Romanization, **268–73**
language, *see* literacy
Laris Pulenas, 103, *104*, 291
Lars Porsenna, 86, 90, 91
Lars Tolumnius, 89
Larth Telicles, 136
Larth Vel Arnies, 173
Larthuza Kulenie, 209
latifundia, *see* agriculture
Latinus, 85
Latium, 35, 96, 118, 124, 131, 134,
    140, 222, 261, 262, 280
lautni, 101–2, 289
Lawrence, D.H., 8, 22, 34
Lemnos, 81, 94, *95*
Levi, C., 37
libri: fulgurales, haruspicini, rituales,
    92
Liguria, 46, 49, *50*, 267
Lipari, 47
literacy, 5, 118; alphabet, 81, 87–8,
    96–7, 126, 293; inscriptions,
    94–7 and *passim*; language,
    80–2, 94–6, 98–9, 293–4;
    origins, 80, 96; of women, 104–5
Livy, 43, 86, 89, 90, 91, 92, 101,
    102, 107, 109, 180–1, 182, 228,
    247, 254, 265, 266, 269, 275,
    294, 296
Loeb tripods, 207
loom weights, 73, 109, 161, 171,
    193, 198, 201; *see also*
    technology, wool
Lucus Feroniae, 311
Luni sul Mignone, 52, 53, 56, 58,
    311
Lycia, 136, 258
Lydia, 123

Magliano in Toscana, *see* Heba
Mantua, 140
Marce Camitlnas, *114*
Marce Unata, 267
Maremma, 16, *17*, 26, 30, 33, *34*,
    143, 198, 262, 275
Marius, Gaius, 266
Marsiliana, 176, 312
Martial, 182
Martignano, Lake, *14*, 38
maru, 99, 100
Marzabotto, 313; rural settlement,
    149; temples, *221*; town
    planning, 140, 156–9, 161
Massa Marittima, 22
Massilia (Marseilles), 214
Mastarna (Macstrna), 113
medieval period, 37, 38, 57, 182,
    210, 275
Megara Hyblaea, 137
Menerva (Athena), 224–5, 280
mesolithic, 45, 46
Mesopotamia, 242
metallurgy: mining, 50, 64, 74, 101;
    ores, 16, 48, 49, 52, 58, 76, 80,
    125, 137, 206; processing, 8, 50,
    201, 205–7, 209; *see also* iron,
    metalwork, technology
metalwork: in burials, 77–9, 133,
    181, 201, 239; copper age, 49; at
    Doganella, 155; early bronze age,
    51, *52*; farm implements, 190,
    193; Homeric, 124; late bronze
    age, 58; at Marzabotto, 158;
    pottery repairs, 134; Sardinian,
    77; Villanovan, 74, 77–9, 133,
    206–9; *see also* iron, metallurgy
Mezzaluna, 38, 39
Micali Painter, *see* pottery, Etruscan
Minns, Sir E., 293
mirrors, 97, *105*, 111, *115–16*, 207,
    228, *230*, 281, 291
Montagnola tumulus, 318
Montarrenti, *18*, *65*, 149; survey, 171
Monte Rovello, *57*, 58
Montecatino, 186
Montereggi, 171
Monteriggioni, Calisna Sepu tomb,
    288
Monterosi, Lake, 38, 40

Montescudaio, 248
Montetosto sanctuary, 166
Monti: Amiata, 12, 16, 22, 25, 206;
    Argentario, 263, 273; Aurunci,
    21; Ausoni, 21; Bibele, 172;
    Cetona, 56; Cimini, 19, 23;
    Lepini, 21; Sabatini, 19; Volsini,
    16–19
Murlo (Poggio Civitate), 100, 109,
    134, 158, **162–6**, *176*, 177, 203,
    222, 251, 313
Musarna, 100, 145, 289, 292, 314;
    families: Alethna, Hulchnie,
    100–1, 292, 293
music, 200, **251–4**, 294
Mussolini, B., 26, 37

Narce, 52, 56, 57, 58, 63, *64*, 73,
    143, 144, 186, 314
neolithic, 47, 82, 184
Nepi (Nepet), 143, 173, 266, 267,
    314
netsvis, 228; *see also haruspex*
Newby, E., 30
Nietzsche, F., 3
Noël des Vergers, A., 3
Nola, 140
Norchia, 101, 145, 267, 282, 289,
    314; Acqualta necropolis, 283,
    284; families: Smurina, 271,
    Tetatru, 271

olive cultivation, 26–9, 37, 183, 190,
    192, 198–9, 214; *see also*
    technology
Orbetello, 263, 315
Orientalizing period, 6, 117–18, 123,
    130, 139, 166, 256
origins, of Etruscans, 5, 43–4, 60,
    80–4, 96
Orvieto (Volsinii), 6, *15*, 16, 56, 61,
    68, 141, *142*, 143, 182, 234,
    266; Belvedere temple, 316;
    cemeteries: Cannicella, 277,
    Crocefisso del Tufo, 97, *98*, 131,
    132, 155, *236*; *see also* painted
    tombs
Osteria dell'Osa (Latium), 72, 76, 79,
    96
Ostia, 25

Oued Miliane (Tunisia), 266
Ovid, 305

Pacciarelli, M., 56
Paestum, 259, 261
painted tombs: (*Chiusi*): Monkey
    (Scimmia), 110; (*Orvieto*): Golini
    I, 110, 251, 316, Hescanas, 316;
    (*Tarquinia*): Augurs (Auguri),
    228, *229*, *241*, 246–7, Baron
    (Barone), 216–19, Blue Demons
    (Demoni Azzurri), 242–3, Bulls
    (Tori), 185, 254–5, Cardarelli,
    107, Chariots (Bighe), 107, 255,
    Dionysus and the Silens (Dioniso
    e i Sileni), 254, Hunter
    (Cacciatore), 199, Hunting and
    Fishing (Caccia e Pesca), 199,
    249–50, 255, *258–9*, Inscriptions
    (Iscrizioni), 245, 254, Jugglers
    (Giocolieri), 110, 255, Leopards
    (Leopardi), 238, Lionesses
    (Leonesse), 238, 251, Moretti,
    270, Mouse (Topolino), 255,
    Olympic Games (Olimpiadi), 246,
    Orcus II (Orco), 239, *240*, 242,
    244, Pulcinella, 246, Querciola II,
    241, Shields (Scudi), 238, Tomb
    1999, 254, Triclinium (Triclinio),
    254, Whipping (Fustigazione),
    254–5; (*Vulci*): François, 3, 100,
    112–*14*, 240, 257, 261, 274, 327
Palestrina (Praeneste), *15*; Barberini
    tomb, 120; Bernadini tomb, 118,
    120, 209
Pallottino, M., 8, 218, 228, 240
Panionion, 91
pasture, 25, 26, 28, 31, 38, 40, 52,
    155, 195, 197
Pausanias, 90, 91, 92, 238, 240
Pech-Maho, 139
Perkins, P., 177, 195, 197, 202
Persephone (Phersipnei), 239, 246
Perugia, *13*, *15*, 20, 23, 143, 181,
    207, 316; tombs: Cutu, 288–9,
    San Manno, 316, Velimna
    (Volumnii), 288–9, 316; urns,
    290, *291*; walls, 149–51, 153,
    316
Petriolo, 46

phersu, 246
Phillips, K.M., Jr., 166
Phoenicians, 44, 75–7, 83, 96, 119, 137; *see also* trade
Phrygia, 249, 285
Piacenza, bronze liver, 229, 231–2
Pian della Conserva, 324
Pianezze, 316
Pieve Socana, 317
Pindar, 245
Piombino, 64
piracy, 86, 89, 94, 96, 137, 214; *see also* shipping
Piranesi, G.B., 2
Pisa, *15*, 22, 24, 147, 182
Pithecusa (Pithekoussai), *see* Ischia
Pittore dei Caduti, *see* pottery, Etruscan
Pleistocene, 11, 39, 41
Pliny, 28, 86, 111, 182, 209, 232
Pliocene, 11, 16, 21
Plutarch, 93, 273
Po plain, 21, 24, 26, 33, 38, 40, 42
Podere Tartuchino, **167–71**, 178, 182, 269; bronze, 211; food production, 184, 185, 186, 190–2, 197, 199, 210; *pithos*, *191*, 195; pottery, 203, 212; walls, 201–2
Poggialtri Vallelunga, 49–50
Poggio Buco, 265, 317
pollen analysis, 11, 38–9, 41, 50, 52, 58, 198, 210; *see also* archaeobotany
Polybius, 86, 182
Pompeii, 140
Pontecagnano, 139, 140
population: DNA analysis of, 82; estimates, 22–3, 53–4, 155, 161; increase, 41, 74, 103, 144, 149, 193, 194, 200; origins, 44, 140
Populonia, *15*, 143, 149, 210; burials, 72, 75; butchery, 187–8; coinage, 211; excavation, 273; faunal samples, 186, 207; metal processing, 206; Roman siege, 266; temple, 318; tombs, 317; walls, *152*, 318

portraiture, 291
ports, 136, 167, *168*, 173, 214, 215, 265
Posidonius, 108
Potter, T.W., 63, 195, 273
pottery: funerary, 70–2, repairs, 134, technology, 201–5, 209, trade in, 136, 181, 214; Greek: Athenian figured, 134, 136, 181, 203, Caeretan *hydriai*, 136, 259, Corinthian, 120, 214, 248, Geometric, 125, *126*; Phoenician: 77, 215; prehistoric: bronze age, 52, 192, copper age, 49, iron age/Villanovan, 63, 77, neolithic, 46
pottery, Etruscan: amphorae (storage, transport), 137, 166, 171, 190, 199, 202, 214; black-figure, 86, 97, 134, 203, 247, 252–3, Micali Painter, 212, *213*, 252–3; black-glazed (black-gloss), 134, 269, 274–5; *bucchero*, 102, 113, *133–4*, 137–8, 140, 144, 166, 203–5, 214, 269; coarse ware, 63, 171, 202–3, 269; cream ware, 210, 212; *dolia*, 161, 191, 192; Etrusco-Corinthian, 134, 137, 140, 203, Bearded Sphinx Painter, 205, *Pittore dei Caduti*, 256; *impasto*, 63, 132, *135*, 202, 203–4, 210, *256*; Italo-geometric, 202, 203; *pithoi*, *191*, 192, 195, 202, 210, 212; red-figure, 134, 327; shapes: askos (aska), 203, kantharos (zavena), 99, kothon (qutum), 203, krater, 76, 327
Pratomagno, 19, 20, 25
priest (priestess), 97, 111
principes, *see* burial: 'princely', chiefdoms, elites
Punta della Vipera, *280*
purth, 99
Pyrgi, 136, 167, 318; *colonia*, 263, 265; gold tablets, 89–90, 94, 167; sanctuary, 111, 187, 224; temples, 89–90, *221*

Quinto Fiorentino, 318

ramo secco bars, 212; *see also* coinage
Ramtha Vestirikina, 103, 104
Randall-MacIver, D., 44
Rascino basin, *21*
Rasenna (Rasna), 83, 85
razors, 71, *78*, 79
Regisvilla, 136, 153, 167, *168*, 319
Rekyavik, 103
Rieti, 23, 24
ritual: as boundary, 176–7; funerary, 58–9, 70–3, 123, 187, 245, 283; Greek, 93; obligations, 212; Roman, 294; sites, 47, 52; in texts 5, 92; wine in, 199; *see also* burial
roads, 24, 172–4, 210, 296; drove-roads (*tratturi*), 31–3; Roman, 23–4, 267–8, 271, 275, 276; *see also* technology
Rome, 12, *13*, *15*, 16, 37, 51, 63, 79, 181, 197; 209, 319; Capitoline temple, 220; Circus Maximus, 294; crops, 183; Etruscan dancers at, 253; Etruscan kings, *see* Tarquin dynasty; Villa Torlonia, 328; walls, 151
Roselle (Rusellae), *15*, 134, 143, 149, 151, 156, *176*, 181, 182, 276, 319; walls, *152*, 274–5
Rutile Hipucrates, 137

Sabine hills, 24, 53, 61
sacrifice, 224, 228–32; human, 257
saecula, doctrine of, 93, 112
St Blaise, 137
San Gimignano, 22, 289
San Giovenale, 158–61, 183, 186, 269, 319; Spring Building, 187
San Giuliano, 124, 320; Tomba Cima, 320; Tomba della Regina, 320
San Polo d'Enza, 143
sanctuaries, 94, **219–27**, **276–81**; faunal samples, 187; as ritual boundaries, 176–7; *see also* temples, votive offerings
Santa Marinella, 265, 280
sarcophagi, **288–91**; *see also* Cerveteri, Tarquinia, Tuscania, Vulci

Sardinia, 2, 47, 74, 75, 77, 137, 206, 214
Sardis, 123
Saturnia, 65, 203, 210, 211, 263, 265, 267, *268*, 269, *270*, 321
Scylla, 284
Seianti Hanunia Tlesnasa, *108*, 109, 291
Serrabottini, 205
Sethre Vipinans, 104–5
Settefinestre, 273
sexual behaviour, 179–80, 254–5, 259
shipping, 135–7, 173, 214–15, *258*, 260; *see also* piracy, trade
Sicily, 2, 74, 75, 86, 125, 137, 158, 214, 260
silver, 79, 102, 118, 120, 123, 180, 205, 207, 212; silver-gilt, 120
slaves, 101, 102, 108, 109, 206, 273, 289
society, *see* aristocracy, elites, family, kinship, slaves
Sorgenti della Nova, 56–8, 68, 172, 321
Sostratos, 87
South Etruria survey, 144–5, 269
Sovana, 100, 113, 281; tombs: Ildebranda, 284, 312, Pola, 284, 322, Silen, 322, Siren, 284, *285*, 322, Typhon, 322
Spain, 74, 75, 206, 214
Sparta, 124, 214
Spina, 140, 143, 158
spindle whorls, 47, 50, 71, 73, 109, 161, 193, 198, 201; *see also* wool
Spivey, N., 3, 261
sports, *see* games
Statonia, 265
stele (gravestone), 49, 70, 261, 309
Stoddart, S., 3, 175, 261
Strabo, 232, 266
Sulla, L. Cornelius, 266
Sutri (Sutrium), 144, 266, 267, 322
symbolism, 70, 89, 97, 293; *see also* cult
symposium (*symposion*), 81, 93, 107, 180, 199, 244, 248–51, 255, 290
Syria(n), 128, 214

Tacitus, 86, 87, 93
Tages, 228
Talamonaccio, *17*, *189*, 211, *270*, 277, 281, 322
Talamone (Telamon), *see* Talamonaccio
Tarchon, 116, 229
Tarquin dynasty, 86–7, 90, 107, 113, 139, 177, 220, 294
Tarquinia, *15*, 99, 144–6, *176*, 323; Ara della Regina temple, 277–9; bronze age, 54, *55*; *elogia*, 100, 112, 274; families: Pulena, 286, Spurinna, 112, 286, Velcha, 286; iron age (Villanovan), 61–2, 67, 68–70, 77; sarcophagi, *104*, *105*, 110, 289; street system, 152–3, *154*; walls, 274; *see also* painted tombs
technology: agricultural, 80, **189–93**; boat, 173; domestic, 58, 74, 87, 109, *110*, 171, **201–10**; drainage, 197–8; *see also* craft, metallurgy, olive cultivation, pottery, roads, vine cultivation
Teiresias (Teriasa), 239
temples, 153, **219–24**, 276–81; *alae*, 219; *cella*, 153, 219; 'tuscanic' style, 219–20; *see also akroteria*, antefix, sanctuaries
Terracina, 24
Tharros, 137
Thefarie Velianas, 89, 90
Theopompos, 107, 179
Thera, frescoes, 258
Theseus (These), 242
Thucydides, 94
tiles, 153, 156, 161, 162, 164, 169, 171, 201, 202, 234
tin, 76, 205, 206; *see also* bronze
Tinia, 227
Todi (Umbria), 20, 23, 207
Tolfa, 19, 47, 161, 205, 206, 324
tombs: barrel-vaulted, 284–5, 295; chamber, *passim*; corbelled, 235–6; façade (cube, *tomba a dado*), 281–5; Villanovan, 70, 172; *see also* burial, cemeteries, tumuli
Toms, J., 70

Torre Spaccata, 51
Torrionaccio, *57*, 58
town planning, **151–8**, 167
trade, 210–15; Carthage treaty, 90; emporia, 135–6, 140; Greek and Phoenician, 76, 83, 87, 119, 124–6, **135–9**, 203, 213–14; pottery exports, 137–9; *see also* exchange, shipping
transhumance, 31–3, *35*, 52, 198
transport amphorae, *see* pottery, Etruscan
tribes, Roman, 292
tripod, 124, 192, *193*, 207, 214
Troilos, 254
tumuli, 118, 120, 126–7, 131, 167, 234; fields, 123; *see also* tombs
Tuscania: families: Curuna, 271, 287, 288, 324, Statlane, 271, Treptie, 271, Vipinana, 271, 288; food production, 192, 210; political landscape, 101, 175–7; roads, 172, *174*; San Pietro acropolis, 54; sarcophagi, 104, *105*, 111, 248, 289; survey, *18*, 61–3, 69, 99, 144–7, 171, 182, 195–6, 211, 271–2; tombs and cemeteries: Ara del Tufo, 324, Peschiera, 324, Regina, 324
Tuscany, 20, 46
Tyrrhenian Sea, *2*, *15*, 86, 173, 265
Tyrrhenoi, 85–6, 95

Umbria, 20, 143, 149, 212
underworld, **238–44**, 255, 282, *290*; *see also* afterlife
Uni, 90, 97, 224
urbanization, 56, 61–4, 139, 140, 141, 156, 176; *see also* cities, city state
urns: ash (cinerary, funerary), **288–91**, 327; canopic, 128, *130*; hut, 69–71, 164; for ash-urns, *see also* Chiusi, Perugia, Volterra

Val di Chiana, 16, *17*, 20, 143, 182
Valle di Castiglione, 38
Varro, 26, 91, 93, 112, 182
Veii: acropolis, 151; fall of, 261, 266; Greek trade, 125; kings, 89;

Ponte Sodo, 325; Portonaccio sanctuary, 70–1, 78, 113, 125–6, 209, 220–5, 277; sculptors, 220; settlement type, 15, 55, 56, 61–3, 65–6, 68, 143, 161; survey, 63, 69, 144, 145, 147, 195, 269; territory, 61–3, 176, 266; tombs and cemeteries: Campana tomb, 296, 325, Monte Michele, 120, 121, Quattro Fontanili, 70–1, 77–9, 125–6; town planning, 152–3, 156; Valle la Fata track, 176; walls, 151, 273–4; wine, 182, 192

Velleius Paterculus, 139

Vetulonia: burial rite, 72; decline of, 151; Diavolino 2 tumulus, 326; mining, 64; Pietrera tumulus, 127–8, 326; settlement type, 15, 143, 149, 176, 325; stele, 261; town planning, 152

Vibenna brothers, 113, 115–16

Vico, Lake, 19, 38

Villanova, 61

Villanovan Iron Age, see Iron Age

vine cultivation, 26–9, 37, 73, 182, 184, 190, 192, 193, 195, 198–9; see also technology, wine

Virgil, 89, 139, 180, 247

Viterbo, 281, 326

Vitruvius, 219, 220

Voghiera, 143

Volnius, 112

Volsinii, see Bolsena, Orvieto

Volterra (Volaterrae): acropolis, 277, 326; Ceicna (Caecinae) family, 287, 288, 293; gates, 209, 326; Inghirami tomb, 288; Roman siege, 266; settlement type, 15, 143, 176, 325; urns, 112, 277, 288, 290; walls, 149–52, 326

von Hase, F.W., 137

votive offerings, 136, 193, **224–7**, 277, 280; see also sanctuaries

Vulca, 209

Vulci: bronze production, 207, 208, 214; Cuccumella tumulus, 327; Cuccumelletta tumulus, 238; landscape, 34; pottery production, 137, 203–5, 212; sarcophagi, 248, 289; settlement type, 15, 55, 61–2, 68, 143, 145, 272; temple, 277; territory, 147, 176, 177, 207, 214, 263, 269; trade, 76–7, 214; see also painted tombs

Walberg, G., 218

walling: ashlar (stone block), 151, 153, 161, 162, 232, 273; defensive, 158, 273; galestro, 201–2; hut-urns, represented on, 70; mud-brick, 151, 153, 162, 169, 273; polygonal, 149–52, 263, 264; wattle and daub, 70, 156, 158, 161, 162, 201

Ward-Perkins, J.B., 65

warfare, 226, **259–71**, 274

weaponry: production, 58, 78, 206–7, 209; in tombs, 49, 72, 252, 286; see also armour

Wedgwood, J., 2

wine: export, 137, 214; production 73, 80, 182, 191–2, 195, 215; in rituals, 199; see also vine cultivation

women, **103–11**, 249, 290–1 and *passim*

wool, 73, 80, 186, 198, 215; see also loom weights, spindle whorls

writing, see literacy

Zagreb text, 92

Zeus, 90, 227

zilac (zilath), 90, 99, 100, 101

Zonaras, 101